Natalie Alvarez
Claudette Lauzon • Keren Zaiontz
Editors

Sustainable Tools for Precarious Times

Performance Actions in the Americas

palgrave
macmillan

Editors
Natalie Alvarez
Ryerson University
Toronto, ON, Canada

Claudette Lauzon
Simon Fraser University
Vancouver, BC, Canada

Keren Zaiontz
Queen's University
Kingston, ON, Canada

Contemporary Performance InterActions
ISBN 978-3-030-11556-2 ISBN 978-3-030-11557-9 (eBook)
https://doi.org/10.1007/978-3-030-11557-9

Cover illustration: Martin Savoie. The Yellow House, Fin Novembre installation. 2012 © ATSA

This Palgrave Macmillan imprint is published by the registered company Springer Nature Switzerland AG.
The registered company address is: Gewerbestrasse 11, 6330 Cham, Switzerland

This book is dedicated to the memory of ATSA cofounder Pierre Allard (1964–2018).
Rest in peace and power.

Acknowledgments

We extend our warmest thanks to colleagues who participated along the way in the development of this book: the members of our 2015 working session at the American Society for Theatre Research in Portland, Oregon (Samer Al-Saber, T.L. Cowan, Peter Dickinson, Serap Erincin, Miriam Felton-Dansky, Catherine Graham, Kimberley Jannarone, Debra Levine, Duygu Erdogan Monson, Christian Nagler, Julie Salverson, Alexis M. Skinner, and J.B. Spiegel) and our 2015 panel at the Association for Theatre in Higher Education in Montreal, Quebec (Pierre Allard and Annie Roy of ATSA, Amy Sara Carroll, Naila Keleta-Mae, Srimoyee Mitra, Kimberly Ramirez, and Tamara Underiner). We'd also like to thank Jennifer de Freitas for her beautifully designed artist pages in this collection, Mick Agustin for the illustration of Fred Moten and Stefano Harney in conversation, Suné Woods for her stunning photograph, and the artists whose provocations are interspersed between the chapters of this volume—L.M. Bogad; ATSA; Hank Willis Thomas and Eric Gottesman; subRosa; Escola de Ativismo; micha cárdenas, Patrisse Cullors, Chris Head, and Edxie Betts; Syrus Marcus Ware; Fred Moten and Stefano Harney; Cannupa Hanska Luger; and Leah Decter with Stop Violence Against Aboriginal Women Action Group. Claudette Lauzon would like to thank her research assistants, Yani Kong and Micaela Kwiatkowski, and Natalie Alvarez and Keren Zaiontz thank their research assistant Sydney Hart—Yani, Micaela, and Sydney were instrumental in bringing this book to fruition. Sydney Hart played an especially critical role transcribing the interviews and securing permissions for us in the final hours; we're very grateful for his professionalism and careful work. We also thank Beatriz

Pizano for taking the time to interview Patricia Ariza during her trip to Bogotá and Bruce Gibbons Fell for his wonderful translation of this conversation. For financial support of this project, we are grateful to the Social Sciences and Humanities Research Council of Canada Insight Development Grant program and the Simon Fraser University Publications Fund.

Contents

List of Figures

CHAPTER 1

On Sustainable Tools for Precarious Times: An Introduction

Natalie Alvarez, Claudette Lauzon, and Keren Zaiontz

As we prepare this collection for publication, thousands of students, parents, family members, and teachers in cities and towns across the US are marching against gun violence. One month has passed since the February 14, 2018 shooting at Marjory Stoneman Douglas High School in Parkland, Florida, which claimed 17 lives. Fading flowers, stuffed teddies, and condolence letters remain on the grass outside the school and affixed to fences as symbolic reminders both of the tragedy itself and of the students' sustained resolve to instigate radical changes in gun control legislation. The students' social media shrewdness has allowed them to take control of the narrative, organize effectively en masse in a short amount of time, and

N. Alvarez (✉)
Ryerson University, Toronto, ON, Canada
e-mail: natalie.alvarez@ryerson.ca

C. Lauzon
Simon Fraser University, Vancouver, BC, Canada
e-mail: claudette_lauzon@sfu.ca

K. Zaiontz
Queen's University, Kingston, ON, Canada
e-mail: keren.zaiontz@queensu.ca

N. Alvarez et al. (eds.), *Sustainable Tools for Precarious Times*,
Contemporary Performance InterActions,
https://doi.org/10.1007/978-3-030-11557-9_1

keep the topic of gun control in the headlines for weeks, defying the typically fickle attention span of the news cycle. The March for Our Lives rallies by students not yet old enough to vote and not yet old enough to be dissuaded by cynicism have raised the prospect of a new, politically engaged generation of activists with a slate of creative tactics at the ready. These include the familiar repertoires that use their own bodies as the medium for marches and die-ins, but they also extend into the domain of networked media to circulate stories, jokes, memes, and video clips that leave NRA (National Rifle Association) spokespersons scrambling for rejoinders and members of Congress, clinging to their Second Amendment rights and their millions in NRA campaign contributions, stumped. But in the wake of President Donald Trump's flaccid response to gun control proposals and the non-response of the Republican-controlled houses of Congress, the question remains as to whether students will manage to sustain the efforts of their movement and, if so, how?

Following the wave of people-powered millennial movements such as March for Our Lives, this volume responds to an emergent concern among the progressive Left: How to sustain and keep alive activist interventions in unsustainable and precarious times? How to create direct actions that effectively support the ongoing labor of political and social movements? How to create art and performance within the changing frontiers of activism that make effective use of their 'remains,' to invoke Rebecca Schneider, as a vehicle for personal and collective endurance?[1]

The episodic rise and fall (and determined continuance) of global movements have led organizers on the ground to raise questions as to whether political change can be accomplished through street protests, temporary occupation of sites, and online petitions alone. These direct actions have a crucial function, but they are necessarily limited to the time and space of protest, or to maintaining the momentum of burgeoning movements. Moreover, these same actions often suffer from having been rehearsed in the public realm one too many times. In the words of Ash Amin and Nigel Thrift, "Too often lately, the Left has been unsuccessful because it has allowed itself to be constrained by a politics

[1]We refer here to Rebecca Schneider's work *Performing Remains: Art and War in Times of Theatrical Reenactment* (London: Routledge, 2011), which questions how performance, typically understood as ephemeral and transient, *remains* in ways that exceed the logic of archival thinking.

that is grounded in habitual ways of thinking and acting—to the advantage of conservative forces.'[2] Nick Srnicek and Alex Williams concur: protest, in their minds, is often too predictable, habitual, and fleeting; moreover, they contest, it has become 'increasingly repetitive,' even feeding anti-progressive sentiments when its 'messages are mangled by an unsympathetic media smitten by images of property destruction.'[3] This commitment to habit has contributed, these scholars argue, to the Left's marked inability to protect citizens' core public and private institutions. For decades, governments and corporations have undermined constitutional laws and regulations with the primary aim to 'elevate' and serve the 'financial sector relative to the real sector.'[4]

Sustainable Tools for Precarious Times responds to these concerns by investigating work in the Americas that meets the shifting demands of activism through the creation of art activist tools, sustainable spaces, and adaptable tactics that exceed the space-time of the action itself. These pages are both an archive and a how-to-manual documenting ways of keeping effective interventionist strategies in circulation. These efforts can be grounded, as the title of this collection suggests, in shared, interrelated concepts—namely, tools and tactics, rights and their violations, sustainability and precarity. With a specific focus on the geopolitics of the Americas, we join current efforts in performance studies scholarship to engage a more inclusive hemispheric optic that takes account of the ways in which transnational migrations, economic systems, and cultural practices imbricate seemingly discrete nation-states. Operating within the macro-structures of various trade deals such as NAFTA (the North American Free Trade Agreement) and ALADI (Asociación Latinoamericana de Integración, or the Latin American Integration Association), as well as state initiatives such as Canada's Americas Strategy that have formalized cross-border agreements in the name of economic security and opportunity, the performance actions documented in this volume map the micro-movements of artists, activists, and art activists who use the tools of their disciplines to build cross-continental alliances for the precarious conditions these very agreements have, in many cases, produced. Our contributors

[2] Nigel Thrift and Ash Amin, *Arts of the Political: New Openings for the Left* (Durham, NC: Duke University Press, 2013), ix.

[3] Nick Srnicek and Alex Williams, *Inventing the Future: Postcapitalism and a World Without Work* (New York: Verso, 2016), 6.

[4] T.J. Palley, 'Financialization: What It Is and Why It Matters' (Working Paper 252, Annandale-on-Hudson, NY: The Levy Economics Institute, 2007).

examine how artists and activists have responded to the interrelated forces of economic restructuring, globalization, and neocolonialism across the continents, North and South. Most importantly, the hemispheric focus of this volume marks our effort to redress how national borders, as colonial constructs, have often stood as necessary and 'natural' delimitations of scholarly inquiry foreclosing Pan-American and Indigenous methodologies, paradigms, and practices. This volume's geopolitical vantage point unveils how activist and art activist tactics have been—and can be—put to work in the shared struggles of precarity that transcend borders.

Over the past 40 years, social movements in the Americas have modeled different methods of sustained action against the combined forces of neoliberalism's market-liberal policies of privatization and deregulation, authoritarian regimes, and forms of neocolonialism advanced by extractive industries. Bolivia's Cochabamba Water War series of protests in 1999 and 2000 in response to the privatization of water; the ongoing efforts since 1994 of the Zapatista Army of National Liberation in Chiapas, Mexico, to secure Mayan sovereignty over resources and land; the Indigenous movements in Ecuador, which organized under the Confederation of Indigenous Nationalities of Ecuador in 1986 to effect broad social reform agendas; the mothers of Soacha, Bogotá, whose continued performance actions with director Patrizia Ariza, interviewed in this collection, have brought international attention to the *falso positivos* murdered by Colombia's military forces, a plot uncovered in 2008; the Idle No More movement in 2012, which involved the occupation of public spaces to demand Indigenous sovereignty in response to failed treaty agreements in Canada—these are just a few of the many protest movements that demonstrate how a well-organized, structured, and choreographed public theatre can be put to work to effect widespread political change. Progenitors of the sustained power of protest can be found in the persistent, decades-long actions of the Mothers and Grandmothers of the Plaza de Mayo who, since 1977, have demanded accountability and justice for the disappeared during Argentina's military dictatorship (1976–1983) and in the US civil rights movements of the 1950s and 1960s, which managed to dismantle public segregation policies and reduce employment discrimination through long-form, collective, and piecemeal planning over time.

But a genealogy of sustained social action and mobilization reaches back further still to the centuries-long resistance and *survivance* of First

Peoples.[5] Michi Saagiig Nishnaabeg scholar and activist Leanne Betasamosake Simpson traces this history in her various writings about Indigenous struggle: 'We have been resisting colonial imposition for four centuries. I think our communities know something about organizing, mobilizing, and strategizing. I think our communities know a lot about *living* through the most grievous of circumstances.'[6] Simpson's comment reveals that Indigenous activism on Turtle Island (or North America) occupies an altogether different category, if not ontology, of action. The temporality of Indigenous struggle puts into question the very notion of 'precarious times' as a bounded crisis that, while marked by moments of tumult, possesses a distant horizon or endpoint.[7] Settler colonialism is not a problem to be neatly 'solved' but a system that, in Glen Coulthard and Betasamosake Simpson's words, is 'partly predicated on the ongoing dispossession of Indigenous peoples' lands and the forms of political authority and jurisdiction that govern our relationship to these lands.'[8] Activism, in this context, unfolds through what these authors call 'grounded normativity'—practices that are 'inherently informed by an intimate relationship to place' expressed through 'other people and nonhuman life forms in a profoundly nonauthoritarian,

[5] Gerald Vizenor coined the term 'survivance' in his edited book by the same name to argue for Indigenous modes of self-determination that can be enacted in the present through expressive cultural and material practices. See Gerald Vizenor, ed., *Survivance: Narratives of Native Presence* (Lincoln: University of Nebraska Press, 2008).

[6] Leanne Betasamosake Simpson, *Dancing on Our Turtle's Back* (Winnipeg: ARP Books, 2011), 16. For texts that chronicle contemporary Indigenous activism and survivance on Turtle Island see the Kino-nda-niimi Collective, Niigaanwewidam James Sinclair, Leanne Betasamosake Simpson, Tanya Kappo, Wanda Nanibush, and Hayden King, eds., *The Winter We Danced: Voices from the Past, the Future and the Idle No More Movement* (Winnipeg: Arbeiter Ring Publishing, 2013). See also Dylan Robinson and Keavy Martin, eds., *The Arts of Engagement: Taking Aesthetic Action In and Beyond the Truth and Reconciliation Commission of Canada* (Waterloo: Wilfrid Laurier University Press, 2016).

[7] This experience of grinding colonialism shares more than one parallel with the slavery of African-American people. Imagining the figure of the 'enslaved woman,' Ta-Nehisi Coates writes in *Between the World and Me*, 'Never forget that we have been enslaved in this country longer than we have been free. Never forget that for 250 years black people were born into chains—whole generations followed by more generations who knew nothing but chains' (70).

[8] Glen Coulthard and Leanne Betasamosake Simpson, 'Grounded Normativity/Place-Based Solidarity,' *American Quarterly* 68, no. 2 (June 2016): 249–255, 251.

nondominating, nonexploitive manner.'[9] In this volume, Jessica Jacobson-Konefall draws on the concept of 'grounded normativity' in her analysis of how First Nations such as the Pimicikimak Cree Nation engage in strategies of performative sovereignty to make manifest modes of self-governance and self-determination that operate outside the structures of settler colonialism.[10] And in the interview that closes this book, Cheryl L'Hirondelle describes her collaboration with inmates in *Why the Caged Bird Sings*—working on the 'inside' to share her knowledge as a singer-song writer—in terms of 'sonic survivance.' This is itself an expressive mode of 'grounded normativity' that facilitates resilience in the confines of the prison through joyful compositions.

The Participatory Theatre of Prefigurative Politics and Its *Back* Back Stage

Keeping in mind this broader historical horizon of sustained Indigenous activism over the centuries, the contributions to this anthology channel our attention on characteristics and tendencies of activism and art activism that have emerged over the last decade, particularly in the aftermath of the global Occupy movement. This was a protest movement motored by Occupy Wall Street, which began in New York City's Zuccotti Park on September 17, 2011, and centered on issues of uneven wealth distribution and corporate governance. Occupy Wall Street agitated for economic equality in the wake of austerity measures in Europe, untenably high food and fuel prices in the Middle East and North Africa, and the collapse of subprime lending in the US. In the North American context, where local Occupy encampments spread across public squares and private plazas throughout the summer of 2011, the revolutionary call of its protestors, 'We are the 99 percent,' was deliberately majoritarian. The net was cast wide to encompass diverse constituencies who, burdened by student debt, mortgage payments, insupportable market rents, consumer debt, car loans, and medical bills, were bound together in a struggle to *get by*. The profits of free market capitalism were not felt by 'the People' whose wages had stagnated and working lives

[9] Ibid., 251.

[10] For more information about the Pimicikimak Cree Nation (which we consider a prefigurative political enactment of nationhood), see Jacobson-Konefall's chapter and visit the Pimicikimak's website: https://www.pimicikamak.ca.

were defined by temporary stints, self-employment, and service work. The most visible encampment, Zuccotti Park, located in the heart of Wall Street, the financial district of New York and financial capital of the nation, was a rebuke against what the movement called 'the 1 percent.' These were the corporations and financial institutions that had spun the economy into recession and the environment into peril. The physical occupation of parks was part of a mass direct action and commentary on the 2008 financial crisis and the very system of finance capitalism. In a recession that surpassed the Great Depression preceding the Second World War, banks and automotive companies were direct beneficiaries of bailout packages by the federal government (drawing from the public purse to stabilize financial markets), even as millions of people lost their jobs, defaulted on their mortgages, and risked homelessness. Occupy responded by squatting in the public square, thus setting the stage for a nationwide performance that openly tested alternatives to capitalism—as tent cities installed communal kitchens, libraries, and medical tents—and alternatives to liberal democracy, as each Occupy encampment was organized around consensus-based General Assemblies. Occupiers installed the material infrastructure that the present had failed to provide and the horizontal, participatory politics they imagined as a future system of governance. At its height, before the mass evictions and police raids in late November 2011, more than a thousand camps took root in cities across the globe.[11]

Occupy Wall Street was a massive stage for the enactment of 'prefigurative politics.' Kamilla Petrick, a former Occupy Toronto activist, explains that 'the internal functioning of the Occupations was meant to prefigure the kind of future society desired by the activists—building a new society in the shell of the old.'[12] For almost three months, the Occupy camps were a bricks-and-mortar example of how prefigurative living—initiated through a networked call by *Adbusters* magazine to 'bring [a] tent'—could take shape as daily, embodied living. In retrospective analyses of the movement, former Occupy Wall Street activists such as Jonathon Smucker have described the social life in the public square as a 'brilliant theater' of

[11] See 'Occupy Movement: From Local Action to a Global Howl of Protest,' *Guardian*, October 18, 2011. https://www.theguardian.com/world/2011/oct/17/occupy-movement-global-protest.

[12] Kamilla Petrick, 'Occupy and the Temporal Politics of Prefigurative Democracy,' *tripleC* 15, no. 2 (2017): 495.

'a visibly participatory people's movement'[13] that brought the 'backstage' work of activism 'front stage' (using Erving Goffman's language). But Smucker differentiates the actions of 'decision-making processes, general meetings, working groups, planning, and so on' from the '*back* back stage' work undertaken by subsets of activists at different encampments who sought change on a macro-economic level.[14] He evaluates this split in terms of the '"prefigurative" public spectacles' in the camps and the 'concrete political goals and accompanying political strategies' that would bring broad-based prosperity to millions of working and middle-class people. For many, the site-specific theatre in the square, which 'enact[ed] desired social changes in the present moment,'[15] came at a cost to the movement itself. The revolution could not be realized because the politics practiced at the camps did not actually force the hand of the government. If anything, the court orders that authorized the police to evict protestors, carting tents, and tarps into garbage trucks only confirmed the power of the state. The centrality of 'big business,' and the web of industry subsidies, corporate lobby groups, flimsy regulations, and closed-door trade agreements—what Jodi Dean describes as the 'various distributed combinations of state use of market and market reliance on state'[16]—remained intact.

More worrisomely, despite the message of income inequality, and the claim to represent everyone, Occupy failed to galvanize Black and brown communities. Laura Grattan, in *Populism's Power: Radical Grassroots Democracy in America*, enumerates why:

> Whiteness permeated most Occupiers' presumptions about politics: the belief that they had a stake in American democracy to begin with, the assumption that they could assemble in public without immediate state repression, their shock and outrage at seeing police attack 'law-abiding' citizens. Whiteness also permeated Occupy's rhetoric (including its central tropes of 'occupation' and 'the 99 percent'); their priorities (student loan debt, for example, rather than basic primary education); and even their cul-

[13] Jonathan Matthew Smucker, 'Occupy: A Name Fixed to a Flashpoint,' *The Sociological Quarterly* 54, no. 2 (2013): 220.

[14] Smucker, 'Occupy,' 219–220.

[15] Petrick, 'Occupy and the Temporal Politics of Prefigurative Democracy,' 495.

[16] Jodi Dean, *Crowds and Party* (New York: Verso, 2016), 163.

turally specific forms of protest (from playfulness and spontaneity to consensus-based politics).[17]

Indeed, for Eve Tuck and K. Wayne Yang, Occupy and its whiteness represented yet another form of settler occupation on stolen land. The movement's overriding call for mass wealth redistribution, they insist, 'camouflages how much of that wealth is land, Native land.' Tuck and Yang go on to state: 'In Occupy, the "99%" is invoked as a deserving supermajority, in contrast to the unearned wealth of the "1%". It renders Indigenous peoples (a 0.9% "super-minority") completely invisible and absorbed, just an asterisk group to be subsumed into the legion of occupiers'.[18] Tuck and Yang examine a widely circulated Occupy meme showing a wide swath of US territory owned by the 1% in comparison to the smaller parcels owned by the 90% and 9%, and take issue especially with the accompanying text, 'If US land were divided like US wealth'.[19] The graphic is emblematic of entrenched settler-colonial views of land as property and occupation as a right—assumptions that Indigenous countermovements across the Americas have sought to dismantle by resisting the expropriation of Native lands.

In the years following Occupy, resistance movements have prioritized what we call 'performative conduct' alongside prefigurative living, a tactical turn Natalie Alvarez and Keren Zaiontz examine in their chapter for this book. The politics of futurity, with its utopian horizon, has given way to unapologetically instrumentalist and disruptive tactics. In an attempt to live that future now, Occupy movement cofounder Micah White proposes a ceaselessly adaptive approach to direct action that emphasizes the redistribution of capital and, by extension, the social order. In the interview for this collection, White argues that it is no longer enough to raise political awareness in a world that is universally acknowledged to be in the midst of a 'global rights

[17] Laura Grattan, *Populism's Power: Radical Grassroots Democracy in America* (Oxford: Oxford University Press, 2016), 207.

[18] Eve Tuck and K. Wayne Yang, 'Decolonization Is Not a Metaphor,' *Decolonization: Indigeneity, Education & Society* 1, no.1 (2012): 23.

[19] Ibid., 24.

emergency.'[20] Sustainable tools and time-sensitive tactics that defy the habitual ***and*** enact more democratic futures are needed to aid communities caught in the throes of political violence, manufactured austerity, and environmental disasters.

From Contingent Tactics to Sustainable Tools: Challenging Critical Orthodoxy

This collection examines the development of new tools and tactics, particularly those based in the arts that may, on the surface, appear as if they are too *frivolous* or *excessive* for activist purposes. Mock funerals and activists in panda costumes are much harder for the 'other side' (e.g., the conservative right, police and military, violent regimes) to co-opt because such actions are not always recognized as explicitly political.

These scenarios are preceded by a rich tradition of tactical interventions designed to dodge capture by institutions of power like government and corporations. Philosopher Michel de Certeau viewed these evasions of power as among the few remaining routes to cultural expression and difference available to 'ordinary' people. Part one of *The Practice of Everyday Life* theorizes a world of creative, tactical acts that daily weave through the 'proper' spheres of power without leaving a trace. Tactics do not have a place, but are mobile, temporary actions that avoid contact with systems of visibility or recognition. De Certeau views these temporal operations as the 'weapons of the weak' and sets them in relation to strategies—sites of power that can exercise control over people, resources, and territories through visible, calculable means.[21] When it was first translated into English in 1984, the tactical worldview in *The Practice of Everyday Life* bolstered arguments already in circulation that viewed subjects as agents capable of resisting institutional, governmental, or corporate entrapment. Tactics soon assumed a critical orthodoxy that aligned well with other

[20] Daniel Fischlin, Ajay Heble, and George Lipsitz, *The Fierce Urgency of Now: Improvisation, Rights, and the Ethics of Cocreation* (Durham, NC: Duke University Press, 2013), xiii.

[21] Michel de Certeau, *The Practice of Everyday Life*, trans. Steven Rendall (Berkeley: Berkeley University Press, 1984), 30.

existing frameworks that sought to claim victory for the everyday person through indeterminate acts and spaces. Within performance studies, Jon McKenzie in *Performance or Else* (2001) famously refers to this oversubscription of transgressive or resistant practices as the 'liminal-norm.' These are practices in which the 'in between' and 'marginal' count as the highest form of politically efficacious art. This disciplinary thrall to transgression is often at odds with the situation on the ground where risk is co-opted as a point of market differentiation within the creative economy. The political limitations of tactics are, in part, what compel Michael Hardt and Antonio Negri to call for an inversion of the roles of strategy and tactics and, in turn, the relationship between the powerful and the weak. The potential of social movements lies in their ability to occupy sites of power by organizing at the strategic—that is, the systemic and structural—level and engage tactically as situations require it.[22]

This collection aims to broaden the conversation from contingent tactics to strategic, sustainable tools in three ways. First, sustainable tools often entail a turn toward visibility as part of a wider call 'for the reconstruction of the plane of visibility' both for juridical recognition and mediation.[23] This investment in what Andrea Mitropoulos calls a 'thematics of inclusion, visibility, and recognition' emerges in response to a widespread acknowledgment that the conditions of precarity—such as those experienced by the undocumented migrant worker or, as Carla Melo and Jimena Ortuzar examine in these pages, the *catadores*, *cartoneros*, and 'sanmen'—are 'a result of their "invisibility" and "exclusion."'[24] Both Melo's and Ortuzar's chapters document ongoing partnerships and long-term artist residencies in Brazil, Argentina, and New York City, which we also see in Patricia Ariza's practices of community-engaged performance activism in Bogotá and Cheryl L'Hirondelle's account of her five-year residency with the Meadow Lake Tribal Council in Northwest Saskatchewan, Canada. Such work reminds us that sustainable models of social practice rely on relationships that develop over time and have the capacity to redefine the

[22] Michael Hardt and Antonio Negri, *Assembly* (Oxford: Oxford University Press, 2017), 22.

[23] Mitropoulos, 'Precari-Us?'At the same time, Mitropoulos and others recognize the need for 'clandestinity which remains an imperative for the survival of many undocumented migrants and workers in the informal economy.' Ibid.

[24] Ibid.

'plane of visibility' in terms that are self-determining, mutually beneficial, and sustainable.

A second characteristic of sustainable tools is their structure as repertoires, as explained by Diana Taylor in her analysis of performances that are primarily contingent upon the presence of 'people [to] participate in the production and reproduction of knowledge by "being there," being a part of the transmission.'[25] In her chapter on the Quebec Student Movement in 2012, Jennifer Beth Spiegel examines how the performance repertoires of protest play an important role in producing affective climates that allow social movements to reproduce, sustaining 'multigenerational and multi-sited advocacy grounded in strong social bonds and transformed social logics' (117). Finally, sustainable tools in these precarious times are disseminated, circulated, discussed, and adapted online. The political movements described in these pages are linked to networked communication technologies that make it possible for specific repertoires to be taken up and repeated across different regions. Sustainable tools, unlike contingent tactics, do not withdraw from sight, but announce their status as open-source resources. In her examination of the Chilean student movement, Daniella Wittern Bush notes how the activist umbrella group Confech created a website that not only served as a digital archive of their performance actions for international circulation but also offered a resource kit for users to create their own demonstrations.

The life of social justice movements online has also changed the very temporality of collective struggle. Networked technologies make it possible to access and take part in political action anywhere and any time. One of the distinct benefits of digital activism is that it can keep a movement ticking during and beyond the event horizon of immediate political interventions that performance actions stage and it can allow performance actions to move and take effect quickly through a participatory groundswell that is oftentimes leaderless. As Micah White observes, within 12 hours of the Brooklyn Bridge arrests of 700 Occupy marchers in 2011 social media made it possible for the movement to travel to over 50 countries (and, eventually take root in more than eighty): 'The capacity of movements to spread so quickly, and the way they're able to sustain without official leadership, is because [...] embedded in the movement is the

[25] Diana Taylor, *The Archive and the Repertoire: Performing Cultural Memory in the Americas* (Durham, NC: Duke University Press, 2003), 20.

tactic itself' (31). However, this same activity online can devolve into what Dean calls a 'circulating data stream' of clicks, messages, and posts in which 'action and application' come second to connectivity: 'A contribution need not be understood; it need only be repeated, reproduced, forwarded.'[26] User-driven digital culture can oftentimes reduce the messages of activism to the mediums (and spectacles) of YouTube, Twitter, Tumblr, and Facebook or, in White's words, to mere 'clicktivism.'

The privileging of circulation over content has been accompanied by the raiding of social media platforms, which traffic daily in disinformation. Tactics are no longer the tools of the 'ordinary' person but the territory of authoritarian regimes, conspiracy theorists, and social media trolls that create measurable damage by undermining what digital users can assume to be truthful. Not so long ago, the infiltration of press conferences, the poaching of corporate letterhead, and the copying of government websites was seen as a 'win' for underdogs of the Left. Art activist teams such as The Yes Men (1999-present) perfected these tactics and nominated their interventions as 'identity correction' in an effort to rewrite bankrupt narratives and political dithering on issues such as climate change. Identity correction often takes the form of hoaxes masterminded by the duo, known by the aliases Andy Bichlbaum and Mike Bonanno, who regularly pose as official representatives of government agencies and corporations. What The Yes Men (and, really no one!) could not have predicted was how the hoax could shift from a satirical stunt to the undoing of US democracy and the rise of what is now commonly referred to as 'fake news.' This turn to mimicry in order to bolster far Right agendas is just one example of how no tactic is intrinsic to a political side.

Precarity, Sustainability

While precarious work and living conditions have long been a feature of life under capitalism, the term 'precarity' has emerged in the past decade as the predominant (albeit hotly debated) term to describe the effects of neoliberal expansion in the post-Fordist age. Its increased circulation can be traced to the EuroMayDay protests that ignited across the European Union (EU) in 2005 in response to widespread rollbacks of social welfare systems. The political idea of 'precarity,' most notably promulgated by UK

[26] Dean, *Democracy and Other Neoliberal Fantasies*, 26–27.

social scientist Guy Standing, has become a way of describing a new social formation characterized by a move away from the predictable, punch-clock kinds of full-time and long-term employment of the industrial era to the 'flexible,' insecure, unpredictable, immaterial, and affective realm of labor-without-limits in the knowledge economies of the post-industrial era. Within the discourse of 'neoliberal freedom,' flexible labor becomes a mechanism for creating a dispensable class of laborers—the 'precariat'—who, Standing argues, 'have fewer and weaker civil, cultural, social, political and economic rights than others in the pecking order of average income.'[27] 'The precariat,' he adds, 'is the first mass class in history that has systematically been losing rights built up for citizens.'[28]

The historical uniqueness and characteristics of Standing's 'precariat' have been contested, but its pervasive uptake, coinciding with the public actions that have swept across regions in Europe, the Middle East, Asia Pacific, and the Americas, enjoins us to investigate the variegated impacts of neoliberalism. As a regulating system of financial and corporate power that prioritizes speculative investment and profit over human rights, and the privatization of government industry over welfare supports, neoliberalism is a constitutive force that shapes social realities and political subjectivities.[29] This volume joins recent work on precarity and neoliberalism in performance studies scholarship, spurred by Nicholas Ridout's and Rebecca Schneider's 2012 special issue of *TDR* as well as recent monographs on the subject of performance and neoliberalism, such as Maurya Wickstrom's *Performance in the Blockades of Neoliberalism*, Jen Harvie's *Fair Play*, and Patricia Ybarra's and Lara Nielsen's edited collection *Neoliberalism and Global Theatre*. These works collectively demonstrate how theatre and performance have responded to the erosion of social welfare under the always contextually-specific operations of neoliberalism. Our contributors extend these conversations by examining how the tools of our discipline have been put to work in arming those members of the precariat whose rights have been severely compromised by the twin forces of neoliberalism and neocolonialism.

[27] Guy Standing, 'Why the Precariat Is Not a "Bogus Concept",' *openDemocracy*, March 4, 2014. https://www.opendemocracy.net/guy-standing/why-precariat-is-not-%E2%80%9Cbogus-concept%E2%80%9D.

[28] Ibid.

[29] Nicholas Ridout and Rebecca Schneider, 'Precarity and Performance: An Introduction,' *TRD: The Drama Review* 56, no. 4 (2012): 8.

Sustainable Tools for Precarious Times asks how 'precarity' as a political idea can serve as the means for alliances and coalition building. But this collection is also mindful of the potential dangers that attend the notion of precarity when it is deployed to describe a broad class of citizen-laborers as the 'precariat.' Its sweeping invocation runs the risk of erasing the critical differences between the artist and the undocumented laborer, for example, just as it risks re-entrenching the hierarchical differences between them. Echoing Mitropoulos' concern as to whether it is 'in the best interests,' for example, 'for the maquiladora worker to ally herself with the fashion designer,'[30] our contributors probe the relational politics at work when 'sustainable tools' are created by artists who may find themselves in comparatively less precarious places than those of the 'precarious subjects' they attempt to aid. In her analysis of the inSITE biennial, which shifted its curatorial focus in 2005 to socially engaged interventionist art addressing the needs of its local Mexico-US border populations, Jennie Klein examines the fraught politics of corporately funded art projects led by star artists who come to the aid of precarious communities.

Precarity, our contributors remind us, is a concept that can train our attention on the ways in which late capitalism produces uneven conditions in which some suffer more than others from failing social welfare networks. With these cautions in mind, Ridout and Schneider nevertheless insist that '"precarity" has long been a vital and necessary tool in actions that critique capitalism, at the same time that life in neoliberal capitalism appears increasingly precarious.'[31] Precarity's '"positive qualities"—leaning away from habit, stepping outside of comfort zones, changing the speculative and uncertain act of critical thinking—can be used to undermine or interrupt neoliberalism's negative, fear-mongering mode of precarity that imposes insecurity for the many in the interest of enormous wealth for the few.'[32] As Martha Herrera-Lasso and Kimberly Skye Richards ask in their chapter, 'How might precariousness be used as a basis for exercises, alliances, and coalitions that seek to overcome precarity?' (233). In the face of widespread anxieties concerning sustainability—both economic and environmental—the contributors to this collection archive artists' efforts to harness the conditions of precarity to produce the tools necessary for its undoing.

[30] Mitropoulos, 'Precari-Us?'.

[31] Ridout and Schneider, 'Precarity and Performance,' 8.

[32] Ibid., 9.

Chapter Overview

This volume features a range of case studies that testify to the diversity and inventiveness of tools being used to foster a 'sustained social world.'[33] The contributions—which traverse Canada, the US, the US-Mexico border, Chile, Argentina, Brazil, Cuba, Colombia, and Indigenous territories on Turtle Island—invite readers to identify networks, clusters, and continuities of art activist tactics that surface across the chapters and across the Americas. Each contributor has taken up the call to analyze strategies of sustainable activism in ways that are specific and responsive to the immediate political and cultural circumstances, allowing the notion of sustainability to take on multivalent meanings from the durational to the environmental, depending on the context in which they are situated. The chapter contributions are interrupted by brief artist's pages, which serve as animated, first-person perspectives of artists working on the 'frontlines' of interventionist art. This movement between scholarly inquiry and first-person artist perspectives is designed to encourage conversation between academics and practitioners and enrich cross-disciplinary interactions between contemporary art and performance. Taken together, the contributions offer a vibrant picture of emergent tactics and strategies over the past decade that allow art activists to sustain the energy and press of political resistance in the face of a whole host of rights emergencies across the Americas.

In the interview that launches this collection, 'Protest *After* Occupy: Rethinking the Repertoires of Left Activism,' Micah White discusses the fallout of Occupy Wall Street. White characterizes the movement as a 'constructive failure,' and reflects upon the lessons he carried forward in his ongoing activist work and brief foray, between 2012 and 2016, into municipal politics in rural Oregon. Among those lessons is that social movements must be willing to reinvent themselves—'never protest the same way twice,' he instructs—or risk defeat at the hands of the state. White's criterion for what constitutes an effective tactic is contextual: so long as a given tactic is '*perceived* as protest,' then it can find traction in the revolutionary moment in which it surfaces. But it is not just the imperative to adapt and outwit; social movements must also be willing to engage the various arms of the state, and this is perhaps White's more controversial 'lesson' from Occupy:

[33] Judith Butler and Athena Athanasiou, *Dispossession: The Performative in the Political* (Cambridge: Polity, 2013), 4.

'I think we should use protests to win elections' (33). While many activists would resist engaging a system they seek to oppose or exist apart from (whether by squatting, living off the grid, or enacting prefigurative alternatives), White sees in elections another backstage, an entry point that, over the long term, has the potential to transform into a consensus-based mode of representational governance.

In 'Performative Conduct for Precarious Times,' Alvarez and Zaiontz examine the proliferation of post-Occupy strategies that have surfaced on smart phones and in the streets. These include the *Debt Resistors Operations Manual* (2012) by Strike Debt, an art activist collective identified as an extension of Occupy Wall Street that aims to dismantle the system keeping the 99% shackled to debt; and *A Practical Guide for Resisting the Trump Agenda* (2016) by Indivisible, a movement founded by former staffers of progressive Members of Congress who deliberately repurposed the obstructionist strategies of the Republication party Tea Party movement. Alvarez and Zaiontz's analysis also includes the tools generated by subscriber-based social enterprise *Safety Pin Box* (which closed in 2018) by Black Liberationists Marissa Johnson and Leslie Mac. Together, these movements and enterprises signal a proliferation of 'how to' manuals that are scripting forms of resistance, modes of 'performative conduct,' for what Zephyr Teachout calls the 'newly political.'

The two chapters that follow undertake close examinations of student movements in Chile and Canada, inviting a comparative look at strategies and tactics that helped sustain ongoing resistance in support of educational reform. In 'Their Dissidence Remains: Lessons from the 2011 Chilean Student Movement,' Daniella Wittern Bush synthesizes key lessons to be learned from a student movement that involved the entire spectrum of Chilean youth (from elementary and high school to university students), and generated enduring forms of protest in the face of constant turnover due to the precarious and liminal positions of its dissidents. Through a vivid analysis of a range of performance actions—from kiss-ins and superhero battles to beach days and marathons—with a particular focus on a choreographed zombie dance to Michael Jackson's *Thriller* that involved thousands of students, Wittern Bush investigates how the students' fusion of performance, digital archive, and charisma attracted international attention to the extreme inequalities of wealth and resources perpetuated by Chile's education system. In 'Beyond the Strike: Creative Legacies of the 2012 Quebec Student Protests,' Jennifer Beth Spiegel examines a range of creative tactics that fueled the 'Maple Spring,' the

Quebec student strike of 2012 against proposed university tuition hikes and the privatization of public services it was thought to signal. In rallies that gathered crowds of up to 500,000, students donned the now famous red squares that symbolized that they were 'squarely in the red' (or squarely in debt) due to rising tuition fees. Written from her own first-hand perspective as an organizer and participant, Spiegel shares insights into how creative tactics produced a *rêve général illimité* or 'unlimited general dream,' that is, a space where alternative social and affective configurations could be set in motion to shape collective futures.

The promise of alternative social configurations often lies in long-term, cross-sector collaborations and the chapters of this volume by Jimena Ortuzar and Carla Melo demonstrate how partnerships can serve as a bedrock for sustainable actions that redress precarious and invisible labor. In her chapter, '"After the revolution, who's going to pick up the garbage on Monday morning?" Cartoneros and Sanmen in the Age of Financial Crises,' Ortuzar undertakes a comparative analysis of Mierle Laderman Ukeles's maintenance art with 'sanmen' during her artist residency with New York City's Department of Sanitation (DSNY) and a partnership between Eloísa Cartonera, a small, artist-run press in Argentina, and local *cartoneros* (or cardboard pickers) to create hand-made books from the cardboard they collect. In bringing these collaborations between artists and waste management workers into conversation with one another from their respective corners of the hemisphere, Ortuzar draws our attention to 'the materiality of waste [and] the invisible labor it demands' as well as 'a particular geography of waste through which power relations and identity constructions become visible' (128). In 'Your Trash is my Sustenance: Recycling the Image of "Waste Pickers,"' Melo examines the Pimp My Carroça movement in Brazil. Melo observes how 'an alliance between the often criminalized art form' of graffiti and a 'stigmatized informal occupation' of *catadores* or 'waste pickers' removed these laborers from invisibility and resignified their social role as 'one that can reflect on the material conditions that have produced their predicament and potential agency' (168).

The alliances between artists and communities of sanmen, *cartoneros*, and *catadores*, respectively detailed by Melo and Ortuzar, demonstrate how socially engaged art often attends to issues of sustainability in terms of the broader maintenance of everyday life. The commitment by the likes of Ukeles and Mundano (of Pimp My Carroça) to *staying* in a given community makes them unique advocates of stigmatized laborers. (And for those artists who work in the long tradition of making objects out of detritus, there is a mutuality here in ***making do*** with what others see as disposable.) But what of those artists who seek to make instrumental art objects for communities in crisis in the absence of a sustained relationship? This is, in part, the focus of Jennie Klein's contribution, 'Sustainable Practices on the US-Mexico border: inSITE_05, Intervention, and Precarious Communities.' Based in San Diego, inSITE is a contemporary art festival and community network that, since 1992, has curated five editions that directly engage the politics of the San Diego/Tijuana border. The emphasis on border art for inSITE_05 (2005) took the form of both site-specific and highly relational modes of public art. In Klein's words, 'artists were encouraged to identify communities, ad-hoc industries, needs and spaces around and along the border and encouraged to conceptualize and design clothing and/or tools that could be worn/used' (186). The results included *Dirty Water Initiative*, a water fountain and recycling installation at the Tijuana pedestrian border crossing by SIMPARCH; *Maleteros*, facilitated by Marc Bradford, which (similarly to Pimp My Carroça, but with less success) attempted to literally and figuratively formalize the work of luggage handlers that cross the US-Mexico border; and Judy Werthein's *Brinco*, running shoes complete with compass, light, painkillers, and border maps designed to help immigrants navigate smuggling routes from Tijuana to San Diego. These works, Klein shows, conceptualize 'ready-made' tools for precarious living that can, however, often yield more for art-going publics than for communities on the margins.

As Klein also shows, artists and art activists regularly navigate between their own investments and those of a community. This describes aspects of the work of Cuban artist Wilfredo Prieto. In 'Art as Process in Everyday Life,' a conversation with Zaira Zarza, Prieto discusses his diverse range of projects from redeveloped live-work spaces to his 2015 land-art piece, *Infinite Journey* (*El viaje infinito*), which functions as a highway in rural Cuba. Works such as these tarry between Prieto's experiments in form and his interest in serving local communities. But they also show sustainability to be specific to the material practices of an island nation where sustainability under the (1962) United States embargo is a necessary way of life. In this context, the art-going public is also the community in need of a road to 'invigorate the local economy' (213), showing artists like Prieto to be powerful mediators between state resources and the constituencies in need of them.

Prieto has been active in biennials around the globe, and it is at these festival sites that bifurcations between the local and global risk being imposed by curatorial teams that pay lip service to the former through tokenistic gestures. This is the ground for Martha Herrera-Lasso and Kimberley Skye Richard's chapter, 'CAVCA buries BIACI': Activating Decolonial Tools in Cartagena de Indias.' The authors examine the artist collective Las Meninas Emputás, whose actions disrupted the International Biennial of Contemporary Art Foundation of Cartagena de Indias in Colombia in 2014. They observe how the collective's engagement with questions of sustainability—both in their lives and in their tactics—required a full-scale assault on an art institution that participates in the 'colonial machinery,' which normalizes an uneven distribution of precariousness. Herrera-Lasso and Richards raise important questions concerning the privileges imbedded in thinking along a thematic of sustainability when conditions of precarity often render such planning impossible: 'What does it mean,' they ask, 'to seek out "sustainable" practices from subjects living in such precarious situations that they do not have the resources to plan for the long term?' (233). Their contribution is followed by a conversation about a very different kind of festival in Colombia. In an interview with the Colombian-Canadian actor-director-playwright Beatriz Pizano, internationally renowned performance activist Patricia Ariza reflects on how creative resistance and community action are foregrounded on the festival stage. Their conversation surveys the state of art activism in Colombia today and the ways in which Ariza's Festival Alternativo (or FESTA) has become both a 'festival of resistance' and an 'encounter festival,' often featuring large-scale public actions involving members of the community with whom her company, Teatro La Candelaria, has formed long-standing relationships. For Ariza, performance actions in public spaces are effective forms of persistent resistance, since they are collective, mobile, immediate, and responsive to the political needs of the moment particularly as Colombia contends with the prospect of sustaining peace in the wake of the 2017 signing of its revised peace agreement with FARC (the Revolutionary Armed Forces of Colombia).

While Indigenous activism in the Americas is a vast and centuries-long process of resistance against forces of colonialism and extractivism, the final chapters of this collection telescope on strategies within very specific localities of the Cree, Algonkian speaking First Peoples in Northern Manitoba. In her chapter on the vital links between sovereignty and sustainability, Jessica Jacobson-Konefall documents how a northern Cree community, which has witnessed the devastation of their lands due to ostensibly 'sustainable' hydroelectric development, runs boat tours to educate Canadian settler-allies and activists on the ways in which they have been the beneficiaries of expropriated Indigenous land and how they might agitate alongside these communities for Cree sovereignty. Such performative strategies, as Jacobson-Konefall argues, consolidate alternative modes of self-governance based in Indigenous land practices. The final chapter of this collection offers insights into the ways in which a land-based praxis grounds the work of Cree/Metis artist Cheryl L'Hirondelle. In her interview, L'Hirondelle discusses how migratory, vocal pieces, such as *songs because of the land*, allowed her to engage in a sonic mapping of the land, effectively 'sounding' *nêhiyawin* (a Cree worldview) out in all directions, substantiating herself in the process. 'Sounding,' for L'Hirondelle, is a strategy of Indigenous survivance, which she translates as 'already-(continuing)-and' (or *âsay mîna* in Cree), underscoring the ways in which the strategies documented in these final two chapters serve as a means of practicing and sustaining sovereignty. The interviews that bookend this collection offer illuminating counterpoints from radically different contexts, worldviews, and perspectives. While Micah White gives us a glimpse of prefigurative alternatives that might shape future forms of representational governance in the context of a settler state, L'Hirondelle shows us how Indigenous land-based strategies engage in what might be called a 'refigurative politics' that make manifest the 'already-(continuing)-and' of Indigenous rights to sovereignty and self-determination.

Artist Pages

This collection is a necessarily incomplete archive of performance activism in the Americas. To attest to the extraordinary breadth and diversity of tools and tactics employed by cultural activists today, the 13 essays that follow are punctuated with a series of ten creative interventions—curated and with introductions by editor Claudette Lauzon—that form a compendium of recent performance actions. The artists profiled range widely across the spectrum of art activism, from Montreal's ATSA, whose *Le Temps d'une Soupe* is an ongoing series of public performances in which passersby are invited to share a conversation and a bowl of soup with a stranger, to Sao Paolo-based Escola de Ativismo, whose *Journey for Sustainability and Activism* in Manaus, Brazil, was a multi-day event with environmental NGOs that workshopped creative strategies for activism and advocacy. Together, the interventions are intended to unsettle any stable definitions of art activism, while creating a space to tell stories of grassroots activism in a non-discursive format that will ideally provoke new ways of thinking/feeling about the mobilizing power of creative collaboration and activism. Sustainable activism must incorporate not just cognitive but also affective elements, and this cross-section of interventions highlights art's capacity to put these very elements into play.

These ten interventions furthermore attest to an urgent conviction that sustainable practices must also be *joyful* practices. Whether it is veteran performance activist Larry Bogad advocating playfully for a *Great Collective Cough-In* (68–69) in the struggle for labor rights, or the feminist collective subRosa taking to the streets as 'cyberswamp escapees' seeking real-life connections in *Down with Self-Management! Re-Booting Ourselves as Feminist Servers* (150–151), artists are injecting what Bogad refers to as 'serious play' into activism. In the process, as he suggests, these practices 'inspire desire, collective stories, group cohesion, and identity formation—making a movement that has denser social networks and is more sustainable and adaptable through hard times.'[34]

In their recent book *Joyful Militancy*, Carla Bergman and Nick Montgomery ask us to consider 'the connections between fierceness and love, resistance and care, combativeness and nurturance.' 'Friendship,' they insist, 'is a root of freedom.'[35] This call for a kind of radical conviviality as essential for the sustenance of long-term activist engagement is echoed in several of our artist projects, perhaps most passionately in Syrus Marcus Ware's appeal to *Listen to Black Women* (226–227)—part of an ongoing series of larger-than-life drawings of otherwise invisibilized Black women activists. Accompanying the drawings is an excerpt from a public talk Ware delivered at the 2017 Creative Time Summit in Toronto, in which he emphasizes the importance of 'love and living' through acts as simple as 'sit[ting] outside on apartment stoops and tell[ing] stories,' and as profound as embracing the 'loving concept' that Black lives matter. In a similar vein, Fred Moten and Stefano Harney's poetic contribution to the volume advances a convivial militancy, which might entail 'forming a band [or] hosting a barbecue,' or might 'be a farm and a daycare, an experimen-

[34] L.M. Bogad, *Tactical Performance: The Theory and Practice of Serious Play* (New York: Routledge, 2016), 97.

[35] Carla Bergman and Nick Montgomery, *Joyful Militancy: Building Thriving Resistance in Toxic Times* (Oakland, CA: AK Press, 2017). See also Benjamin Shepard, *Radical Friendships: Outsider Networks and Social Movements* (New York: Palgrave Macmillan, 2015) and Niharika Banerjea, Debanuj Dasgupta, Rohit K. Dasgupta, and Jaime M. Grant, eds., *Friendship as Social Justice Activism: Critical Solidarities in a Global Perspective* (Kolkata, India: Seagull Books, 2018).

tal writing collective, or a mechanics shop' (254). What matters, they insist, is the retreat into fugitive states of 'welcome and visitation' as a way of circumventing what they refer to, after W.E.B. DuBois, as 'democratic despotism.'[36] Indeed, what emerges throughout the compendium of art interventions, and this collection at large, is the strong sense that creative activism, which begins so often with an ordinary, playful, and/or spontaneous act of defiance or resistance, becomes the seed for radically rethinking long-term sustainability.

References

Banerjea, Niharika, Debanuj Dasgupta, Rohit K. Dasgupta, and Jaime M. Grant, eds. *Friendship as Social Justice Activism: Critical Solidarities in a Global Perspective*. Kolkata, India: Seagull Books, 2018.

Bergman, Carla, and Nick Montgomery. *Joyful Militancy: Building Thriving Resistance in Toxic Times*. Oakland, CA: AK Press, 2017.

Bogad, L.M. *Tactical Performance: The Theory and Practice of Serious Play*. New York: Routledge, 2016.

Butler, Judith, and Athena Athanasiou. *Dispossession: The Performative in the Political*. Cambridge: Polity, 2013.

Coates, Ta-Nehisi. *Between the World and Me*. New York: Spiegel & Grau, 2015.

Coulthard, Glenn, and Leanne Betasamosake Simpson. 'Grounded Normativity/Place-Based Solidarity.' *American Quarterly* 68, no. 2 (June 2016): 249–255.

de Certeau, Michel. *The Practice of Everyday Life*. Translated by Steven Rendall. Berkeley: Berkeley University Press, 1984.

Dean, Jodi. *Crowds and Party*. New York: Verso, 2016.

———. *Democracy and Other Neoliberal Fantasies: Communicative Capitalism and Left Politics*. Durham, NC: Duke University Press, 2009.

DuBois, W.E.B. 'The African Roots of War.' *Atlantic Monthly* 115 (1915): 707–14.

Fischlin, Daniel, Ajay Heble, and George Lipsitz. *The Fierce Urgency of Now: Improvisation, Rights, and the Ethics of Cocreation*. Durham, NC: Duke University Press, 2013.

Grattan, Laura. *Populism's Power: Radical Grassroots Democracy in America*. Oxford: Oxford University Press, 2016.

Hardt, Michael, and Antonio Negri. *Assembly*. Oxford: Oxford University Press, 2017.

[36] W.E.B. DuBois, 'The African Roots of War,' *Atlantic Monthly* 115 (1915): 707–714. See also Stefano Harney and Fred Moten, *The Undercommons: Fugitive Planning and Black Study* (New York: Minor Compositions/Autonomedia, 2013).

Harney, Stefano and Fred Moten. *The Undercommons: Fugitive Planning and Black Study*. London: Minor Compositions/Autonomedia, 2013.
Harvie, Jen. *Fair Play: Art, Performance and Neoliberalism*. Basingstoke: Palgrave Macmillan, 2013.
Kauffman, L.A. 'The Theology of Consensus.' *Berkeley Journal of Sociology*, May 26, 2015. http://berkeleyjournal.org/2015/05/the-theology-of-consensus/.
Kino-nda-niimi Collective, Niigaanwewidam James Sinclair, Leanne Betasamosake Simpson, Tanya Kappo, Wanda Nanibush, and Hayden King, eds. *The Winter We Danced: Voices from the Past, the Future and the Idle No More Movement*. Winnipeg: Arbeiter Ring Publishing, 2013.
Mitropoulos, Angela. 'Precari-Us?' EIPCP: European Institute for Progressive Cultural Policies, March 2005. http://eipcp.net/transversal/0704/mitropoulos/en.
Nielsen, Lara D., and Patricia A. Ybarra, eds. *Neoliberalism and Global Theatres: Performance Permutations*. Basingstoke: Palgrave Macmillan, 2012.
Palley, T.J. 'Financialization: What It Is and Why It Matters.' Working Paper 252. Annandale-on-Hudson, NY: The Levy Economics Institute, 2007.
Petrick, Kamilla. 'Occupy and the Temporal Politics of Prefigurative Democracy.' *tripleC* 15, no. 2 (2017): 490–504.
Ridout, Nicholas, and Rebecca Schneider, eds. 'Precarity and Performance: An Introduction.' *TDR: The Drama Review* 56, no. 4 (2012): 5–9.
Robinson, Dylan and Keavy Martin, eds. *The Arts of Engagement: Taking Aesthetic Action In and Beyond the Truth and Reconciliation Commission of Canada*. Waterloo: Wilfrid Laurier University Press, 2016.
Shepard, Benjamin. *Radical Friendships: Outsider Networks and Social Movements*. New York: Palgrave Macmillan, 2015.
Simpson, Leanne Betasamosake. *Dancing on Our Turtle's Back*. Winnipeg: ARP Books, 2011.
Smucker, Jonathan Matthew. 'Occupy: A Name Fixed to a Flashpoint.' *The Sociological Quarterly* 54, no. 2 (2013): 219–225.
Srnicek, Nick and Alex Williams. *Inventing the Future: Postcapitalism and a World Without Work*. New York: Verso, 2016.
Standing, Guy. 'Why the Precariat Is Not a "Bogus Concept".' *openDemocracy*, March 4, 2014. https://www.opendemocracy.net/guy-standing/why-precariat-is-not-%E2%80%9Cbogus-concept%E2%80%9D.
Taylor, Diana. *The Archive and the Repertoire: Performing Cultural Memory in the Americas*. Durham, NC: Duke University Press, 2003.
Thrift, Nigel, and Ash Amin. *Arts of the Political: New Openings for the Left*. Durham, NC: Duke University Press, 2013.
Tuck, Eve, and K. Wayne Yang. 'Decolonization Is Not a Metaphor.' *Decolonization: Indigeneity, Education & Society* 1, no. 1 (2012): 1–40.

Vizenor, Gerald, ed., *Survivance: Narratives of Native Presence*. Lincoln: University of Nebraska Press, 2008.

White, Micah. *The End of Protest: A New Playbook for Revolution*. Toronto: Knopf, 2016.

Wickstrom, Maurya. *Performance in the Blockades of Neoliberalism: Thinking the Political Anew*. Basingstoke: Palgrave Macmillan, 2012.

Yankah, Ekow N. 'Can My Child Be Friends with White People?' *New York Times*, November 11, 2017. https://www.nytimes.com/2017/11/11/opinion/sunday/interracial-friendship-donald-trump.html.

CHAPTER 2

INTERVIEW
Protest *After* Occupy: Rethinking the Repertoires of Left Activism

Micah White, Natalie Alvarez, and Keren Zaiontz

Micah White is a lifelong activist who co-created Occupy Wall Street, a global social movement that spread to 82 countries, while an editor of *Adbusters* magazine. White has a 20-year record of innovative activism, including conceiving the debt-activism tactic used by the Rolling Jubilee, popularizing the critique of clicktivism, and identifying the emerging trend of 'social movement warfare.'

M. White (✉)
Activist Graduate School, New York, NY, USA
e-mail: micah@activistboutique.com

N. Alvarez
Ryerson University, Toronto, ON, Canada
e-mail: natalie.alvarez@ryerson.ca

K. Zaiontz
Queen's University, Kingston, ON, Canada
e-mail: keren.zaiontz@queensu.ca

N. Alvarez et al. (eds.), *Sustainable Tools for Precarious Times*, Contemporary Performance InterActions,
https://doi.org/10.1007/978-3-030-11557-9_2

Natalie Alvarez: During OWS, you found yourself at the center of a large-scale global social movement. Can you talk about what concrete changes you hoped to accomplish through mass organizing?

Micah White: Now that we're in 2017 it's hard to remember the intense, magical, revolutionary moment that Occupy emerged out of in 2011. The Arab Spring was raging and all of these autocrats like Hosni Mubarak [former Egyptian President, 1981–2011] were forced to step down, which had been previously deemed impossible, and then the protests spread to Spain and there were people going into their squares having general, consensus-based assemblies. The goal of Occupy was really revolution. We believed that there was going to be a regime change in America just like there had been in the Middle East, and that the regime we were going to overthrow was finance capitalism and its domination over our democracy. I tell people that we had this revolutionary goal for America in mind and they say, 'No, no, we don't believe that that's true.' The proof I give is that right after Occupy collapsed, *The Washington Post* asked me and the founder of *Adbusters* (Kalle Lasn, the other person who came up with the idea of Occupy), to write an editorial.[1] In that editorial, we talk about how we were dreaming of soft regime change in America. I say that not because it's proof that we said it, but to say that *The Washington Post* printed it. So, the point here is that in 2011 even the *Washington Post* confirmed, 'Oh yeah, that's what you guys were going for.' [*laughs*] Looking back, it does seem absurd. What we wanted was to overthrow the financiers' control of our democracies, and it was a response to Citizens United, which just happened a year earlier in America, so it was a revolutionary movement.[2]

Keren Zaiontz: In your book, *The End of Protest: A New Playbook for Revolution* (2016), you describe OWS as a 'constructive failure.' Why was it important to you to narrate the fallout of Occupy in 'constructive' terms?

Micah White: If you look at the history of American activism, and the collapse of the anti-globalization and anti-war movements [between 1999 and 2003], there was a period of stasis. Occupy was this huge rebirth of American activism in a way that hadn't been seen in a generation. So, when it collapsed in 2011, a lot of activists led by progressive NGOs and union people wanted to use the momentum of Occupy for their own ends. They would say, 'Occupy was a success, and the reason it was a success is

[1] 'Why Occupy Wall Street Will Keep Up the Fight,' *The Washington Post*, November 18, 2011.

[2] Citizen's United refers to the 2010 US Supreme Court ruling that enabled unlimited spending by corporations and unions on ads to influence elections.

because it changed the discourse: it brought income inequality into the mainstream discourse, and now people are talking about this thing that they previously weren't talking about.' To me, that was a really dangerous and hurtful thing for them to say because the goal of Occupy, as I said earlier, was not to change the discourse. The goal of Occupy was an actual change in the political regime, and actual transformation of who had power in our world. I started to say instead that Occupy was a failure, but it wasn't a total failure, because I think it's really important to acknowledge that Occupy did a lot of good things: it *did* change the discourse, it *did* train a new generation of activists who became organizers for Black Lives Matter, and the [2017] Women's March. But the most important thing that it did, and why I called it a 'constructive failure,' is that it illuminated the limitations of our contemporary ways of thinking about activism. That, I think, is a real gift; for decades, activists have been chasing the same narrative and the same story line about how social change will be achieved through mass action on the streets, with millions of people. Once we did that with Occupy, and realized that it doesn't work, it allows people to try something else! So that's why I called it a 'constructive failure.'

Keren Zaiontz: One of the criticisms of the Occupy movement was that the commitment to participatory politics in the General Assemblies proved a barrier to radical political change. (The kind of change that would see the state be more accountable to its constituencies rather than corporations, or what you describe in your writing and other contexts as 'getting money out of politics.') Both activists within and outside the movement openly questioned the efficacy of participatory processes such as horizontal decision-making, arguing that the time of consensus was at odds with the time of revolution. What was your own experience with consensus decision-making in OWS, and do you see it as compatible with large-scale social movements?

Micah White: Well, it's a really important question because there is a real danger in not learning the correct lessons from Occupy, and then not continuing the experiment. With Occupy, we were right about the necessity for social movements to be led by the participants, and that the participants themselves should be dictating the direction and this, ultimately, was the strength of our movement. The reason why Occupy spread so far, so quickly (to every city on Earth practically), is because it was based on consensus-based decision-making, which meant that if you wanted to create an Occupy [encampment], you didn't have to get anyone's approval: you just showed up in the square, then anyone else who showed up there with you […] that was Occupy in your town. There was no central leadership. Had there been a central leadership, I very much doubt it would have spread so quickly and so far, and been so sustained. Things like the Women's March, which does have a central leadership, were able to do a one-day action, but they weren't able to do more than 24 hours of protest. Occupy was sustained for a few months. At the same time, it is important to acknowledge that the way that consensus-based decision-making was practiced during Occupy was inadequate and broken. Another way that Occupy was a constructive failure that we can learn from is that we don't have to do a militantly naive General Assembly model where anyone can block everything. My experience at Occupy Berkeley was that there was one guy who obstinately blocked everything, and he would try to say why he blocked everything and, ultimately, it's because he could. That was his contribution: to just block everything. On top of that, there was no authority to kick anyone out, because with a purely open social movement, who's to say that this person isn't part of Occupy. It became very messy, very quickly. But going forward, we know that social movements need to solve the problem of how to make collective decisions together. I don't think it should be based on strict consensus, where everyone has the power to veto everything. But I do think that we shouldn't swing to the other extreme of trying to give power back to a single charismatic leader, whether it be Dr. Martin Luther King Jr. or Donald Trump. I think that's flawed. What I anticipate is that some sort of social movement emerges out of Spain or Italy or China—who knows?—that will have a process for making decisions together as a group that will work, and enables a much more sophisticated social movement to emerge (Fig. 2.1).

Natalie Alvarez: You were implying a linkage between the lack of a centralized leadership and the possibility of a sustained action. Can you elaborate on that?

Micah White: Well, one of the things that's remarkable is the speed at which ideas spread around the world. You can actually do really interesting studies about the speed at which social protests have spread throughout human history. For example, in 1848, Europe erupted in this revolutionary wave led by the tactic of barricade-creation. Historian Mark Traugott figured out how long it took the barricades to move from Paris to Berlin. (Basically, it took about seven days for this tactic to spread across Europe.) If you compare that to OWS, and what happened when 700 people were arrested on the Brooklyn Bridge, that's the moment when Occupy became

Fig. 2.1 Occupy Bank of America, March 15, 2012, rally and march in New York City. Activists 'moved in' to a branch by setting up a sidewalk living room on the theory that 'the bank took our homes so we're moving in with them.' A half dozen people were arrested. Credit: Michael Fleshman

a global news story. That's when the movement really spread everywhere. So, it took 12 hours, or something like that, to go from the Brooklyn Bridge arrests to, practically overnight, 50 countries that had Occupys. The capacity of movements to spread so quickly, the way they're able to sustain themselves without official leadership, is possible because—like the barricades, and like Occupy—embedded in the movement is the tactic itself. It's not like a traditional thing where people don't know what to do and have to ask someone. Instead, with Occupy, you already know what to do: you occupy the financial district, you do the General Assembly, and you can go online and learn about the twinkle finger gesture if you like, but even that's not obligatory [...] All the rules in the game are embedded in the idea for the protest itself. Even the Women's March has these simple steps: 'I'm going to participate in the Women's March. How do you do that? You march, with women.' It's obvious. It's not like other, older forms of social protest, where, 'We're going to have a communist revolution. How do you do that? You ask your [...] Leadership team.' [*laughs*]

There's no clear idea about what that is and what that means. One way I look at the Consensus Assemblies is that they were a way of slowing down time: their inability to create a decision is the very reason why the movement lasted so long, because we couldn't do anything, we we're stuck in the square trying to figure it out. If the police said 'Do you want to leave?' we would be like, 'I don't know, we need to talk about it.' It would take two days to figure out what we're doing with ourselves. That's part of the problem. It's part of the strength too, you know.

Keren Zaiontz: In your writings, you urge activists on the Left to never protest the same way twice. Why is it crucial *not* to repeat the same tactics when demonstrating?

Micah White: I'll give an anecdote. I was living in Berkeley with my wife while she was doing her graduate studies. And they had these student occupations, these student protests, where the students would go into a classroom, lock themselves in the classroom, and shout out demands from the upper windows. Obviously, the tactic failed because in the history of military science there's never been a battle won by people who have locked themselves in a space or been completely encircled. It was interesting to know about this experience, because they kept doing it, and they kept losing because eventually you run out of food or they just kick down the door. One day, though, I was walking down the street near campus, and there was this abandoned building, and there were all these police in tactical gear going into the building, and I said to one of them, 'Oh my gosh, what is going on, is there a kidnapping situation in there?' and he said, 'No we're training.' And I realized that they were training on how to deal with the student occupation tactic. They were literally using a campus building to train how to neutralize the tactics that these students had been using against them. This is why it's so important to never repeat the same tactic twice, because the government invests a lot of energy and training in learning what tactics are being used and how to defeat them. That's what they do. They wait for tactics to be effective, and then they learn how to defeat them. Throughout human history what happens is that a new tactic emerges among protesters, and then the state figures out how to neutralize it and it's never effective again. After 1848, the barricades were never again effective. Never. It's the same with Occupy, it will probably never again be effective to occupy a financial district. And so, as an activist, you have to acknowledge that and say, OK, I can't protest the same way again, because I will be defeated. It's tricky because I think you can combine elements together, and I don't exactly know at what threshold something becomes a new tactic. The larger point is that we can't just replicate exactly the same thing over and over again.

Natalie Alvarez: We'll come back to the question of sustained action and the repertoires and tactics of actions in a little bit, but I want to move onto the aftermath of Occupy and the fact that you've now turned to the electoral process. We want to hear more about your own experience engaging with municipal politics in rural Nehalem, Oregon: why are you encouraging activists and social movements to engage directly with the state?

Micah White: I think that activists have been chasing this idea that we can manifest this kind of collective power over our government—a collective sovereignty—through protest in the streets. I trace this idea back to the core principles of democracy: the idea that the authority of government is based on the collective will of the people. It's written into the [1776] Declaration of Independence in America; it's written into the Universal Declaration of Human Rights passed in 1948 by the United Nations after World War II. How do you manifest the collective will of the people? Well, you do that with street protests and large-scale marches. It's a kind of logic that I think is no longer true. Maybe that logic came to an end in 2003 with the failed anti-Iraq-war march. What I'm saying is that if you can't manifest sovereignty through collective action in the streets, then there's only two ways left: you can win elections or you can win wars. Those are the only two ways that our society passes power to someone who is not currently in power. Maybe it used to be true that you could manifest large-scale protests and that the government would finally say, 'You know, by seeing the large-scale of your protest, you really are a legitimate authority.' But I don't think that's true anymore, at least not in Western democracies. After you realize that as an activist then you also understand that we have to use protest to win wars or win elections. I think we should use protests to win elections. Trying to win wars is not only immoral, it is also foolhardy. Viably speaking, it just seems impossible to win a war and have a positive outcome. So, we have to figure out elections. I don't think that means voting for [US Senator] Bernie Sanders. I think that means, literally: how would you have a social movement like OWS, for example, also engage in electoral politics? What would that look like? How would you do that without just becoming the standard parties? I put this forward to activists because I think it's a strategic necessity, and that you have to figure it out. Even though we don't want to, you still have to do it.

Keren Zaiontz: Have you had conversations with other activists or pictured what it would look like if a movement like Occupy took power in electoral terms?

Micah White: To test this idea out, I lived in rural Oregon for about four and a half years (2012–2016), and I ran for mayor. One thing that's interesting about the rural community I was living in is that there were only 210 voters. It's an easier test case than, you know, New York City, where there's millions of voters. It was also a nonpartisan election, which now that I'm learning more about the electoral process, I'm realizing how important that is too. In cities like New York where elections are partisan, and you have to be part of a party, it's much harder to break through. But this was a nonpartisan election. So, I ran for mayor, but I didn't say, 'Vote for me because I'm such a good person.' I said, 'I'm going to create something called the Nehalem People's Association. This is a community discussion group; we'll have community meetings before each city council meeting and talk about what city council has on their agenda for the next day. We'll also talk about what we think they should do, and if I'm elected mayor, then I promise to abide by the decisions of this group.' That was the basic concept. So, when the mayor of such and such city proposes some sort of reform, they're really putting forward what the group told them to do. That's what I think it would look like: a social movement that elects delegates of itself. The Five Star Movement in Italy is a really great example of that because they call themselves a movement, but they are also the third largest political party in Italy, and they have got people elected into power, and those people have submitted to the decisions of the movement. So, it is possible, but it challenges that notion of representative democracy, which is so important to American politics and, more generally speaking, Western democracy, and I think it challenges progressive electoral strategy that is so invested in charismatic individuals like Bernie Sanders. It's something we could put our hopes and dreams in but it's a challenge.

Natalie Alvarez: How receptive were locals to that model?

Micah White: In my town, I got 20 percent of the vote, which obviously means I lost, but it was still 20 times better than the Green Party, and 10 times better than what DeRay [Mckesson], a famous Black Lives Matter activist, did when he ran for office in Baltimore (he didn't even make it through the primary). On top of that, he spent an insane amount of money, whereas in my tiny town I got 20 percent of the votes, and spent under a thousand dollars, something like that. Some people loved it, they were really receptive. But the way the opposition fought it was horrible; *they* actually made a movement of it! They called all the people they knew and made up a story, 'Did you know that he's cheating on his wife and that he's a satanist?' Those were the two stories they spread around. By the time I heard about it everyone else had heard it three times [...] Again, that doesn't mean that it couldn't work. I was naive about the degree to which they would just make something up. I found that very hurtful and I don't know how to reply to someone who says, 'You're cheating on your wife,' other than to say, 'That's just not true'. But you also don't want to go out onto the street saying, 'I'm not cheating on my wife!' So, it's a weird conundrum.

Natalie Alvarez: Well, the fact that they had to resort to smear campaigns is a kind of perverse testament to the power of your idea. They probably recognized the potential of the model you were proposing, so they had to resort to that, unfortunately.

Micah White: The community meetings, we had several of them, and a *ton* of people came out. I calculated, and at some point, I think 30 or 40 percent of all the voters in the community came to at least one meeting. This is in contrast to city council meetings, where one, or no people, go to them. You can look up the minutes, and literally no one goes to them. The community is not involved in the decision-making process at city council. So, people would come to our meetings and they would leave interested, because it would be the first time that someone said to them, 'What do you think we should do in our community?' They are 210 voters but there's still a tiny group within that tiny group that controls everything, and has convinced people that that's the way it should be. So, I do think they were threatened that some people said, 'Hey, we'll get together, we'll talk about the future, and we'll do it.'

Natalie Alvarez: We want to move now into questions that more directly respond to the themes of *Sustainable Tools for Precarious Times*. Part of the book attempts to grapple with how artists, activists, and communities can sustain themselves in the face of manufactured crises such as government scandals, and austerity measures, and naturally occurring ones, such as environmental disasters. Can you talk to us about what sustainable activism looks like to you?

Micah White: Yeah, again, a really important question. I've been an activist since I was 13; it's all I've ever done. And now that I'm 35, one thing that I've noticed is that there are fewer and fewer people who are able to sustain activism into their 30s. Activist burnout is a huge problem.

I think I've never burned out partly because I've always been an outsider. I always switched tactics and switched campaigns whenever I got bored with what I was doing. I have a mental device to ward off burnout, and this is what it is: revolution is a social phenomenon that has several interesting features. One of those features is that it often comes as a surprise. Revolutionary moments often come when they seem least likely and most distant. This is true of the Russian Revolution [1917], of Occupy, of Black Lives Matter [2013-present], it's even true of the Women's March. These things emerged when they seemed least likely. So, one way to ward off burnout is to say, 'When the revolution seems least likely, it's most likely to happen.'

I think the other way to maintain sustainability is to question one of the core assumptions about activism: that it's all up to us, it's all up to human action. A lot of what creates revolutionary moments is outside of human control, like food prices, and causes the social organism to be more conducive to social protest, to going into the streets en masse. A lot of times those are factors outside of human control, and so if you're able to say, 'It's just not a revolutionary moment right now,' [*laughs*] it makes it easier to sustain yourself than to constantly think, 'I'm not creating the revolution right now, it's my fault, because I didn't do the right action.'

Keren Zaiontz: Do you think also that revolution is a young person's sport? You say you're not seeing as many of your contemporaries as you did when you were in your 20s. Is there something about the ways in which different priorities take over when you're in your 30s?

Micah White: I have a distorted view on this because I'm completely sustained by my activism, which is very rare, and much different than someone who is trying to be an activist in their 30s and also works a full-time job, and supports their family on top of that. But I do think that within activism, a very pernicious idea started to percolate in the 1960s, which is that the young people were the vanguard of the revolution. The youth and students and universities and college campuses would be the place from which the next great revolution would emerge. I think that people like [Herbert] Marcuse really promoted this idea, and it obviously won them a lot of acclaim from young people who were a large part of these social movements, because all of a sudden they were being told, it's not the peasants, or the workers, it's the 19-year-old student who is going to be the revolutionary vanguard. And it sounds great when you're young, but I think it's a really dangerous and incorrect view. Young people might be a heavy component of social movements, but they have no historical context. And I say this as someone who was a young person protesting: you have no understanding of what's really going on and, moreover, you completely underestimate the power of the status quo.

That's another thing that young people do. They don't realize that power in our society is really held by people in their 60s who have been doing this their entire lives, who have large cash resources, who have networks of control and power, and who will do anything to defeat you. So, we need to shift back our concept of the revolutionary vanguard, and I think it's safe to say that the revolutionary vanguard is someone who's more like 30 or 40 or 50. You would see the emphasis change from activists in their 20s trying to lead the revolution to putting themselves in a position to lead the revolution when they are 40. A lot of people think, 'Well, I didn't lead the revolution when I was 25, it's over,' and that's a big part of the burnout.

Keren Zaiontz: It's an interesting way to think about sustainability within activism: in your 20s, you enter into a kind of apprenticeship, and you then mature into a leadership role over time. I want to slightly shift tracks to consider yet another facet of sustainability. The contributors in our book examine tools and strategies that are sustainable in a durational sense, that are designed to *exceed* the moment of protest, and enter the sustained press of resistance a political movement demands. This emerges in part from the post-protest malaise of 'Now what?' that so often follows marches and other direct actions. How can art-activists avoid falling into the kind of predictable, outmoded repertoires that your book decries?

Micah White: It's a good question. Going back again to this idea that revolution is a social phenomenon and that it has characteristics that are constant throughout human history, one of those that I mentioned earlier is that it comes as a surprise. Another characteristic that's also constant is that it always comes back. It's a recurring phenomenon. We know that because we can go all the way back: from Ancient Egypt, there are records of social unrest and revolution, and we know it's happened every so often since. So, we can rest assured there's going to be a revolutionary moment in the future. It may not be a successful revolution, but there will be a moment when people rush into the streets and start protesting in whatever way it then looks like to protest. For me, the question of sustainable action has more to do with what to do between those revolutionary moments. However we protest, it's historically contingent and kind of arbitrary. We can march in the streets because that's what they did in the

1960s [...] or we could be doing something else, because that's what they will do in the future. The realization that the specific tactics we use are arbitrary is liberating. As long as it's *perceived* as protest, and it's done consistently, then we can make art if we want, we can try to build clandestine insurgent movements if we want, until some sort of revolutionary moment emerges. I'm really big on not engaging in the 'drudgery' mindset; instead, I think that it's really important to realize that Occupy, or Black Lives Matter, or the Women's March, or even the Russian Revolution, these are moments that just *took off*. So if the things we're doing are not taking off, that means it's just not the right moment: not that we need to keep pushing on it. There's a kind of grinding that people do but we can have a little bit more joy, take a break right now, and, you know, prepare.

Keren Zaiontz: But don't you see something like Black Lives Matter and the Black Liberation movement as an extension of the civil rights movement? As part of a long historical arc of struggle as opposed to recurring boom and bust cycles?

Micah White: I do, in the sense that I think that there's a revolutionary story line that goes back to Ancient Egypt. We are all part of that multigenerational struggle. Everyone who protests is part of that multigenerational struggle, and sometimes it's taken the form of anti-segregation activism, or sometimes it's taken the form of the women's right to vote. But these have all been efforts by humanity to achieve greater collective freedom and liberty, and most importantly to transform the way power functions in those societies. So I think we're all part of this grand movement, for sure. What I want to push against is a belief held by a lot of community organizing oriented people who think that it's all up to us, and that we need to exert a lot of energy. Occupy increased in size dramatically, but creating it did not take a lot of energy. Even the creation of the Arab Spring didn't take a lot of energy to get started. Revolutions just *take off*. Know what I mean?

Keren Zaiontz: In other words, you didn't have to *convince* people in 80-plus countries about the merits of Occupy.

Micah White: It caught their imagination. I think there are times in human history when people are more susceptible to social protest, and we don't fully understand what makes that happen. We don't know exactly why people become, en masse, more susceptible. As activists, it's a question of, 'What do we do between the moments when people are susceptible?' People have been talking about income inequality for a long time, then it takes Occupy for people to think that it's worthy of protesting. If you talk to people about it today, they're not going to go protest. [*laughs*] Why were you protesting about it in 2011 but not in 2017? It's because they're not susceptible to that kind of mass hysteria. That's interesting and worthy of researching.

Natalie Alvarez: It seems that we're currently witnessing what might be called a new frontier of activism characterized by tactics of mimicry and camouflage. I'm thinking, for example, of your recent encounter with Black Matters, the front group for Russian trolls that successfully posed as an activist organization. We're seeing the Trump administration study the playbooks of the Left for social media strategies and groups like Indivisible reverse engineer the tactics of the Tea Party. How do you see these emergent tactics shaping the future of protest?

Micah White: It's important for activists to realize that this is happening. I think the experience of Occupy, which impacted the governments of 82 countries [...] 82 countries, their governments, their police forces had to go out and deal with the fact that their people were protesting, and that they were protesting in a movement that wasn't created in their country! [...] We live in a world where, all of a sudden, very powerful forces—nation-states, militaries, and governments—have woken up to the fact that they can create social movements in other people's countries to achieve their strategic objectives. This is not a new thing, because Russia has been accusing America of doing that since the color revolutions.[3] The US State Department would train activists, they would fund activists, they would provide resources. The difference now is all you need to do is post something on Facebook and *boom* it spreads. (We didn't train anyone in America to create OWS.) So, now we see Russia trying to do that in America. They're mimicking social movements, social protests, and I think that's a really dangerous development. The obvious benefit for Russia is, well, maybe they will create something that takes off and influences American politics. The second benefit for them is maybe they will end up completely

[3] In his article for *The Guardian*, 'I started Occupy. Russia tried to co-opt me' (November 2, 2017), White contextualizes the color revolutions in the following way:

> Russia's attempts to foment, stage and manage social protest in western democracies is a strategic response to allegedly American-funded "color revolutions" like the Rose, Orange and Tulip revolutions against Russian-allied governments in Georgia (2003–2004), Ukraine (2004–2005) and Kyrgyzstan (2005) along with, arguably, the Arab Spring (2010–2012) and Euromaidan Revolution (2013–2014).

de-legitimizing American protests, which would be a major blow to American democracy, and would also benefit them strategically, because if people start to think that every protest is just created by some foreign government, and it's not real, then they won't participate in them. So I think that activism is in a dangerous situation where it is being used as a pawn by greater forces.

At the same time, I wonder if that's one of those necessary evils. Maybe a revolution in America would require the support of an outside force [...] I think that the only option is for American activists and activists everywhere to become more sophisticated in how we think about what we're doing, and cognizant of the geopolitical implications of what we're doing. It's not just a game. It has real consequences for other governments around the world, and they're invested in dealing with that.

CHAPTER 3

Performative Conduct for Precarious Times

Natalie Alvarez and Keren Zaiontz

The swiftness with which Donald Trump, the 45th President of the United States, has used his office to undermine immigrant and migrant rights, broad-based access to health care, reproductive rights, and safeguards to the environment, testifies to the speed at which democracies can be undone. The art of government can shift quickly from managing institutions to banning bodies and building walls. Daily scandals generated by the Twitter President have only fueled the coalitional voices of the Left to *act now*, to move fast to salvage social and environmental safety nets. The precarious present requires an active citizenry in the United States that is one step ahead of the next legislative maneuver, executive order, or hateful tweet. The groundswell of anticipatory activism was instanced in rallies such as the post-inauguration Women's March in Washington and cities beyond, and the People's Climate March, which took place on Trump's 100th day in office. Taking to the streets is, of course, a time-tested practice of social justice movements in which protesters insist on their right to

N. Alvarez
Ryerson University, Toronto, ON, Canada
e-mail: natalie.alvarez@ryerson.ca

K. Zaiontz (✉)
Queen's University, Kingston, ON, Canada
e-mail: keren.zaiontz@queensu.ca

N. Alvarez et al. (eds.), *Sustainable Tools for Precarious Times*,
Contemporary Performance InterActions,
https://doi.org/10.1007/978-3-030-11557-9_3

the public sphere. In her *Notes Toward a Performative Theory of Assembly*, Judith Butler argues that this action is always invested in futurity; in other words, when we assemble in times of struggle, it is over '*what will be* public space [...] how bodies *will be* supported in the world.'[1]

Our disastrous present was, in part, precisely what the anti-austerity movements of 2011 sought to avert. This was a period marked by a commitment to public models of support from communal kitchens at the heart of Occupy Wall Street in Lower Manhattan to the early morning 'red line dances' (*ligne rouge*) in the Metro by Université du Québec à Montréal students during the Maple Spring, to the use of the public square as a democratic laboratory in Cairo and across the Arab world. These movements were not just reacting to their respective financial crises and hardline regimes; they were establishing the material conditions for a future free from authoritarian, privatized governments. We now know the fallout of these futures. The sustained physical presence of protesters in the streets was almost universally met with police pepper spray, truncheons, and heavy fines for gathering in public. In response to the kettling of the body politic, many groups in the United States have turned to hardcopy and hypertexts to reflect on the failures of the present and map out strategies for new futures.

The publication of *The End of Protest: A New Playbook for Revolution* by Occupy Wall Street co-founder Micah White;[2] the open source *Debt Resistors' Operations Manual* by Strike Debt; the downloadable agenda, *A Practical Guide for Resisting the Trump Agenda* by Indivisible; and videos and tasks by *Safety Pin Box*, formerly run by Black liberationists Marissa Johnson and Leslie Mac, point to how the Left is regrouping (and bringing about a new politics) through *tactical texts*. These examples signal a proliferation of 'how to' manuals that script forms of what we refer to here as 'performative conduct,' or modes of histrionic dissent that overturn social scenarios underpinned by politeness and complicity. Precarious times call for 'bad acting' or, to be more precise, oppositional expressive behaviors that can sustain movements against the distribution of inequality that defines the present. As a tool frequently found in the kind of nuts-and-bolt texts named above, performative conduct marks a return to the

[1] Judith Butler, *Notes Toward a Performative Theory of Assembly* (Cambridge, MA: Harvard University Press, 2015), 72.

[2] See also our interview with White in this volume, 'The Protest Repertoires of Left Activism after Occupy.'

genre of the advice manual—now adapted to user-driven platforms such as Google Docs, YouTube, blogs, wikis, and photo-sharing sites. These texts guide, train, and prepare the 'newly political'[3] on how best to comport themselves in their role as agents of political resistance.

Genealogies of Performative Conduct

Digital culture has enabled new modes of self-administration in which we teach ourselves by watching others. The self-taught content user finds her mimetic antecedent in the reader of advice manuals from the Victorian period, which proved valuable to middle-class publics, particularly women who ran households and sought advice on marriage, mothering, and social etiquette. Just as the Victorian advice manual made a claim on women's lives by attempting to shape their domestic conduct—revealing the home to be no less regulated than public space—contemporary movements such as Facebook COO Sheryl Sandberg's Lean In have also made claims on women's lives, by attempting to shape their workplace conduct. This top-down movement, based on the principles outlined in Sandberg's bestselling self-help book *Lean In*,[4] promotes the advancement of women in the workplace through actionable tips such as 'proceed and be bold,' peer support groups (called 'circles'), marketing campaigns, and open source resources. Those resources include 'expert videos,' or what might best be described as 'conduct videos': instructional reels that help cisgendered, predominately white women steer their way through the white-collar workplace. Salary raises and making the most of team dynamics can be achieved by following expert advice on effective body language, affect, and word choice. Not surprisingly, feminist scholars such as Angela McRobbie have roundly criticized Sandberg's movement for placing the burdens of systemic inequality in the workforce onto the personal behaviors of women. The fault largely lies with the female employee's inability to perform with confidence, not the corporate world itself and its reproduction of both hostile and benevolent forms of sexism. Women are poor performers, ***bad actors*** in need of coaching lessons. What McRobbie and other critics have been quick to point out is that the tools of Lean In take the activist techniques of second-wave feminism and gut them of their

[3] We refer, here, to what Zephyr Teachout calls 'the newly political,' or people who were drawn to politics for the first time.

[4] Sheryl Sandberg, *Lean In: Women, Work, and the Will to Lead* (New York: Knopf, 2013).

politic. McRobbie notes how the 'Lean In circles taking place in many US cities, [are] a ghostly version of its more overtly feminist predecessor the consciousness-raising group of the 1970s.'[5] Similarly, Lean In advice pages, such as 'How to be a workplace ally,' neutralize the labor of allyship—historically connected to supporting feminist, queer, Black, and Indigenous liberation movements—into a series of workplace tips. Here, acting as an ally means not interrupting your female coworker at a meeting or acknowledging that her ideas are in fact *hers*. From consciousness-raising groups to self-help circles, from activist tactics to handy business tips, from intersectional ally to coworker enthusiast, Lean In is an example of how neoliberal culture empties the medium of its message by recasting the Left for the purposes of economic competition.

Indivisible

Perhaps because neoliberalism has so ably mimicked progressive politics—only to radically alter its conditions, concentrating wealth and privilege upwards—less attention has been paid to how a subset of social justice movements are playing their own game of copycat. Mimicking the operations of neoliberal culture and the Far Right, these movements reveal (yet again) that appropriation is *not* a one-way crossing between the powerful and the dispossessed. Indivisible is one such example of how Leftist movements are poaching from the powerful. Founded by former staffers of progressive Members of Congress who experienced first-hand the successful strategies of Tea Party activists, Indivisible borrows from the Tea Party's core tactics—reverse engineering the Far Right with the aim of re-establishing a future for progressive politics.

The Tea Party first surfaced in 2009 to oppose President Barack Obama's administration (2009–2017), a rejection that unfolded through aggressively anti-Black means. Donald Trump's 'birtherist' claims—that Obama was not born in the United States and therefore could not hold the office of President—were culled from conspiracy theories first circulated at national Tea Party conventions and news sites. That 'black-lash' against the first African-American President was paired with obstructionist tactics that bordered, at times, on the very abolition of government. Parsing the racist politics from its activist strategies, Indivisible has pursued

[5] Angela McRobbie, 'Feminism, the Family and the New "Mediated" Maternalism,' *New Formations: A Journal of Culture/Theory/Politics* 80, no. 8 (2013): 133.

what they call 'replicable practices' of the Tea Party.[6] The collectively authored Indivisible guide literally scripts congressional advocacy for its grassroots members by taking their cue from the very playbook that 'paved the way for the Republican takeover' and 'Donald Trump today.'[7] Downloaded over one million times to date (as of June 2017), the open source guide highlights 'four advocacy tactics to put pressure on your three Members of Congress (MoCs)': town halls, local public events, district office visits, and coordinated calls.[8]

It was through these four tactics that small groups of Tea Partiers engaged in what Indivisible authors call 'defensive actions.' Constituents noisily disrupted town halls and ribbon-cutting ceremonies, flooded staffers with phone calls, and showed up en masse at state offices demanding meetings with their MoCs. The goal of these tactics was not legislative reform but the end to the Obama government and, by extension, the reach of the federal government. The Indivisible guide not only divides the practices of the Tea Party from its regressive politics but also repurposes them as tools of resistance to secure against a 'damaged future,' to borrow Butler's words.[9] These advocacy tactics are visible, real-time acts that, through public assembly and *performative conduct*, become an instrument for Leftist resistance.

Pressing performative conduct in service of protest, Indivisible activists are encouraged to be bad actors and histrionic constituents in tactical manuals tailored to district office visits, coordinated phone calls, local public events, and town halls. Early in 2017, in what would be the first in a series of attempts by the Republican-controlled House of Representatives to repeal the Affordable Care Act (ACA), colloquially referred to as Obamacare, Indivisible was quick to publish resistance resources on its site, including the 'Save the ACA [Affordable Care Act]: Die-In Planning Guide.' The ACA was Obama's signature domestic policy legislation, making private health insurance more affordable and expanding the remit of Medicaid to cover more adults. In June 2017, the legislative push by Republicans succeeded in installing what is now (derisively) referred to as Trumpcare. The repeal, which could poten-

[6] Indivisible, *A Practical Guide for Resisting the Trump Agenda*, updated March 9, 2017 (2016): 6. https://www.indivisible.org/guide/.

[7] Ibid.

[8] Indivisible, 'Chapter Four: Local Advocacy Tactics That Work,' 2016. https://www.indivisible.org/guide/advocacy-tactics/.

[9] Butler, 67.

tially leave up to 23 million Americans uninsured, remains to be approved by the Senate.[10] In an attempt to stave off a future that imperils the bodies of those with so-called 'pre-existing conditions,' Indivisible has called on its participants to 'publically pretend to die [in order to] highlight a deadly problem.' Citizens are encouraged to *act badly* in the fullest sense of the word: to engage in public dissent outside the district office of their Representatives and to do so with markers and cardboards. The Die-In Planning Guide recommends fashioning 'cardboard tombstones,' a 'grim reaper costume,' and 'tissue paper wreaths and bouquets for deceased constituents.' The campy spectacle of the die-in is the perfect antidote to a government invested in acting against the bodies of its own citizens.

Well before participants were stitching grim reaper costumes and drawing tombstones, the tactics of Indivisible largely focused on the scene of the town hall. The original guide provides step-by-step notes on how to script questions, where to sit in the venue, when to boo or hiss, what personal stories and testimony to share, and the importance of recording footage for local reporters and social media sites. Town hall claques have become particularly important forms of congressional advocacy in the lead up to, and aftermath of, legislation to repeal the ACA. In the months following Trump's inauguration, many town halls served as vital sites of public assembly to contest the deregulation of the federal safety net. As town hall events gained traction on social media, one could witness how Indivisible was shifting the performative conduct from public relations platform to heart-wrenching testimonials.

In a February 2016 Arkansas town hall with Republican Congressman Tom Cotton, a local constituent from the national advocacy group, Better Medicare Alliance, demonstrates the Indivisible playbook with its repertoire of tactics in full effect. She stands up confidently but neutrally, raising her hand to attract the staffers with the microphone: 'Look friendly or neutral,' the Indivisible guidelines insist, 'so that staffers will call on you.'[11]

[10] That figure is according to the findings by the nonpartisan Congressional Budget Office, released June 26, 2017. As of the writing of this chapter (April 2018), the Affordable Care Act remains to be fully repealed. The Kaiser Health News includes a timeline that tracks how the legislation has been altered at state and federal levels since Donald Trump took office. See Julie Rovner, 'Timeline: Despite GOP's Failure to Repeal Obamacare, The ACA Has Changed,' April 5, 2018. https://khn.org/news/timeline-roadblocks-to-affordable-care-act-enrollment/.

[11] Indivisible, 18.

But once the constituent gets a 'firm hold on the mic,' as the playbook urges, her neutrality gives way to unapologetic anger as she addresses Cotton who stands alone receiving questions on the apron of a proscenium stage facing a full house.[12] From the center of the auditorium, she introduces herself as an ambassador of the Better Medicare Alliance and an angry constituent. In keeping with the Indivisible playbook, the constituent has prepared an incisive question designed to be difficult to evade and she demands answers. But before she gets to the question, she establishes the life-or-death stakes of the repeal: 'I can tell you about three family members who would be dead—dead and homeless—were it not for the ACA.'[13] The rousing supportive applause to these opening remarks elicits a well of emotion in the constituent, which only fuels her anger—'I am an angry constituent,' she repeats—demonstrating the ways in which anger is rarely a 'singular emotional state' but a 'mobile affective intensity,' as Dylan Robinson has argued in the context of Indigenous activism and public assembly, which finds many forms of expression.[14] Anger often 'invalidates the speaker through the perception of being unjustifiably resentful'; but anger, as Robinson observes, is never merely anger.[15] As this constituent's affect makes clear, anger serves as a way of shoring up a well of emotions in a moment that demands bravery in the face of policies that produce precarious and vulnerable citizens. 'I am an angry constituent' is a refrain that must be reiterated to insist upon its justification, the right to be angry, and to refuse invalidation.

The constituent is transparent about her own family's health problems, including her husband's dementia, and she expresses her resentment that folks should be expected 'to remain calm, cool, and collected' with a potential repeal on the horizon.[16] Indivisible's guidelines account

[12] Ibid.

[13] A full recording of the town hall can be accessed on the YouTube channel, Live Satellite News. The constituent from the Better Medicare Alliance Group can be heard at the 20-minute mark of the video. See 'Arkansas Tom Cotton Hostile Town Hall (PT1),' YouTube video, 56:19, posted by Live Satellite News, February 22, 2017. https://youtube.com/watch?v=lwuE_yD3Rg8./.

[14] Dylan Robinson, 'Enchantment's Irreconcilable Connection: Listening to Anger, Being Idle No More,' in *Performance Studies in Canada*, ed. Marlis Schweitzer and Laura Levin (Kingston and Montreal: McGill-Queen's University Press, 2017), 217.

[15] Ibid., 217.

[16] See Indivisible's Facebook recording of this exchange, 'Woman Asks Senator Tom Cotton (Arkansas) "What Insurance Do You Have?"' Facebook, posted by Indivisible, February 22, 2017, online video. All quotes from the constituent that follow in this chapter

for the risks of too much affect and too much anger, which MoC staffers will quickly try to suppress: *'Don't give up the mic until you're satisfied with the answer,' the guide instructs*, 'If you've asked a hostile question, a staffer will often try to limit your ability to follow up by taking the microphone back immediately after you finish speaking.'[17] The guide offers a script of suggested lines to say if the staffers attempt to stifle speakers: 'I'm not finished. The MoC is dodging my question. Why are you trying to stop me from following up?' The self-identified 'angry constituent' and ambassador for the Better Medicare Alliance has no need for this script, however; she is enveloped by adrenalized supporters who jump to their feet in uproarious applause when she poses her question to Cotton—'What kind of insurance do *you* have?'—a question that is meant to reveal just how remote the Member of Congress is from the folks he represents. Note that the guide stresses that '[a]fter one member of your group asks a question, everyone should applaud to show that the feeling is shared throughout the audience'[18] and that unity is demonstrated powerfully in this moment.

Cardboard Cories

Importantly, Indivisible offers this repertoire as advocacy tactics that are intended to be ongoing, as evidenced in its motivational tagline, 'Let's KEEP DOING this' (upper case emphasis theirs).[19] Even after the devastating repeal in 2017, Indivisible continued to generate texts, including scripted dialogue with MoCs, to hold them accountable for their decisions.[20] Performative conduct entails the training and preparation of expressive behaviors for the persistent press of activist action. That Indivisible's repertoire works within an explicit mandate of sustained—and sustainable—action is made apparent by the guides it offers constituents on what to do *between* events; performative conduct, in other words, encompasses a sustained mode of engagement that works to secure the

can be accessed on this video or through the full town hall recording on YouTube, cited in the note 14.

[17] Indivisible, 18.

[18] Ibid.

[19] To see the collective imperative for resistance, scroll to the bottom of the homepage for Indivisible Front Range Resistance under the section 'Taking Action.'

[20] See the Sample Call Dialogue on the Indivisible resource page, 'Hold your Senators Accountable for their TrumpCare Votes,' https://www.indivisible.org/resource/hold-senators-accountable-trumpcare-vote/.

efficacy of the event itself. This extends to Indivisible's 'Cardboard Cory' conceit, an ongoing action that effectively allows constituents to practice performative conduct; and when they are not engaging with Cardboard Cory directly, constituents are given a list of actions to undertake in the interim: 'Here's what you can do between Cardboard Cory events,' an Indivisible website reads.[21]

Members of Indivisible Front Range Resistance (IFRR), representing communities and cities in Colorado's Front Range, created six 'Cardboard Cories'—life-sized cardboard cutouts of Senator Cory Gardner—in response to his chronic absenteeism. The senator had failed to hold a town hall with constituents in more than one year (from the time of the divisive 2016 elections well into the summer of 2017). IFRR members maintain a rigorous tour schedule for the Cardboard Cories to appear in public forums, whether on the streets or in town halls across Colorado, offering citizens an opportunity to ask questions and voice concerns, which are recorded on camera and posted on social media for the not-cardboard Cory to see and hear. The actively involved and available Cardboard Cory is often pictured at community events affectionately embraced by constituents. He has participated in the cleanup of a roadway in Colorado Springs, marched the streets of Denver, and visited the Douglas Springs Fair and Rodeo; he holds interviews, has a Twitter account, and a Facebook page, as well as an online Cardboard Cory Events Calendar.

While the cardboard cutout may be an old gimmick, as Dan Njegomir remarks in *Colorado Politics*,[22] it serves a critical function within the emergent repertoires of performative conduct: it allows constituents to rehearse how best to approach congressional representatives and articulate their concerns effectively and persuasively. At a February 2017 town hall in Denver that proceeded without the senator and attracted over a thousand citizens, the smiling Cardboard Cory was placed behind a podium with the US flag draped behind him. Constituents approached the microphone placed in front of the podium and directly addressed the cutout with their questions to rounds of supportive applause. The predominantly respectful direct addresses to Cardboard Cory are encouraged by Cory's 'handlers'

[21] Visit the website, Cory Gardner: Absentee Senator for Colorado, http://gardnertown-hall.com/.

[22] See Dan Njegomir's, 'Coming to Your Town Soon: The Cardboard Cory Gardner!' *Colorado Politics*, July 27, 2017. https://coloradopolitics.com/coming-town-soon-cardboard-cory-gardner/.

who seem acutely aware that the growing anger and frustration in response to their absentee senator could be cathected on the cutout. As Cardboard Cory observes in an interview: 'my handlers make sure that I am treated like an actual child when I am at my various events. That means someone is with me at all times while I am out in the community. No one can walk off with me who isn't a trusted adult. No one should abuse me or verbally attack me, even in jest.'[23] The Cardboard Cories are not intended to serve as effigies that are subjected to ritual burnings (one of the Tea Party's actual tactics), but proxies that allow citizens to rehearse civil disobedience through persuasive performative conduct.

Some recorded engagements with Cardboard Cory have attracted widespread attention for the constituent's histrionic embrace of candor and frankness, made easy by the presence of a smiling cardboard facsimile. A month after Senator Gardner ordered the arrests of ten disability rights activists who staged a 57-hour sit-in at his Denver office demanding that he oppose the Republican Party's plan to repeal and replace the Affordable Care Act, a woman took the opportunity to confront Cardboard Cory outside the office about his discriminatory behavior. With her arm placed gently around the cutout, in the way a mother might hold a child during a disciplinary moment of tough love, the woman looks Cardboard Cory straight in the eyes and asks, 'I would like to know why you actually discriminate against people with disabilities. I mean, you don't just blow them off, you keep them out of the building, you get them arrested, and you don't *talk* to them. I just don't understand what this bigotry toward people with disabilities is about. Can you explain yourself?'[24] The silent cutout with its impassive smile stands next to the woman as comical evidence of the senator's reluctance to *talk* about disability rights. In other recorded engagements, constituents can be seen gently placing their hand on Cardboard Cory's shoulder as they try to persuade the proxy to recognize what is at stake. In a form of Boalian rehearsal theatre, citizens strengthen their resolve and steel their nerves in practiced direct addresses to state representatives with Cardboard Cory. These rehearsals encourage a key aspect of performative conduct that is inextricably tied to the speech

[23] See 'An Interview with Cardboard Cory,' *Indivisible* (IndivisiBlog), October 17, 2017. https://indivisible.org/blog/interview-cardboard-cory/.

[24] Cardboard Cory, Twitter post, July 27, 2017, 3:30 p.m. https://twitter.com/CardboardCoryCO/status/890700949815263232.

Fig. 3.1 Community activist Sylvia questions Cardboard Cory in connection to the senator's indignant treatment of people with disabilities, July 27, 2017. Video by Katherine Farnan and the Indivisible Front Range Resistance of Colorado (@ CardboardCoryCO)

act, namely, giving the newly political agency to self-authorize an injunction and demand the right to be heard (Fig. 3.1).[25]

The Cardboard Cory stunt worked: Senator Gardner succumbed to the pressure of his screened photograph taking the limelight and finally appeared at town halls in Colorado Springs, Greeley, and Lakewood in August 2017. Despite the actual senator's belated appearance, Cardboard Cory's presence remains in demand. In December 2017, Cardboard Cory appeared with concerned citizens outside the field office of Senator Gardner in Denver when it appeared closed without explanation days before the Republican 'Tax Cuts and Jobs Act' was scheduled to go to the Senate floor. Cardboard Cory will, it seems, live on—perhaps because he is serving as such an effective surrogate.

[25] We allude here to J.L. Austin's formulation of the performative speech act whose felicity is contingent upon a number of conventions and conditions, most notably, its proper authorization; that is, the individual issuing the performative must be appropriate for the invocation and authorized to make it. See J.L. Austin, *How To Do Things With Words* (Cambridge, MA: Harvard University Press, 1975, Second Edition), 34–35.

Though writing in the context of circum-Atlantic performance, Joseph Roach offers a useful distillation of the dynamics of surrogation that helps pinpoint how a cardboard cutout, which might otherwise seem like a hollow political stunt, has proven to be so tactically effective. Surrogation is, after all, the means by which a culture 'produces and reproduces itself' in response to a perceived absence or loss, and collectively negotiates expectations: 'In the life of a community, the process of surrogation does not begin or end but continues as actual or perceived vacancies occur in the network of relations that constitutes the social fabric. Into the cavities [...] survivors attempt to fit satisfactory alternatives'; he adds, 'surrogation rarely if ever succeeds [...] The intended substitute either cannot fulfill expectations, creating a deficit, or actually exceeds them, creating a surplus.'[26] Cardboard Cory exceeds expectations precisely because, as a cutout, there is no pretense to fulfill them, which allows Cardboard Cory to become, ironically, an icon of a more authentic and honest representative. The cutout gives shape, in other words, to the significant deficit created by Senator Gardner's ineffective leadership. In a July 23, 2017, Facebook post, Cardboard Cory states its commitment to do better:

> When I came on the scene, I thought I was destined to a life of being just like Cory (after all, I am made in his image). But now, I think I can do better. I think I can listen better, I think I can empathize more, and I honestly think I can better represent your concerns.
>
> So, since your Senator isn't responding, please feel free to ask *CardboardCory*. I won't pretend to have all the answers, but I won't pretend you don't exist, and I'll try like heck to understand your concern and respond like I think a real Senator should. I'll do my genuine best, ok?[27]

If performative conduct is constituting ideal forms of activist engagement, Cardboard Cory is becoming its ego ideal, filling the void of effective representation. In an interview, Cardboard Cory proves impressively self-reflective about the key both to its success and, as a cardboard surrogate, failure to succeed. Cardboard Cory 'simply uses the voice of the people'[28] and tries to 'listen better' while modestly noting the unfair advantage

[26] Joseph Roach, *Cities of the Dead: Circum-Atlantic Performance* (New York: Columbia University Press, 1996), 2.

[27] See Cardboard Cory's Facebook page, accessed February 22, 2018. https://www.facebook.com/CardboardCoryCo/.

[28] See 'An Interview with Cardboard Cory.'

he has over his flesh-and-blood counterpart: 'Of course, as a screened photograph, it's easy for me to listen.'[29] Cardboard Cory is, in this respect, figuring the performative conduct of effective governance, as an icon made by the people that uses 'the voice of the people' and listens to the people.

As a sounding (card)board for the people's concerns that provides an opportunity to rehearse performative conduct, Cardboard Cory is representative of a post-Occupy turn toward a more direct engagement with electoral politics, which was largely eschewed during the Occupy movement. As a 'social laboratory,' the global Occupy movement was characterized, as Yates McKee notes, by a 'refusal of representational politics' even as it initiated 'self-organized experiments with political and economic practices […] nevertheless capable of tactically engaging the state.'[30] Indivisible's guide to performative conduct is the means by which a Left populist hegemony is figured and brought into being through the expressive behaviors of its electorate in direct, on-the-ground congressional advocacy.

Strike Debt

The Debt Resistors' Operations Manual, first released in 2012, is positioned by its group of anonymous authors as a 'living document,' a first but nevertheless ongoing edition that is designed to aggregate strategies from readers.[31] It is, they write, 'a project that we will *all* build together—a collectively written manual for collective action.'[32] The project is in development under the auspices of Strike Debt, an art-activist collective identified as an extension of Occupy Wall Street. Strike Debt emerged from a recurring flashpoint among Occupy activists concerning the shared condition of indebtedness that bound them together, some of it documented in the form of testimonials on the Tumblr site 'We Are the 99 Percent.' The impetus for the collective's formation was a desire to find solidarity in this shared condition and investigate the potential of building political alliances on the basis of an identity position of debtor, which a

[29] Ibid.

[30] Yates McKee, *Strike Art: Contemporary Art and the Post-Occupy Condition* (London: Verso, 2016), 19.

[31] Members of the Strike Debt assembly, Occupy Wall Street, Common Notions, and Antumbra Design, 2012. *The Debt Resistors' Operation Manual* (2012): v. http://strikedebt.org/The-Debt-Resistors-Operations-Manual.pdf.

[32] Ibid., vi.

corrupt financial system not only interpellates but also necessitates. The collective initially organized under the idea of a 'debt strike' as a way of mobilizing the power of a mass movement of debtors who would simply refuse to pay their debts and thereby atrophy the financial system. The idea of debt resistance in the form of a 'debt strike' was, in McKee's words, 'inverted into the active verbal phrase *strike debt*, recalling the open-ended injunction to 'occupy Wall Street.'[33] The strike debt moniker placed ~~Debt~~ in struck text in the center of a red square, signaling its coalitional politics with student protestors in Quebec who signified their condition of being 'squarely in the red' due to soaring tuition fees with squares of red felt pinned to their clothes.[34]

The Debt Resistors' Operations Manual acknowledges the atomizing force of debt, which grips debtors with a sense of fear, frustration, and shame; the guidelines it offers on everything from the 'mission creep' of credit reporting agencies to the analysis of credit scores are designed to equip readers with the information necessary to recognize that debt is a systemic condition rather than a personal tragic flaw of financial mismanagement. The manual enables readers to identify themselves as an informed debtor, to overcome the fear and shame, and work from a position of agency to engage in collective debt resistance. Readers are encouraged to share their stories and experiences with 'the way debt affects [them]' to surmount the sense of fear and isolation that the debt system begets: 'Remember,' the manual insists, 'you are not a loan!'[35] As McKee puts it, 'To speak as a debtor, and to address others as debtors, was an empowering process in its own right; the simple act of testifying, building community and solidarity based in a shared experience of refusing to be interpellated as a guilty debtor.'[36]

[33] Members of the Strike Debt assembly et al., x.

[34] See Jennifer Spiegel's sharp analysis of the Quebec student protests in this volume, 'Beyond the Strike: Creative Legacies of the 2012 Quebec Student Protests.'

[35] Members of the Strike Debt assembly et al., vi.

[36] Yates, 161–162. Strike Debt's rolling jubilee events would become pivotal sites for debtor assembly. Launched in the form of a retro 'telethon' variety show in November 2012 titled 'The People's Bailout' at Le Poisson Rouge in New York City's Greenwich Village, the rolling jubilee became an ingenious and enduring strategy of debt resistance and a tactical response to the federal bailout of the Wall Street. The rolling jubilee events raise funds that are used to purchase defaulted debts from collectors on the secondary debt market at discounted prices, which would then never be collected, effectively erasing debt.

The Debt Resistors' Operations Manual offers strategies on how 'resistors, debtors, and allies' can individually negotiate the crush of debt on an ongoing and daily basis. Section 9 of the manual, for example, titled 'Debt Collection: Don't Feed the Vultures,' guides readers on how to push back against the debt collector who assumes that debtors are uninformed about the alternative courses of action available to them and overwhelmed by 'Kafkaesque bureaucracy, harassment, and shame.'[37] The manual guidelines provide debtors with a new discourse, premised on debtors' rights and the legal limits of debt collection, which shapes the performative conduct of debt resistors. Significantly, the manual details how collection agents ought to conduct themselves according to the Fair Debt Collections Practices Act of 1996 (FDCPA) and provides scripts of lawfully required correspondence, such as the mini-Miranda—statements a debt collector must use when contacting an individual to collect a debt; if these statements are not used, the debtor has grounds to sue. In response, the manual provides counter-scripts to debtors for written letters and phone calls, line-by-line tactics on how to dispute the debt, legitimate or not, which often manage to discontinue contact from the collection agent.[38]

The deception, intimidation, and bullying tactics of collection agents, which typically escalate toward the end of the month when they are pressured to meet quotas, are in violation of the FDCPA and the manual guides readers on how to respond to the most common—and illegal—of collectors' tactics. The manual appendices provide templates on how to write 'angry letters'[39] for a variety of circumstances, from requesting a validation of debt, disputing debt, and demanding a cease and desist, to requesting the removal of medical debt. The language scripted in these letters is assertive, angry, and informed, modeling the performative conduct of the debt resistor, fortified by the knowledge of debtors' rights. But while the manual offers tactics that script the performative conduct of individual debt resistors, it returns repeatedly to the ways in which these individual acts of resistance can be put toward '*collective* action and radical transformation,'[40] which is the Manual's over-arching objective: 'Collective action,' they write, 'is the only true solution.'[41]

[37] Ibid., 84.
[38] Ibid., 87.
[39] Ibid., 10.
[40] Ibid., emphasis in the original, 80.
[41] Ibid., 35.

Safety Pin Box

The mobilization of progressive movements like Strike Debt and Indivisible has largely paralleled the rise of open source platforms, which have democratized access to information through wikis, blogs, file sharing, forums, and collaboratively written documents. But while the transparency of open access materials and media is often linked to inherent claims of 'progress,' technology, like power, is not distributed equally across content users. The populist movements rallying in the name of the '99 percent' have been predominately white, and this racially unmarked yet powerful category (and identity) has shaped the types of Leftist manuals, videos, and other digital resources currently in circulation.[42] For people of color, sometimes, radical change must be imposed through a pay wall. That may well appear like a contradictory justification, but it describes how Safety Pin Box enacts its unique brand of performative conduct. In the trio of case studies examined here, Safety Pin Box is an outlier because it was a for-profit business not a social justice movement. It is discussed in this chapter for the ways in which it makes deft use of the culture of actionable self-help to materially aide the cause of Black liberation in a post-Ferguson United States.[43]

Safety Pin Box was a commercial enterprise created by activists Marissa Johnson and Leslie Mac 'for white people striving to be allies in the fight for Black liberation.'[44] The subscription-based business was created in the aftermath of Donald Trump's 2016 election, which saw a proliferation of 'bias-led harassment and intimidation' against the whole panoply of minority society in the United States including immigrants, Muslims,

[42] See Laura Grattan, 'Popular Resonances in the 21st Century: The Tea Party and Occupy,' in *Populism's Power: Radical Grassroots Democracy in America*, especially her razor sharp critique of whiteness and occupy (Oxford: Oxford University Press, 2016), 202–212.

[43] The August 2014 Ferguson Riots in Ferguson, Missouri, were precipitated by the death of 18-year-old Michael Brown, an unarmed African-American teenager shot six times by police. Months later, in November 2014, the grand jury decision not to indict white police officer Darren Wilson in Brown's murder sparked further riots in Missouri and across the United States. The Ferguson Riots were a tipping point for a community that faced daily harassment by police including disproportionate traffic stops, physical searches, ID checks, arrests, and lethal force. Ferguson proved to be a formative moment for the Black Lives Matter movement, a coalition of rights activists and Black liberationists demanding an end to the systemic police violence, mass incarceration, and murder of Black people.

[44] Safety Pin Box, 'What is Safety Pin Box?' (2016). https://www.safetypinbox.com/home/.

Blacks, Jews, LGBTQ2+ people, and women.[45] Johnson and Mac took note, with a sense of moral outrage, as a cottage industry of solidarity pins cropped up overnight that claimed to demonstrate allyship in the face of hate crimes. As they state on their site, for 'little to nothing, financially or emotionally,' white people could wear pins 'identifying them as "safe people" to marginalized populations.'[46] Johnson and Mac saw the pin as a symbolically empty gesture that stood in for concrete action that would make 'tangible, measurable difference in the movement for Black lives.'[47] Safety Pin Box thus arose as an antidote to the fantasy of the solidarity pin as ally work. Johnson and Mac embraced the role of social entrepreneurs, working with individual white clients and groups on a fee-for-service basis.

Safety Pin Box made skillful use of marketing language generally found in a variety of commercial membership programs. Customers could purchase a premium subscription (US $100 per month) in which they gained access to a package of select perks including, 'Exclusive calls to action when urgent ally services are needed.' Other levels included a shared subscription between two users called a Pin Pals box (US $50 per month) and a digital E-Ally box subscription (US $25 per month). Safety Pin Box also sold one-time packages such as the Ally Backpack (US $100), which included videos and a glossary. In full disclosure, one part of this authorial team, Keren, purchased the Ally Backpack and the digital E-Ally box membership for three months throughout 2017–2018. The goal was to learn what kind of conduct Johnson and Mac sought to impart to their clientele. For Keren, the mission of Safety Pin Box spoke to the long-standing issues of racial inequality in her predominately white institution. Indigenous and ethnic studies scholars such as Eve Tuck and K. Wayne Yang have long agitated for dismantling whiteness in the university—and its attendant discourses of innocence and naiveté—by arguing for an end to sym-

[45] See Southern Law Poverty Centre's post-2016 election hate watch page, 'SPLC Hatewatch,' December 16, 2016. https://www.splcenter.org/hatewatch/2016/12/16/update-1094-bias-related-incidents-month-following-election.

[46] See Safety Pin Box, Frequently Asked Questions. https://www.safetypinbox.com/faq/.

[47] Safety Pin Box, Frequently Asked Questions, 'Why Is It Called Safety Pin?' and the comparative chart that follows, 'Wearing a Safety Pin' versus 'Safety Pin Subscription.'

bolic decolonial gestures.[48] Change will not transpire by affixing a pin to one's lapel, nor will it happen through what Tuck and Yang call 'critical enlightenment' (robust discussions that stall at the level of debate), because both point to the appearance of a problem not their solution.[49] In place of appearance, they call for a mode of conduct for which there is no rehearsal: 'the repatriation of Indigenous land and life.'[50] While Johnson and Mac did not, at least within the context of their business, make mention of repatriation, they did frame the transactional nature of their work as 'a form of reparations' in which white people purposely redirect their capital to support Black women. If the most direct route to a socially just future is the redistribution of *white coin*, then what was the purpose of the performative conduct—the self-reflexive tactics—that Safety Pin Box proscribed on a one-time and monthly basis?

One answer is that in a digital culture that makes a virtue of do-it-yourself endeavors, white people *can help themselves*. If, historically, such critical self-transformation has relied upon indiscriminately resourcing people of color for what they know about being racialized ('help me understand...'), then Safety Pin Box insists upon payment for that extraction. This necessarily restricted who could access the company's supply of videos, articles, and facilitated discussions. Safety Pin Box asserted both authorship and ownership over content dedicated to mobilizing white people 'in the fight against white supremacy' through what Johnson and Mac called 'measurable tasks.'[51] The insistence on copyright speaks directly to the ways in which the activist work by women of color across civil rights, feminist, LGBTQ2+, and Black liberation movements has been repeatedly and systematically marginalized and appropriated.[52] Compounding this theft is the consciousness-raising fatigue that surrounds educating white people about genealogies of racial oppression

[48] Tuck and Yang argue that the act of critically engaging in decolonization should not 'attempt to reconcile settler guilt and complicity, and rescue settler futurity,' an argument that also applies to the anti-oppression work of Safety Pin Box. Eve Tuck and K. Wayne Yang, 'Decolonization is Not a Metaphor.' *Decolonization: Indigeneity, Education & Society* 1, no. 1 (2012): 21.

[49] Ibid., 21.

[50] Ibid.

[51] These statements can be found on the 'Subscribe' page of the site, https://www.safetypinbox.com/subscribe/.

[52] See Black Lives Matter co-founder Alicia Garza's article, 'A Herstory of the #BlackLivesMatter Movement by Alicia Garza,' October 17, 2014. https://thefeministwire.com/2014/10/blacklivesmatter-2/.

from the slave plantation to mass incarceration, from the mass lynching of Black men to the murder of Black people at the hands of police, from the white flight to the suburbs to the present day gentrification of urban cores. This race labor carries an affective toll for people of color who, in exposing 'real' historical and present-day wrongs, absorb the stresses of 'white shock' and 'white fragility.' In the Ultimate White Ally Glossary, Volume 1, which is included as part of the Ally Backpack, Johnson and Mac use Robin DiAngelo's definition of white fragility as '[a] state in which even a minimum amount of racial stress becomes intolerable […] often resulting in the outward display of emotions such as anger, fear, and guilt […].' Monetary payment makes the work of mediating these 'intolerable' emotions visible. It disrupts the assumption that anti-oppression work should be like other women's work, free, a *labor of love*. It also points to the ways in which 'open source' does not always resonate as purely democratic for women of color who daily battle for property over their own ideas and bodies—even within those very movements that they have forged—rendering them 'helpmates' or erasing their contributions altogether.

Of course, remuneration ensures material sustainability in the present. Johnson and Mac channeled the profits yielded from the monthly subscriptions to a funding pot they called Black Women Being. These were one-time 'financial gifts' to '[a]ny and all Black women & femmes doing any work towards the liberation of Black people.'[53] Applicants essentially entered a lottery and, if selected, were awarded an amount 'based on the funds raised from that month's subscriptions.' The criteria for eligibility were deliberately broad. There was no formal assessment of a proposed project, for example, because the money itself was meant to function as reparations. Black Women Being addressed the gender and race pay disparity that Black women face as organizers who 'do a majority of the labor for Black liberation work and are also the least likely to be financially sustained while doing it.' Thus, Safety Pin Box established an implicit distinction between white clientele, who were instructed to do their weekly 'tasks,' and focus on critical self-improvement, and the recipients of Black Women Being, who were encouraged to continue their various advocacy efforts. The outcome was not a reinscription of the uneven activist labor noted above, whereby Black women are left (without credit) to do the frontline work, so much as it is an insistence upon separate repertoires of activism.

[53] The quotes in this paragraph are from the Safety Pin Box page, 'Black Women Being.' https://www.safetypinbox.com/black-women-being/.

When compared to the planning guides and manuals of Strike Debt and Indivisible, the internal line drawn here appears antithetical to the coalition building necessary to resist everything from white supremacy to Wall Street. And yet, it is a stance that resonates across communities of color. David Garneau, writing about the politics of reconciliation between Indigenous people and settlers in Canada, writes: 'One lesson: while decolonization and Indigenization is collective work, it sometimes requires occasions of separation—moments where Indigenous people take space and time to work things out among themselves, and parallel moments when allies ought to do the same.'[54] This statement carries over to the subscriber-activist relationship established in Safety Pin Box in which white allies had a different kind of work to undertake than Black liberationists.

Keren's E-Ally box came with a file that contained weekly tasks connected to a specific critical race issue, as well as access to an Ally Q&A on Facebook, or 'Pin Collective,' made up of other subscribers. The purpose of this type of performative conduct was to take stock of one's own actions. For example, the E-Ally file, also entitled the 'Monthly Accountability Card,' included bullet-point instructions to 'spend at least one hour working on your task,' to journal, and 'to share your progress online' through theme-specific hashtags. This is activism meets what Melissa Gregg calls 'productivity self-help,' or the drive toward greater worker efficiency in the modern corporate workforce through personal goal setting. Gregg examines how the rise of goal-setting systems such as SMART, or Smart, Measurable, Actionable, Realistic, and Time-Specific emerged in the early 1980s, at the same time as workers faced greater precarity on the job through the freelancing and casualization of labor.[55] The ideal worker was transformed into an entrepreneurial figure: a confident corporate actor who relied on her 'SMARTs' rather than broader organizational support. Safety Pin Box critically re-imagines SMART through the company motto ('Effective, Measurable Allyship'). In so doing, they also reimagine the 'ideal worker' as an ideal

[54] David Garneau, 'Imaginary Spaces of Conciliation and Reconciliation: Art, Curation, and Healing,' in *Arts of Engagement: Taking Aesthetic Action In and Beyond the Truth and Reconciliation Commission of Canada*, ed. Dylan Robinson and Keavy Martin (Waterloo: Wilfrid Laurier University Press, 2016), 23.

[55] Melissa Gregg, 'The Limits of Self Help Productivity Lit,' *The Atlantic*, April 22, 2016.

ally. In their 11-point guide, 'How To Use This [Ally] Backpack,' they instruct: 'Come up with a list of next steps for yourself whether that be education, reparations, self-work, or joining an organization, and set a timetable for doing these steps. Put them in your calendar and tell a friend so they can hold you accountable.' Worker efficiency is rewired to promote the unlearning of racial domination.

Once in receipt of her Ally Backpack, Keren took seriously the call to *act better*, to be more personally accountable, and side-step the part of the fragile white girl. She studied the definitions included in her Ultimate White Ally Glossary, Volume 1. Printed onto a stack of index cards, the glossary of 20 words includes both a 'Standard Definition,' with descriptions pulled from sites like dictionary.com, and a Safety Pin Box definition co-authored by Johnson and Mac. On the reverse of each card, placed into two neat columns, are examples of the word as well as its use in a sentence. These usages deliberately stray from the presumed objectivity typically associated with dictionary entries. Note, for instance, the definition of 'systemic oppression':

> The school-to-prison pipeline [...] is a good example of how systems incarcerate individual children.

And then the word is used in a sentence:

> We can never deal with systemic oppression if we aren't willing to challenge, change, and dismantle our current systems.[56]

Such definitions take the white ally into the cross-fertilized terrain of radical utterance and aphorism (dare we say daily affirmation?) that calls upon her to move beyond critique. Consider how the vernacular of the self-help industry is underpinned by 'inspirational' quotes that encourage self-improvement. Might the definitions in the Ally Backpack also be thought of as 'inspirational' quotes that, to borrow Sara Ahmed's words, 'bring something into existence'[57] through their categorical use?

[56] These statements can be found on the 'Subscribe' page of the site, https://www.safetypinbox.com/subscribe/.

[57] Sara Ahmed, *The Promise of Happiness* (Durham, NC: Duke University Press, 2010), 11.

It is notable that while many of the resources and tasks that Safety Pin Box made available were online (from video series and tasks to online conversations), the glossary was distributed as a hardcopy text. The Ally Backpack itself comes, rather playfully, with a mesh, drawstring bag. In this scenario of portability, we might imagine the white ally wearing the backpack as a way to indexically mark her privilege, an exercise in which she *gives herself up as an object*, to adapt the words of Frantz Fanon.[58] Of course, the person of color has no such choice, since race, like gender and disability, is not a costume that one can take on and off at will. Rather, the very premise of the backpack is to be aware of such privileges.[59] With her drawstring in tow, reciting parts of her glossary like sides of a script, the white ally is now ready to enact dissent by hailing herself into everyday conversations *with other white people*. Quoting Johnson and Mac's sentence on white fragility, she might say: 'So many people claim to want to be allies, but at the end of the day their white fragility doesn't allow them to really follow the lead of Black people.'[60] The white ally here becomes a *bad actor* but in a different way than the noisy activists of Indivisible. She becomes, to borrow Ahmed's category from *The Promise of Happiness*, a killjoy, 'the one who comes between bodies that would be, or should be, in agreement [...] the one who gets in the way of an organic solidarity.'[61] By referencing the glossary, she will, in all likelihood, 'ruin the atmosphere'[62] of white 'solidarity' in the convivial spaces of the lunchroom or bar or holiday party, and this infelicitous mode of conduct is precisely the point. If taken up as a tactical text, the glossary can and *should* promote 'bad feeling'[63] or discomfort because it is rattling the smooth social relations that underlie white privilege.

[58] Frantz Fanon, *Black Skin, White Masks*, trans. Richard Philcox (New York: Grove, [1952] 2008), 92.

[59] In this way, the Ally Backpack directly cites Peggy McIntosh's 1989 essay, 'White Privilege: Unpacking the Invisible Knapsack.' In this foundational piece, McIntosh notes how she has 'come to see white privilege as an invisible package of unearned assets that I can count on cashing in each day, but about which I was "meant" to remain oblivious. White privilege is like an invisible weightless knapsack of special provisions, maps, passports, codebooks, visas, clothes, tools and blank checks.' See Peggy McIntosh, 'White Privilege: Unpacking the Invisible Knapsack,' *Peace and Freedom Magazine* (July/August 1989): 10–12.

[60] Johnson and Mac, *The Ultimate White Ally Glossary*.

[61] Ahmed, 217.

[62] Ibid., 65.

[63] Ibid., 66.

Few deliberately aspire to a poor performance, but when scripted in terms of 'bettering oneself,' then acting badly becomes a potential marker of self-improvement. Even if the subscribers of Safety Pin Box did not treat their glossaries as an unruly script, they still paid good money to take their lead from Johnson and Mac. Self-help is a hierarchical business populated with aspirational figures. It is not just *anyone* dispensing advice about leadership in the workplace; it is Sheryl Sandberg, the corporate monarch of Facebook, who makes the case for women with a symmetrical smile. Figures such as Sandberg at the 'top' of their respective industry—the CEO, personal coach, preacher, politician, self-styled visionary—can convincingly promise self-transformation. These actors impart dollar- and election-worthy wisdom to their followers. In the case of the team at the center of Safety Pin Box, they too mirror the influencer charisma of self-help gurus by promising a politically progressive version for *how to act* or conduct oneself as a white ally.

As we have detailed, Leftist resistance movements such as Indivisible can also make use of the aspirational figure by inventively turning to cardboard cutout surrogates. The collective can construct their own smiling guru, or, to put it more precisely, they can hold up a frozen mirror to the absentee politician and demand that he does better. This 'bottom up' performative conduct sets the scene for the body politic to *instruct* the politician on how to act or, in the case of Strike Debt, the debt collector, according to the terms of the Fair Debt Collections Practices Act of 1996. Together, these tactical texts, in scripting resistance, put new expressive behaviors and modes of direct action into circulation. As the 'how-to' manuals examined here make clear, performative conduct takes on many shapes, tactics, and strategies since it remains nimble and responsive to the crisis of the moment. More often than not, performative conduct requires taking on the role of the 'bad actor,' the dissenter whose histrionics disrupt felicitous social conditions, demand the right to be angry, or self-authorize the political performative. Importantly, manuals such as *Indivisible* and *Debt Resistors' Operation Manual* craft these roles through content that is collaboratively generated. These shared texts are, in effect, shaping performative conduct and its expressive enactment as a rehearsal for revolution. With its genealogies that lie in conduct manuals and self-help books, performative conduct could play handily into neoliberal agendas that foist responsibilities on individuals to manage the precarity of social insecurities through creative adaptation, were it not for these manuals' insistently collectivist message. As the upsurge of these 'how-to' guides reveal, performative conduct offers ways of sustaining the individual labor of collective resistance. The tactical texts examined here point toward the necessity of repurposing practices the Left has, until recently, ignored as purely oppositional. If there is a future beyond the insupportable present, then it lies in inhabiting the very repertoires that have fractured and diminished constitutional democracies. The resistance movements of the Left in an era of Far-Right populism remind us that while the personal forever remains political, it is also insistently performative.

References

Ahmed, Sara. *The Promise of Happiness.* Durham, NC: Duke University Press, 2010.

Austin, J.L. *How To Do Things With Words.* Second Edition. Cambridge, MA: Harvard University Press, 1975.

Butler, Judith. *Notes Toward a Performative Theory of Assembly.* Cambridge, MA: Harvard University Press, 2015.

Fanon, Frantz. [1952.] *Black Skin, White Masks.* Translated by Richard Philcox. New York: Grove, 2008.

Garneau, David. 'Imaginary Spaces of Conciliation and Reconciliation: Art, Curation, and Healing.' In *Arts of Engagement: Taking Aesthetic Action In and Beyond the Truth and Reconciliation Commission in Canada*, edited by Dylan Robinson and Keavy Martin, 21–41.Waterloo: Wilfrid Laurier University Press, 2016.

Grattan, Laura. *Populism's Power: Radical Grassroots Democracy in America.* Oxford: Oxford University Press, 2016.

Gregg, Melissa. 'The Limits of Self Help Productivity Lit.' *The Atlantic*, April 22, 2016. https://www.theatlantic.com/business/archive/2016/04/the-limits-of-self-help-productivity-lit/479382/.

Indivisible. *A Practical Guide for Resisting the Trump Agenda.* Updated March 9, 2017. https://www.indivisible.org/guide/.

———. 'Chapter Four: Local Advocacy Tactics That Work.' 2016. https://www.indivisible.org/guide/advocacy-tactics/.

———. 'How to Plan a Die-In' From, 'Save the ACA: Die-in Planning Guide.' 2017. https://www.indivisible.org/resource/die-in-planning-guide/.

———. 'What's a Die-In?' From, 'Save the ACA: Die-in Planning Guide.' 2017. https://www.indivisible.org/resource/die-in-planning-guide/.

Johnson, Marissa Janae, and Leslie Mac. *The Ultimate White Ally Glossary.* Volume 1. Safety Pin Box Ally Backpack, 2017.

McIntosh, Peggy. 'White Privilege: Unpacking the Invisible Knapsack.' *Peace and Freedom Magazine* (July/August 1989): 10–12.

McKee, Yates. *Strike Art: Contemporary Art and the Post-Occupy Condition.* London: Verso, 2016.

McRobbie, Angela. 'Feminism, the Family and the New "Mediated" Maternalism.' *New Formations: A Journal of Culture/Theory/Politics* 80, no. 8 (2013): 119–137.

Members of the Strike Debt assembly, Occupy Wall Street, Common Notions, and Antumbra Design. *The Debt Resistors' Operation Manual*, 2012. http://strikedebt.org/The-Debt-Resistors-Operations-Manual.pdf.

Roach, Joseph. *Cities of the Dead: Circum-Atlantic Performance.* New York: Columbia University Press, 1996.

Robinson, Dylan. 'Enchantment's Irreconcilable Connection: Listening to Anger, Being Idle No More.' In *Performance Studies in Canada*, edited by Marlis Schweitzer and Laura Levin, 221–235. Kingston and Montreal: McGill-Queen's University Press, 2017.

Safety Pin Box. 'What is Safety Pin Box?' 2016. https://www.safetypinbox.com/home/.

Sandberg, Sheryl. *Lean In: Women, Work, and the Will to Lead.* New York: Knopf, 2013.

Tuck, Eve, and K. Wayne Yang. 'Decolonization Is Not a Metaphor.' *Decolonization: Indigeneity, Education & Society* 1, no. 1 (2012): 1–40.

White, Micah. *The End of Protest: A New Playbook for Revolution.* Toronto: Knopf Canada, 2016.

L.M. Bogad, *The Great Collective Cough-In*, 1995

L.M. Bogad, *The Great Collective Cough-In*, 1995

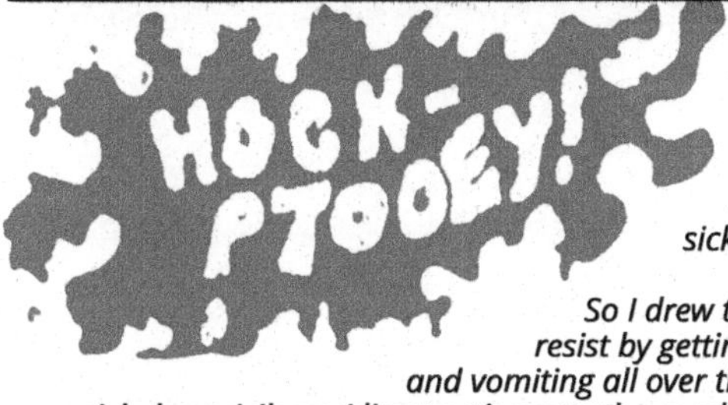

Years ago I worked as a writer/ editor at a comic book company. One day, the management told us we would no longer have any allowed sick days. If we called in sick, we would be docked a day's pay.

So I drew this cartoon, in which the workers resist by getting each other sick, going into work, and vomiting all over the bosses until they win back their sick day privileges (direct action gets the goods!). In the end, a mass of people, sick and ready to vomit, are amassed and marching on Congress to try to get universal healthcare for all in this manner.

I showed the cartoon around the office. After work, I brought it to my grandmother, Margie Bogad. I said, "Grandma, I wanna show you this cartoon I drew. They just told us at work that we can't call in sick, if we do they'll dock us."

"What?" said my grandma, outraged. "Well, then, you should all just get each other sick and then go into work and vomit on them!"
I was stunned. I showed her the cartoon.
We looked each other in the eye.
"That's strange..." she said.
"Yeah..." I said.
Made me think again about the nature-versus-nurture argument.... Is there a gene for creative direct action?

—Larry Bogad

A veteran trickster-mentor of creative performance-based activism, **L.M. BOGAD** embodies the conviction that "unpredictable and participatory actions help create a joyous counterculture that can sustain long-term participation in a movement."* Cofounder of the Clandestine Insurgent Rebel Clown Army and alumnus of the Lincoln Center Theater Director's Laboratory, he has performed on many picket lines in roles such as Saint Francis, Ronald McDonald and the Angry Banker, and has collaborated with the Yes Men, La Pocha Nostra, Reclaim the Streets and other groups. As Professor of Performance Studies at University of California Davis, Bogad teaches classes such as "Satire, Irony and Protest," "Tactical Performance," and "Oppositional Performance and Social Movements"—thus galvanizing and sustaining the next generation of critical pranksters.

Bogad is the author of *Tactical Performance: The Theory and Practice of Serious Play* (2016) and *Electoral Guerrilla Theatre: Radical Ridicule and Social Movements* (2005/2016), as well as the play *COINTELSHOW: A Patriot Act* (2011). He has performed, lectured and led workshops in major museums, theatres, and occupied buildings internationally, from Chile to Finland, from Egypt to Latvia. He is the world's worst, best, and only economusician.

* L.M. Bogad, *Tactical Performance: The Theory and Practice of Serious Play* (London and New York: Routledge, 2016), 91.

CHAPTER 4

Their Dissidence Remains: Lessons from the 2011 Chilean Student Movement

Daniella Wittern Bush

Close your eyes. Imagine: it is June 24, 2011, 5:30 pm. You stand across from *la Moneda*, the Chilean Presidential Palace, in the Plaza of Citizenship. Just another passerby taking in the expanse of green out of which the neoclassical façade of la Moneda rises, you at first barely notice the shadows weaving through the after-work street throngs that fill your field of vision. Soon, though, your eyes track them: raggedly clothed bodies moving in from all angles, faces obscured by white paint and dark eye-makeup. Some smile and converse, while others, already in character, lumber forward with limbs outstretched, growling at those they pass. Suddenly a cheer rises up from their midst, an alarm sounds, and the zombies rush toward the center of the plaza. In the notes that follow, you immediately recognize the bass line: you have stumbled across a re-enactment of Michael Jackson's 1982 hit music video 'Thriller.'

Approaching the action, the tombstones hanging around the zombies' necks come into focus. Instead of the typical dates of birth and death, these tombstones bear unusual inscriptions: 'Morí debiendo $35,000,000

D. W. Bush (✉)
Worcester, MA, USA

N. Alvarez et al. (eds.), *Sustainable Tools for Precarious Times*, Contemporary Performance InterActions,
https://doi.org/10.1007/978-3-030-11557-9_4

QEPD'[1] one epitaph near you reads. Your eye travels from indebted zombie to indebted zombie, falling on a body splayed out across a table, covered in blood, wearing a shirt that declares: 'Vendí mis órganos para pagar mi educación.'[2] Not simply filming a remake of a video, you realize, these zombie dancers are protesting an all too familiar issue in the neoliberal world: student debt. You are witnessing the 'Thriller por la educación,' the first in a series of alternative demonstrations orchestrated by Chilean students to stage the extreme inequalities of wealth and resources perpetuated by Chile's largely privatized, for-profit educational system.

How did we get here, to the Plaza de la Ciudadanía, in Chile? In my case, by word of mouth: friends I made during a research trip to Chile, in 2010, knew I would be interested by the form of the protests as much as by what was at stake. A Latin Americanist by training, from and educated in the United States, I wrote a dissertation[3] on one Chilean artist's political performance from dictatorship through the transition to democracy. Personally and professionally, then, I tracked the Chilean student movement via conversations with friends, social media posts, news reports, and a follow-up visit to Chile in 2014. While I did witness a few minor protests in the city of Concepción during that trip, my experience with the Chilean student movement is largely drawn from publicly available online sources mixed with private social media conversations—pointing to the power of the student movement to convey its message to an audience that is not on the 'scene,' but 'offstage' and online.

Consequently, you, my reader, get to take a much shorter flight to Santiago, thanks to the power of the Internet and social media. Feel free to try it now. Type 'Thriller por la educación' into the search engine of your choice. Go on—I'll wait while you skim through the 2,340,000 plus results. Choose a video, a photograph, an interview, and re-enter the scene. As with the kiss-ins, beach days, super hero battles, marathons, and other protests that formed the 2011 Chilean student movement, you can re-witness the 'Thriller' as many times as you like—even choosing between myriad viewing angles. If you continue to sift through the search results,

[1] 'I died owing 35,000,000. Rest in peace.' This is approximately US$53,500 at today's exchange rate (US$64,000 at the time of the event). All translations that follow are my own.

[2] 'I sold my organs to pay for my education.'

[3] Daniella Wittern Bush, 'Words that Speak, Literature that Acts: Diamela Eltit's Narrative Performances,' PhD diss., Brown University, 2012.

Fig. 4.1 Over 3,000 students perform Thriller in the Plaza de la Ciudadanía across from the Presidential Palace on June 24, 2011 in Santiago, Chile. The tombstones hanging from their necks state the amount of student debt owing when they died. Credit: Archivo y Centro de Documentación Fech

you might learn how the protest was planned and rehearsed, and about its international media afterlife (Fig. 4.1).

Given the precarious and liminal nature of its dissidents, many of them still too young to vote (and therefore, in the eyes of certain members of the Chilean government, to be taken seriously), the Chilean student movement had to stumble on a creative and enduring mode of protest in order to achieve results in the face of constant turnover. This article explores the lessons offered by the Chilean students' fusion of performance, charisma, *fiesta*, and digital archive in order to sustain resistance in an ongoing push for reform of their educational system.

Get This Party Started

'Thriller' was not the first push for educational reform in Chile: in 2006, the *Revolución de los pingüinos* (the 'Penguin Revolution,' so named for the uniform students wore at most schools) united secondary students to protest the *Ley Orgánica Constitucional de Enseñanza (LOCE)*.[4] A vestige from the military dictatorship, General Augosto Pinochet signed the LOCE into effect on his last day in power in 1990. Setting the stage for both the 2006 and 2011 student movements, the LOCE made the state the 'regulator' of Chile's educational system while allowing private corporations to become the principal providers of education. Sixteen years later, between April and October of 2006, *los pingüinos* (as the protesters were fondly called) organized a series of protests against the LOCE that, at its height, amassed the participation of 800,000 students from high schools around the country, culminating in several national strikes.[5]

By May of 2006, the protests had captured the attention of the then-president Michelle Bachelet, who on national television and radio announced a wide package of '*Reforma de calidad a la educación*.'[6] The *Asamblea Nacional Estudiantil*,[7] however, rejected the government's offer since it did not address the protesters' appeals for free tuition for all students, and called for another national strike. Eventually, Bachelet invited student leaders to a newly formed national advisory committee on education, which in September of 2006 presented a report that proposed many—but not all—of the changes demanded by students. Repudiating the report, students returned to the streets, but were unable to achieve the levels of participation of previous rounds of demonstrations. In December, days before the advisory committee was to reveal its final report, the National Assembly of Secondary Students retired from the committee, stating that the students could not partake of resolutions they felt lacked substance. Nonetheless, following the committee's report, Bachelet asked Congress to begin a project of LOCE reform in April of 2007. Two years later, in spite of student and teacher demonstrations against it, the *Ley General de Educación*[8] was signed into law as a revision of the LOCE. This new law did not guarantee high-quality, free public education, however, and students

[4]The 'Organic Constitutional Law of Teaching,' popularly known within Chile as '*la LOCE*.'

[5]While the *pingüinos* only involved high school students, this number means that, given Chile's population at the time, 1 out of every 20 Chileans was involved.

[6]Quality Reform for Education.

[7]The National Student Assembly.

[8]The General Education Law's major provision limited the ability of educational establishments to consider a student's financial background during the admission process. It also made changes to what would be considered elementary- and middle-school curriculum, and to the prerequisites for an educational institution to be recognized by the government.

felt that it was a betrayal from Bachelet's administration rather than the act of support it was intended to be.

Unable to achieve substantial change in Chile's educational laws, the Penguin Revolution had at least two lasting consequences. First, it brought the need for structural change to the educational system into the sphere of national debate. Second, it sparked an interest in activism in a segment of the Chilean population that had until then been presumed to be politically apathetic. The generation '*ni-ni*,' a term designated by Spanish sociologists for youth that—disillusioned by the lack of opportunity around them—neither study nor work, also characterizes the plight of youth globally who face precarious non-salaried, non-unionized, non-pensionable employment.

After the Penguin Revolution, education reform fell to the back burner in Chile—until April of 2011, when chaos broke out at the Universidad Central de Chile. A private university that until then distinguished itself from others in the country by operating on a non-profit and democratic model, the Universidad Central announced a 'strategic alliance' with the Norte Sur group, a private investment firm based in Santiago whose holdings span the realms of real estate, education, and health care. For US$45 million, the corporation would obtain ownership of 45 percent of the school's real estate and 50 percent control of its governance.[9] Unwilling to partake in Chile's for-profit sector of education, students and faculty alike staged a strike that forced the university to cease all activities.

Student unrest quickly spread well beyond the Universidad Central. The *Confederación de Estudiantes de Chile* (Confederation of Students of Chile, also known as the *Confech*) organized a series of mobilizations in response to the financing of education in Chile, delays in the delivery of scholarships and grants, and problems with the cost of the National Student Card, which was intended to lower the costs of public transportation for students. The protests reached national proportions on May 12, 2011: 15,000 students marched in Santiago to demand that the country focus on renewing the possibilities of public education. Through the month of June, marches and strikes were held in all of Chile's major cities. Given the number of students involved, the then-president Sebastián

[9] Juan Pablo Figueroa and Tania Araya detail the significance of Norte Sur's takeover of the Universidad Central in their article, 'Académicos se transforman en accionistas. El negocio que esconde la venta de la Universidad Central,' Centro de Investigación Periodística, April 28, 2011.

Piñera's government was forced to offer proposals for limited reform of the Chilean educational system. Student protesters deemed none of them adequate.

Throwing a *Thriller* Protest

June 15, 2011: Felipe Villaseca, a 20-year-old student of Public Administration at the Universidad de Chile, posts an idea on Facebook. What if, he asks, the next protest takes the form of 'reliving' Michael Jackson's music video 'Thriller'?

A small group of students put together a Facebook page outlining the details of a flash mob protest. Word spreads quickly: within a week, more than 1500 students confirm their participation, and the organizers distribute a video tutorial for the 'Thriller' choreography. On the day of the event, as many as 3000 student 'zombies'[10] convene across from the Presidential Palace and break out into dance. And over the course of the next 48 hours, the students' '*Thriller*' makes headlines not only in Chile's national papers, but also in those of countries such as Peru, Mexico, the United States, Norway, and Russia.

Why was this protest able to garner so much press at national *and* international levels? The Revolución de los pingüinos, by contrast, gained popular support within Chile but was virtually unknown beyond the country's borders. So why would students dancing to a 1983 pop song interest the rest of the world? The 'Thriller por la educación' was not politics or protest as usual; it was fun. Who does not love a party? Who does not want to have the chance to participate in or witness a flash mob? Playing on these desires, the Chilean students pulled off a well-organized spectacle that was beautiful to watch, in the name of a cause that is sympathetic to everyone who recognizes the value of broad-based access to quality education.

The dance that the students re-enacted was the centerpiece of Michael Jackson's mock horror film, in which dreams and fiction alternate with reality, and a teenage boy (who may or may not be a werewolf) courts (or hunts) a teenage girl. Reframed in terms of for-profit educational institutions and student debt, Jackson's storyline becomes a political metaphor revealed by the tombstones the dancers wear around their necks: they are being strangled by their student loans. For the students, Jackson's horror

[10] As reported by the Chilean newspaper *La nación*. Regardless of the official headcount, aerial photographs and videos of the protest confirm that the involvement was massive.

is the debt they have accumulated, which, as the lyrics state, 'close to midnight' (i.e., close to graduation and, therefore, the start of loan repayment periods) 'looks you right between the eyes,' leaving you 'paralyzed.'

What is paralyzing about the current educational system? Only 40 percent of Chilean students have access to free education even at the secondary level—and those that do attend public schools constantly face budget shortfalls. Everyone else pays out of pocket to attend charter, private, or 'subsidized' schools (where there is a combination of public and private—that is to say, parental and, eventually, student—financing). This is before taking into account the costs of university-level education, in a country where only 15 percent of higher education's funding comes from the government. As *The Economist* clarifies in its October 2011 article on the Chilean student movement, 'What makes this harder to stomach is that many educational establishments are profit-making businesses. That is true of a third of secondary schools and of the technical and vocational colleges attended by two-thirds of students in higher education. Three quarters of universities are private.'[11]

But Chile is a wealthy country, right? Thanks to Pinochet's 'Chicago Boys,'[12] a voracious form of capitalism has dominated the country since 1973. As a result, Chile is often touted as one of the most economically stable countries in Latin America. What is less discussed is the larger economic context, succinctly laid out by Francisco Goldman in his *New York Times* article on the Chilean student movement: 'Chile might have the highest per capita income in the region, but in terms of distribution of wealth, it ranks as one of the most unequal countries in the world. A university education in Chile is proportionally the world's most expensive:

[11] See 'The Fraught Politics of the Classroom' from *The Economist* online, October 29, 2011, for a revealing discussion of Chilean student debt.

[12] The 'Chicago Boys' were a group of Chilean economists who studied at the University of Chicago under Milton Friedman and Arnold Harberger as part of the U.S. State Department's 'Chile Project,' an academic effort to influence international economic policies. Upon their return, the 'Chicago Boys' rose to prominent government positions across a number of South American countries, and were strongly embraced by Pinochet. They are credited with what Friedman termed 'the miracle of Chile,' transforming the country into Latin America's strongest economy by advocating the hallmark free-market policies of neoliberalism—privatization and deregulation—to the benefit of large corporations. For further reading, see: The Heritage Foundations' 'Chile, Index of Economic Freedom'; Naomi Klein's *The Shock Doctrine: The Rise of Disaster Capitalism*; Gary Becker's 'What Latin America Owes to the "Chicago Boys"'; *El Ladrillo: Bases de la Política Económica del Gobierno Militar Chileno*; and Carlos Fuentes' 2015 documentary *Chicago Boys*.

$3400 a year in a country where the average annual salary is about $8500.'[13] This cost begins at the secondary level, so as a result the average graduate from the Chilean university system receives $45,000 worth of debt along with his or her college degree.[14]

This is how Chile's educational system converts students into the 'living dead' of neoliberalism. From the time they are toddlers, they are told to work hard to get an education that will supposedly lead them to a good career, thereby getting them 'ahead' in life—only to spend the rest of their lives working to get out of the debt incurred to get that education. Moreover, 'public education'—once a true priority of the Chilean government, especially during Socialist president Salvador Allende's 1970–1973 regime—has become a living dead concept in the Chile that emerged following the 1973 *golpe de estado* (coup) that led to Augusto Pinochet's military dictatorship. Magdalena Paredes, one of the student organizers of the 'Thriller for la educación,' insisted on this point in an interview. We, the students, she explained, 'Somos *zombies* viendo cómo la educación en este país se muere [...].'[15]

Indignant and Kissing: When Parties and Protest Collide

While the zombie metaphor worked for the students, Villaseca's intention in proposing 'Thriller por la educación' was to use the flash mob to generate positive energy in the protesters and public opinion. 'Lo que queríamos,' he indicates, 'era dejar de lado lo malo que siempre se muestra en las manifestaciones y demostrar que los jóvenes podemos comprometernos por una buena causa.'[16] And it worked, as evidenced by the level of

[13] From Francisco Goldman, 'Camila Vallejo, the World's Most Glamorous Revolutionary,' *New York Times*, April 5, 2012.

[14] César Chelala writes, 'Chilean economist Marcel Claude has found that student debt is close to 174% of Chilean students' annual salary upon graduation—and 50% among them are heavily indebted. The average Chilean university student graduates with $45,000 in debt—a larger burden than even in the United States, where the comparable figure is about $27,000.' See 'In Chile, Dissent Has a Woman's Face,' *The Globalist*, August 30, 2011.

[15] 'We [students] are zombies watching how education in this country is dying [...].' 'Thriller por la educación.mpg.flv,' *Endless Video*, accessed October 11, 2017. https://endlessvideo.com/watch?v=JJcOrWaViWg.

[16] 'What we wanted was to push aside the bad that is always shown in protests and demonstrate that we, the youth, can commit ourselves to a good cause.' 'En Chile jóvenes bailan 'Thriller' por una mejora en la educación,' *CubaDebate. Contra el Terrorismo Mediatico*,

participation in 'Thriller' as well as the media onslaught that followed. Student leaders understood the ramifications: five choreographed minutes of fun had garnered an entirely new degree of empathy for and commitment to the Chilean student movement, unlike anything the 2006 Revolución de los pingüinos—or even 2011's earlier mass marches and strikes—had been able to achieve. Whether or not the government was listening now, it soon would have to. Because 'Thriller' was only the tip of the iceberg: after that initial success, students quickly set to work to plan their next intervention.

From the end of June through the end of August of 2011, the movement would continue to build in intensity, forming what would soon be dubbed the Chilean Winter. Not all of the protests were groundbreaking in form. Rather, students combined older and newer modes of demonstration in order to maintain momentum. Following time-honored traditions, students held massive marches, rallies, concerts, and candlelight vigils, all in the name of education—with an outpouring of popular approval and participation not just from students but from parents and grandparents as well.

Garnering and demonstrating community support was essential: without buy-in from the rest of the population, the students' demands would be too easy to dismiss. After all, if ignored long enough, the current student leaders and activists would graduate. As soon as they entered their loan repayment periods, they would be forced to turn their energies to paid employment, and the movement would lose momentum much as it had in 2006. Real change, the students now knew, would only be possible if sustainable strategies could be found that would allow their movement to continue regardless of where *this* particular group of protesters fell in the cycle of study/incurring debt and labor/debt repayment.

With this in mind, students returned to a form of anonymous and sheltered protest, the *cacerolazo*, that originated in Chile in 1971: at a set hour, people lean out of the windows of their homes and bang on pots and pans to indicate their commitment to the cause. Students also worked with faculty to organize strikes at and occupations of schools, as well as student teach-ins within the closed schools. And to ensure that the public knew what they were doing and why, students employed press conferences

June 26, 2011, accessed April 24, 2013. http://www.cubadebate.cu/noticias/2011/06/26/en-chile-jovenes-bailan-thriller-por-una-mejora-en-la-educacion/#.Wd51-q3MzGI.

and platforms on the Internet to articulate demands, researching how much their proposals would cost and how they could be paid for. When the government still did not react, some students held highly publicized hunger strikes to hold the then-president Piñera personally accountable for the lack of educational reform.

Traditional protests took on a new edge in the Chilean student movement, thanks to the Internet, keeping their actions in the public eye and their cause a constant topic of conversation. When students occupied government agencies, schools, or television stations, for example, they live-streamed their interventions via YouTube so that their message could not be reduced and simplified in the edited-down footage that would be shown in the official media. They also re-appropriated a kind of protest that emerged in the aftermath of the dictatorship in which individuals guilty of human rights violations who had received official amnesty were 'exposed' to the public by placing signs outside of their homes enumerating their crimes—only the students used signs that publicized elected officials' records on educational reform. As with the cacerolazo, the Chilean students' public outing of politicians opposed to educational reform reflects a cross-pollination of strategies for dissidence taken from the period of Chile's military dictatorship, demonstrating the sustainability of performative protest as a tool that can transfer between contexts and remain effective.

In spite of the reception of and public support for these more traditional protests, however, it was the range of alternative modes of demonstration that would repeatedly make headlines—in Chile and beyond. What did these protests look like? Villaseca's 'Thriller por la educación' (itself later repeated in smaller cities in Chile as well as by student protestors in other countries) provided the basic formula for many flash mobs to follow: a Facebook invitation would be created for a place and date, interested participants would find links to YouTube video 'rehearsals' that would teach them the choreography, and signage would be created (and/or lyrics rewritten) to make the students' message explicit. Anyone who did not want to dance or sing would take on the task of documentation. From this pattern emerged the July 13, 2011, 'Gagazo por la educación,' a re-rendering of Lady Gaga's song 'Judas' to reflect the government's betrayal of the interests of its citizens by refusing to commit to educational reform[17]; the July 20, 2011, 'Cuecazo por la educación'[18] that encircled Santiago's Plaza de Armas with banners decrying profit in education while students within staged Chile's national dance[19]; and the northern port city Antofagasta's August 12, 2011, 'Regresamos a buscar la educación gratuita,'[20] a re-enactment of a musical medley from *Grease* that sought to take passersby back in time to an era when Chile still had free public education.[21]

While the flash mob style of protest struck a chord with the Chilean students—and with the press that now wanted to cover the movement—student leaders needed to diversify their interventions to maintain momentum. Moving beyond choreographed dances, student demonstrations now tended toward two new themes: protest as party, and protest as a creative interruption of public space and daily life. Coming off of the energy and excitement generated by 'Thriller' and the 'Gagazo,' protest as party offered a logical evolution of the students' work. One of these interventions,

[17] For links to the Facebook event invite, planning videos, and much of the documentation of the event itself, see *Artivismos* (blog), '"Gaga-so por la Educación"/'Gagazo por la Educación' (flashmob USACh),' posted July 13, 2011. http://artivismos.blogspot.com/2011/08/gagazo-por-la-educacion-flashmob.html.

[18] 'The Giant *Cueca* [Andean dance] for Education.' Due to space limitations, this chapter cannot detail all actions of the 2011 Chilean student movement to the present. Nonetheless, students continue to take to the streets in the name of a free, quality education for all, and on July 7, 2017, this took the form of a second *Cuecazo por la educación* in front of the Universidad de Chile's theatre.

[19] The *Cueca* is a partner dance that has long been used to stage protest: during Pinochet's dictatorship, widowed women would dance the *cueca* alone, carrying photographs of loved ones who had 'disappeared.' With the *Cuecazo*, students re-instrumentalized a rite of Chilean citizenship that carries the trace of performed dissent, bringing both connotations into their struggle to guarantee free, equal, and quality education for all Chileans.

[20] 'We Return Looking for Free Education.'

[21] Antofagasta's flash mob breaks with the established pattern in that it built off a separate, *digital* action by a group of students from the Universidad de Chile, who on July 8, 2011, released a YouTube video ad campaign inviting anyone who had not yet joined the student movement to mobilize themselves in the name of education. Rewriting the song 'Summer Nights' from the musical *Grease*, their video portrays Sandy as a participant in the student occupation of the university while her boyfriend relaxes at home and plays video games. Eventually he joins the student movement, and the video closes with the two singing together, 'Somos dos endeudados / pero [...] ah [...] cambiarémos la historia.' ('We are just two debters / but [...] we will change history'). See '"Grease" De La Toma Estudiantil En Chile,' *El Centinela*, July 8, 2011, accessed December 10, 2016. https://centinela66.com/2011/07/08/grease-de-la-toma-estudiantil-en-chile/.

'Ven a salvar la educación—héroes por la educación,'[22] extended the original flash mob theme. Two hundred student protesters dressed as well-known super heroes or as their own 'super' creations (such as '$uper Endeudada'[23]) and super villains standing in for the government—ranging from the Joker to a masked villain demarcated by a '$' symbol to others who carried signs such as, 'Los Super Villanos somos dueños de las universidades.'[24] Singing and dancing alternated with individual combat and battles that embroiled all of the supers, at times pulling in many of the 1500 spectators.

While the costumes, signs, and new lyrics to 'We Will Rock You' articulated a clear message, it would nonetheless have been easy to mistake the Héroes' gymnastics, capoeira, chanting, and mix of choreographed and spontaneous dance for a street festival rather than a protest. A similar feel permeated the kiss-in or *besatón por la educación* staged by students from the Universidad de Santiago de Chile on July 6, 2011. Nearly 4000 students gathered in the Plaza de Armas, faces and signs painted with slogans such as 'Enamorado pero endeudado' or 'Con pasión para la educación,'[25] to kiss for 1800 seconds to publicize how much money ($1.8 billion) it would take to finance the tuition of higher education for all Chileans.[26] Likewise, a sense of festivity lined the 'Genkidama for la educación,' a battle based on the Japanese anime series *Dragon Ball Z* for which 3000 students gathered in Santiago's Plaza de Armas on July 11, 2011.

A quick look at photo or video documentation of any of these interventions might lead you to assume they were street festivals or outdoor

[22] 'Come to save education—heroes for education' in Santiago's Plaza de Armas. See *Artivismos* (blog) for organizing details and videos of the event. 'Superhéroes y Villanos por la Educación, flashmob,' posted July 18, 2011. http://artivismos.blogspot.com/2011/08/superheroes-y-villanos-por-la-educacion.html.

[23] 'Super Indebted.'

[24] 'We, the Super Villains, own the universities.'

[25] 'In love but in debt', 'With passion for education.'

[26] The *besatón* was replicated in Concepción and Antofagasta. Santiago's sequel in September of 2011 carried a new undertone: the re-kiss-in denounced the violence between the *encapuchados* (hooded rioters) and police that had turned tragic at the end of August with the death of 16-year-old Manuel Gutierrez. Instigating chaos at the end of many student protests, the rioters' identity remains under debate: Piñera's government cited them to discredit the movement as a whole, while student leaders suggested they were either state infiltrators inciting violence to break up demonstrations and challenge the public's empathy toward the students, or anarchists taking advantage of their cause.

performances—the images overflow with joy, movement, and color. Chilean students had discovered that protest could merge with *fiesta*, with spectacle, and fun—and while it was winning them both attention to and more involvement in their cause, it also helped them maintain energy and morale among protesters, enabling the movement to build rather than run out of steam. Diana Taylor emphasizes this need: 'The art projects and collaborative activities keep the protestors emotionally strong and focused enough to keep up their activism day after day.'[27] The fiesta protest reminds us that we are not alone and that even in the midst of disappointing official or public reactions, there can be joy just as much as struggle as we work to create change.

Drawing on pop culture—whether Michael Jackson or Lady Gaga, anime plots or comic book super heroes—Chilean students cast casual passersby as spect-actors[28] rather than spectators. Stumbling upon a protest completely unawares, you could probably at least hum along or dance a few steps yourself. Or you could choose to stand back as a witness, documenting the interventions and their repercussions with photographs and videos. Even leaving the scene would not be a passive act but an active refusal to engage. In her discussion of political spectatorship, Taylor reminds us that, 'Revolutions take place (for good or bad),' as Immanuel Kant reminds us, when they arouse 'in the hearts and desires of all spectators who are not themselves caught up in it a sympathy which borders almost on enthusiasm.'[29] And if the spectators' empathy and enthusiasm can get them directly involved, the stronger the revolution will be.

On June 16, 2011, a group of civil engineering students from the University of Bío-Bío bridged the student movement's party as protest into an unexpected interruption of public space, freezing in place for six minutes in the atrium of a mall. Shopping was temporarily suspended as consumers paused to question what was happening around them. As in many of the other protests, there were signs to let people know what they were

[27] 'The Politics of Passion,' *E-misférica*, special issue 'Dissidence,' 10, no. 2 (Summer 2013). http://hemisphericinstitute.org/hemi/en/e-misferica-102/taylor.

[28] Term taken from Augusto Boal's *Theatre of the Oppressed* (New York: Theatre Communications Group, 1985). In Boal's 'forum theater,' audience members did not simply watch a drama unfold, but could stop a performance at any time to suggest ways to alter the action, or even step onstage themselves, becoming part of the performance.

[29] Taylor, 'The Politics of Passion'; Taylor cites Kant's 'The Contest of the Faculties (1798),' in *Kant's Politics Writings*, ed. Hans S. Reiss (Cambridge: Cambridge University Press, 1991), 182.

agitating for, although in this case most of the signs came out after the students unfroze, perhaps so that the six silent, 'frozen' minutes could make people think before the message was made totally explicit. Briefly, students were able to interrupt the otherwise incessant flow of the neoliberal market, whose firm control of education in Chile is at the heart of the students' protest.

Likewise, another group of students in Santiago chose to disrupt tourism to draw attention to the student cause. In mid-June, when one student protester—a runner—heard how much money would be needed to revitalize public education ($1.8 billion), he tied his shoes and set off to run around la Moneda for 1800 hours. Others immediately jumped in, calling themselves the 'maratonistas por la educación' and making the '1800 horas de corrida por la educación'[30] a relay that lasted without lapse from June 13 to August 27, such that every tourist visiting Chile's Presidential Palace during that time was confronted by the students' plea for public education for all.

This repertoire of creative protest strategies, ranging from the disruption of tourism and commerce to the staging of beaches or music videos in public plazas, emanated primarily from Santiago's Plaza de Armas. As it migrated north and south, distinct Chilean cities chose which interventions to re-enact and how to go about them. Building on the metaphors brought up by '*Thriller*,' for example, students organized collective 'suicides' for education, in which students lay down 'dead' along central streets in Santiago, Valparaíso, Concepción, and Valdivia. Likewise, 'funerals' for education spotted the country, burying what the students called the 'dead promise' of public education in Chile. Other demonstrations were in and of themselves a migration, as in the case of the group of students from Concepción that walked the 500 kilometers to Santiago to hand-deliver a letter to the then-president Piñera; others walked from distant cities to Valparaíso to deliver letters to the seat of Congress. Not even the borders of the country could limit the student movement, as seen in the so-called exiled student[31] demonstrations that were held in Argentina,

[30] 'Marathoners for education' and '1,800 hour race for education.'

[31] In 2011, 5000 Chileans lived in Argentina, where public education is free at all levels, because it was dramatically cheaper to pay rent in Argentina than to live at home and pay tuition in Chile. Calling themselves 'exiliados económicos y sociales' (economic and social exiles), these Chileans saw themselves as forced to live abroad due to the exorbitant cost of education in Chile. For more, see 'Los exiliados del modelo chileno,' *La Pulseada*, October 12, 2011, accessed January 8, 2017. http://www.lapulseada.com.ar/site/?p=2585.

and the 'continental demonstration'[32] on November 24, 2011, that staged simultaneous marches in Chile, Colombia, Ecuador, Peru, Argentina, Mexico, and Brazil.

Digital Traces

The 2011 Chilean student movement did not just stage creative interventions in their work toward the reform of their educational system; they also carefully planned and managed the portrayal of the protests in the public eye. While only nine days passed between the conception and staging of the event, for example, the 'Thriller para la educación' was organized with rare insight running the gamut from the location in which it took place to the ways in which it should be documented. Given that the student movement centers on the premise that access to a high-caliber education is a basic right of every Chilean *ciudadano* or citizen, the Plaza de la Ciudadanía—Citizenship Square, located directly across from the seat of government—was particularly apt to be 'Thriller's' setting. While 'Thriller' physically occupied the public space of the Plaza de la Ciudadanía, it also engaged with two other highly influential public spaces: the media and the Internet. Like many of the alternative protests that were staged in its aftermath, 'Thriller' was extremely mediatized, as student organizer Magdalena Paredes explains, 'porque se vende mucho mediático en Chile.'[33] Appropriately, in a country that over the last 40 years has been the model for Latin American neoliberalism, students realized that the only way to combat a profit-driven model of education is through interventions that they know will *sell.* Their musical selection reflects this principle: Michael Jackson's album 'Thriller' is still 'the best-selling album of original music ever recorded' and the single made it into the Guinness World Records list in 2006 as the 'most successful music video,' having sold more than nine million copies at that point.[34] Not a bad choice for a flash mob when 'selling' the event to the public is your intention.

[32] A Facebook event for this protest was titled, 'Jornada continental de movilización en defensa de la eduación' ('Day of Continental Mobilization in Defense of Education'), and used to publicize the action throughout Latin America.

[33] 'Because media sells so much in Chile.' 'Thriller por la educación.mpg.flv,' *Endless Video.*

[34] See Mike Celizic, '"Thriller" Video Remains a Classic 25 Years Later,' *Today Show—Today Entertainment* online, April 26, 2008, accessed April 30, 2013. Similarly, John Lynch's article for *Business Insider*, 'The 50 Best-Selling Albums of All Time,' September 23,

No matter how appealing a product is, you need a marketing team to sell it to the public. Chilean students ensured that the event was photographed and filmed from numerous angles by participants, bystanders, and local media alike. By creating a sizable video and visual archive of the protest, the students were able to get their 'Thriller' into local television and radio news pieces, as well as into regional papers throughout Chile (such as *El Concecuente* and *El Ciudadano*), magazines (e.g., *Sangría*), at least one daily tabloid (*La Cuarta*), and a national digital paper (*El Mostrador*).[35]

While the immediate media coverage in traditional formats extended throughout Chile and was in itself a triumph, the students involved in 'Thriller' had a more significant trick up their sleeves. They curated a digital record that would disseminate the news of this protest and others like it far beyond national borders, and ensured that they would remain available to the public consciousness long after each intervention ended. Consequently, a Google search today for 'Thriller por la educación' brings up more than 2,000,000 results that include videos, photographs, newspaper articles, blog entries, and twitter links.[36] Not leaving their online footprints to chance, the umbrella group representing all Chilean university students, Confech, constructed a website with pages[37] explaining who the student protesters were; articulating the movement's ten goals; contextualizing the movement through videos about the crisis in Chilean higher

2016. http://businessinsider.com/50-best-selling-albums-all-time-2016-9, confirms that even today, 'Michael Jackson's "Thriller" currently boasts a sales mark that no album is likely to touch anytime in the near or distant future.'

[35] I cannot discuss Camila Vallejo (former president of the University of Chile's student federation) at length here, but her leadership was an essential factor contributing to the 'marketing' of the Chilean student movement to the international media. Francisco Goldman's *New York Times* article from April of 2012 sums up Camila's aesthetic 'marketing' appeal, although failing to convey her intelligence and determination, in his title: 'Camila Vallejo, the World's Most Glamorous Revolutionary.' Adored by many, Camila's face has appeared on the front pages of myriad international publications—she was *The Guardian*'s 2011 'Person of the Year'—and in video interviews with media from around the world; yet she is hated by others who dismiss her for being a Communist, or disregard her work for education reform as the demands of a spoiled child who would rather go on strike than actually attend school.

[36] As conducted from the United States. Google search results vary across time and space, so a search from Chile or Argentina, for example, may turn up different results.

[37] When I first began working on this topic, www.reformaeducacional.cl was an active website constantly being added to and regularly accessed. Six years later, the URL no longer works, but I believe that the type of archive they created offers a useful model for other movements.

education; documenting the student proposals sent to the government as well as the counter-proposals received; sharing links to independently conducted reports on the Chilean educational system; sharing links to articles that appeared in the press and to the debate on educational reform as covered by the mainstream media; and providing a direct-action resource kit for organizing your own physical demonstrations, or printing and distributing posters, stickers, and other promotional materials.

The Federación de Estudiantes de la Universidad de Chile (Federation of Students of the University of Chile, known as the FECH) went further in digitizing the students' protest. At the height of the movement, the FECH maintained a YouTube feed (youtube.com/user/FECHComunicaciones) with video footage from all of the interventions in which the FECH participated, editorial-style videos on the subject of the educational system and reform, short documentaries, official communications made by FECH representatives to the press, and more; a Tumblr stream comprised of photographs, memes, and Photoshopped caricatures of government figures opposed to educational reform; a Flickr photostream where student activists shared images from demonstrations[38]; a Facebook page liked more than 116,000 times; and a Twitter feed, Comunicaciones FECh, with over 65,700 followers, where new events and inspirational words are posted to keep the movement rolling.

As a result, the 'Thriller por la educación' and the other alternative demonstrations that have followed were not simply formulated and organized online, but assumed a digital afterlife through Facebook posts, tweets, photographs, videos, blog entries, and articles. This was essential because while, as Rebecca Schneider indicates, performed actions can leave traces behind for participants and witnesses after an action has ended,[39] they only imprint on those who were present. Students needed a strategy to extend their protest beyond the event horizon itself, into the wider public consciousness. Consequently, the intended spectator in many of the student protests, as in the case of '*Thriller*,' is not so much the local passersby as the camera, and the global online audience it facilitates. By extension, an action from a single day in a single place becomes an endlessly

[38]Neither lafech.tumblr.com nor the Fech's Flickr stream are currently available, as the student movement has consolidated its social media presence to platforms that have broader reach and offer more capabilities—at present, Facebook, Twitter, and YouTube.

[39]See Rebecca Schneider, *Performance Remains: Art and War in Times of Theatrical Reenactment* (New York: Routledge, 2011).

repeatable digital performance, and in this way protests such as the 'Thriller por la educación' have been able to generate an impact that has crossed, and continues to cross, political and geographic borders.

From Political *Fiestas* to Political *Partidos*

Piñera's administration (2010–2014) did not want to take the students seriously, publicly dismissing the flash mobs and street party demonstrations as the actions of a vocal yet ignorant minority who would rather cause trouble and skip classes than enter into dialogue with the government. Besides, Piñera would insist, 'No siempre la voz de la calle es la voz de la nación.'[40] After demonstrations ended in violence and police repression, Piñera was quick to label the protesters 'delinquents,'[41] proposing a law in October of 2011 (the 'Ley Antiencapuchados' or 'Anti-Hoods Law') that would criminalize social protest with penalties of up to three years in jail. Piñera maintained that education was a consumer good that should be regulated only by the demands of the market. Yet in spite of his reticence to work with the student protesters, their cause was validated time and again by public opinion polls showing overwhelming support on the part of Chileans, while the former president's approval ratings dropped precipitously. Eventually, the attention attracted by the students would force Piñera to change his tone, if only when faced with a critical international audience.[42]

Far from over, the student movement lasted longer than Piñera's term as president. Educational reform became the top issue in the 2013 general elections: upon announcing her candidacy, Michelle Bachelet—who won

[40] 'The voice of the street is not always the voice of the nation' (December 2011).

[41] See 'Chile: Piñera censura a 'minoría de delincuentes' durante protesta estudiantil,' *América Economía*, June 26, 2013, accessed September 1, 2013. https://www.americaeconomia.com/politica-sociedad/politica/chile-pinera-censura-minoria-de-delincuentes-durante-protesta-estudiantil.

[42] Before the United Nations in September 2011, two weeks after violence at the protests ended in the shooting of a 16-year-old by the police, Piñera declared: 'En las últimas semanas han sido miles los jóvenes chilenos que han salido a las calles a manifestarse en favor de una causa noble, hermosa y legítima como es una educación de calidad para todos, que les permita ser protagonistas y no meros espectadores de esta sociedad del conocimiento y la información.' ('In the last weeks, it has been thousands of young Chileans who have gone out into the streets to demonstrate in the name of a cause that is as noble, beautiful, and legitimate as a quality education for all, a cause that allows them to be protagonists and not mere spectators in this society of knowledge and information.').

the presidency with 62 percent of the second-round vote—made haste to proclaim that 'El primer proyecto que voy a enviar al Congreso pondrá fin al lucro y avanzará en la gratuidad de la educación en todos su niveles.'[43] Four former student leaders—Camila Vallejo, Karol Cariola, Gabriel Boric, and Giorgio Jackson—were elected to Congress in the same election cycle. Building on this momentum, Bachelet submitted a reform package within two months of being sworn in. The May 2014 legislation aimed to limit profit in the education system by making primary and secondary school free, eventually discontinuing government funding of private schools unless they move to non-profit models, end discrimination in the school selection process, and replace family co-payments for education with greater government subsidies. Students rejected the package, insisting that it did not address the true problems with education in Chile: that it is dominated by the market and perpetuates the inequalities built into the constitution orchestrated by Pinochet's military regime just before he left power. Moreover, Bachelet's proposal failed to address the intense debate around university-level education.

So, the protests continue. On May 8, 2014, at least 40,000 protesters marched through the streets of central Santiago, with simultaneous marches held in other cities. The movement's former student leaders absented themselves from Congress to participate in the demonstrations. That same month, the visual artist known as 'Papas Fritas,' Francisco Tapia—who over the course of a year had secretly burned $500 million worth of tuition contracts from the private, for-profit Universidad del Mar—toured through Santiago and Valparaíso in his van-turned-mobile-art installation to curate the ashes from those now-destroyed student debt obligations. Massive demonstrations in May of 2015 resulted in two student deaths. Strikes closed down over one hundred universities and secondary schools in 2016, and the most recent national march, this past April of 2018, brought students back into the streets by the thousands—although there has been complete turnover of both student leaders and government officials.

[43] 'The first project that I am going to send to Congress will put an end to profit and advance free education at all levels.' Rocío Montes, 'El movimiento estudiantil marca la campaña presidencial en Chile,' *El País*, April 13, 2013. https://elpais.com/internacional/2013/04/13/actualidad/1365815591_316625.html.

Questions and Lessons

How much more can the students demand of the government, beyond the 2015 School Inclusion law and Bachelet's 2016 program financing education tuition for nearly 80,000 university students? The Chilean government must walk a fine line with policy as major investors worry that education reform will combine with a slowing demand for copper to impede Chile's economic growth.[44] And, given the hefty majorities required by Pinochet's still-regnant constitution to pass large-scale reforms, there are stark limits to what she can get through Congress to be signed into law.

Meanwhile, as members of Congress, the former student leaders face their own challenges. They must work with the system with which they have long been at odds, side-by-side with right-wing politicians who will do everything in their power to hamper them. While their goals of sweeping reforms begin with free education for all, their platforms extend to a new constitution and reform of the electoral system itself—neither of which will be any small feat to achieve. And in addition to the enemies they know and expect, there is another test ahead: many of the current student protesters feel that the government will only betray them, and that true change will never be accomplished from within the system. Will Vallejo, Cariola, Boric, and Jackson be able to win the trust of new student leaders?[45] Can they take what they have learned from their successes in the streets and make it work for them in the legislature? These are some of the questions that are before us. What is the future of the Chilean student movement? What will its final evolution be? Will it have moved from youthful disillusionment with party (*partido*) politics to the party (*fiesta*)

[44] See Benedict Mander's article in *The Financial Times* online, 'Chile's President Aims to Soothe Investors over Reforms,' June 2, 2014. https://www.ft.com/content/28013328-e9d9-11e3-99ed-00144feabdc0.

[45] Just before the elections, Melissa Sepulveda, the then-president of the Universidad de Chile's student federation, went on record as saying she would not vote for any of the former student leaders, because 'Creo que las posibilidades de transformación no están en el Parlamento.' ['I believe that the possibility of transformation doesn't reside in Congress.'] See 'Presidenta electa FECh: No votaría por Giorgio Jackson ni Camila Vallejo,' *Cooperativa.cl*, November 13, 2013. https://www.cooperativa.cl/noticias/pais/educacion/universidades/presidenta-electa-fech-no-votaria-por-giorgio-jackson-ni-camila-vallejo/2013-11-13/092648.html.

politics of the street, only to return to the party (*partido*) politics of government once again? Or can the fiesta find a way to go on, crossing borders and finding new sources of inspiration, until change is finally achieved?

These answers remain to be seen, but from where we stand on the brink of the student movement's history, I believe there are some lessons the Chilean students can share with the rest of us striving to achieve social, political, and/or economic reforms:

1. Clearly articulate your goals. Do the research to know exactly what it will cost to implement them, and make your plan to achieve those goals easily accessible.
2. Aesthetics are important. Dissidence can be fun, appealing, and beautiful without losing its meaning.
3. Make neoliberalism work for you. Know what sells and how to market it.
4. Everyone can be a spect-actor. Find forms that encourage engagement, that pull bystanders into participation or make them consciously choose to walk away.
5. Democratize the process. Whether through social media or other formats, allow anyone to propose an event, contribute to planning, and show up to participate and/or document.
6. Curate a digital archive and link it everywhere. Make mainstream media pay attention to you, but don't let what your message looks or sounds like be determined by the media's chosen frames.
7. Play both sides. Change does not *have* to come from beyond the system. It's vital to have feet on the street, but those voices might be louder when complimented by hands in government chambers.

Take what you will from this list, improvising on and playing with these suggestions to continue to create and share new tools that effect social and political change. While the Chilean students have not yet written their own story's ending, I hope these strategies can both inspire new action and sustain the energy of ongoing resistance wherever it is needed to make this world a better place for us all to live in.

References

Boal, Augusto. *Theatre of the Oppressed*. New York: Theatre Communications Group, 1985.

Bush, Daniella Wittern. 'Words that Speak, Literature that Acts: Diamela Eltit's Narrative Performances.' PhD dissertation, Brown University, 2012.

Chelala, César. 'In Chile, Dissent Has a Woman's Face.' *The Globalist*, August 30, 2011. https://www.theglobalist.com/in-chile-dissent-has-a-womans-face/.

'Chile: Piñera censura a 'minoría de delincuentes' durante protesta estudiantil.' *América Economía*, June 26, 2013. https://www.americaeconomia.com/politica-sociedad/politica/chile-pinera-censura-minoria-de-delincuentes-durante-protesta-estudiantil.

'En Chile jóvenes bailan 'Thriller' por una mejora en la educación.' *CubaDebate. Contra el Terrorismo Mediatico*, June 26, 2013. http://www.cubadebate.cu/noticias/2011/06/26/en-chile-jovenes-bailan-thriller-por-una-mejora-en-la-educacion/#.Wd51-q3MzGI.

Figueroa, Juan Pablo, and Tania Araya. 'Académicos se transforman en accionistas. El negocio que esconde la venta de la Universidad Central.' Centro de Investigación Periodística, April 28, 2011.

Goldman, Francisco. 'Camila Vallejo, the World's Most Glamorous Revolutionary.' *The New York Times*, April 5, 2012. https://www.nytimes.com/2012/04/08/magazine/camila-vallejo-the-worlds-most-glamorousrevolutionary.html?mtrref=www.google.com&gwh=E7B97FE19CA96906869EB9F3E9A6FEB1&gwt=pay.

Mander, Benedict. 'Chile's President Aims to Soothe Investors over Reforms.' *The Financial Times*, online, June 2, 2014. https://www.ft.com/content/28013328-e9d9-11e3-99ed-00144feabdc0.

Montes, Rocío. 'El movimiento estudiantil marca la campaña presidencial en Chile.' *El País*, April 13, 2013. https://elpais.com/internacional/2013/04/13/actualidad/1365815591_316625.html.

Sepulveda, Melissa. 'Presidenta electa FECh: No votaría por Giorgio Jackson ni Camila Vallejo.' *Cooperativa.cl*, November 13, 2013. https://www.cooperativa.cl/noticias/pais/educacion/universidades/presidenta-electa-fech-no-votaria-por-giorgio-jackson-ni-camila-vallejo/2013-11-13/092648.html.

Taylor, Diana. 'The Politics of Passion.' *E-misférica*, special issue 'Dissidence.' 10, no. 2 (Summer 2013). Accessed January 13, 2018. http://hemisphericinstitute.org/hemi/en/e-misferica-102/taylor.

'Thriller por la educación.mpg.flv.' *Endless Video*, n.d. Accessed October 11, 2017. https://endlessvideo.com/watch?v=JJcOrWaViWg.

ATSA (Annie Roy and Pierre Allard), *Le Temps d'une Soupe* 2015-present

"By transforming the simple act of eating a bowl of soup into an interlude offering quality interaction in an aesthetic setting, this installation sets the stage—the table, if you will—for social encounters on a more human and egalitarian basis. It serves as an opportunity for taking that small yet brave step toward connecting with a perfect stranger, in a world where such connections are often virtual."

ATSA (Annie Roy and Pierre Allard), *Le Temps d'une Soupe* 2015-present

LE TEMPS D'UNE SOUPE (While Having Soup) begins with a deceptively simple premise: that sharing a meal and a conversation with a complete stranger can catalyze social action. Since 2015, artists Pierre Allard and Annie Roy have been staging public interventions in Montreal and beyond that invite passersby to partake in what they call a three-course dialogue experience. On a large raised platform with pairs of seats, participants are matched with strangers, offered bowls of soup prepared by neighborhood restaurants, and given a menu of "conversation starters" related to locally relevant social-justice topics ranging from homelessness to climate change. At the end of each exchange, the pairs are photographed along with a short caption that summarizes their encounter.

Le Temps d'une Soupe emerges from a series of sustained art actions that have their basis in providing frontline services to homeless and under housed Montrealers. The work was preceded by the large-scale actions *État d'Urgence* (1998–2010) and *Fin Novembre* (2011-2013), set in the heart of Montreal's Quartier Latin. In freezing temperatures, Allard and Roy curated a full suite of free arts programming for the public, enlisted the services of public health, charitable, and activist organizations, and coordinated the participation of hundreds of volunteers. By mobilizing different communities through artistic exchange, ATSA models the possibility of a more socially just world.

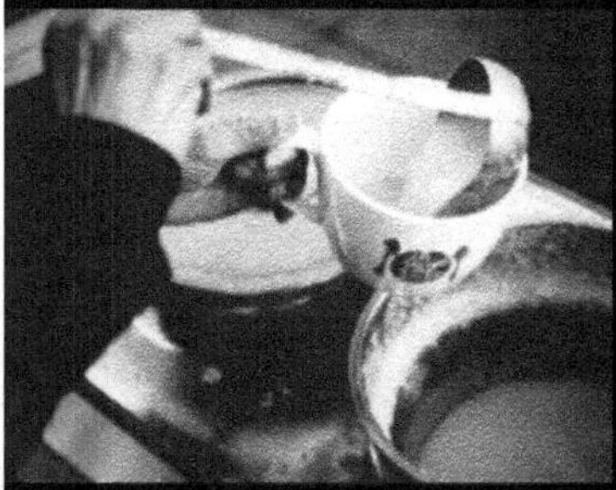

"The world is changing: tensions are flaring up, be they for economic, cultural or other reasons. All too often, we evolve in isolation from one another through virtual conversations that ultimately leave us disconnected, and incomprehension forms a great divide between us. We need to speak to one another, on a human scale, one to one, in order to reconnect and stimulate respectful encounters between people and in public spaces."
—Annie Roy and Pierre Allard, cofounders of ATSA

ATSA is a Montreal-based not-for-profit organization founded in 1998 by artists Pierre Allard and Annie Roy. The pair create transdisciplinary works and events for the public realm that take the form of interventions, installations, performance art and realistic stagings. Their actions are born of a desire to raise public awareness of urgent social, environmental and heritage issues. ATSA has received numerous awards, including the inaugural Prix du Jury on the occasion of the 33rd Grand Prix of the Conseil des Arts de Montréal (2018), the Prix du maire de Montréal en démocratie (2013), the Giverny Capital prize (2011), the Pratt & Whitney Canada Nature de l'Art Prize awarded by the Conseil des arts de Montréal (2010), the Citoyen de la Culture (2008), and the Artistes pour la Paix award (2008). ATSA is the subject of the 2010 documentary film *Art in Action*, directed by Magnus Isacsson and Simon Bujold.

CHAPTER 5

Beyond the Strike: Creative Legacies of the 2012 Quebec Student Protests

Jennifer Beth Spiegel

In the spring of 2012, the province of Quebec, Canada, was awash with red squares. In the streets and across social and mainstream media, students and their supporters protested rising tuition through a range of tactics from picket lines and occupations to street theatre and art installations, emphasizing that they were already 'squarely in the red'—squarely in debt—and could not accept higher fees. A year earlier, on March 17, 2011, the Quebec government had proposed substantial changes to university finances,[1] tying research funding to corporate investment and a 75 per cent tuition hike to be applied over a three-year period. While the government argued that this increase was warranted and just made Quebec fees comparable with tuition in most other Canadian provinces, students opposed the move towards privatization of education and argued that the hike would not only make education less affordable to many, but, importantly, constituted a significant ideological shift away from the gains made during Quebec's Quiet Revolution of the 1960s when accessible education

[1] A Fair and Balanced University Funding Plan to Give Québec the Means to Fulfill Its Ambitions, Gouvernement du Québec, 2011.

J. B. Spiegel (✉)
Simon Fraser University, Burnaby, BC, Canada

N. Alvarez et al. (eds.), *Sustainable Tools for Precarious Times*,
Contemporary Performance InterActions,
https://doi.org/10.1007/978-3-030-11557-9_5

was heralded as a fundamental value. At that time, a promise had been made to freeze tuition at a low rate and eventually abolish user fees for education as a means of reversing systemic inequities that disproportionately impacted women and Quebec's majority francophone population.[2]

In February 2012, after the government refused to negotiate with student associations, a student strike began that would last over six months. At its height, nearly 300,000 students, almost 75 per cent of Quebec's student population, were on strike. During what would become known as Quebec's 'Maple Spring,'[3] a diverse range of tactics were used, including blocking access to classes and buildings, daily marches, street theatre interventions, and videos on social media to mobilize popular support. Organizers estimated that the largest march was attended by as many as 500,000 people.[4] On May 18, 2012, the government passed a 'special law,' Bill 78, prohibiting the picketing of classes, as well as making it an offence to refuse to teach during the strike.[5] The bill further outlawed the encouraging of civil disobedience as well as all public gatherings of more than 50 people unless police were provided with detailed trajectories eight hours prior. Denounced as an infraction of human rights by Amnesty International[6] and as unconstitutional by the Quebec Bar Association,[7] fines for transgressing were up to $5000 for individuals, $35,000 for authority figures including professors and student spokespersons, and

[2] See Radio-Canada, 'Les Élections du Québec,' June 22, 1960, accessed October 11, 2017. http://archives.radio-canada.ca/emissions/1537.

[3] The term 'Maple Spring' (*printemps érable*) was controversial amongst activists and organizers, many objecting to the false equivalence it suggested with the Arab Spring (*printemps arabe*), where the stakes, risk, and sacrifice far exceeded that experienced in Quebec.

[4] Ethan Cox, '400,000+ in the Streets? Quebec's Students Are Winning […]' *Citizen's Press*, May 24, 2012. http://rabble.ca/blogs/bloggers/ethan-cox/2012/05/500000-streets-quebecs-students-are-winning.

[5] Québec National Assembly, 'Bill 78: An Act to Enable Students to Receive Instruction From the Postsecondary Institutions They Attend,' Québec City: Québec National Assembly, 2012.

[6] Amnesty International, 'Quebec Law Breaches Canada's International Human Rights Obligations,' *Amnesty International News*, May 25, 2012. https://www.amnesty.org/en/latest/news/2012/05/quebec-law-breaches-canada-s-international-human-rights-obligations/.

[7] Le Barreau du Québec, 'PL 78: Loi permettant aux étudiants de recevoir l'enseignement dispensé par les établissements de niveau postsecondaire qu'ils fréquentent: Le Barreau du Québec formule de sérieuses inquiétudes,' *Barreau du Québec: Activités Médias et Positions*, May 18, 2012. http://www.barreau.qc.ca/fr/actualites-medias/communiques/2012/05/18-etudiants.

$125,000 for organizations and associations, with fines doubled for a second offence.

On May 10, 2012, Stefan Christoff of Howl Arts Collective, a Montreal-based collective of cultural workers, artists, and activists working for social justice via artistic expression, published an article entitled '*Rêve général illimité* in Quebec' (roughly translating to 'unlimited general dream'), emphasizing the 'broader dreams of a student movement now sparking the popular imagination'.[8] Over the past several decades, numerous scholars have detailed the importance of cultural memory and the development of performative protest repertoires in mobilizing resistance and challenging modes of social organization.[9] The role of play and creativity in transforming a sense of possible social configurations,[10] as well as the relationships between the personal and the political has increasingly been stressed,[11] though the risk that such playful resistance could act as a distraction has also been noted.[12] This chapter examines the plethora of creative repertoires of protest invoked and transfigured during the Quebec student strike, the debates they occasioned, and their manifold legacies. Specifically, I analyse the ways in which creative tactics alter divisions of labour by transforming the relationship between 'private care' and 'public participation.' Through engaging in various creative social movement activities, I argue that how such divides are resisted ultimately reshapes the dynamics of cultural reproduction, labour, education, and the social relations that traverse these spheres, with deep implications for the sustainability of movements.

[8] Stephan Christoff, "Rêve général illimité" in Quebec,' in *Le fond de l'air est rouge*, ed. Stephan Christoff (Montreal: Howl Arts Collective, 2013), 31.

[9] See Diana Taylor, *The Archive and the Repertoire: Performing Cultural Memory in the Americas* (Durham, NC: Duke University Press, 2003); Charles Tilly, *Contentious Performances* (Cambridge: Cambridge University Press, 2008); and Benjamin Shepard, *Play, Creativity, and Social Movements: If I Can't Dance, It's Not My Revolution* (London: Routledge, 2012).

[10] See Baz Kershaw, 'Fighting in the Streets: Dramaturgies of Popular Protest, 1968–1989,' *New Theatre Quarterly* 13, no. 51 (1997): 255–276; and Richard Schechner, 'Invasions Friendly & Unfriendly: The Dramaturgy of Direct Theatre,' *South African Theatre Journal* 6, no. 1 (1992): 4–24.

[11] Kolonel Klepto and Major Up Evil, 'The Clandestine Insurgent Rebel Clown Army Goes to Scotland Via a Few Other Places. *Shut Them Down*!' in *The G8, Gleneagles 2005 and the Movement of Movements*, ed. David Harvie, Keir Milburn, Ben Trott, and David Watts (Autonomedia/Dissent!), 243–254.

[12] See David Graeber, *Direct Action: An Ethnography* (Oakland, CA: AK Press, 2009); and Shepard, *Play, Creativity, and Social Movements.*

The arguments here are based on insights collectively generated during the six-month period I was on strike as a post-doctoral member of the Graduate Students Association at McGill University, as well as a part-time lecturer active in organizing with Professors Against the Tuition Hikes at Concordia University. It also draws on my involvement in local social movements in the years that followed. Throughout these periods, I attended meetings and events, taking field notes and collecting materials about creative protest repertoires, and facilitated workshops and discussions with students and other activists concerning histories of creative interventions as well as debates on tactics emerging in the scholarly literature and 'on the ground'. In keeping with the fluidity between academic analysis and the activist discourses produced during the strike, I consider the theorizations of activists, editorialists, and academics, as well as activist performance itself, all of which, I argue, intertwined to transform activist discourse and practice. Throughout the chapter, I detail how events of 2012 not only created 'temporary autonomous zones'[13] but also influenced subsequent thought and action concerning student mobilization, protest culture, and the divisions of public and private within the popular lexicon more broadly.

From '*Grève Générale*' to '*Rêve Général*': Spatialized Tensions of Collective Visioning

The first formal *Rêve Général Illimité* event of the Quebec student strike was not launched until July 2012, at the outset of the Montreal Jazz Festival during the height of Montreal's tourism season, as a collaboration between Howl Arts and L'École de La Montagne Rouge.[14] However, it highlighted the invocation of discourses and imagery historically associated with creativity in social movements that had been re-deployed in the months preceding the event. While the introduction of the concept of the '*rêve général*' during the Quebec student movement resurfaced a collective questioning of the role of play and creativity in seizing public space, it was not an invention of the 2012 Quebec student strike. The concept of the *rêve général*, prefigured by Surrealist and Situationist movements, was used in 2006 in France by students on strike against the precariousness of

[13] Hakim Bey, *The Temporary Autonomous Zones, Ontological Anarchy, Poetic Terrorism* (Brooklyn, NY: Autonomedia, 1985).

[14] Raphael Dallaire Ferland, 'Premier Rêve général illimité,' *Le Devoir*, June 12, 2012.

modern life, and rapidly spread in response to the financial crisis of 2009.[15] Writing about this phenomenon from within the Occupy movement (coincidentally, at the very moment that the Quebec 2012 student movement was gaining visibility, although no connection was made at the time), Mirzoeff explains the pun and its relevance to anti-austerity movements. He argues that the interchangability of the words for strike and dream—by simply adding or subtracting the G and/or the e at the beginning and/or end of *(G)rève Général(e)*—sparks a re-imagining of the future.

Near the onset of the 2012 Quebec student strike, L' École de la Montagne Rouge had been formed by design students and became a hub for the development of posters, slogans, and images, many of which directly referenced the iconography and slogans of the May 1968 student strike in Paris. Various other initiatives extended this tradition of creatively seizing public space to illustrate the social debates at play. Students from the Theatre Department at the Université de Québec à Montréal (UQAM) conducted a daily event called La Ligne Rouge (the red line): every morning at 8:30 a.m., students dressed in red spread themselves out along the southbound subway station platform in Montreal's Jean-Talon Metro Station. After other passengers had boarded, the red-clad protestors would silently enter the subway together, getting on and off at every station for maximum visibility until they arrived at their university. This allowed the commute to school, and the commitment of students to accessible education, to be made visible, maximizing peaceful yet politicized interchanges between students and those commuting to work. Dance students formed the 'Red Line Dancers' and performed such symbolic actions as slow-motion Butoh walks down busy Saint Catherine Street, illustrating the catch phrase 'don't slow down our education' (with a tuition hike). 'Theatre Struck,' a group of Concordia theatre students, built giant puppets, while 'Archicontre,' students from the Université de Montréal, constructed giant red cubes and posed in public spaces, lying down, crushed beneath the weight of the red cube—crushed, that is, beneath the weight of debt. In each case, the very act of putting education to work in the service of the common goal of the strike was itself a statement.[16]

[15] Nicholas Mirzoeff, 'Vive la Rêve générale,' *Occupy 2012: A Daily Observation on Occupy*, April 20, 2012. http://www.nicholasmirzoeff.com/O2012/2012/04/20/vive-la-reve-generale/.

[16] Jennifer Beth Spiegel, 'Quebec's Noisy Revolution: Social Dramaturgies of the "Maple Spring",' *Wi: Journal of Mobile Media* 6, no. 2 (2012). http://wi.mobilities.ca/quebecs-noisy-revolution-socialdramaturgies-of-the-maple-spring/.

Such usages of street art within social movements have a long history in Quebec.[17] Indeed, much of the discourse and tactics used on the streets of Quebec that spring were borrowed and adapted from previous student strikes and social movements. With the anti-World Trade Organization (WTO) Seattle protests at the end of the twentieth century, 'swarm' theories of street activism began to proliferate,[18] rethinking traditional notions of a 'bloc' (the most common in contemporary protest lexicons being the Black Bloc, but also 'pink blocs' of queer groups, 'circus blocs,' 'baby blocs' comprising parents and young children, etc.). This choreography departed from that of previous movements, such as labour movements, that tended to march organized behind banners. These groups were not functioning according to cleanly divisible bloc choreographies, but swarmed, filling available spaces, creating a kind of tactical contamination. During the 2012 student strike, such swarms rapidly multiplied, springing up 'unexpectedly everywhere.'[19]

The changing nature of protest choreographies and creative tactics speaks to the shifting nature of social movements themselves. These transformations parallel changes in the workforce and the increasing pressure on precarious workers to become 'creative entrepreneurs' and find their own contracts.[20] Protests are now increasingly organized via multiple splinter groups, or affinity groups, self-organized and functioning in tandem. Swarms unite through a common desire to generate an alternative model of socio-political life, confronting state policies that they mutually find punitive. The motto of anti-corporate globalization activists made popular at the anti-WTO protests had become 'another world is possible.' The protests that followed against the Summit of the Americas in Quebec City 2001, as well as the anti-G8 events of the same year, repeated much of the alter-globalization and anti-capitalist discourse. For many Quebec activists, the 2012 student movement was a particular,

[17] See Ève Lamoureux, 'L'art de la manif réinventé? Analyse de l'importance actuelle des pratiques culturelles et artistiques,' *Bulletin d'histoire politique* 21, no. 2 (2013): 70–81.

[18] See John Arquilla and David Ronfeldt, *Networks and Netwars: The Future of Terror, Crime, and Militancy* (Santa Monica, CA: Rand Corporation, 2001) as well as Michael Hardt and Antonio Negri, *Multitude* (New York: Penguin, 2004).

[19] Timothy Beeler, 'Unexpectedly Everywhere: Reflections on Alternative Learning,' *Transmutations* 1, no. 1. (2013). http://transmutations.org/site/123-2/.

[20] Mauricio Lazzarato, *The Making of the Indebted Man: An Essay on the Neoliberal Condition* (Cambridge, MA: MIT Press, 2012).

localized moment within this broader global movement.[21] It was at these protests that the Quebec activist art group 'artivistic' was formed,[22] providing activist art-making and skill-trade workshops in Montreal, keeping the tradition alive in ways that would proliferate during the 2012 student movement.

In the case of the Seattle protests, as Lazzarato noted, signs, images, and statements did not just represent a state of affairs, but rather created the world in which things and people function.[23] The force of the anti-WTO Seattle protests reminded audiences worldwide that even in America people were capable of conceiving of 'another world.' The Occupy Wall Street movement of 2011 had sought to reclaim space from the corporate elite, explicitly tying the disappearance of public space to growing wealth inequity. Occupy Montreal was amongst the largest and longest-standing Occupy sites in Canada, and had, from day one, been frequented by student organizers distributing red squares. In the case of the Quebec student movement, the occupation of public space for collective visioning was catalysed by a very precise rejection of the government's funding plan. The streets became the extension of the university and a site to contest the future of universities in spaces that were, in principle, public and accessible. Techniques for stopping classes were thus combined with various other tactics.

In the larger marches that occurred monthly for six months, during which hundreds of thousands of people would coalesce in support of the movement, people did often gather behind particular banners designating particular student associations, workers' unions, professors against the tuition hike, mothers, and other self-identified groups. In the daily protest events, however, as well as the various 'family days,' the choreography tended to be that of the swarm. Each of these configurations repeated and adapted refrains from previous eras, from union hierarchies and the affiliations they rehearsed and inspired in other non-syndical groups, to the swarm and art happenings re-invented from the avant-garde and taken up

[21] Anna Kruzynski, Rachel Sarrasin, Sandra Jeppesen and Research Group on Collective autonomy (Collectif de recherche sur l'autonomie collectif or 'CRAC'), 'It Didn't Start with Occupy, and It Won't End with the Student Strike! The Persistence of Anti-authoritarian Politics in Quebec,' *Wi: Journal of Mobile Media* (June 2, 2012). http://wi.mobilities.ca/category/2012-6-2-out-of-the-mouth-of-casseroles-i/page/3/.

[22] Lamoureux, 'L'art de la manif réinventé?'

[23] Maurizio Lazzarato, 'Struggle, Event, Media,' *republicart*, May 2003. www.republicart.net/disc/representations/lazzarato01_en.htm.

by a generation accustomed to 'user-generated content.' While protests began on campuses and spread first to student and working-class neighbourhoods, by May, marches were weaving through even the wealthiest areas of town.[24]

The universities, the streets, the Internet—spaces at risk of becoming corporatized—were reclaimed as places where students, workers, and all those concerned about the future of the province could converge. Both the goals of the movement and the tactics deployed were, however, subject to heavy critique from both within and without. The movement had created a plethora of spaces of 'dissensus'[25] (rather than consensus), where diverse and occasionally conflicting perspectives were embodied through heterogeneous tactics and counter-tactics, as well as the conjoining of multiple sites of occasionally convergent and often conflicting activity.

On May 22, a few days following the adoption of Bill 78, in a large-scale act of civil disobedience, the march of several hundred thousand people that month did not follow the set trajectory. Shortly thereafter, the tradition of *tintamarre* or cacerolazo—the communal banging of pots and pans—was introduced into the local repertoire, appropriated from the ongoing student struggle in Chile, thereby solidifying performative links between the two. The tactic, popularized in Chile when police tactics became too threatening for the general population to join street protests, spread across the province and particularly across Montreal, renamed as '*les casseroles*.' These casserole protests started precisely at the threshold between the 'private' space of the home and 'public' space—on the balconies and front steps of a wide range of dwellings across the province. As Thain aptly noted, the casserole protests introduced a 'coming into discourse of noise'; the message that rings out through the expansion of such festive protests is the frequently heard chant '*avec nous, dans la rue*!' ('join us in the streets!').[26] Within this schema, symbolic acts, such as the casserole protests, chants, the symbol of the red square, as well as the various forms of street theatre and street art, function as collective excitement whereby the symbolism triggers affective responses, generating collective action based primarily on emotional rather than analytic factors.[27]

[24] Alanna Thain, 'Press Play,' *Society and Space*, July 6, 2012. http://societyandspace.org/author/alanna-thain/.

[25] Jacques Rancière, *Dissensus: On Politics and Aesthetics*, trans. S. Corcoran (Cambridge: Polity, 2010).

[26] Thain, 'Press Play.'

[27] Herbert Blumer, 'Social Psychology,' in *Man and Society: A Substantive Introduction to the Social Science*, ed. Emerson Schmidt (New York: Prentice Hall, 1937), 144–198.

Such a call to boost the noise and number in the streets was particularly important due to the opposition the movement was facing both within Quebec and in the rest of Canada. Much of the mainstream Canadian media portrayed protestors as 'spoiled babies' unwilling to pay tuition on par with that of students elsewhere in Canada let alone the US where tuition was much higher. Student protests were repeatedly framed as imposing themselves on the 'silent majority' of citizens whose will the new Bill was purported to defend.[28] Within this context, the casseroles became a form of symbolic warfare, aimed at countering dominant rhetoric on an affective level. Through the casserole protests, residents—with no special political status or claim within the movement—were able to deploy the most ordinary of household items to act as guardians of community values. Here, harkening to pre-modern community rituals, this rhythmic banging became a modern day political act of publicly shaming the forces that were undermining the 'public good.' The casserole protests altered the terms of participation in civic life itself, bringing protest into domestic spaces and allowing people to participate easily from their homes, with their neighbours.

The apparent spontaneity and event-focused 'taking of the streets' has historically threatened to occlude the work of long-term organizing, mobilization and the restructuring of institutions that are required to realize the demands.[29] Nonetheless, as will be discussed, it can also serve to strengthen ties of solidarity for the movement's renewal. The tension gestures towards the stakes in thinking of the re-creation of spaces as public political spaces of dissensus in terms of a '*rêve général illimité*'—a space for unlimited collective visioning. During the Québec mobilization of 2012, the Rêve Général Illimité of July 5 sought to democratize not only the consumption but also the production of cultural visions and collective affects. It contested the social logic of arts events that rely on corporate sponsorship to bring art to the people—the same dynamic increasingly being imposed on education where rising user fees were also accompanied by mounting reliance on corporate research funds.[30] The play on words invoking an unlimited general strike works only when the collective visioning is viewed in

[28] Tasha Kheiriddin, 'Quebec Student Protests: Silent Majority Needs to Make Some Noise about Violent Demonstrations,' *National Post*, May 23, 2012.

[29] See Barbara Epstein, *Political Protest and Cultural Revolution: Nonviolent Direct Action in the 1970s and 1980s* (Berkeley: University of California Press, 1991) and Shepard, *Play, Creativity, and Social Movements.*

[30] Ferland, 'Premier Rêve général illimité.'

tandem with the stoppage of habitual institutional functioning. As Mirzoeff writes, 'the general strike is the limit of the dream image, its enactment as social life' while the general dream of transformation and the renunciation of domination founds the possibility of a new politics.'[31]

Dissensus: Divisions of Labour and the Time for Participation

On April 7, 2012, the 54th day of the strike (that would last another five months), a student spokesperson, Gabriel Nadeau-Dubois, elaborated on its meaning: 'Our strike is just a step, a stopping point along a path that is much, much longer. Our strike is already victorious because it enables us to see that path, the path of resistance.'[32] Nadeau's speech unpacked the world-making at the heart of the strike, the rejection of 'your commercialized education, your laboratory schools, and your society of "Me, Inc.,"' underlining the renewal and strengthening of the tradition of struggle in Quebec. The confluence and occasional tensions between the immediate material demands of the strike and the long-term socio-cultural transformations it embodied and propelled, however, led to a multiplicity of positions.

The *time* of engagement is intractable from the question of participation, shaping who can transform the politics of public life, how, and at what cost. In this case, students (and professors to some extent) had the time to engage precisely because the primary tactic for opposing the educational and economic reforms was to stop the regular functioning of the system. As a result, the time normally spent in class could be spent on the streets. The power of the Red Line, for instance, was not just that it spatialized and dramatized a commitment to schooling akin to having a full-time job (travelling the morning rush hour Metro with those hurrying to work), but that this ritual was maintained in a visible manner every morning for months, allowing others to identify the practice and to join in. Time, re deployed, allowed for the creation of protest repertoires that could indeed become visible and intelligibly draw on the short- and long-term cultural memory of social movements. Some chant, such as 'so-so-so

[31] Mirzoeff, 'Vive la Rêve générale.'

[32] Gabriel Nadeau-Dubois, 'Staying Power (Le souffle le plus long),' trans. Susan Ruddick, *Society and Space*, July 6, 2012. http://societyandspace.org/2012/07/06/staying-power-le-souffle-le-plus-long-gabriel-nadeau-dubois/.

so-li-dar-i-ty' and 'you're sexy, you're cute, take off your riot suit' pre-date the student movement and have been used around the world. 'New' interventions also exploited repetition, their meaning transforming over time, producing their own fissures.

Towards the beginning of the 2012 strike, Jean Charest, Quebec Premier at the time (2003–2012), used the 'disruptions' caused by daily marches during the day, public teach-ins often held on the streets, and blockades of ports and bridges to declare that students were harming workers.[33] In response, labour unions came out in support of students, helping to de-stabilize this argument. Daily marches were relegated to the evening when they would not disrupt the nine-to-five working crowd, and when more workers could participate in solidarity—as indeed a great many did. For over a hundred consecutive nights from early March 2012, marches would depart at 8 p.m. from Place Emilie Gamelin. By May, there was hardly a moment, day or night, when there was not a protest action somewhere in the province. Night marches continued, often into the early hours of the morning. Shortly thereafter, the morning shift began with demonstrations at 8 a.m.

The question of time remains deeply linked to issues of division of labour, as those with the duty to care for increasingly privatized survival needs of self and family face ever-growing demands on their time. While, as Lazzarato suggests, in the age of privatization, expectations that we will all engage in the unpaid labour of preparing ourselves for the workforce is becoming a social leveller of the multitude,[34] as feminist movements have been arguing for decades, this labour and the associated precariousness with which it is linked remains deeply gendered.[35] The privatization of social services further inscribes the work of social and cultural production as a private good. During the 2012 strike, feminist and women's groups in Quebec thus highlighted the historical importance of women's struggles to gain access to education and enable women to fully participate in shaping society rather than being confined to the private realm of unpaid

[33] Tom Gagné, 'Quebec Students on the March,' *Socialist Worker*, March 22, 2012. http://socialistworker.org/2012/03/22/quebec-students-on-the-march.

[34] Lazzarato, 'Struggle, Event, Media.'

[35] Charlotte Bunch, *Passionate Politics: Feminist Theory in Action* (London: Palgrave Macmillan, 1987), Epstein, *Political Protest and Cultural Revolution*, and Silvia Federici, 'Precarious Labor: A Feminist Viewpoint,' 2008. http://inthemiddleofthewhirlwind.wordpress.com/precarious-labor-a-feminist-viewpoint/.

caregiver.[36] The official 'Statement on Tuition Fees in Québec and their Impact on Women' of the Simone de Beauvoir Institute at Concordia University highlighted the disproportionate effect that raising tuition would have on women due to the statistically lower incomes that women still earn relative to men, as well as the serious effects this would have, in particular, on single mothers and their children. Given the tendency for women to have to juggle greater family duties, work more hours for the same revenue, and hence work longer and/or incur higher debt load for the same education, the tuition hikes would further reduce women's access to education—especially those from low-income families including Indigenous women.[37] The relevance of the cuts for parents in the age of austerity hovered beneath the surface of every 'family friendly' event and every space created by parents who arrived on the scene with their children, dissolving the difference between the private time of family responsibilities and the public act of creating collective futures.

This division between private and public was, however, heavily policed. Parents who took their children to protests were occasionally chastised on social media for 'bad parenting,' while threats of being reported to the authorities for putting their children at risk also spread—despite the fact that the 'risk' that many feared was precisely brutality at the hands of the police accuser.[38] As demanding that people 'stay in their place' (at home to raise well-behaved children, at work to pay their debts, etc.) reduces participation in reshaping collective visions, transforming this dynamic requires attention to how time and space can be reshaped for such participation. While the strike liberated time for students to participate in political pressure tactics, the 'real test' would be the extent to which public services would remain available and public participation active, beyond the strike. Within the context of austerity budgets and the ongoing privatization of

[36] Martine Delvaux, Gabrielle Desrosiers, Garlerand Elsa and L'écuyer Vanessa, 'Militantes féministes grévistes. Du Comité femmes de l'ASSÉ au Comité femmes GGI de l'UQAM,' in *Un Printemps rouge et noir: Regards croisés sur la grève étudiante de 2012*, ed. Marcos Ancelovici and Francis Dupuis-Déri (Les Editions Écosociété, 2014), 115–149.

[37] Simone de Beauvoir Institute. *Statement on Tuition Fees in Québec and Their Impact on Women*, Simone de Beauvoir Institute, Concordia University, February 2012. http://wsdb.concordia.ca/about-us/official-position-on-issues/documents/2012SdBITuitionFees.pdf.

[38] La Ligue des droits et Libertés, Associations des juristes progressistes, Associations pour une solidarité syndicale étudiante, 'Répression, discrimination et grève étudiante: analyse et témoignages,' 2013. http://liguedesdroits.ca/wp-content/fichiers/rapport-2013-repression-discrimination-et-greve-etudiante.pdf.

services, this would require reorganization of social life and the public/private dichotomies that have come to be accepted. In this respect, the techniques and technologies of participation popularized during the strike became important contributing factors to the possibility of long-term engagement.

Legacies of Creative Disruption: Artfully Out of Place

'Artivism,' as coined by the Quebec-based group during the G8 Counter Summit, focuses on transforming space-time relations, emphasizing intervening on-site, where things are taking place.[39] This tradition of creatively transforming time and space was the dominant cultural correlate to the direct action interventions that sought to disrupt the business-as-usual of privatizing institutions in Quebec. Various tactics transformed the politics of participation in the 2012 protests, an important dimension of which was how 'safe space' was created or destroyed, including how risk was experienced and distributed. While direct action was, in principle, open to all, various factors influenced who was able to invest the time and take the risk.

The use of laughter and playfulness has been amply theorized as strategically incorporated into activists' resistance movements to change the affective tenor. For example, proponents of activist clowning note that these activities help sustain movements across time and space by re-humanizing, personalizing, and bringing care and laughter into situations where anger and confrontation often dominate.[40] Groups like the Vermont-based Bread and Puppet Theatre (who made a brief appearance in night protests in Montreal), the Clandestine Insurgent Rebel Clown Army (CIRCA), and the Wombles in the UK have become famous for using costuming and the absurd to raise morale in often-confrontational demonstrations. This tradition was extended during the Quebec student movement, with affective protest furthered by the presences of such 'protest mascots' as Anarchopanda—a protestor in a giant panda suit who became famous for giving hugs to protestors and police alike. The re-personalization of the political, however, threatened to return the question of collective futures to that of interpersonal interaction between individuals and their case-by-

[39] Lamoureux, 'L'art de la manif réinventé?,' 71.

[40] Klepto Kolonel and Major Up Evil, 'The Clandestine Insurgent Rebel Clown Army.'

case negotiations. Figures like Anarchopanda attempted to maintain separation between their public role and the personal story of the individual human that inhabited the role, with marginal success.[41]

Social media allowed student and community groups to disseminate creative and informational material to wider audiences. For instance, Docteur Chaussette, a sock puppet from the small northern city of Rimouski and 'head of the union of socks,' started a YouTube channel where she spoke humorously of the personal considerations of engagement in activist life, from the perspective of the socks worn by activists as they marched for hours, day after day.[42] Drawing attention to the unseen personal aspects of labour and risk involved in transforming the time and space of political engagement—tired feet, vulnerability to police attack, the strain on family and romantic relationships when one's time is devoted to the collective cause—was able to be humorously explored by the learned 'indebted' puppet. A scene of confrontation was dramatized in which the puppet sat down with a hand-puppet version of the puppeteer's boyfriend wherein the boyfriend-puppet complains that the puppeteer is spending more time engaged in creative, unpaid, activism than with him. A plan was thus developed in which the puppeteer would take a break from her creative activism to attend to the relationship (go fishing) and the boyfriend would, in return, accompany the puppet and puppeteer to a protest. Such creative interventions allowed for broader participation while reaching friends and other viewers through humour, provoking a rethinking of divisions between public and private time.

While the strike created time for heightened devotion to social movements, the real test would be the changes that remained beyond the strike. The strike saw some 'victories.' The government called a snap election in the middle of the strike and was defeated. The first day after taking office, the new government repealed the infamous Bill 78 and cancelled the tuition hikes. However, tuition was indexed to the rate of inflation and $250 million was still cut from university operating grants.[43] While not discounting the importance of the achievements, many claimed that the

[41] Alanna Thain, 'Anarchopanda's Soft Subversions,' *Wi: Journal of Mobile Media* 6, no. 2 (June 2012). http://wi.mobilities.ca/anarchopandas-soft-subversions/.

[42] Docteur Chaussette, 'Marionnette engagée, Docteur Chaussette,' *Transmutations* 1, no.1 (2013). http://transmutations.org/site/123-2/.

[43] Micheal Wrobel, 'Quebec's Political Parties on Tuition Fees and University Funding,' *The Link*, March 25, 2014. https://thelinknewspaper.ca/article/quebecs-political-parties-on-tuition-fees-and-university-funding.

real gain of the strike was cultural—the sense that it was possible to mobilize against austerity and collectively hold discussions on the fate of societal services and educational institutions. The countless acts of coming together to creatively revise education were far-reaching.

On March 22, 2013, exactly one year from the first of the monthly mass protest marches that became legendary during Quebec's Maple Spring, some of us came together to launch a bilingual online platform that I co-edited/curated along with other professors and students, entitled Performing the Student Strike.[44] We asked: 'what does it mean to perform a movement—or to perform with a movement?' Contributions included videos of Docteur Chaussette; a collective video class project created by UQAM students exploring the collective creation that so many had learned during the strike; reflections by undergraduate and graduate student artists and scholars; and a host of video art works by local artists who had participated in the protests. As we stated in our editorial: 'We lived the re-negotiations of 'performance' in both the sense of performing one's role or identity as a multiple of student/professor/leader/citizen, etc., as well as in the artistic sense, in which a large range of creative techniques were deployed to augment or challenge particular visions of society.'[45]

The platform was intended as a space 'to extend and inspire the ever-changing repertoire of collective possibilities.' The 'real test' of such efforts, however, occurs in the public spaces of contestation themselves. That night students were protesting anew the educational reforms and the consultation process staged by the new government, widely deemed unsatisfactory by those who had only recently ended their six-month strike. The march was stopped by police within minutes, and the protesters held in a 'kettle,' surrounded by riot police for hours. Eventually protestors were arrested and released with $637 fines each for being in a protest that had not given an itinerary to police. This charge issued from an amendment to the municipal bylaw passed the previous year (P6) alongside the repealed Bill 78. The arrests thus shed light on two legacies: one institutional and the other grassroots. During the Maple Spring, even the most moderate of supporters had marched banging pots and pans without prior itinerary. In contrast, following on the heels of the mass

[44] See transmutations.org.

[45] Jennifer Beth Spiegel, Alanna Thain, Sophie Castonguay, and Magda Olszanowski, 'To Perform in/with a Movement,' *Transmutations* 1, no. 1 (2013). http://transmutations.org/site/.

arrests at the March 15 anti-police brutality protests, a new era of political repression had begun; the municipal anti-protest legislation, largely unused during the 2012 student strike, would be applied liberally.

The police kettle and subsequent arrests of March 22, 2013, propelled a second wave of cultural activism in Montreal. A cast of activist characters happened to have been kettled together. They had refined their powers of cheerful resistance and resilience the spring before, armed with musical instruments, rabbit ears, panda suits, and snacks. The police detention served to re-energize creative resistance. Two days later, I received a text that read: 'We need the "circus bloc". Make it happen.' At the first meeting, a name for the collective was adopted by consensus: a self-kettle would be enacted by *Les Souris Fières*, a name gesturing towards the double meaning of what the group was trying to actualize. In French, the police tactic of circling protestors (known in English as a 'kettle') is colloquially called a '*souricière*,' which translates literally to mousetrap. The word '*souris*' means both mouse and smile. '*Souris Fières*' thus not only rhymes with '*souricière*' but translates both to 'proud mice' and 'proud smiles.' Dressed as clown police and other playful and ridiculous characters, protestors would encircle and 'arrest' other protestors. The antics were to be a demonstration of resolve, joy, and catharsis, counteracting the fear instilled by the laws against protest and the policing tactics that upheld them (Fig. 5.1).[46]

The event staged a coming together of disparate groups opposing anti-protest legislation and reached out to other non-affiliated individuals. In the preceding weeks, a clown battalion offered free training in slapstick violence wherein participants learned how to appear to attack one another without risking injury. On the day of the event, there were thus a handful of newly trained clowns. Costumes and cardboard police shields were provided so that others could safely participate. With circus artists performing outreach, the event was, in many ways, classically carnivalesque. The inversion and dissolution of social hierarchies, the sharing of skills, and the celebration of bodily freedom, often with base-level comedy, pervaded the spirit of the activities. The target of the event, however, was extremely precise: the laws that would limit unsanctioned bodily demonstrations of dissent in public space. Much like other interventions, it must be seen as part of an array of tactics that included, in this case, community mobiliza-

[46] Jennifer Beth Spiegel, 'Masked Protest in the Age of Austerity: State Violence, Anonymous Bodies, and Resistance "In the Red,"' *Critical Inquiry* 41, no. 4 (2015): 786–810.

Fig. 5.1 The clown police handcuff Anarchopanda at *Sourisfest*. Credit: Marco Simonsen-Sereda (@blogocram)

tion to remove the burden of fines from individuals, as well as an eventually successful campaign to repeal the bylaw amendment and cancel the fines. The debates on the efficacy of such carnivalesque tactics raged throughout the 2012 Quebec protests and beyond.[47] A threat of movement involvement being reduced to engagement in the affective immediacy of carnival, instead of focusing on the, often long, series of meetings needed to formulate and lobby for policy alternative persists. Nevertheless, these moments of political 'belonging' were intensely transformative for building collectivity and maintaining networks able to be re-activated on short notice, precisely because of the affective labour and collective care that such events perform.

In her 'Manifesto' on 'mothering as revolutionary praxis,' Cynthia Dewi Oka[48] advises movements to 'reclaim the process of creating art for

[47] See Spiegel, 'Of Spectacle and Collective Resistance.'

[48] Cynthia Dewi Oka, 'Mothering as Revolutionary Praxis,' in *Revolutionary Mothering: Love on the Front Lines*, ed. Alexis Pauline Gumbs, China Martens, and Mai'a Williams (Toronto: Between the Lines & PM Press, 2016), 56.

facilitating collective critical reflection, connectedness and inspiration.' She argues that the capacity of collective art to give voice to the multigenerational yearnings for a community becomes essential for creating a more equitable future. It was, indeed, the further deepening of multigenerational networks that was sought by creative actions, and by the reconvergence of local movements more broadly in the years following the 2012 strike. Shortly after the tuition hike was officially cancelled, student groups began mobilizing against the broader social logic of austerity that had taken hold of public institutions. The following spring, cuts to daycare funding were occurring at the same time as reductions to university funding. Alongside accessible education, affordable childcare had been a core achievement of the aforementioned Quiet Revolution, and in particular, the feminist movements that were nurtured at that time. Although some tried to pit one against the other, the conjoining of protest networks that were deepened through the existence of groups like '*mère en colère et solidaire*' (Angry Mothers in Solidarity) organized during the 2012 student strikes and persisting for years to follow, resisted this dichotomy, and instead highlighted the hypocrisy of austerity at a time when corporate taxes were at an all-time low.

In the spring of 2015, after a year of mobilization, a much smaller contingent of students went on strike again. This time the strike was part of a much broader cross-sector mobilization and against the more pervasive austerity budgets that were gutting public services including universities but also daycares, the public school system, and most public sector institutions. The emblem of the anti-austerity movement was the wolf because—as was noted in their cross-sector website—wolves are not sheep, but they move in packs or collectives. This new wave of mobilizations echoed many of the tactics and visions of the 2012 protests, including some of the artistic practices leveraged to forge solidarity and creatively diffuse messages. After months of organizing, the 2014 anti-austerity movement garnered public attention with a colourful Halloween march rife with familiar satire under the official name: 'Austerity: a horror story.' Concordia University's student paper, the *Link*, reported that 'an estimated 10,000 disgruntled zombies, witches, students and public sector employees took to the streets of Montreal Friday to protest austerity measures imposed by the Quebec Government.'[49]

[49] Noelle Didierjean, 'Over 10,000 Costumed Anti-Austerity Protestors March in Montreal: Public Sector and Students Upset over Government Austerity Measures,' *The Link*, November 1, 2014.

More targeted art interventions delved into the current state of affairs, re-using designs and networks formed in 2012 to quickly respond to subsequent events. For example, an interactive performance piece, entitled '*Prêter l'oreille*' ('Lend an Ear'), led by Sophie Castonguay in 2012, invited participants to communally recite texts proliferating on the web to take over time and space collectively. Participants would download recorded speeches from student leaders, literary texts produced by striking students, editorials, and the like; they would then gather together at a designated time and place, usually in the context of a larger protest, march, or 'family day' of solidarity, and subsequently walk, repeating the texts out loud in synchrony. The 'flashmob' style of the protest combined with its use of personal technologies—first the downloading of speeches from the internet, Castonguay's re-parsing and rerecording of the text to make time for the listener to repeat it, and finally the downloading of the newly constructed text to a personal audio player worn in public to generate collective speech. While Castonguay had previously initiated similar events in other cities around the world, the 2012 protests had occasioned its launch in the city of Montreal where she studied and taught. The methodology developed became a technology for collective dissent that continued in the following years. During the 2015 anti-austerity campaign, for instance, it provided a peaceful and rich means to build bridges between sectors. For instance, professors took their critique of the cuts to hospital entrances and public squares as well as university foyers. This technique offered a collective experience of re-spatializing critical thought—an act that, in the context of institutional discourses and policies that promoted individualization and fear of dissent (e.g. criminalization of picket lines and protest itself), provided a site for generating sensuous solidarity. While the message was not always clear for onlookers, it became a means of rehearsing collective resolve and performing counter-discourses.

While ties to workers' movements and neighbourhood organizations were arguably much deeper this time than in 2012—May 1, 2015, saw the first workers' wild cat strikes in Montreal since the 1970s—students failed to get the broad support of left-wing academics that had been mobilized in the highly mediatized Maple Spring. If only for a day, however, a general strike in the true sense of workers' and students' disgruntled dissidence, not only found a common target in austerity budgets, but also broke institutional protocol to resist.

Beyond Performance: Building 'Self-Reproducing' Movements

The 2012 student protests were, above all, sparked by the desire to secure accessible public education for future generations—the vast majority of students on strike would have graduated by the time the full force of the tuition hikes had come into effect. It was, as such, a series of protests launched in the interest of futurity, in the interest of resisting a further privatization of collective futures, redirecting who would be able to study what and to whom such studies would be accountable: to the individual or to the collective. The various performative interventions thus staged different modes of performing one's personal and social identities and responsibilities in ways that echoed into the future. Those who became active during the 2012 strike and remained active in social movements beyond the end of the strike are sometimes affectionately called the '*bébés de la grève*' (babies of the strike). The term does not so much gesture towards their youth, but to the cutting of political teeth. It parallels and subverts the demeaning designation of 'spoiled babies' levelled against them by the government that had introduced tuition hikes. These babies 'grew up' during the strike. No longer obedient children content to receive the divisions of power and resources as handed down, they had learned to demand a place in creating the future they, and subsequent generations, would inherit.

During the 2012 protests, much creative energy was placed in generating sites of liberatory public education. Such experiments included 'alternative universities' projects[50] and the participation of young children as emerging protest chroniclers.[51] The creativity of the 2012 student strike altered the affective tenor of space, thus aiding the redistribution of time and ultimately the redistribution of roles, wherein diverse populations were able to take their place in the movement. Arguably, creative actions individually had a minor impact, each galvanizing relatively few participants and spectators. However, their proliferation was symptomatic of the spirit of decentralized organizing and projected a desired democratization of movements and societal dynamics. Such techniques turned care into a pub-

[50] Timothy Beeler, 'Unexpectedly Everywhere: Reflections on Alternative Learning,' *Transmutations* 1, no. 1 (2013). http://transmutations.org/site/123-2/.

[51] See, for example, Dayna McLeod's, 'This is my Friend Ethan,' *Transmutations* 1, no. 1 (2013). http://transmutations.org/site/83-2/.

lic, political, and collective act, destabilizing the dichotomy between the personal and the political. In so doing, they helped generate an affective climate that made critique and sustained engagement possible, creating the conditions of possibility for self-reproducing movements.

The long duration of the Quebec student strike offered the time for cultures of care to be extended and techniques of 'togetherness' to be developed. 'Private' aspirations and limitations were brought repeatedly into view as 'publicly' reproduced and governed, and vice versa. Within the temporary zones of recreated space/time division—the 'private time' of caring for self and the family—was extended into the collective political space. In the aftermath of the 2012 protests, the 'heightened' engagement was unable to be maintained. However, legacies of artful networking remain. The affective power of collective political acts of solidarity, sensitive to differences in positionality and modes of engagement had helped generate spaces of care that produced networks through which to sustain multigenerational and multi-sited advocacy grounded in strong social bonds and transformed social logics. The creative legacy of the 2012 strike thus included a lexicon through which institutional structures could be re-imagined. As artful protest movement, it has thus helped alter horizons of futurity across generations.

Acknowledgements This chapter extends work I first published in 2015 as an article in *Antipode* (47.3) 'Rêve Général Illimité? The Role of Creative Protest in Transforming the Dynamics of Space and Time During the 2012 Quebec Student Strike,' pp. 770–791.

References

Amnesty International. 'Quebec Law Breaches Canada's International Human Rights Obligations.' *Amnesty International News*, May 25, 2012. https://www.amnesty.org/en/latest/news/2012/05/quebec-law-breaches-canada-s-international-human-rights-obligations/.

Arquilla, John, and David Ronfeldt. *Networks and Netwars: The Future of Terror, Crime, and Militancy*. Santa Monica, CA: Rand Corporation, 2001.

Beeler, Timothy. 'Unexpectedly Everywhere: Reflections on Alternative Learning.' *Transmutations* 1, no. 1 (2013). http://transmutations.org/site/123-2/.

Bey, Hakim. *The Temporary Autonomous Zones, Ontological Anarchy, Poetic Terrorism*. Brooklyn, NY: Autonomedia, 1985.

Blumer, Herbert. 'Social Psychology.' In *Man and Society: A Substantive Introduction to the Social Science*, edited by Emerson Schmidt, 144–198. New York: Prentice Hall, 1937.

Bunch, Charlotte. *Passionate Politics: Feminist Theory in Action*. London: Palgrave Macmillan, 1987.

Chaussette, Docteur. 'Marionnette engagée, Docteur Chaussette.' *Transmutations* 1, no. 1 (2013). http://transmutations.org/site/123-2/.

Christoff, Stephan. '"Rêve général illimité" in Quebec.' In *Le fond de l'air est rouge*, edited by Stephan Christoff, 29–31. Montreal: Howl Arts Collective, 2013.

Clough, Nathan L. 'Emotion at the Center of Radical Politics: On the Affective Structures of Rebellion and Control.' *Antipode* 44, no. 5 (2012): 1667–1686.

Cox, Ethan. '400,000+ in the Streets? Quebec's Students Are Winning…' *Citizen's Press*, May 24, 2012. http://rabble.ca/blogs/bloggers/ethan-cox/2012/05/500000-streets-quebecs-students-are-winning.

Crossa, Veronica. 'Play for Protest, Protest for Play: Artisan and Vendors' Resistance to Displacement in Mexico City.' *Antipode* 45, no. 4 (2013): 826–843.

Delvaux, Martine, Gabrielle Desrosiers, Garlerand Elsa and L'écuyer Vanessa. 'Militantes féministes grévistes. Du Comité femmes de l'ASSÉ au Comité femmes GGI de l'UQAM.' In *Un Printemps rouge et noir: Regards croisés sur la grève étudiante de 2012*, edited by Marcos Ancelovici and Francis Dupuis-Déri, 115–149. Montreal: Les Editions Écosociété, 2014.

Didierjean, Noelle. 'Over 10,000 Costumed Anti-Austerity Protestors March in Montreal: Public Sector and Students Upset over Government Austerity Measures.' *The Link*, November 1, 2014.

Drapeau-Bisson Maire-Lise, Dupuis-Déri Francis and Marcos Ancelovici. '"La grève est étudiante, la lutte est populaire!" Manifestation de casseroles et assemblée de quartier.' In *Un Printemps rouge et noir: Regards croisés sur la grève étudiante de 2012*, edited by Marcos Ancelovici and Francis Dupuis-Déri, 150–184. Montreal: Les Editions Écosociété, 2014.

Epstein, Barbara. *Political Protest and Cultural Revolution: Nonviolent Direct Action in the 1970s and 1980s*. Berkeley: University of California Press, 1991.

Federici, Silvia. 'Precarious Labor: A Feminist Viewpoint.' *In the Middle of a Whirlwind*, 2008. http://inthemiddleofthewhirlwind.wordpress.com/precarious-labor-a-feminist-viewpoint/.

Ferland, Raphael Dallaire. 'Premier Rêve général illimité.' *Le Devoir*, June 12, 2012.

Gagné, Tom. 'Quebec Students on the March.' *Socialist Worker*, March 22, 2012. http://socialistworker.org/2012/03/22/quebec-students-on-the-march.

Graeber, David. *Direct Action: An Ethnography*. Oakland, CA: AK Press, 2009.

Hardt, Michael, and Antonio Negri. *Multitude*. New York: Penguin, 2004.

Kershaw, Baz. 'Fighting in the Streets: Dramaturgies of Popular Protest, 1968–1989.' *New Theatre Quarterly* 13, no. 51 (1997): 255–276.

Kheiriddin, Tasha. 'Quebec Student Protests: Silent Majority Needs to Make Some Noise about Violent Demonstrations.' *National Post*, May 23, 2012.

Klepto, Kolonel, and Major Up Evil. 'The Clandestine Insurgent Rebel Clown Army Goes to Scotland Via a Few Other Places.' *Shut Them Down! The G8,*

Gleneagles 2005 and the Movement of Movements, edited by David Harvie, Keir Milburn, Ben Trott, and David Watts, 243–254. Autonomedia/Dissent!, 2005.

Kruzynski, Anna, Rachel Sarrasin, Sandra Jeppesen and Research Group on Collective autonomy (Collectif de recherche sur l'autonomie collectif or 'CRAC'). 'It Didn't Start with Occupy, and It Won't End with the Student Strike! The Persistence of Anti-authoritarian Politics in Quebec.' *Wi: Journal of Mobile Media* 6, no. 2 (2012). Accessed October 11, 2017. http://wi.mobilities.ca/category/2012-6-2-out-of-the-mouth-of-casseroles-i/page/3/.

La Ligue des droits et Libertés, Associations des juristes progressistes, Associations pour une solidarité syndicale étudiante. 'Répression, discrimination et grève étudiante: analyse et témoignages,' 2013. http://liguedesdroits.ca/wp-content/fichiers/rapport-2013-repression-discrimination-et-greve-etudiante.pdf.

Lamoureux, Ève. 'L'art de la manif réinventé? Analyse de l'importance actuelle des pratiques culturelles et artistiques.' *Bulletin d'histoire politique* 21, no. 2 (2013): 70–81.

Lazzarato, Maurizio. *The Making of the Indebted Man: An Essay on the Neoliberal Condition*. Cambridge, MA: MIT Press, 2012.

———. 'Struggle, Event, Media.' *Republicart*, May 2003. www.republicart.net/disc/representations/lazzarato01_en.htm.

Le Barreau du Québec. 'PL 78: Loi permettant aux étudiants de recevoir l'enseignement dispensé par les établissements de niveau postsecondaire qu'ils fréquentent: Le Barreau du Québec formule de sérieuses inquiétudes.' *Barreau du Québec: Activités Médias et Positions*, May 18, 2012. http://www.barreau.qc.ca/fr/actualites-medias/communiques/2012/05/18-etudiants.

Mirzoeff, Nicholas. 'Vive la Rêve générale.' *Occupy 2012: A Daily Observation on Occupy*, April 20, 2012. http://www.nicholasmirzoeff.com/O2012/2012/04/20/vive-la-reve-generale/.

Nadeau-Dubois, Gabriel. 'Staying Power (Le souffle le plus long).' Translated by Susan Ruddick. *Society and Space*, July 6, 2012. http://societyandspace.org/2012/07/06/staying-power-le-souffle-le-plus-long-gabriel-nadeau-dubois/.

Oka, Cynthia Dewi. 'Mothering as Revolutionary Praxis.' In *Revolutionary Mothering: Love on the Front Lines*, edited by Alexis Pauline Gumbs, China Martens, and Mai'a Williams, 51–57. Toronto: Between the Lines & PM Press, 2016.

Québec National Assembly. 'Bill 78: An Act to Enable Students to Receive Instruction From the Postsecondary Institutions They Attend.' Québec City: Québec National Assembly, 2012.

Radio-Canada. 'Les Élections du Québec.' June 22, 1960. Accessed October 11, 2017. http://archives.radio-canada.ca/emissions/1537/.

Rancière, Jacques. *The Politics of Aesthetics*. London: Continuum, 2006.

———. *Dissensus: On Politics and Aesthetics*. Translated by S. Corcoran. Cambridge: Polity, 2010.

Schechner, Richard. 'Invasions Friendly & Unfriendly: The Dramaturgy of Direct Theatre.' *South African Theatre Journal* 6, no. 1 (1992): 4–24.

Shepard, Benjamin. *Play, Creativity, and Social Movements: If I Can't Dance, It's Not My Revolution*. New York: Routledge, 2012.

Simone de Beauvoir Institute. *Statement on Tuition Fees in Québec and Their Impact on Women*. Simone de Beauvoir Institute, Concordia University, February 2012. http://wsdb.concordia.ca/about-us/official-position-on-issues/documents/2012SdBITuitionFees.pdf.

Spiegel, Jennifer Beth. 'Quebec's Noisy Revolution: Social Dramaturgies of the "Maple Spring".' *Wi: Journal of Mobile Media* 6, no. 2 (2012). http://wi.mobilities.ca/quebecs-noisy-revolution-socialdramaturgies-of-the-maple-spring/.

———. 'Masked Protest in the Age of Austerity: State Violence, Anonymous Bodies, and Resistance "In the Red".' *Critical Inquiry* 41, no. 4 (2015): 786–810.

———. 'Rêve général illimité? The Role of Creative Protest in Transforming the Dynamics of Space and Time During the 2012 Quebec Student Strike.' *Antipode* 47, no. 3 (2015): 770–791.

Spiegel, Jennifer Beth, Alanna Thain, Sophie Castonguay, Magda Olszanowski. 'To Perform in/with a Movement.' *Transmutations* 1, no. 1 (2013). http://transmutations.org/site/.

Taylor, Diana. *The Archive and the Repertoire: Performing Cultural Memory in the Americas*. Durham, NC: Duke University Press, 2003.

Thain, Alanna. 'Anarchopanda's Soft Subversions.' *Wi: Journal of Mobile Media* 6, no. 2 (2012). http://wi.mobilities.ca/anarchopandas-soft-subversions/.

———. 'Press Play.' *Society and Space*, July 6, 2012b. http://societyandspace.org/author/alanna-thain/.

Tilly, Charles. *Contentious Performances*. Cambridge: Cambridge University Press, 2008.

Wrobel, Micheal. 'Quebec's Political Parties on Tuition Fees and University Funding.' *The Link*, March 25, 2014. https://thelinknewspaper.ca/article/quebecs-political-parties-on-tuition-fees-and-university-funding.

Hank Willis Thomas and Eric Gottesman, *For Freedoms*, 2016-

For Freedoms with Spider Martin, Pearl, Mississippi, 2016

"We believe that artists, and art, play an important role in galvanizing our society to do better. We are frustrated with a system in which money, divisiveness, and a general lack of truth-telling have stifled complex conversation. We believe it's time for artists to become more involved in the political process."

For Freedoms Lawn Signs, Brooklyn Museum, New York, 2016

Kameelah Janan Rasheed and Norman Rockwell at For Freedoms Exhibition, Jack Shainman Gallery, New York, 2016

For Freedoms Town Hall: Collective Thinking, Aperture Foundation, New York, 2017

For Freedoms Town Hall, Freedom From Fear: Migration, MOCA Cleveland, 2017

Hank Willis Thomas and Eric Gottesman, *For Freedoms*, 2016-

How can art intervene in political discourse? During the 2016 presidential elections in the US, artists Hank Willis Thomas and Eric Gottesman decided to find out by registering For Freedoms as the first artist-run Super PAC (or Political Action Committee), raising funds to insert art directly into the political media landscape. The group organized several events and campaigns, producing subway advertising, Internet memes, yard signs, and billboards—including the *Make America Great Again* billboard in Pearl, Mississippi, which superimposes Donald Trump's campaign slogan over a famous Spider Martin photograph depicting the 1965 Bloody Sunday civil rights protest in Selma, Alabama.

What started as an experiment in becoming part of the political system has since grown into a collective platform for civic engagement and direct action. Now operating as an LLC, For Freedoms has partnered with dozens of institutions and artists (including Carrie Mae Weems, Trevor Paglen and Pablo Helguera) to curate a series of town halls, exhibitions, public programs and artist residencies, with an overriding agenda of equality, dialogue and political action. In 2017, For Freedoms was awarded the ICP Infinity Award for New Media and Online Platform.

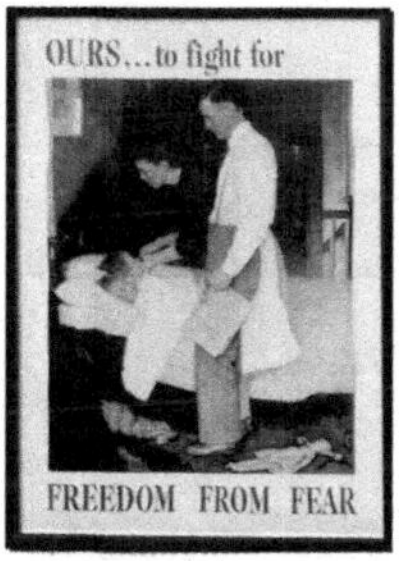

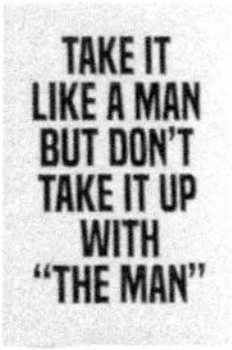

"Norman Rockwell's paintings depicting Roosevelt's Four Freedoms are part of a long lineage of artistic practices and movements that have used fine art as a vehicle for political engagement and social change. For Freedoms aims to act as a hub for other artists, arts institutions, and activists who want to be more engaged with the current political system in all of the fifty states. The medium for this project is American democracy, and our mission is to engage artists, the public, and policy makers to help make our democracy more transparent and responsive."
—Eric Gottesman

HANK WILLIS THOMAS has exhibited internationally, including the International Center of Photography, Guggenheim Museum Bilbao, Musée du quai Branly and the Cleveland Museum of Art. His work is in numerous public collections including the Museum of Modern Art New York, the Solomon R. Guggenheim Museum, the Whitney Museum of American Art and the National Gallery of Art in Washington DC. Thomas is the recipient of the 2017 Soros Equality Fellowship and the 2017 AIMIA | AGO Photography Prize. **ERIC GOTTESMAN** was named a 2015 Creative Capital Artist and has won a Fulbright Fellowship, an Artadia Award, a Light Work Residency, the Aaron Siskind Foundation Artist Fellowship, and other awards. His work is in various collections including the Museum of Fine Arts, Boston. His first book, *Sudden Flowers*, was published in 2014. He is currently a Visiting Associate Professor at Hampshire College. **FOR FREEDOMS** also includes a core team of five—Elizabeth Baribeau, Michelle Woo, Taylor Brock, Emma Nuzzo and Evan Blaise Walsh.

CHAPTER 6

'After the revolution, who's going to pick up the garbage on Monday morning?' Cartoneros and Sanmen in the Age of Financial Crises

Jimena Ortuzar

A gleaming New York City garbage truck clad in mirrored glass paraded in front of the Queens Museum in the fall of 2016, kicking off the opening of artist Mierle Laderman Ukeles's exhibition (September 18, 2016, to February 19, 2017), a survey of her work that spans five decades of 'maintenance art.' The mobile artwork, titled *The Social Mirror*, was created in 1983 with the help of the New York City Department of Sanitation (DSNY), where Ukeles has been artist in residence for 40 years and counting. Its reflective surface prompts viewers to see themselves within the waste disposal process rather than outside of it, implicating them in the invisible work of sanitation that maintains their own lifestyles of consumption. Struck by the invisibility of waste collectors, who are 'out performing

J. Ortuzar (✉)
Ryerson University, Toronto, ON, Canada
e-mail: jimena@nyu.edu

N. Alvarez et al. (eds.), *Sustainable Tools for Precarious Times*,
Contemporary Performance InterActions,
https://doi.org/10.1007/978-3-030-11557-9_6

their work in public every day' yet remain largely unseen,[1] Ukeles seeks to counter the public's disavowal of such work, which she sees in relation to women's hidden labor (including her own) in maintaining the private sphere of the household. In recognizing that as a mother and wife, she too is a 'maintenance worker,' Ukeles links private and public spheres. Her body of work repeatedly shows how the structural relations that govern both realms conceal the quotidian labor needed to sustain them—a view that also extends to the art world. In her iconic *Manifesto for Maintenance Art 1969!*[2] Ukeles questions the very foundations of the avant-garde by drawing attention to the labor of maintenance that makes it possible. Her much-quoted text asks what many feminists have often wondered: 'after the revolution, who's going to pick up the garbage on Monday morning?'[3]

One surprising response to this rhetorical question comes from the Southern hemisphere, with the rise of the *cartonero* movement in the wake of Argentina's 2001 economic and political crisis—an event more often associated with violent protests and loud *cacerolazos* that brought an enraged public to the streets banging pots and pans, effectively toppling down the government.[4] In the aftermath of this uprising, the cartoneros (cardboard pickers) indeed picked up garbage, as the practice of waste collection became a means of survival in the brutal conditions of austerity and mass unemployment that ensued. Entire families of cartoneros appeared in affluent neighborhoods pulling carts of cardboard in the streets, making the marginalized group highly visible. But unlike other social phenomena that emerged at this time and soon faded from view—cacerolazos, *piquetes, assambleas barriales*[5]—the cartoneros remained active long after the crisis, striving to formalize their trade and organizing into cooperatives that continue to operate today.

Among these is the editorial Eloísa Cartonera founded by poet Washington Cucurto and artists Javier Barilaro and Fernanda Laguna in 2003 as a response to the problem of social degradation and sustainability for both workers and artists—the precarious position of the cartoneros and the lack of cultural capi-

[1] Tom Finkelpearl, 'Interview with Mierle Laderman Ukeles,' in *Dialogues in Public Art* (Cambridge, MA: MIT Press, 2000), 313.

[2] Mierle Laderman Ukeles, *Manifesto for Maintenance Art 1969!, Proposal for an Exhibition 'Care'* (1969).

[3] Ibid.

[4] Cacerolazos—street protests involving the loud banging of pots and pans—have a history of making private concerns public in Latin America. More recently they have been used by movements elsewhere as an effective means of protest.

[5] Piquetes are a form of direct action that involve blocking roads to disrupt circulation; assambleas barriales are neighborhood assemblies engaged in direct democracy to address issues affecting daily life in the community.

tal of emerging writers.[6] The small press produces inexpensive books made by hand from the cardboard collected by cartoneros, thus making them accessible to a wider readership while resisting the growing influence of transnational publishing conglomerates in Argentina's literary field. Like Ukeles's sustained collaboration with the 'sanmen' in New York City, which also began in the midst of a fiscal crisis, Eloísa Cartonera has proven to be a lasting project between artists and cartoneros that shares with Ukeles the desire to legitimize a culture of work that has long been reviled around the globe.

Curiously, popular interest in Ukeles's maintenance art and the cartonero movement is on the rise. The aforementioned retrospective at the Queens Museum is the first in-depth exhibition of Ukeles's work, which has also prompted new writing and public talks about her practice. Meanwhile in Argentina, cartoneros are the subject of a new television series (titled *Cartoneros*), which is rather unusual for a group rarely represented in the media. Traces of the cartoneros and Ukeles are also evident outside popular culture and across national borders. Eloísa Cartonera has inspired the creation of *cartoneras* across Latin America and as far as Sweden and Mozambique, and these in turn have instigated new interventions and events such as literary workshops in Boston's public schools and an international *cartonera* conference at the University of Wisconsin-Madison in 2009. Ukeles's unprecedented residency at DSNY, and the attention her projects there received, has not only helped advance initiatives and improvements in sanitation, but has more recently served as a model for organizations and embedded artists in the US and beyond.[7]

These forms of social phenomena and cultural production have outlasted financial and political crises at home and abroad. That they persist in a world where nearly every field of activity is seen in market terms of speculative value suggests they share an imaginative potential worth exploring for those interested in creative tactics that remain effective over time. This chapter investigates how the practice of *cartoneo*[8] came about and what made collaborations between waste collectors and artists possible in opposite poles of the hemisphere. To do so, I examine the conditions of their emergence, which bracket key moments in the development of global capitalism and significant changes in waged labor as it moves into increasingly

[6] Djurdja Trajkovic, 'Made in Buenos Aires: Eloísa Cartonera and Literary Production in the Post-2001 Crisis in Argentina,' PhD diss., University of Wisconsin-Madison, 2012, 2.

[7] Patricia C. Phillips, 'Making Necessary Art: Collisions of Maintenance and Freedom,' in *Mierle Laderman Ukeles: Maintenance Art* (New York: Prestel, 2016), 23.

[8] Cartoneo refers to the practice of gathering and selling recyclable waste; cartoneros are the people doing it—the cardboard pickers.

precarious forms of employment. In light of current struggles against neoliberal political and economic hegemony across the Americas, understanding how embodied practices have responded to the dynamism and power of capital in its shift to speculative finance seems more urgent than ever. Such diffused economic networks and global flows of speculative capital are increasingly difficult to decode, but their effects are very real. What, then, might we learn from a small cartonero/artist-run cooperative and an artist in residence at a large municipal organization in the era of financial crises? As different as these sustained practices and collaborations are in terms of historical context and discursive framing, each confronts the social stigmas that alienate waste workers associated with the trash they handle, engaging with the performance of maintenance on the one hand and the production of a material culture of waste on the other. What links these different scenarios, then, is not only the materiality of waste or the invisible labor it demands; it is also a particular geography of waste through which power relations and identity constructions become visible.

Staying Alive in Times of Debt: New York's Fiscal Crisis and Argentina's Fall

When Ukeles wrote her manifesto in 'a quiet rage,' frustrated by the seemingly irreconcilable positions of artistic freedom and maintenance work that would define her radical approach to artistic practice, it was clear that she was already interested in the conceptual possibilities of waste.[9] The text was drafted as a proposal for an exhibition that included bringing various kinds of refuse (including the contents of a garbage truck) into the museum to be 'purified, dipoluted [sic], rehabilitated, recycled and conserved'[10] there. While these ideas would have to wait more than three decades to materialize in her ongoing projects with the massive Staten Island landfill, a fiscal crisis was brewing in New York City in the mid-1970s, which set the stage for her entry into the public service sphere of sanitation.

In 1973, when Ukeles began staging her first maintenance art performances in art institutions,[11] New York City was billions in the red—a debt incurred from years of borrowing to compensate for the slow growth, declining profits, and high unemployment that followed the post-Second

[9] Mierle Laderman Ukeles, Queens Museum Programme, 2016.

[10] Ukeles, *Manifesto for Maintenance Art 1969!*

[11] For instance, washing and mopping the floors of the Wadsworth Atheneum Museum of Art in Hartford, Connecticut.

World War boom along with an exodus of manufacturing jobs and tax revenues that left the city. As the debt burden deepened and the likelihood of federal aid grew slim, the banks that had largely funded New York's municipal budget 'used their financial leverage to foster a major political crisis' pushing elected officials into austerity programs against their will.[12] A new agency (the Municipal Assistance Corporation) led by investment bankers and business elites (and hence dubbed the 'Big MAC') was established in the summer of 1975 to oversee the city's financing, though its real purpose, as historian Kim Phillips-Fein observes in her recent account of the crisis, was to 'force the city and unionized workers to accept a staggering array of budget cuts.'[13] Protests erupted across the city, and when layoffs were confirmed, 10,000 sanitation workers walked off their jobs, leaving piles of garbage rotting in the streets.

On October 17, 1975, the city braced for imminent default and the sanitation department was ordered to stop issuing payroll checks. But hours before bankruptcy and 'with no one else coming forward to save the city,' the teachers' union conceded to make up the city's $150 million shortfall with their pension fund, averting the immediate catastrophe.[14] A month later, Washington finally agreed to provide loans, retreating from President Ford's previous threats to veto any bailout.[15] With federal help and deals struck with the banks and the unions, New York managed to avoid fiscal collapse, but not without severe austerity measures attached that would end the welfare liberalism of the postwar golden age.[16] Social services were slashed, wages were frozen, and thousands of public workers lost their jobs.

Such sacrifices were necessary, or so the narrative goes, to protect a city whose expansive network of public institutions and services aimed at supporting the working classes was no longer sustainable in what was becoming an increasingly market-driven world. But as Phillips-Fein argues, this was not a foregone conclusion at the time and the assault on the city's long

[12] Chris Maisano, 'The Fall of Working-Class New York,' *Jacobin Magazine*, November 7, 2017.

[13] Kim Phillips-Fein, *Fear City: New York's Fiscal Crisis and the Rise of Austerity Politics* (New York: Metropolitan Books, 2017), 128.

[14] Albert Shanker quoted in Jeff Nussbaum, 'The Night that New York Saved Itself from Bankruptcy,' *The New Yorker*, October 15, 2015.

[15] See the infamous 'Ford to City: Drop Dead,' headline in *The New York Times*, October 29, 1975.

[16] Maisano, 'The Fall of Working-Class New York.'

tradition of social democracy was not met without resistance.[17] For at the heart of the crisis was the will of a ruling-class agenda to disempower local elected officials and assert the power of capital in the political field. It was a conflict between two opposing poles still present today: 'the harsh limits of the political sphere and the delusional boundlessness of the market.'[18] Ultimately, the crisis served to 'justify a brutal austerity program that became the template not just for domestic Reaganism, but for neoliberal "structural adjustment" measures in Latin America,'[19] as we shall see shortly in the case of Argentina.

In response to New York's dire fiscal circumstances, Ukeles made *Maintaining NYC in Crisis: What keeps NYC Alive?* (1976), a performance with more than 40 participants and audience volunteers at the Whitney Museum of American Art, which aimed to measure the 'thickness' of the situation. To do so, Ukeles orchestrated a dissonant sequence of voices and movement, with participants in parallel 'reading lanes' pacing across the gallery while simultaneously reading aloud passages of the mayor's budget citing public jobs that could be eliminated.[20] The effect was a fragmented and somatic experience of the city's painful state, which Ukeles hoped would help visitors understand 'the scale of the maintenance of the city's vital services.'[21] Among such essential services was the department of sanitation, and Ukeles would soon shift from *what* maintains the city to *who* maintains it, in a year-long performance thanking each individual waste collector for keeping New York City alive.

Unexpectedly, it was the amusing suggestion of an art critic that sparked the possibility of a partnership with the city's sanitation workers. In an exhibition review of Ukeles's work with 300 service workers at the Whitney Museum in 1976,[22] David Bourdon jokingly called on 'the city's financiers [to] pursue the implications of Ukeles's Maintenance Art. If the Department of Sanitation, for instance, could turn its regular work into conceptual performance, the city might qualify for a grant from the National Endowment for the Arts.'[23] Ukeles took up the idea immediately and wrote to DSNY

[17] Phillips-Fein, *Fear City*, 6–7.

[18] Kim Phillips-Fein, 'The Legacy of the 1970s Fiscal Crisis,' *The Nation*, April 16, 2013.

[19] Maisano, 'The Fall of Working-Class New York.'

[20] Ukeles had planned to include the individual names of city personnel whose jobs were at risk with the proposed budget cuts but city officials threated to sue her if she proceed to do so. Phillips. "Making Necessary Art," 87.

[21] Ukeles quoted in Phillips, 'Making Necessary Art,' 87.

[22] *I Make Maintenance Art One Hour Every Day*, 1976.

[23] David Bourdon, 'Art,' *Village Voice*, October 4, 1976, 105.

Commissioner Anthony Vaccarello, citing Bourbon's review and asking if he would be interested in having an artist in residence. She proposed that he apply directly for a National Endowment for the Arts grant, as Bourbon had joked, while she in turn would apply directly for a federal grant in maintenance-research systems, anticipating that 'the only way an artist might qualify for any other federal grant would be under the guise of pure research.'[24] Ukeles received an invitation from the commissioner's office asking, 'How would you like to make art with 10,000 people?' A more felicitous reply to an artist's cold call is hard to imagine, hence her response: 'I'll be right over.'[25] New York Sanitation was for her 'the major leagues.'[26]

Thus began Ukeles's long journey into the waste disposal process of a major city, spanning eight commissioners and six mayors. Ukeles delved deep into the systems and infrastructure of sanitation, its technological, cultural, and social dimensions, and its multiple sites: marine transfer stations, incinerators, and landfills, not to mention the infinite number of collection routes along the five boroughs of the city. But the serendipitous beginnings of this story should not be taken to mean that her engagement with the sanmen happened by chance. From the time she wrote her manifesto in 1969 to the start of her residency at DSNY nearly a decade later, Ukeles moved from personal performances of maintenance that documented her domestic tasks at home (such as rinsing a diaper or bundling up her children to go out in the cold) to performances involving the invisible workforce responsible for the maintenance of institutions. In a matter of a few years, her art practice had amplified both in scale and scope, and the turn from household maintenance to public maintenance was simply 'the domestic on an urban scale.'[27] Sanitation work presented an opportunity to explore maintenance at a municipal level and further develop her 'maintenance art' as a systems-oriented art practice.

Moreover, the vital work of sanitation workers was impossible to ignore during the agonizing fiscal crisis: mounds of fetid refuse piled up on sidewalks and garbage fires blazed through the city, as angry residents began throwing trash in the middle of the streets and incinerating the waste themselves.[28] Garbage collection eventually resumed but DSNY had suf-

[24] Phillips, 'Making Necessary Art,' 89.

[25] Finkelpearl, 'Interview with Mierle,' 311.

[26] Ibid., 296.

[27] Jeffrey Kastner, 'The Department of Sanitation's Artist in Residence,' *The New York Times*, May 19, 2002.

[28] Charles Kaiser, '292 Fires Set in City in a Day,' *The New York Times*, July 31, 1975.

fered major cutbacks as a result of the crisis. Consequently, the city became increasingly and noticeably dirtier, with anger and frustration often directed at the workers.[29] It was clear, then, as Commissioner Norman Steisel recounts, that efforts to restore the sanitation department and build public support 'would have to involve getting people to understand the nature of the work.'[30] And Ukeles was indeed the perfect candidate to do so, not only because her 'maintenance art' was bringing invisible labor into view, but also because she understood that maintenance, even if performed entirely by men, was a feminized form of labor and hence of little value. Service work, as Ukeles later observed, 'confers low status on anyone, regardless of gender, wherever it occurs.'[31] That the sanmen she encountered were blind to this reality revealed a deep disconnect both inside and outside the sanitation department, and it convinced Ukeles that she could not have found 'a more valid place to make an art that aims to create a new language.'[32]

Though Ukeles's legendary role as the first and only official artist in residence of DSNY is widely considered pioneering and has led to new avenues for local artists to work with government agencies in Boston and New York, art historian Carol Phillips reminds us that it was cultivated rather naively and dreamily, both by Ukeles's deep belief in her connection to a 'maintenance class' and Vaccarello's 'why not' and 'let's see attitude' that together opened up an unlimited sphere of possibilities.[33] Such openness to the new and unknown appears in stark contrast to the sense of fear that had engulfed the city during the crisis, where arguably a lack of imagination precluded the pursuit of alternative paths. For if the abandonment of social democracy was a political choice rather than the inevitable evolution of the world economic order, as Phillips-Fein convincingly argues, then Ukeles's radical initiative prompts us to ask: what other possibilities may have been on the horizon for the city's leaders?

The embrace of austerity politics would have repercussions that reached far beyond New York City. Fiscal austerity, along with privatization and market liberalization, became the foundation of the 'Washington

[29] Tom Finkelpearl, 'Interviews with New York City Department of Sanitation Commissioners,' in *Mierle Laderman Ukeles*, ed. Patricia C. Phillips (New York: Prestel, 2016), 196.

[30] Ibid., 197.

[31] Mierle Laderman Ukeles to Lucy Lippard, December 15, 1980.

[32] Finkelpearl, 'Interview with Mierle,' 313.

[33] Phillips, 'Making Necessary Art,' 23, 90.

Consensus' policies throughout the 1980s and 1990s in response to serious economic problems in Latin America.[34] Emerging from years of poverty and dictatorship, countries in Latin America were faced with huge deficits. As they sought relief from the International Monetary Fund (IMF) for debts incurred by previous regimes, they were required to implement structural adjustment programs that imposed austerity measures as a condition of the loans.

Argentina became a model case for the efficacy of the Washington Consensus and remains a prime example of the neoliberal rationality that informs the actions of governments today. Washington eagerly supported the 'conservative revolution' headed by President Menen, which privatized everything from oil to water.[35] With approval from the IMF, Argentina opened the national economy to global markets and pegged its currency to that of the US—a convertibility plan launched in 1991, which set the exchange value of the peso at one to one with the US dollar in order to bring hyperinflation under control. The problem with this fixed-rate exchange system is that it is susceptible to the volatility and havoc of financial markets, as lenders insist on high interest rates to compensate for the exchange risk, which in turn heightens the risk of devaluation.[36] This situation created a boom in times of high inflation, particularly for the middle class, but it had little relation to the economic conditions of the poor.

For the next decade, Argentina faithfully followed IMF policies, liberalizing trade and trimming expenditures to reduce the deficit, which only exacerbated the economic downturn by causing a decline in employment and tax revenues. By 2001, the unemployment rate had reached historical levels, nearly three times what it had been in 1991. Neoliberal reforms had only worsened the debt and the country was headed for bankruptcy and political turmoil. In anticipation of the default, investors moved their money out of the country, leaving the government in no position to pay off foreign debts. Bank accounts were frozen and a state of panic took over the nation as people saw their savings evaporate. The Argentine middle classes, long known as the silent majority for both their connivance and indifference to politics throughout the 1990s,[37] took raucously to the streets with

[34] Joseph Stiglitz, *Globalization and Its Discontents* (New York: W.W. Norton, 2002), 53.

[35] Edward Epstein and David Pion-Berlin, *Broken Promises? The Argentine Crisis and Argentine Democracy* (Lanham, MD: Lexington Books, 2008), 36.

[36] Joseph Stiglitz, 'Argentina, Shortchanged,' *The Washington Post*, May 12, 2002.

[37] Sebastián Carassai, 'The Noisy Majority: An Analysis of the Argentine Crisis of December 2001 from the Theoretical Approach of Hardt & Negri, Laclau and Žižek,' *Journal of Latin American Cultural Studies* 16, no. 1 (2007): 45–62.

pots and pans, car tires, and even human waste. The violent *coup* they staged forced president de la Rua to flee his presidential quarters in a helicopter as images of riots and looting circulated in the news around the world.

Todos Somos Cartoneros: Picking Up the Garbage after the Crisis

With more than half of the population falling into poverty, the number of cartoneros in Buenos Aires rose drastically as waste recovery became a strategy for survival for the thousands of unemployed. While waste pickers had long existed in Greater Buenos Aires—they were known as *cirujas* (surgeons), for their surgical-like process of sorting through garbage—the crisis reconfigured the traditional figure of the ciruja into the new social subject of cartonero. Waste, as Gay Hawkins observes, has a role in reorganizing social value and, as he further notes, waste matters when it can be made profitable.[38] With the devaluation of the currency, the price of imported raw materials, including paper, became unaffordable for corporations, thus making recycling a necessity. This in turn made cartoneo a more lucrative option than it had been previously. As cartoneros moved from invisibility to hypervisibility, they came to embody the national sentiment of a country deep in crisis. Cartoneros were the new face of the marginalized brought about by the collapse of the economy on the one hand and a crisis of political representation on the other. A sense of solidarity with the cartoneros developed, not least because many people who took up this informal occupation were those displaced from the formal economy. Few were those who had been spared in the country's fall from grace, and the popular slogan '¡*Todos somos cartoneros*!' (We are all cartoneros!) captured the general feeling of being left behind across social classes.

However, this new visibility brought new problems, for, as Verónica Paiva observes, what had made the practice of *cirujeo* possible had been precisely its invisibility.[39] A criminalized activity, scavenging had previously remained largely a clandestine endeavor. And while the phenomenon of cartoneo was often perceived as a novel strategy for poverty-stricken sec-

[38] Gay Hawkins and Stephen Muecke, *Culture and Waste: The Creation and Destruction of Value* (Lanham, MD: Rowman & Littlefield, 2003), xi.

[39] Verónica Paiva, *Cartoneros y Cooperativas de Recuperadores: Una Mirada Sobre la Recolección Informal de Residuos, Área Metropolitana de Buenos Aires, 1999–2007* (Prometeo Books, 2008), 109.

tors of society to earn a living, the proliferation of cartoneros flooding the streets in search of recyclable valuables raised fears among middle and upper-middle classes who suddenly saw the *villa miserias* (shantytowns) encroaching on their neighborhoods. As much as the public identified with the plight of the cartoneros and blamed the government's negligence for their existence, concerns with the unsanitary conditions of waste recovery were more difficult to overcome.[40] The increased presence of poor families in relatively affluent neighborhoods was often seen as polluting the urban landscape—undesirable others associated with contamination not only because of their proximity to waste but also because they were deemed to be out of place, even if, paradoxically, they were converting trash into material that could be reused and recycled.

The fear of being plagued by a reterritorialized 'third world' had gripped Buenos Aires well before the crisis, when middle classes increasingly faced their own impoverishment and tried desperately to safeguard the social integrity of a city they associated with their own class identity.[41] That thousands of cartoneros were now descending from the peripheries into the city was a highly visible transgression. As the producer of a news program recounts in the Argentine newspaper Clarín, 'it was as if poverty had jumped out of the shantytowns and was rubbing shoulders like never before with the middle class.'[42] More than just a strategy for survival, then, doing cartoneo meant resisting public exclusion in middle-class Buenos Aires. For as Tim Cresswell reminds us, the concept of transgression is 'an inherently spatial idea.'[43] The boundary that is crossed is not only sociocultural but also geographic. Hence, establishing a pattern of movement through the city was key in creating a public presence. By following daily collection routes, the cartoneros slowly transformed stigma into trust.[44] Though the right of cartoneros to recover waste in public spaces remains contested, attention to the way they walk through the city has enabled forms of affinity with many citizens whose waste they collect for their live-

[40] Natalia Cosacov and Mariano D. Perelman, 'Struggles over the Use of Public Space: Exploring Moralities and Narratives of Inequality. *Cartoneros* and *Vecinos* in Buenos Aires,' *Journal of Latin American Studies* 47 (2015): 538.

[41] Emanuela Guano, 'The Denial of Citizenship: "Barbaric" Buenos Aires and the Middle-class Imaginary,' *City & Society* 16, no. 1 (2004): 87.

[42] Emilio Fernandez, 'Cartoneros en Contacto,' *Clarín*, May 22, 2007.

[43] Tim Cresswell, *Place: An Introduction* (Malden, PA: Blackwell, 2004), 103.

[44] Cosacov and Perelman, 'Struggles over the Use of Public Space,' 531.

lihood.[45] The paths made by their circulating bodies transform the streets into a site for potential solidarity, which may be limited to facilitating movement and access to collectible materials, but is nonetheless vital to the cartoneros' economic activity.

Their presence in the city is therefore negotiated and quite different from that of formal waste collectors whose access to the city is implicit in the municipal service they provide.[46] Both types of workers, however, are less likely to be tolerated if they divert from their routes or linger behind. Ukeles quickly discovered this while listening to the sanmen's stories, for instance, being scolded by a resident for resting on the steps of her home. Their tolerance is predicated on their passing through neighborhoods, not remaining in them. However, a transient but ever-present workforce, as migrant workers around the world have shown, can nonetheless claim a place in the urban sphere.[47] The political practices of today, notes Saskia Sassen, have much to do with 'the production of "presence" by those without power and with a politics that claims rights to the city.'[48] Cartoneros assert their right to the city by casting themselves as legitimate workers and the trash they recover as a shared public resource.[49] Their informal labor provides a public service, and hence a legitimate reason for inhabiting the streets. But more importantly, in viewing household waste as a shared resource, cartoneros reclaim the streets as an urban commons for the marginalized, a powerful act that resists the ongoing corporatization of public spaces into sites of consumption for the well-off sectors of society.

The enduring presence of cartoneros in Buenos Aires is a visible embodiment of deep inequalities that exist in Argentine society. It is not surprising, then, that an encounter with a cartonero in the streets is what gave rise to the idea of a 'cartonera'—an editorial that uses the cardboard collected in the streets and enlists the people who collect it to publish handmade books of stories by Latin American writers. According to Mexican poet

[45] Ibid.

[46] Though in Buenos Aires, official waste management is operated by private sanitation companies.

[47] For instance, Filipina domestic workers in Hong Kong take Central District for their own use every Sunday.

[48] Saskia Sassen, 'The Global Street: Making the Political,' *Globalizations* 8, no. 5 (October 2011): 574.

[49] Katherine M. Parizeau, 'Urban Dirty Work: Labor Strategies, Environmental Health, and Coping Among Formal Recyclers in Buenos Aires, Argentina,' PhD diss., University of Toronto, 2011, 235.

Hernán Bravo Varela, who recalls the encounter, Cucurto and Barilaro mistook a cartonero for a beggar, offering him the little pocket change they could muster together.[50] The cartonero refused the offer but suggested they purchase a sheet of cardboard from him.[51] The recovered cardboard, and the image of the cartonero it embodied, became the starting point for Eloísa Cartonera—an attempt to take the logic of recycling waste and create, like the cartoneros, an alternative economic space.

The sociopolitical histories behind cartonero initiatives and Ukeles's work with sanitation workers illustrate how embodied practices respond to and counteract the circulation of finance capital that has contributed to conditions of precarity.[52] While immediate reactions manifested in large mobilizations such as cacerolazos and piquetes in Buenos Aires or wildcat strikes and garbage fires in the streets of New York, Ukeles's response 'NYC in crisis' reveals the consequences of fostering financial growth at the expense of social services that sustain the city. Similarly, artists and activists in Argentina engaged the speculative economics that led to very real consequences, as Marcela Fuentes observes in her analysis of highly structured performance protests that appeared alongside manifestations.[53] However, the cartoneros and Ukeles's subsequent collaboration with DSNY propose responses outside trajectories of political interventions—a stable income alternative in the case of the cartoneros and a revalorization of sanitation work in the case of Ukeles's extended residency. Such responses involve ordinary acts that do not necessarily cause a rupture with everyday life; in other words, practices and gestures that are not initially made with a political objective but which nonetheless contribute to new subjectivities and forms of sociality. What, then, is the combined or cumulative effect of sustained everyday acts? In what follows, I consider Ukeles's maintenance art at DSNY and the cartonero-artists project Eloísa Cartonera as sites of sustained collaborations in everyday action, suggesting their endurance may have much to do with how they engage the material circumstances of daily life.

[50] Hernán Bravo Varela, 'Abelardo y Eloísa,' *Blog de Letras Libres*, September 8, 2009. http://www.letraslibres.com/mexico-espana/cartones-abelardo-y-eloisa.

[51] Ibid.

[52] I owe this point to Marcela Fuentes's brilliant analysis of protests in post-crisis Argentina. 'Investments Toward Returns: Protest and Performance in the Era of Financial Crises,' *Journal of Latin American Cultural Studies* 21, no. 3 (2012): 449–468.

[53] Ibid.

Lending a Hand: *Touch Sanitation Performance*

The uneventful gestures of daily activities are precisely what Ukeles considers in *Follow Your Footsteps* (1979–1980), an act that involved walking with the sanmen on their collection routes as they picked up garbage. Side by side with the workers, she would mirror the gestures and movements of picking up, carrying, and emptying waste containers (Fig. 6.1). Her gestures attend to the particular daily rhythms of urban life that remain largely unperceived, no doubt linked to the repetitive gestures of domestic work and maintenance she had performed both at home and in the gallery space. Attention to the quotidian had flourished in postwar culture, becoming a significant concern for feminists and cultural critics while gaining theoretical currency with Henri Lefebvre's influential writings on

Fig. 6.1 Mierle Laderman Ukeles, *Touch Sanitation Performance*, July 24, 1979–June 26, 1980. Citywide performance with 8500 sanitation workers across all 59 New York City Sanitation districts. January 20, 1980; Photo Day 6, Sweep 5, Queens 60. Photo by Marcia Bricker, courtesy the artist and Ronald Feldman Gallery, New York

the critique of everyday life. Underpinning this interest is a Marxist impulse to analyze the material conditions of concrete reality and social existence. Everyday life, argued Lefebvre, must be at the center of a true revolution.[54] Much like Lefebvre, Ukeles saw the creative potential in the quotidian, the site from which art should originate. The only way to 'make a revolution with everyone in the picture,' she maintains, is 'by walking out into the city and facing each worker, and walking out into the streets, and staying behind the trucks, and listening to people, and seeing the city from garbage can to garbage can, from bag to bag, from street to street, through all the weather.'[55]

This immersive fieldwork led Ukeles to her first and most celebrated artwork with the sanmen, *Touch Sanitation Performance* (1979–1980). The yearlong performance involved Ukeles shaking hands with 8500 sanitation workers in every corner of the city. With each handshake of acknowledgment, she expressed her gratitude: 'Thank you for keeping New York City alive!' Traveling to the 59 sanitation districts of the city, Ukeles mapped out her movement in a series of 'sweeps' she developed through her extensive research in the department. While the number of workers she reached each day varied, she was shaking about 40 hands a day.[56] Each and every worker would be touched, not just a select few, she announced in her invitation to them.[57] Through the tactile gesture of the handshake, Ukeles engaged the space between herself and the sanmen 'honor[ing] them with the living structure of relationships.'[58] For the sanitation workers so often treated like the garbage they handle, taking their gloves off and 'pressing flesh' with the artist was 'a huge turn of events' that even brought some men to tears.[59] According to commissioner Steisel, '[t]here had never been this kind of sustained interest in recognizing what they did [...] that's when I kind of designated her as artist in residence.'[60]

[54] Henri Lefebvre, *Critique of Everyday Life: From Modernity to Modernism, Volume 3* (London: Verso, 2008), 29.

[55] Finkelpearl, 'Interview with Mierle,' 314.

[56] Phillips, 'Making Necessary Art,' 99.

[57] Ibid., 101.

[58] Jennifer Fisher, 'Tangible Acts: Touch Performances,' in *The Senses in Performance*, ed. Sally Banes and Andre Lepecki (Hoboken, NJ: Taylor and Francis, 2012), 171.

[59] Finkelpearl, 'Interviews with Commissioners,' 196.

[60] Ibid.

The gesture of touching every last worker through the repetition of ordinary affects reveals Ukeles's sensitivity to the temporality of laboring bodies engaged in the maintenance of urban life. But behind what we understand as the performance—the artist extending her hand to each and every sanman—is a wealth of activity Ukeles undertook to imagine and plan the work, including the study of labor processes involved in the pickup, delivery, compression, and transfer of waste, as well as a substantial amount of time spent observing and listening to the sanmen. This expansive fieldwork, emblematic of conceptual art in the late 1970s, need not be considered separate from the work. This is because Ukeles's exploration of the sanitation system through the tools of conceptual art 'emphasizes not only registers of performance such as liveness, ephemerality or display,' but also, as Shannon Jackson incisively observes, 'the sense of performance as a provisional and fragile system, as coordination, and as hyper-contextual form that is embedded in a network of coordination in space and over time.'[61] This sense of performance as a 'reciprocally sustaining infrastructure' has implications for what performance does outside the time-space of the event. To think of performance as that which sustains is also to expand its possibilities for remaining, that is, as something more than the ephemera of traces, echoes, affects, and spectral meanings that live acts are thought to leave behind—in other words, performance remains because it is always already there, as a process that exceeds the live events it supports.

Hence, rather than a series of interventions that make visible the essential but undervalued work of sanitation in the city, Ukeles's work at the DSNY can be seen as a mode of ongoing performance (in this sense of a sustaining system) that not only 'lends a hand' to every worker, but also reaches into every aspect of their labor in its various spaces and temporalities. *Touch Sanitation Performance* is often considered an early iteration of what would soon be called 'social practice,' and yet Ukeles's strategy in undertaking this project was to consciously run against the grain of social science, which 'samples, abstracts, selects.'[62] Instead, Ukeles went to every sanitation facility in New York and faced every sanitation worker, mapping out 'the entire mind-bending operation.'[63] Her unparalleled access to DSNY gave her a distinct perspective of the institution and a specialized

[61] Shannon Jackson, *Social Works: Performing Art, Supporting Publics* (New York: Routledge, 2011), 78.

[62] Finkelpearl, 'Interview with Mierle,' 314.

[63] Ibid.

knowledge of the waste disposal system that would inform subsequent projects. What Ukeles seems to propose as a sustainable strategy for collaboration between social and aesthetic systems is a lifelong learning process of mutual support. Though she remained unpaid for the duration of her residency and funded her projects through grants, Ukeles received a great deal of assistance and in-kind help from DSNY, most importantly the time and trust of the workers as well as unfettered access to all sanitation facilities, but also materials, equipment, operational support, and space. In return, she engaged the public in a process that allowed people to see the work of sanitation and its value to society while making the sanitation department a place where art could be made. This reciprocally sustaining infrastructure is what makes this collaboration between two widely diverse social institutions so significant, and, as Jackson points out, it is 'the fundamental link to a larger socio-political consciousness on the role of maintenance in sustaining human welfare.'[64] Like the vital work of the sanmen in keeping the city alive, Ukeles's sustained collaboration with maintenance workers rests on her continued action and ongoing labor—it's what keeps the art alive.

Ukeles's DSNY residency has inspired the creation of a new residency program titled Public Artists in Residence (PAIR), which was launched in 2015 by the New York Department of Cultural Affairs (DCLA). The year-long residency, which aims to build meaningful links between municipal agencies and the public they serve, clearly takes Ukeles's residency as a model: it includes a research phase during which 'the artist spends time at the agency meeting staff and learning about its operations and initiatives' and concludes with a 'public-facing' participatory project in partnership with the agency.[65] Now in its pilot phase, this program has rectified the issue of wages, an important step for artists whose affective labor has gone too often unrecognized as work. But it has also drastically revised the crucial component of time, precisely that which is a scarce and highly exploitable commodity in the 24/7 world of late capitalism. In contrast to the extended duration of Ukeles's four-decade stay in DSNY, this model reminds us of global capitalism's dramatic shrinkage of time, where a year seems rather generous but is really only a short-term investment—a source of potential value for the cultural capital that an artist can bring quickly. And yet, Ukeles's project suggests that time is what allowed her to develop

[64] Jackson, *Social Works*, 78.

[65] DCLA. http://home2.nyc.gov/html/dcla/html/public_artists/pair.shtml.

in-depth knowledge of the workforce she engaged as well as the nature of its labor. It is thus an approach that is completely at odds with the time pressure of high productivity that constantly propels us to move on to the next project, the next grant, the next show, the next breakthrough. In such a high-speed world where the affective energies and creative capacities of workers and consumers alike are marshaled toward the production of value, even free time takes the form of urgency.

But here is where perhaps duration itself, sustainable as long as it can be made to last, is valuable as a strategy that can resist the relentless compression of late capitalist temporality on which finance capital depends. Durational art in 1970s and 1980s spawned a new form of cultural resistance to the regulation and acceleration of 'capitalized time.' By taking place across time, performances of long duration 'stall [...] the cultural economies of instantaneous meaning and reception' and 'reassert [...] the living labor of meaning making.'[66] If Ukeles's exploration with the time of performance is largely overlooked, it is because maintenance—the content of her work—is often seen as being equivalent to its meaning. 'What has not been fully appreciated,' suggests Helen Molesworth, 'are the ways in which this usually "degraded" content actually *permits* an engagement with questions of value and institutionality that critique the conditions of everyday life as well as art.'[67] Recovering the potential of duration in her process-based practice may prove useful if we consider that today financial power is primarily asserted through the use of derivatives – instruments that modify duration in relation to capital's exposure to risk. And to minimize this risk, explain Edward LiPuma and Benjamin Lee, speculative capitalism 'must continually turn itself over in the shortest time possible.'[68] This accelerated temporality alters not only capital circulation but also cultural production. Ukeles's work appears remarkably immune to the rhythms and tempo of global capitalism, not least because her intervention in the sanitation of New York never seems to end, much like the work of maintenance itself.

[66] Adrian Heathfield, 'Then Again,' in *Perform, Repeat, Record: Live Art in History*, ed. Adrian Heathfield and Amelia Jones (Bristol: Intellect, 2012), 29.

[67] Helen Molesworth, 'House Work and Art Work,' Globalizations 92 (2000), 82.

[68] Edward LiPuma and Benjamin Lee, *Financial Derivatives and the Globalization of Risk* (Durham, NC: Duke University Press, 2004), 129.

Eloísa Cartonera: 'Disidentes del ISBN'

From the time she wrote her manifesto, Ukeles has insisted that maintenance/survival work is at the core of art and culture. It was the message she brought to the sanmen by thanking them for keeping the city alive. Her contention that art 'begins at the same time as basic survivals systems,' was coincidentally one of the consequences of the crisis in Argentina, which saw the emergence of artist collectives and grassroots movements aiming to reorganize the social fabric of the nation through cultural and labor practices. The convergence of aesthetic and political aims and the move toward collectivization characterize the post-crisis context in which Eloísa Cartonera participates, both symbolically and practically. The small independent press describes itself as 'a social and artistic project in which we learn to work together in a cooperative manner,'[69] in line with the open spaces of collective activity that formed in the rubble of fiscal collapse. Like Ukeles, Eloísa bridges the spheres of cultural production and waste collection, integrating both the waste and the workers in the process of cultural production.

The scale of the cartonera's operation may seem insignificant in contrast to Ukeles's ambitious projects with the DSNY, which remains one of the largest sanitation departments in the world. But considering the particularly small size of the editorial team and the bare bones structure on which it survives, Eloísa Cartonera has a remarkably wide reach. Although few cartoneros are permanently employed in the making of books, the press engages the cartonero community at large through the purchase of cardboard, offering cartoneros five times the price that recycling factories pay. The press, which until recently was located in the working-class neighborhood of La Boca, operates as a workshop open to the local community and a growing public that participates in the book-making process. Sold at the cost of production, the 'no logo' books 'accumulate readers rather than capital.'[70] Available on site as well as in bookstores, cafes, street stands, and book fairs, the low-priced books make literature accessible to those unable to afford the escalated prices of the publishing conglomerates.

[69] Historia de Eloisa Cartonera, 2007. http://www.eloisacartonera.com.ar/historia.html.

[70] Ksenija Bilbija and Paloma Celis Carbajal, *Akademia Cartonera: A Primer of Latin American Cartonera Publishers* (Madison, WI: Parallel Press, 2009), 30.

The renowned writer and provocative journalist Tomás Eloy Martínez describes Eloísa as 'an artistic and social community that has done much more for the people at the margins of a society of consumption than municipal and national politics since the economic cataclysm of 2001.'[71] However, Barilaro is cautious about framing Eloísa in terms of social responsibility, insisting he never uses the verb to 'help' when referring to the cartonera; 'the proper verb is to share,' he asserts.[72] This emphasis on the shared experience of collectivity runs across the cartonera movement inspired by Eloísa. In her study of Latin American cartoneras, Ksenija Bilbija discovered that all the editorials share this view: 'there is nothing more fascinating than to sit together, listen to music, sing, cut cardboard, fold it, insert the pages of a story or a poem recently printed or photocopied, paint the covers, and finish up with a book in hand.'[73] The experience of working together in a collective space becomes as important as the book, which finds itself 'uprooted from the center of the literary encounter.'[74] As its own slogan proclaims, Eloísa Cartonera is '*Mucho mas que libros*' (Much more than books!), pointing to the live act of collective creation that extends the field of publishing into that of performance.

The books produced are thus not just cardboard books; they are *libros cartoneros* that, in addition to the written text, carry traces of their collective production. If mass-produced books guarantee the precedence of the literary work over its copy through the uniformity of the print edition,[75] cartonero books call attention to their own material emergence—their rough edges and textures constantly pointing to the cartoneros and the collaborative creativity that follows from the recovery of waste. The materiality of the book is thus a reminder that the point of the cartonera as an editorial project is more about incorporating the labor of the cartoneros in the creative process than it is about their representation. Nevertheless, in assuming the name 'cartonera,' the project sutured its identity to that of the cartoneros on whose labor it depends. And as this editorial concept transmigrates northwards—there are now more than 60 cartoneras in over 20 countries—the 'cartonera' designation remains and with it the figure of the cartonero.

[71] Tomás Eloy Martínez, 'Creadores Ante La Crisis,' *La Nación* 30, February 28, 2009.
[72] Ibid., 50.
[73] Ibid.
[74] Craig Epplin, *Late Book Culture in Argentina* (New York: Bloomsbury, 2014), 59.
[75] Ibid., 64.

What makes Eloísa Cartonera significant as an instance of cultural agency is that the project is one of the few responses to the post-crisis turmoil that continues to be self-sustainable. The independent press refuses financial donations, grants, or subsidies, and relies solely on the alternative market it creates for vanguard literature. This is possible not only because its costs are low but also because it is based on the idea of *copyleft* in which writers give permission to have their work published rather than sell a copyright to the publisher. Both established and emerging writers have donated their work to the project. The cooperative, in turn, has reintroduced Latin American authors omitted by transnational publishing companies while making visible a new generation of young Argentine authors. In doing so, it responds to the commercialization of literature by the publishing conglomerates that formed in the 1990s as a result of neoliberal doctrine and began to influence literary taste. Eloísa's intervention into the literary field opens up a space to (re)discover old and new literature by making it accessible and affordable. Hence poet Edgar Altamiro's moniker for the cartoneras: '*disidentes del ISBN*' (dissidents of ISBN).[76]

Eloísa Cartonera received the 2012 Prince Claus Fund Award for its dedication to culture and development. But perhaps in light of Ukeles's manifesto, it would be more appropriate to say culture and development along with maintenance and survival. For the cooperative has managed to achieve and sustain in concrete terms what Ukeles has long argued: that the two systems go hand in hand. Avant-garde art has long claimed absolute development: 'pure individual creation; the new; change; progress,' but as Ukeles identified in her manifesto, it 'is infected by strains of maintenance ideas, maintenance activities, and maintenance materials.'[77] Eloísa Cartonera's success is largely due to this recognition, which it makes an integral part of its project.

Toward Sustainable Ecologies of Waste

Waste collection remains a culture of work that is vilified and those doing the work are considered 'dirty,' punished for having transgressed the border of the sanitary. The concept of dirt is linked to how we act in space.

[76] Aurelio Meza, 'Editoriales Cartoneras: Hacia una possible genelología,' *Radiador Magazine*. http://www.radiadormagazine.com/2014/04/editoriales-cartoneras-en-mexico.html.

[77] Ukeles, *Manifesto for Maintenance Art*.

As Mary Douglas famously argued: dirt is matter 'out of place' and the attempt to get rid of it is about how we separate and order our environment.[78] However, Eloísa Cartonera and Ukeles have managed to invert the ways in which waste reorganizes social values, bringing new visibility and recognition to those engaged in its collection. Their practices increasingly expand toward sustainable and ecological visions of the urban. Eloísa has plans to buy a piece of land that can house the growing visitors (along with a vegetable garden that can feed its members) while Ukeles expands her projects to the massive Fresh Kills landfill in Staten Island and its ongoing transformation into a public park. The cartoneros too have taken on a new ecological role as actors in Buenos Aires's waste management, which coincides with a general shift toward sustainable societies and changing social views of waste through concepts of green economies. These sustained practices and collaborations insist that waste does not disappear; however, it can be transformed into new modes of sociality that counteract the social erosion caused by the havoc of neoliberal expansion and offer the possibility of sidestepping the seemingly inescapable logic of free markets.

References

Bilbija, Ksenija, and Paloma Celis Carbajal. *Akademia Cartonera: A Primer of Latin American Cartonera Publishers*. Madison, WI: Parallel Press, 2009.

Bourdon, David. 'Art.' *Village Voice*, October 4, 1976.

Bravo Varela, Hernán. 'Abelardo y Eloísa.' *Blog de Letras Libres*, September 8, 2009. http://www.letraslibres.com/mexico-espana/cartones-abelardo-y-eloisa.

Carassai, Sebastián. 'The Noisy Majority: An Analysis of the Argentine Crisis of December 2001 from the Theoretical Approach of Hardt & Negri, Laclau and Žižek.' *Journal of Latin American Cultural Studies* 16, no. 1 (2007): 45–62.

Cosacov, Natalia, and Mariano D. Perelman. 'Struggles over the Use of Public Space: Exploring Moralities and Narratives of Inequality: *Cartoneros* and *Vecinos* in Buenos Aires.' *Journal of Latin American Studies* 47 (2015): 521–542.

Cresswell, Tim. *Place: An Introduction*. Malden, MA: Blackwell, 2004.

Department of Cultural Affairs, New York City. http://home2.nyc.gov/html/dcla/html/public_artists/pair.shtml.

Douglas, Mary. *Purity and Danger: An Analysis of Concepts of Pollution and Taboo*. New York: Praeger, 1966.

[78] Mary Douglas, *Purity and Danger; An Analysis of Concepts of Pollution and Taboo* (New York: Praeger, 1966).

Eloísa Cartonera. 'Historia de Eloisa Cartonera.' 2007. http://www.eloisacartonera.com.ar/historia.html.

Epplin, Craig. *Late Book Culture in Argentina*. New York: Bloomsbury, 2014.

Epstein, Edward, and David Pion-Berlin. *Broken Promises? The Argentine Crisis and Argentine Democracy*. Plymouth: Lexington Books, 2008.

Fernandez, Emilio. 'Cartoneros en Contacto.' *Clarín*, May 22, 2007.

Finkelpearl, Tom. *Dialogues in Public Art*. Cambridge, MA: MIT Press, 2000.

Finkelpearl, Tom. 'Interviews with New York City Department of Sanitation Commissioners.' In *Mierle Laderman Ukeles*, edited by Patricia C. Phillips, 195–209. New York: Prestel, 2016.

Fisher, Jennifer. 'Tangible Acts: Touch Performances.' In *The Senses in Performance*, edited by Sally Banes and Andre Lepecki, 166–178. Hoboken, NJ: Taylor and Francis, 2012.

Fuentes, Marcela. 'Investments Toward Returns: Protest and Performance in the Era of Financial Crises.' *Journal of Latin American Cultural Studies* 21, no. 3 (2012): 449–468.

Guano, Emanuela. 'The Denial of Citizenship: "Barbaric" Buenos Aires and the Middle-class Imaginary.' *City & Society* 16, no. 1 (2004): 69–97.

Hawkins, Gay, and Stephen Muecke. *Culture and Waste: The Creation and Destruction of Value*. Lanham, MD: Rowman & Littlefield, 2003.

Heathfield, Adrian. 'Then Again.' In *Perform, Repeat, Record: Live Art in History*, edited by Adrian Heathfield and Amelia Jones, 27–39. Bristol: Intellect, 2012.

Jackson, Shannon. *Social Works: Performing Art, Supporting Publics*. New York: Routledge, 2011.

Kaiser, Charles. '292 Fires Set in City in a Day.' *New York Times*, July 31, 1975.

Kastner, Jeffrey. 'The Department of Sanitation's Artist in Residence.' *New York Times*, May 19, 2002.

Lefebvre, Henri. *Critique of Everyday Life: From Modernity to Modernism, Volume 3*. London: Verso, 2008.

LiPuma, Edward and Lee, Benjamin. *Financial Derivatives and the Globalization of Risk*. Durham: Duke University Press, 2004.

Maisano, Chris. 'The Fall of Working-Class New York.' *Jacobin Magazine*, July 11, 2017.

Martínez, Tomás Eloy. 'Creadores Ante La Crisis.' *La Nación*, February 28, 2009.

Meza, Aurelio. 'Editoriales Cartoneras: Hacia una possible genelología.' *Radiador Magazine*. http://www.radiadormagazine.com/2014/04/editoriales-cartoneras-en-mexico.html.

Molesworth, Helen. 'House Work and Art Work.' Globalizations 92 (2000): 71–97.

Nussbaum, Jeff. 'The Night that New York Save Itself from Bankruptcy.' *The New Yorker*, October 15, 2015.

Paiva, Verónica. *Cartoneros y Cooperativas de Recuperadores: Una Mirada Sobre la Recolección Informal de Residuos, Área Metropolitana de Buenos Aires, 1999–2007*. Buenos Aires: Prometeo Books, 2008.

Parizeau, Katherine M. 'Urban Dirty Work: Labor Strategies, Environmental Health, and Coping Among Formal Recyclers in Buenos Aires, Argentina.' PhD dissertation, University of Toronto, 2011.

Phillips, Patricia C. 'Making Necessary Art: Collisions of Maintenance and Freedom.' In *Mierle Laderman Ukeles*, edited by Patricia C. Phillips, 23–193. New York: Prestel, 2016.

Phillips-Fein, Kim. *Fear City: New York's Fiscal Crisis and the Rise of Austerity Politics*. New York: Metropolitan Books, 2017.

———. 'The Legacy of the 1970s Fiscal Crisis.' *The Nation*, April 16, 2013.

Sassen, Saskia. 'The Global Street: Making the Political.' *Globalizations* 8, no. 5 (October 2011): 573–579.

———. 'Argentina, Shortchanged.' *The Washington Post*, May 12, 2002.

Stiglitz, Joseph. *Globalization and Its Discontents*. New York: W.W. Norton, 2002.

Ukeles, Mierle Laderman. *Manifesto for Maintenance Art 1969! Proposal for an Exhibition 'Care'*, 1969.

———. Queens Museum Programme, 2016.

subRosa, *Down with Self-Management! Re-Booting Ourselves as Feminist Servers*, 2014

Image credit: ESC Medien

"What are the politics of a Feminist Server? Can we hack the very concept of a 'Server' to think differently about how the collective itself is a Server? How do feminist theories of the reciprocity of the personal and the political shift our perspective, and craft feminist solidarity?"

Cyberswamp Escapees. Image credit: subRosa

subRosa, *Down with Self-Management! Re-Booting Ourselves as Feminist Servers*, 2014

"What does it feel like to live in this moment of compulsory self-management, self-marketing, and the enforced enhancement, upgrading, and 'connectivity' of all aspects of our lives? How does being too busy to care for the self, and for others, actually play out in our everyday lives, our relationships at home, our labour, our communities, our politics and the ability to create the world we want to live in? How can collective feminist organizational savvy, critical insights, and creative energy, be used to craft a Server with a new 'operating system' that can re-connect us in mindful, collaborative, and pleasurable ways? And how can we instigate active, nurturing, convivial being-in-common, both in the *here* where we live, and in ever-expanding global territories both virtual and embodied to which we are connected?" For the past twenty years, the feminist art collective subRosa has been exploring both the rapid development of what they call pseudo techno-sociality *and* the ways in which feminist theory and practice are uniquely equipped to interrogate contemporary regimes of enforced connectivity.

In 2014, subRosa took to the streets of Graz to propose the Collective-as-Server as a model for sustained activism in real and virtual spaces. Cheekily clad in the detritus of techno-materialism, a team of so-called cyberswamp escapees interviewed passersby to generate suggestions for a Feminist Server, and these conversations—along with a curated series of public "Kaffee und Kuchen" (coffee and cake) gatherings—were themselves used to produce an installation of objects and ideas toward rethinking the idea of the Server through a feminist lens. *Down with Self-Management*! was commissioned for *Ministry of Hacking*, a series of events and installations organized around the theme of feminist hactivism at the ESC Medien Kunst Labor in Graz, Austria, in 2014.

> ***"subRosa proposes that the Collective-as-Server can foment feminist struggle and practices in the public/virtual sphere, as well as in personal life. The Collective-as-Server can support solidarity and collective action, and make common cause with the many different struggles for environmental, economic, social and political justice."***

SUBROSA is a reproducible cyberfeminist cell of cultural researchers committed to combining art, activism, and politics to explore and critique the effects of the intersections of the new information and biotechnologies on women's bodies, lives, and work. subRosa's name honors feminist pioneers in art, activism, labor, science, and politics: Rosa Bonheur, Rosa Luxemburg, Rosie the Riveter, Rosa Parks and Rosie Franklin. subRosa produces artworks, activist campaigns and projects, publications, media interventions, and public forums that make visible the effects of the interconnections of technology, gender, and difference; feminism and global capital; new bio and medical technologies and women's health; and the changed conditions of labor and reproduction for women in the integrated circuit. subRosa practices a situational embodied feminist politics nourished by conviviality, self-determination, and the desire for affirmative alliances and coalitions.

CHAPTER 7

Your Trash Is My Sustenance: Recycling the Image of 'Waste Pickers'

Carla Melo

Long before sustainability became a central concept for the environmental movement and the green industry, most of us privileged to live in the Global North viewed recycling as an empowering duty—as the only step that consumers learned they could take, from the comfort of their home, to 'save the Earth.' In the Global South, most people have not had such a privilege. While in developed countries residential waste is generally separated by the consumers and collected by municipalities, in the developing world, material, political, and cultural conditions have not allowed for such a practice to develop in a *significant* manner. Thus, historically speaking, the burden of collecting and separating recyclable materials has been largely taken up by waste pickers who make up approximately 1 to 2% of the population in developing nations.[1] Although most of these precarious subjects live in dire conditions, they have, particularly in the last two decades, begun to mobilize both locally and globally. Whether they are

[1] Sonia Maria Dias, 'Gestão de resíduos sólidos, catadores, participação e didadania—novas articulações?' *Políticas Urbanas* 18 (July 2010): 2. http://www.wiego.org/sites/default/files/publications/files/Dias_WIEGO_WP18_Portugues.pdf.

C. Melo (✉)
Arizona State University, Tempe, AZ, USA

N. Alvarez et al. (eds.), *Sustainable Tools for Precarious Times*, Contemporary Performance InterActions,
https://doi.org/10.1007/978-3-030-11557-9_7

called 'waste pickers' (for the purposes of international alliances)[2] or *catadores* (Brazil), *recolectores* (Chile), *recuperadores* (Peru), *classificadores* (Uruguay), *zabaleen* (Egypt), *cartoneros* (Argentina), *recicladores* (Colombia), *mikhali* (Morocco), *minadores* (Ecuador), or *pepenadores* (Mexico),'[3] those who belong to the informal recycling sector have invariably been stigmatized and, not unlike garbage itself, been pushed to the margins of society.

In spite of *and* because of this stigmatization and the significant parallels to precarious living and labor conditions found across borders, there is a growing transnational network of waste pickers that has been struggling to resignify their image and the very notion of trash in order to claim social inclusion.[4] But the process is quite slow. In Brazil, a country that is a leader both in waste production[5] and in the struggle to organize waste pickers (besides presenting 'high rates of recycling'),[6] it wasn't until 2010 that the federal government began to take the plight of these informal laborers into account[7] through the launching of a 'National Policy on Solid Waste.' Nonetheless, most still work either on landfills or on the streets sifting through residential and commercial discards independently and without any labor protection or safety.

Some in the Global North may have become familiar with those catadores who work at landfills through the famous *Wasteland* (2010)—a documentary that follows the interactions of Vik Muniz, an internationally renowned visual artist with a community of catadores that lived by and worked in what used to be the largest landfill in Latin America[8]—Rio de Janeiro's Jardim Gramacho. Although Muniz's two-year intervention and

[2] Ibid., 6.

[3] Jutta Gutberlet, *Urban Recycling Cooperatives: Building Resilient Communities* (London: Routledge, 2016), 6.

[4] Mari Aparecida Bortoli, 'Processos de organização de catadores de materiais recicláveis: lutas e conformações,' *Revista Katálysis* 16, no. 2 (July 2013): 250. https://doi.org/10.1590/S1414-49802013000200011.

[5] Ann M. Simmons, 'The World's Trash Crisis, and Why Many Americans are Oblivious,' *Los Angeles Times*, April 22, 2016. http://www.latimes.com/world/global-development/la-fg-global-trash-20160422-20160421-snap-htmlstory.html.

[6] Sonia Maria Dias, 'Statistics on Waste Pickers in Brazil,' *WIEGO Statistical Brief* 2 (May 2011): 1. http://www.wiego.org/sites/default/files/publications/files/Dias_WIEGO_SB2.pdf.

[7] Gutberlet, *Urban Recycling*, 57.

[8] *Wasteland*, directed by Lucy Walker, performed by Vik Muniz, England/Brazil: Midas Film, 2010, film.

the Oscar nomination of the film brought great visibility and some benefits to the community, those were arguably short-lived and limited to a few of his subjects.[9]

In this reflection, I explore a more sustained and wide-reaching intervention that has been engaged with the other class of catadores, which, in the city of São Paulo alone, constitute 'a quiet army of 20,000 waste collectors [who] roam the streets day and night collecting recyclable material' in human powered carts known as *carroças* (which translate as carts or wagons).[10] As these *carroceiros* (as they are often pejoratively called) take up the road, invading the space territorialized by cars, trucks, and motorcycles, they are generally perceived, particularly by the middle and upper classes, as subhuman scavengers and/or archaic intruders obstructing the flow of traffic. Consequently, they can become the object of harassment through verbal abuse and violence.

Given this tense scenario, it was with great irony that the well-known graffiti artist, who goes by the artistic name of 'Mundano,' (and who had long moved from spray-painting city walls to painting carroças) decided to expand his up until then unnamed interventions into a collaborative, community-engaged project that referenced a car subculture. In a parodic gesture to MTV's widely popular *Pimp My Ride*,[11] a reality show in which old or poorly conditioned cars were refurbished and customized, he named his project Pimp My Carroça. Thanks to extremely successful crowdfunding campaigns and community participation, the project, centered on the painting of vibrant images and impactful phrases upon the surface of the carroças, has accomplished much more than simply 'pimping' the carts.[12]

Moved by the simple idea of forming an alliance between an often criminalized art form—in spite of graffiti's infiltration into high art spheres—and a stigmatized informal occupation, Pimp My Carroça has been staging public events in urban space that bring together catadores and graffiti

[9] Josiane Gothardo, 'O Olhar Sobre o Outro Descartável: A Representação da Categoria dos Catadores de Materiais Recicláveis na Mídia,' *Razon y Palabra* 19, 2_90 (June 2015), 483. http://www.revistarazonypalabra.org/index.php/ryp/article/view/333.

[10] Frederick Bernas and Enrique Castillo, 'Pimp My Carroça: One Artist's Campaign to Clean up Sao Paulo,' *BBC Brasil*, July 10, 2014. http://www.bbc.com/news/magazine-28203419.

[11] It's important to note that MTV's version (2004–2007) was reproduced in the country as *Pimp My Ride Brasil*.

[12] Mundano, *TEDGlobal*.

artists, plus a host of volunteers. Their goal is not only to resignify the catadores' instrument of labor through street art aesthetic, but also to help improve their working conditions and promote a shift in public perception in regard to these subjects, their urban practice, and the environmental cause they embody.[13] The growing popularity of these events has led Pimp My Carroça (which I will, from here on, refer to as PMC) to develop a number of other live and virtual participatory tools and tactics, mobilizing an increasingly broader spectrum of civil society. Since 2012, these interventions, which began in São Paulo, have, by early 2017, travelled to many cities in Brazil and around the world, including Colombia, Peru, Argentina, USA, Morocco, Kosovo, and South Africa.[14]

From its very origins the project has been deemed a success, not only by the media, but also from a variety of scholarly perspectives. In his investigation on the changing functions of crowdfunding (from private to social projects), Rodrigo Davies has claimed that PMC is 'one of the best examples of how civic crowdfunding can be used as a powerful movement-building mechanism.'[15] In this sense, what started in 2012 as a 'social, environmental and cultural project that [sought] to remove catadores from invisibility through art and collective participation,'[16] began, within two years, to reach the cultural status of a movement.[17] Although, in the age of social media, not all mobilizations last beyond the first protest, in this case, the 'movement' denomination does point to sustained forms of actions with *and* alongside communities struggling to overcome precarious conditions.

While existing studies have either focused on the project's micropolitics,[18] funding structure,[19] or the semiotics of the messages inscribed on the carts,[20] my aim is primarily to situate PMC within a broader local context of practices and discourses related to street art, waste picker mobilization,

[13] 'Pimp My Carroça—São Paulo + Rio de Janeiro,' posted by 'Parede Viva' in 2013, Vimeo video 15:50. https://vimeo.com/45878176.

[14] Aline Silva (Pimp My Carroça team), e-mail message to author, January 26, 2017.

[15] Rodrigo Davies, 'Case Study: Crowdfunding Civic Action—Pimp My Carroça,' in *Civic Media: Technology, Design, Practice*, ed. Eric Gordon and Paul Mihailidis (Cambridge, MA: MIT Press, 2016), 609.

[16] Quoted from their Instagram page: https://www.instagram.com/pimpmycarroca/.

[17] Term deployed by Davies and the PMC group.

[18] Gabriela Roberto Alves dos Santos, 'Micropolítica da arte pública: Pimp My Carroça e a remodelagem da realidade,' in *Pasados presentes: Debates por las memorias en el arte público en América Latina*, ed. Teresa Espantoso Rodríguez and Carolina Vanegas Carrasco, vol. V (Cali: Editorial Universidad del Valle, 2016).

[19] Davies, 'Case Study,' 2016.

[20] Luciana Stefaniu and Luciana Di Raimo, 'O espaço urbano, o grafite e a identidade do sujeito catador,' *Revista Rua* 1, no. 22 (June 2016).

urban policies, and environmentalism, in order to pose the following questions: How has a project that seeks to visibilize invisible environmental agents been able to sustain its practice within a sociopolitical context that, while welcoming the discourse of sustainability, remains resistant to notions of environmental justice? What are the various cultural, political, and material factors that have allowed the project its longevity, expansion, and popularity? And what is the role of the *catador* in sustaining the 'movement'?

Although other analyses and, in certain instances, even the organizers, have deployed a paternalistic lens to examine the efficacy of Mundano's endeavor in regard to benefits produced for the catadores,[21] I posit that their agency within the collaboration plays an important role in the project's 'sustain-ability.' Equally crucial in this regard are the shifting cultural appeal of graffiti, the power of the coalition between two marginalized constituencies, and the multiplicity of the project's tools and tactics (all of which I will explore later)—not to mention its efficacious publicity, the cool factor of its title, and the cultural capital of its founder. But these factors cannot be examined without situating them in a wider context that includes the support of the influential national movement of catadores, Movimento Nacional dos Catadores de Materiais Recicláveis (MNCR) or the National Movement of Recyclable Waste Pickers, the installment of a national waste management policy, the growing awareness of urban populations in regard to the environmental urgency of our times, and the rise of crowdfunding as a way of mobilizing civil society toward confronting social injustices.

Biopolitics of Erasure

Before teasing out the elements sustaining the encounter between 'artivists' and these invisible protagonists, or 'heroes' behind the scenes of waste management, as Mundano has called them, I will recycle three news stories that, juxtaposed, provide useful clues into the contextual factors of the project's sustainable practices.

Story #1: In 2007, Gilberto Kassab, a former right wing mayor of São Paulo, instituted a law named 'Cidade Limpa' (Clean City) that, in its quest to eliminate visual pollution created by large ads, also waged a war against street art. Mundano, who would later found PMC (2012),

[21] In various sources, Mundano has stated that he wishes to *give* voice and dignity to catadores, although he has also spoken on how much he has learned from them.

outraged by the cultural erasure, repainted a wall from which the work of two renowned graffiti artists had been censored. Each time he repainted it, the city erased his work. As the game continued, he began to add critical sentences to his iconic imagery: 'Erase extreme poverty, not graffiti' and 'Clean the city of its corrupt politicians,' and so on. This 'verbal war' even gained space in newspapers and he eventually acquired a criminal record. Soon afterwards, he began to forge connections with catadores, transferring his work to their mobile tools with the goal of endowing them with visibility and respect.[22]

Story #2: On August of 2009 in São Paulo, a BMW hit a 20-year-old catador, killed him instantly, and fled the scene. A witness took down the car's license plate. Upon being apprehended, the driver underwent alcohol tests and claimed that he was not speeding, displacing the blame onto the victim. Since it was the words of an executive against those of a taxi driver—the only witness who attested that the BMW was speeding at least 100 km per hour—the driver was released on bail.[23]

Story#3: On his second day in office, João Doria, the 52th mayor of Brazil's largest city (often called the Donald Trump of São Paulo), joined a team of street sweepers in the early hours of January 2, 2017, dressed in their full attire. This 'photo op' performance, produced after its 'stage' was cleared of homeless catadores,[24] sought to promote a set of public policies titled 'Beautiful City'[25]—a new version of hygienism costumed in its literal garments. On the occasion of the mayor's first appearance, Gabriel dos Santos, a catador and member of the PMC team, delivered him a letter titled: 'Manifesto: From the Trash, I Live':[26]

[22] Bruno Abbud, 'Mundano: como um grafiteiro se tornou símbolo da arte que muda o mundo,' *GQ Brasil*, September 30, 2013. http://gq.globo.com/Cultura/noticia/2013/09/mundano-como-um-grafiteiro-se-tornou-simbolo-da-arte-que-muda-o-mundo.html.

[23] Andre Caramante, 'Empresário atropela, mata, foge e é preso,' *Folha de São Paulo*, August 31, 2009. http://www1.folha.uol.com.br/fsp/cotidian/ff3108200911.htm.

[24] 'Doria veste uniforme de gari e faz varrição simbólica em São Paulo,' *Estado de Minas*, January 2, 2017. http://www.em.com.br/app/noticia/politica/2017/01/02/interna_politica,836571/doria-recolhe-algumas-folhas-e-varricao-fica-so-no-gesto.shtml.

[25] Eduardo Gerarque, 'Doria se veste de gari e diz que vai limpar as ruas de SP todas as semanas,' *Folha de São Paulo*, January 2, 2017. http://www1.folha.uol.com.br/cotidiano/2017/01/1846329-doria-promete-se-vestir-de-gari-e-limpar-as-ruas-todas-as-semanas.shtml.

[26] 'Catadores de São Paulo desafiam João Doria a ser #CATADORpor1dia no primeiro dia de mandato,' *Estadão*, January 2, 2017. http://economia.estadao.com.br/noticias/

> Mayor João Doria, imagine what would be of the most populous city in America without the public and private service provided by twenty-five thousand CATADORAS and CATADORES of recyclable materials, who work the streets of São Paulo with their carts? [They] can neither remain invisible to the 12 million inhabitants nor to their new mayor. In spite of [...] the National Policy of Solid Waste (PNRS), we need public policy measures that are truly effective and innovative in promoting the social and economic value of these professionals. For this reason, the independent movement Pimp My Carroça—which brings culture and humor through actions that seek to bring the reality of the catadores closer to the population—delivers this 'Manifesto From Trash I Live!' and challenges João Doria to become #CATADORfor1day [...] in order for him to experience the difficulties that catadoras and catadores face in their work.[27]

The war against graffiti in a city famous across the world for hosting a very unique brand of street art has never ended.[28] It is unlikely that the executive that killed that young catador in 2009 has ever been sentenced.[29] The former mayor accepted the challenge but never fulfilled his promise.[30] Ironically, what he did, dressed as a street-maintenance laborer,[31] was to 'help' turn the city's largest graffiti mural gray. Nonetheless, performances of resistance continue. Looking back at Mundano's earlier artivism in protest to the program 'Cidade Limpa,' it is easy to see how his reaction to the erasure of graffiti, framed as a cleaning process, would lead him to collaborate with urban agents whose jobs and identities are often associated with trash.

The juxtaposition of these events spanning a decade seeks to contextualize the creation of PMC as a response to public policies and judicial practices that foreground a very specific biopolitics,[32] one in which urban

releases-ae,catadores-de-sao-paulo-desafiam-joao-doria-a-ser-catadorpor1dia-no-primeiro-dia-de-mandato,10000097805.

[27] Found in the project's website: http://pimpmycarroca.com/o-manifesto-de-sp/.

[28] For more on this 'war,' see the documentary *Cidade Cinza* (2013), directed by Marcelo Mesquita and Guilherme Valiengo.

[29] No record of his sentencing has been found.

[30] Aline Silva (Pimp My Carroça team), e-mail message to author, January 26, 2017.

[31] 'Doria manda apagar grafites dos Arcos do Jânio e da av. 23 de Maio,' *UOL Notícias*, January 14, 2017. https://noticias.uol.com.br/cotidiano/ultimas-noticias/2017/01/14/doria-manda-apagar-grafites-dos-arcos-do-janio-e-da-av-23-de-maio.htm.

[32] I deploy the Foucaultian notion of biopolitics to foreground the links between the law's devaluing of the bodies at society's margins with 'hygienism,' a public policy pervasive in the late nineteenth century Brazil. During that period, the threat of contagious diseases served

hygienism and its demagogic performances are connected to cultural erasure, censorship, and the extreme precarization of some lives. It is precisely for embodying a resistance to these interwoven ideologies of erasure that PMC has harnessed such unexpected support; in other words, beyond representing a coalition between two marginalized urban constituencies, the project foregrounds the very interdependency of their marginalizing processes. When life is erased just as easily as the vibrant expressions of graffiti are painted gray, we are reminded that beyond the hard physical labor, poor living conditions, and prejudice catadores suffer, precarity for them also lies in the vulnerability of their bodies and their carts vis-à-vis the traffic.

Since the positions of carroças and carroceiros are fragile spots within a tense nexus of urban space and power, it is not surprising that at the core of PMC's endeavors are activities that seek to make the carts safer and more visible, in both the literal and connotative sense of visibility. As a practice that constitutes an effort to reclaim the catadores' right to the city, the project has been able to sustain itself across time while expanding its geographical reach. I will now explore the broader factors that have contributed to this phenomenon, to then turn to a closer reading of the central event and its multiple tools and tactics, with an emphasis on the catadores' agency and the role that the cultural status of graffiti plays as a sustainable tool of artivism.

Riding on the Shoulder of a Giant

PMC's fight to promote greater visibility for this class of workers has not been staged in a vacuum. Grounded in a history of local resistances that took its first steps in the mid-80s, MNCR was officially founded in 2001.[33] Presently, the MNCR is recognized as the largest national organization of waste pickers in the world[34] and has built strong coalitions across Latin America in addition

as an excuse to evict unwanted populations from the cities. The war against graffiti, waged under the guise of 'cleaning' and embellishing the city (as the policies of 'Cidade Limpa' and 'Cidade Linda' convey) not only brings forth echoes of an ideology of segregation, but also indirectly controls the performative bodies of graffiti artists.

[33] Bortoli, 'Processos de organização de catadores,' 251.

[34] Sandro Pereira Silva, Fernanda Lira Goes and Albino Rodrigues Alvarez, 'Situação Social das Catadoras e dos Catadores de Material Reciclável e Reutilizável: Brasil,' Federal Report from the IPEA: Instituto de Pesquisa Econômica Aplicada, 2013. http://www.ipea.gov.br/

to obtaining a socioenvironmental status.[35] This new rank might be a result of a brilliant performative move that has consisted in promoting a shift in self-representation through the renaming of waste pickers' occupation. Instead of *catadores de lixo* (trash pickers) or other pejorative terms, they have become *catadores de materiais recicláveis* (recyclable waster pickers) and, as such, environmental agents. As their performance of identity has lent them greater agency, their demands for access to better working and living conditions and the institution of waste management policies that position the catador as a crucial player, have gained greater visibility. Consequently, the movement has been pivotal in the installment of public policies that have improved levels of social inclusion, particularly for catadores who are members of cooperatives.

One of these policies is the National Policy on Solid Waste (PNRS), instituted in 2010 by the then Leftist Brazilian government led by President Lula of the PT (Workers Party). The policy mandates that municipalities 'adopt selective waste collection and composting' while backing 'the involvement of catadores in actions for shared responsibility for product life cycles and prioritize[ing] recycling cooperatives in formal recycling programs.'[36] However, various sources agree that this population represents, approximately, only 10% of the estimated total number of catadores in Brazil[37]—a highly contested figure, varying from 300,000 to 1,000,000.[38] Besides, as many policies in Brazil, this legal victory is poorly enforced and slowly implemented. The PMC manifesto delivered to the mayor of São Paulo in early 2017 translates this concern as it stated that, 'in spite of [...] the PNRS, we need public policy measures that are in fact effective.' It is also important to note that this program 'defines recycling as the reprocessing of waste that allows for its reuse' and thereby overlooks the importance of collection or waste picking.[39] The irony is that by downplaying the centrality of the catador that actually does the waste picking, the policy ignores the largest portion of its constituency.

agencia/images/stories/PDFs/situacao_social/131219_relatorio_situacaosocial_mat_reciclavel_brasil.pdf.

[35] Pereira Silva, et al., 'Situação Social das Catadoras,' 31.

[36] Gutberlet, *Urban Recycling*, 75.

[37] Silva, IPEA report, 20.

[38] Ibid. Numbers vary according to sources and are difficult to access due to the stigma around the occupation.

[39] Bortoli, 'Processos de organização de catadores,' 254.

Nevertheless, the policy furthers the growing dissemination of sustainable discourses and practices—a diffusion that is partly due to Brazil's prominence in the staging of these narratives, as hosts of the United Nations Conference on Environment and Development, Rio 92[40] (also known as Earth Summit) and, more recently, the United Nations Conference on Sustainable Development, Rio+20 (2012), as well as the 2016 Summer Games. Yet, as these discourses 'trickle down' into the mainstream, they are often perceived as disconnected from issues of social justice. It is precisely in this aspect that PMC's success owes much to the climate of resistance that was already in place, particularly through MNCR's performative reinvention of the catador as environmental agent. This is just one of the ways in which this intervention turned 'movement' has benefited from the national struggle. In fact, much of Mundano's impetus to broaden his project was fueled by the greater consciousness he gained through attending MNCR's symposiums.[41] And even though PMC largely assists and collaborates with those catadores who work independently,[42] it has received support of the MNCR and often acted as a partner in initiatives that seek to contest social exclusion.[43]

Multiple Tactics and Tools

PMC came out of Mundano's five-year solo practice, during which he had already painted over 150 carts in Brazil and abroad. Within a few months of crowdfunding to expand the project, the graffiti artist and his team had exceeded their goal by 167%.[44] While these funds were largely derived from 792 single civil donations,[45] the first event also counted with the political support and presence of the MNCR, in addition to goods and services from 42 private sponsors and non-profit organiza-

[40] Larissa de Brito Feitosa, 'Sentidos atribuidos às políticas públicas de inclusão dos catadores,' Master's thesis, Universidade Federal do Paraná, 2011, 27. http://www.repositorio.ufc.br/handle/riufc/2119.

[41] Mundano, 'Arte como instrument de revolução social,' filmed August 27, 2011, YouTube video, 11:07, posted by TEDx Talks. https://www.youtube.com/watch?v=CXwstjBc2sw.

[42] Silva, e-mail message to author, January 26, 2017.

[43] MNCR and Pimp My Carroça have been partners in a few actions, from protesting confiscation of carts to promoting events. More details here: http://www.mncr.org.br/artigos/inclusao-social-na-formula-indy?searchterm=pimp.

[44] Gathered from the project's website: http://pimpmycarroca.com/o-pimp-my-carroca/.

[45] Ibid.

tions. The first PMC experience took place on June 3, 2012 at one of São Paulo's most politically active squares[46] gathering 40 catadores with their carts, 60 artists, and a total of 300 volunteers.[47] At the end of the event, there was a long street parade of the 'pimped' carts, only this time the carts—many of which are quite heavy—were pulled by community participants. Accompanied by a street percussion band, they paraded the streets for nearly 10 kilometers all the way to the City Council, where Mundano delivered a 'manifesto' to the mayor—not radically different from the one I narrated earlier.[48]

This first 'edition,' which gathered considerable mainstream and social media attention, served as a model for numerous other events at similar or smaller scale that have taken place in Brazil and abroad in the last five years. Volunteers generally assist in providing an array of services to refurbish the carts as well as nourish safer work conditions, thereby improving the catadores' quality of life. In the midst of a festive atmosphere, these informal workers often receive food, health and well-being assistance, including vision tests, massages, haircuts, and counseling. Each catador also gets a T-shirt and safety items, including a rain jacket, socks, sneakers, rubber gloves, and reflective tape. After the carts are cleaned and fixed, having passed through thorough mechanical checkups and installation of safety features (such as rear-view mirrors, horns, and reflective tape), each catador joins an artist and they begin a dialogue on the kind of imagery and message that the worker would desire on his/her cart. Some of these events also host musical performances, displays of artwork or clothes made with recycled materials, group dialogues and talks by organizers, and waste specialists.[49] As this urban action becomes a cultural event, it attracts passersby and local residents.[50]

For this reason, I posit that the awareness-raising role of the project takes place not only from the moment the 'pimped' carts begin to circulate, but also during the events, as residents engage and learn more about

[46] 'Vale do Anhangabaú.'

[47] Project's website.

[48] 'Pimp My Carroça,' Vimeo video, 2013.

[49] An important parallel can be traced to the Québécois urban interventionist non-profit organization, known as ATSA, who have staged similar events (known as 'Etat d'urgence'), which brought politics, public awareness, and celebration together. Like Pimp My Carroça, these events consisted of street marches and parades and involved the participation of public health and social justice groups, as well as high profile political figures, including Montreal's mayor. See their project page, *Le Temps d'une Soupe* in this volume.

[50] Ibid.

those who perform such a valuable service to their neighborhoods. A great portion of this function also takes place virtually, via news and social media. Other similar initiatives included 'Pimp Our Cooperative' and 'Pimp Our Ecoponto,' which have taken place in São Paulo—the last referring to neighborhood recycle collection stations.[51] Besides raising awareness through these PMC events, the team, along with catadores who have become further involved in the project, also perform direct forms of activism, including marching and making public demands—many of which have been quite successful, as I shall demonstrate in the next section of this chapter.

Two years following the first event (and many alike in several cities), Mundano and his group multiplied their idea through the creation of 'Pimpex.' For this, they created a PMC channel within the same crowdfunding site (catarse.me) that helped them launch the project. Through their channel, interested individuals or collectives can raise funds to acquire a kit that allows them to produce small-scale versions of the original event. As of early 2017, there have been over 40 'Pimpex' interventions—all of which reached over 100% of their funding goal.[52] The sustainability of this branch of the project comes out of how it draws from PMC's popularity to obtain funding and allow easy access to the tools. One need not be a graffiti or professional artist to engage with a local catador and collaborate in the 'pimping' process. As the intervention is reproduced and multiplied by those not linked to the PMC team, it becomes a sustainable tool that not only reproduces the action but also produces new artivists. Besides, the project as a whole has become a model that has been reproduced by others not associated with 'Pimpex.'[53]

It is also important to note that PMC also engages in forms of artivism that, through territorial and semiotic appropriation, intervene into the politics of access and visibility within urban spaces. Although (as of 2017) most of the actions I will briefly analyze were events bound in time, they were framed as seeds for broader actions. One of them, titled 'The Name of the Streets,' consisted in creating replicas of street signs and renaming streets after catadores. Another intervention that paid homage to these

[51] Project's website.

[52] Numbers drawn from examining the projects at their channel in the crowdfunding website, Catarse. https://canalpimp.catarse.me/#created.

[53] One such project was titled '*Projeto Catadores Saudáveis*,' produced by the City council in partnership with various non-profits: http://www.mncr.org.br/noticias/blog-sudeste/mncr-participa-de-evento-em-prol-da-saude-e-inclusao-do-catador.

workers was the distribution of street posters that depicted larger than life photographs of catadores. The cart also became the center of focus for a few interventions that performed a twist on the transgressive practice of graffiti as the PMC group created parking spots for carroças and stenciled their iconic images into bike lanes.[54] The last action gained significant repercussion as they painted 'over four hundred icons along twenty-five kilometers of bike lanes in São Paulo.' With this intervention the group demanded that a law that authorizes the use of the city's bike lanes for tricycle, skates, and wheelchairs, be altered to include carroças as well.[55] These interventions perform critiques through estrangement, as they appropriate and transgress into official spaces and, in the last case, become a vehicle for making demands for political change. For instance, whether or not it eventually changes the law, the efficacy of the last action lies in the support catadores have gained from cyclists to share the bike lanes—an effect that has outlasted the performance. As these punctual actions leave performative traces on the urban ground, they function as seeds that infiltrate and transgress the norms of public space, inspiring responses that demonstrate the ways in which the efficacy of a one-shot action can be sustained beyond itself. In this sense, these interventions propose a different way of thinking about the intersections of sustainability and activism.

Beyond *Assistencialismo*

Given the ways in which the project is based on aiding precarious subjects, can it escape the label of *assistencialismo*? And to what extent do the catadores themselves participate in their own empowerment? What role do they play in sustaining the project? Following Paulo Freire's groundbreaking work with disadvantaged communities, the critique of assistencialismo has become a strong current in both the academy and society at large. As Freire himself has put it, assistencialismo is 'a term used in Latin America to describe policies of financial or social assistance which attack symptoms, but not causes of social ills.'[56] With the explosion of non-profits that has, since the neoliberal expansion in the nineties, brought civil society to the

[54] Project's website.

[55] 'Ativistas fazem intervenção para pedir liberação de carroças de catadores em ciclovias paulistanas,' *Radar Nacional*, June 3, 2015. http://www.radarnacional.com.br/ativistas-fazem-intervencao-para-pedir-liberacao-de-carrocas-de-catadores-em-ciclovias-paulistanas/.

[56] *Education for Critical Consciousness* (New York: The Seabury Press, 1973), 15.

fore of social assistance, this diagnosis has been often transferred to them, based on the claim that some of these NGOs were not able to break away from pre-established models.[57]

At first glance, one could tentatively place PMC within this category, since it does seek to remedy the consequences of the informalization of labor, providing both the carts and their carriers an aesthetic and functional makeover. However, this is only one aspect of this multi-tactical project and just one way of reading this feature. Certainly the 'pimping' is based on a provision of goods and services that seek to improve the labor conditions of catadores. But it is also centered on fostering their visibility and thereby addressing their marginalization. By challenging a long-seated process of stigmatization, the project tackles not only the 'symptoms,' but also one of the many factors (along with structural inequality) that reproduce and maintain exclusionary practices. And while the material assistance could be seen as remedial and leading to potential dependency, it has actually provided many catadores with greater material outcomes from their labor, potentially allowing them to continue the maintenance measures while helping spread awareness of the project.

An iconic example of such a collaborator was Rafael dos Santos, known as 'Bahia,' who sadly passed away in 2016 after engaging with PMC for over four years.[58] He, like many others, was quite vocal about the efficacy of the project, as his interview with BBC Brasil demonstrates: 'We used to be humiliated, treated *like a horse* [idiom that means: in a brute manner]. "Illiterate, you have to eat trash," they use to tell me.' He continues by proposing that this perception has shifted and that 'the population treat us with more respect. Drivers curse less. And this has happened thanks to the work of graffiti artists, folks who are also criticized in the city.'[59] Following his participation in the first event, he volunteered to help 'pimp' other carroças, brought dozens of catadores to the project, and joined the group in their protests and mobilizing actions.[60] One of these actions was the demand for the return of some hundred carts that had been confiscated by the city government in early 2015—a demand initiated by Bahia, which, along with support of PMC and important political figures, they've even-

[57] Ruth Cardoso, 'Sustentabilidade, o desafio das políticas sociais no século 21,' *São Paulo em Perspectiva* 18, no. 2 (2004): 43. https://doi.org/10.1590/S0102-88392004000200005.

[58] Project's website.

[59] 'Projeto 'turbina' mais de 160 carrinhos de catadores,' *BBC Brasil*, July 28, 2014. http://www.bbc.com/portuguese/videos_e_fotos/2014/07/140725_galeria_pimpmycarroca_pai.

[60] Project's website.

tually achieved.[61] Bahia also gave interviews to national and international channels as well as public talks, including a TEDx talk in which he narrates his nearly 30-year trajectory as a catador and his encounter with the project. His politicization and redefinition as an environmental agent as a result of this encounter is clearly demonstrated as he lists estimated natural resources that were saved, thanks to his labor along the decades: '100,224 trees, 902.016 kilograms of petroleum, 1809.043 kilograms of iron ore.' Even though he framed PMC as a savior,[62] it is clear that Bahia played a pivotal role in legitimizing the project as an intervention that gives agency to those they help, primarily through education and by inviting them to spread awareness and join their efforts.

This empowerment of the catadores that has led many to become advocates of the movement begins during the Pimp events, where a dialogue on the catadores' views in regard to their own labor and identity is set in motion between themselves and the artists as they look for a critical sentence, designed to provoke and engage viewers, to be inscribed on the carts. According to one of the coordinators, sometimes the impact phrases may be the result of this collaboration or come from Mundano or the artist painting the cart or solely from the catador.[63] Either way, the phrases have to appeal to the catadores, who must feel that they constitute a message that represents them, such as: 'Your Trash is my Sustenance,' 'Environmental agent working; Don't honk,' 'I am world champion of the recycling World Cup,' 'Recycling habits,' 'The biggest burden is not trash but prejudice,' 'Proud to be a catador.'[64] While reflecting on the ways in which the visibility produced by the images is transferred from the cart to the catador, some authors have pointed out that this gesture of including critical phrases 'allows for the emergence of a new role for the catador and trash collection itself: that of circulating new relations of meanings in and through the city.'[65]

Given the long-seated class biases of Brazilian culture it is not surprising that this analysis limits the role of the catador as a simple carrier of messages, instead of viewing him as an author or coauthor. It is important to note that

[61] Rafael do Santos, 'Catadores e a invisibilidade social,' filmed in August 2015, posted by TEDx, YouTube video, 18:15. http://www.tedxdantealighierischool.com.br/catadores-e-a-invisibilidade-social-rafael-dos-santos-bahia-tedxdantealighierischool/.

[62] do Santos, 'Catadores e a invisibilidade social.'

[63] Silva, e-mail communication with author, January 2017.

[64] PMC's Instagram page.

[65] Stefaniu and Di Raimo, 'O espaço urbano,' 23–24.

another possible reading is one that resignifies catadores, shifting them from a subject position that is always-already lacking in intellectual capacity to one that can reflect on the material conditions that have produced their predicament and potential agency. In this sense, the performance of the 'pimped' catador may signal a destabilization of the naturalized equation between poverty and ignorance or diminished intellectual capabilities.

Mobile *Grafite* as Sustainable Tool

Whether 'pimped' catadores are viewed as authors or carriers, it is clear that the complex cultural capital of graffiti is also transferred to them. I contend that the efficacious and sustained character of the project owes a great deal to this transfer of value, stemming from graffiti's 'cool factor' and dialogical power. These attributes, in turn, derive from both its ambiguous position between marginality and art, and the ways that such ambivalence has shifted in the last two decades, moving toward greater artistic recognition (Fig. 7.1).

Such a shift is expected given the widely recognized innovative character of Brazilian *grafite*, which has placed it at the forefront of the art world's assimilation of the art form. São Paulo occupies second rank in terms of best cities to witness street art.[66] Its reputation allegedly derives from an irreverent assimilation of modernist aesthetics combined with Afro-Amerindian influences that generate 'a hybrid of graffiti and mural art [...] a distinctly Brazilian aesthetic' which, nonetheless, has strong sociopolitical engagement.[67] Within this scenario the municipal government's erasure, in 2008, of a seven-year-old, collectively created graffiti panel of 700 square meters, seemed highly anachronic. Ironically, in the same year, renowned Brazilian street artists known as 'Os Gêmeos' (The Twins) were invited to create work for the façade of the Tate Modern in London, one of the central sites of contemporary art. The mayor at the time, clearly embarrassed, quickly declared that the erasure had been 'an error' and invited the original artists (including Os Gêmeos) to repaint the wall[68]—a

[66] Holly Eva Ryan, *Political Street Art in Latin America* (London: Routledge, 2017), 32.

[67] Ana Christina DaSilva Iddings, Steven McCafferty and Maria Lucia Teixeira da Silva, 'Conscientização Through Graffiti Literacies in the Streets of a São Paulo Neighborhood: An Ecosocial Semiotic Perspective,' *Reading Research Quarterly* 46, no. 1 (2011): 5–6. https://doi.org/10.1598/RRQ.46.1.1.

[68] Daniel Drummond Ribeiro, 'Cidade cinza: a guerra entre o graffiti e a prefeitura de São Paulo,' *Cinéfilos*, January 22, 2014. http://cinefilos.jornalismojunior.com.br/cidade-cinza-a-guerra-entre-o-graffiti-e-a-prefeitura-de-sao-paulo/.

Fig. 7.1 Valdemar Costa da Silva, proud of his pimped 'carroça'. Credit: Thiago Mundano

wall that, having been once again erased in early 2017, has become emblematic of the 'changing and ambiguous relation of the government with graffiti,' 'oscillating between prohibition and incentive.'[69]

These fluctuations have been moved by a growing legal divide between *pixação* (a form of tagging with very specific local characteristics) and grafite.[70] Pixação, inscribed in coded black letters by authors who remain fully anonymous to outsiders, is invariably viewed by practitioners as radical resistance and framed by the law as vandalism; grafite is distinct from hip-hop-influenced graffiti and akin to what is known elsewhere as street art. Still, even when authorized, as we've seen in the account above, it runs the risk of getting erased. In fact, some scholars (when analyzing phenomena similar to the erasure of authorized grafite) suggest that

[69] Lucrécia D'Alessio Ferrara, *Cidade, entre mediações e interações* (São Paulo: Paulus, 2016), 23.

[70] D'Alessio Ferrara, *Cidade*, 32–33.

> In the absurdity of these accounts we begin to see something else as well: that the contradictions are also dialectical. It is not only that graffiti and street art are both legal and illegal, condemned and encouraged; it's that these contradictory processes entangle and intertwine, with each remaking the other as part of the ongoing cultural dynamic by which graffiti and street art are produced and perceived. To begin with, graffiti writers and street artists don't simply accept the dilemma of legality and illegality in which they are caught; they regularly negotiate it, contest it, and prank it, in the process reshaping the very nature of what they do.[71]

In this sense, the processes of criminalization and assimilation seem to be contingent upon each other. The back-and-forth mobility from legitimate public art to vandalism adds to the polemic it generates, and consequently to the attention and the 'cool factor' that it gathers, while the growing acceptance within the art market lends it cultural capital.

In addition to these processes, there is yet another feature of grafite that may lend PMC its appeal and longevity, particularly to the audience that most needs to be affected by the project—middle class drivers with strong class prejudice, largely invested in maintaining their privilege within a very unequal society, who are, nonetheless, exposed to the growing urgency of environmental issues. In her counterhistory of Brazilian grafite, Holly Eva Ryan views the renaissance of grafite in the 1990s and the first decade of the twenty-first century as one that is radically different from a more politicized expression that took place during previous decades, forged against the grain of dictatorial repression. Under her lens, contemporary grafite, unlike its predecessor, is largely characterized by 'cheerful imaginaries, colorful characters and vectors.'[72] Ryan deploys the work of Sara Ahmed in affect theory to describe this turn in Brazilian graffiti as a shift from a more subversive expression into what Ahmed would call a 'happy object': One that generates good feelings and as such contains an inherent promise of happiness—the problem lies in the presumption that 'bad feelings are backward and conservative and good feelings are forward and progressive.'[73]

Ironically, such happy visuality, when transposed to waste picker's carts, may work toward progressive results. At first, it may provoke a sense of

[71] Jeff Ferrell, 'Graffiti, Street Art and the Dialectics of the City,' in *Graffiti and Street Art: Reading, Writing and Representing the City*, ed. Konstantinos Avramidis and Myrtle Tsilimpounidi (London: Routledge, 2016), 30.

[72] Ryan, *Political Street Art*, 55.

[73] Ahmed, quoted in Ibid., 55.

estrangement in the average middle-class driver, generally accustomed to seeing these subjects as sad scavengers of urban trash who do not seem to fit the image and forward pace of the modern environment. Following this Brechtian logic, this shock in itself may lead to questioning. And while the decorative, happy appeal of grafite draws their gaze to the carts, the potent political statements may incite, as some have found,[74] what Freire has termed *conscientização* (critical consciousness). Nonetheless, there is always the risk that readings produced by those who only view graffiti as a criminalized activity double the marginalization of both graffiti and waste pickers. But given the feedback PMC has received from catadores, this reading seems to be the exception, not the rule.

Sustaining Sustainable Practices

In 2015 PMC was listed by the Brazil Foundation as a 'Project Highlight in Human Rights and Civic Engagement,' having, by then, been able to raise nearly US$80,000 in donations from 11,622 citizens and 25 organizations. As of February 2017, the project has assisted 706 catadores with the help of 577 artists and 1920 volunteers in 39 cities across eight countries. This incredible feat of mobilization has led to important partnerships,[75] including one with MIT, which has made possible the development of a mobile application that will help users contact catadores. PMC's growth has also placed it within Update Politics, 'a map of the ecosystem of political practices in Latin America that depicts the hubs and signals that contribute to reduce the gap between civil society and the government.' The unprecedented success in crowdfunding and the project's popularity have incited, since 2014, both private and public investments as well as grants. In this sense, PMC's trajectory, as performance studies scholar Shannon Jackson would put it, probes 'models of political engagement that measure artistic radicality by its degree of anti-institutionality.'[76] In fact, what has been radical about the endeavor is its undiluted and sustained commitment to the catadores' cause and to reducing the gap between them and society.

[74] Iddings, 'Conscientização Through Graffiti.'

[75] One of these partnerships resulted in an interactive exhibit with renowned street art photographer Martha Cooper that depicted waste pickers from around the world, titled #VivaOsCatadores (São Paulo, December–January, 2016)

[76] Shannon Jackson, *Social Works: Performing Art, Supporting Publics* (New York: Routledge, 2011), 14.

Although funding has been a huge factor in the project's growth and continued action, these would not have been possible without the efficacy of its tools and tactics, the groundwork of the MNCR, the advocacy of catadores, and the power of graffiti. As I have suggested, the multiplying effects of tactics and tools sharing expand the 'movement' through artivist interventions that promote and combine a 'do-it-yourself' attitude with a spirit of collaboration and community, while producing tangible material and cultural benefits to catadores and, ultimately, to society at large. Even though the numbers of catadores involved are still microscopic vis-à-vis their estimated populations in Brazil and the world, the cultural and political effects of PMC are transferable. In other words, if the performance of the 'pimped' catador truly manages to resignify her/his image (even if for one driver or pedestrian), it could affect the ways in which other catadores would be perceived by that person thereafter, whether or not they've been 'pimped.'

This shift in perception owes a great deal to the national movement. The image of the catador, resignified by the MNCR as an environmental agent, was already circulating in the media, web, and on the streets when PMC was launched. The national policy for waste management, which MNCR struggled to make a reality, also works toward destabilizing the stigma around catadores. However, it does not affect the material conditions of 90% of their constituency who work autonomously in precarious conditions. This enormous oversight is partly why PMC has continued to grow: The project fulfills a huge gap in social assistance. That is not to say that these informal workers need handouts. In fact, I have attempted to demonstrate that PMC's sustainability is also due to the ways in which it fosters the agency and political awareness of catadores who, in turn, legitimize the movement as advocates and partners.

As Valdemar Costa da Silva stands proudly for the camera, leaning onto his 'pimped' carroça, the smiling face painted upon the cart's surface seems to mirror his own sentiment. Behind the camera stands Mundano, doubling the visibility of the subject through the photographic gaze, but also registering the ways in which graffiti itself has already been resignified as it stands, free from the walls, without permission, beyond the reach of erasure. With this new freedom of movement, graffiti's inherent mobility between street and gallery, art and crime, center and periphery is amplified, producing new ways of intervening in public space. From this perspective, as carroças are inscribed by graffiti artists, they simultaneously become a 'portable artistic support'[77] and a sustainable tool for

[77] Stefaniu and Di Raimo, 'O espaço urbano,' 23.

graffiti as well. Yet, ultimately, it is Valdemar who performs graffiti's dialogical power; it is he who speaks through its surface; it is he who, performing at the intersections of social and environmental rights, declares that which perhaps he always knew, but never had a stage to do so: 'My car does not pollute!'

References

Bortoli, Mari Aparecida. 'Processos de organização de catadores de materiais recicláveis: lutas e conformações.' *Revista Katálysis* 16, no. 2 (July 2013): 248–57. https://doi.org/10.1590/S1414-49802013000200011.

Cardoso, Ruth. 'Sustentabilidade, o desafio das políticas sociais no século 21.' *São Paulo em Perspectiva* 18, no. 2 (2004): 42–48. https://doi.org/10.1590/S0102-88392004000200005.

Davies, Rodrigo. 'Case Study: Crowdfunding Civic Action—Pimp My Carroça.' In *Civic Media: Technology, Design, Practice*, edited by Eric Gordon and Paul Mihailidis, 609–612. Cambridge, MA: MIT Press, 2016.

Dias, Sonia Maria. 'Gestão de resíduos sólidos, catadores, participação e didadania—novas articulações?' *Políticas Urbanas* 18 (July 2010): 2–22. http://www.wiego.org/sites/default/files/publications/files/Dias_WIEGO_WP18_Portugues.pdf.

———. 'Statistics on Waste Pickers in Brazil.' *WIEGO Statistical Brief* 2 (May 2011): 1–3. http://www.wiego.org/sites/default/files/publications/files/Dias_WIEGO_SB2.pdf.

Dos Santos, Gabriela Roberto Alves. 'Micropolítica da arte pública: Pimp My Carroça e a remodelagem da realidade.' In *Pasados presentes: Debates por las memorias en el arte público en América Latina*, edited by Teresa Espantoso Rodríguez and Carolina Vanegas Carrasco, vol. V. Cali: Editorial Universidad del Valle, 2016.

Dos Santos, Rafael. 'Catadores e a Invisibilidade Social.' Filmed in August 2015 at TEDx, YouTube video, 18:15. http://www.tedxdantealighierischool.com.br/catadores-e-a-invisibilidade-social-rafael-dos-santos-bahia-tedxdantealighierischool/.

Feitosa, Larissa de Brito, 'Sentidos atribuidos às políticas públicas de inclusão dos catadores.' Master's thesis, Universidade Federal do Paraná, 2011. http://www.repositorio.ufc.br/handle/riufc/2119.

Ferrara, Lucrécia D'Alessio. *Cidade, entre mediações e interações*. São Paulo: Paulus, 2016.

Ferrell, Jeff. 'Graffiti, Street Art and the Dialectics of the City.' In *Graffiti and Street Art: Reading, Writing and Representing the City*, edited by Konstantinos Avramidis and Myrtle Tsilimpounidi. London: Routledge, 2016.

Freire, Paulo. *Education for Critical Consciousness.* New York: The Seabury Press, 1973.

Gothardo, Josiane. 'O Olhar Sobre o Outro Descartável: A Representação da Categoria dos Catadores de Materiais Recicláveis na Mídia.' *Razon y Palabra* 19, 2_90 (June 2015): 473–487. http://www.revistarazonypalabra.org/index.php/ryp/article/view/333.

Gutberlet, Jutta. *Urban Recycling Cooperatives: Building Resilient Communities.* London: Routledge, 2016.

Iddings, Ana Christina DaSilva, Steven McCafferty and Maria Lucia Teixeira da Silva, 'Conscientização Through Graffiti Literacies in the Streets of a São Paulo Neighborhood: An Ecosocial Semiotic Perspective.' *Reading Research Quarterly* 46, no. 1 (2011): 5–21. https://doi.org/10.1598/RRQ.46.1.1.

Jackson, Shannon *Social Works: Performing Art, Supporting Publics.* New York: Routledge, 2011.

Mundano. 'Pimp My ...Trash Cart?' Filmed October 2014, TEDGlobal video, 5:22. https://www.ted.com/talks/mundano_pimp_my_trash_cart#t-9178.

'Pimp My Carroça—São Paulo + Rio de Janeiro.' Posted by 'Parede Viva' in 2013, Vimeo video, 15:50. https://vimeo.com/45878176.

Ribeiro, Daniel Drummond. 'Cidade cinza: a guerra entre o graffiti e a prefeitura de São Paulo.' *Cinéfilos*, January 22, 2014. http://cinefilos.jornalismojunior.com.br/cidade-cinza-a-guerra-entre-o-graffiti-e-a-prefeitura-de-sao-paulo/.

Ryan, Holly Eva. *Political Street Art in Latin America.* London: Routledge, 2017.

Silva, Sandro Pereira, Fernanda Lira Goes and Albino Rodrigues Alvarez. 'Situação Social das Catadoras e dos Catadores de Material Reciclável e Reutilizável: Brasil.' Federal Report: IPEA (Instituto de Pesquisa Econômica Aplicada), 2013. http://www.ipea.gov.br/agencia/images/stories/PDFs/situacao_social/131219_relatorio_situacaosocial_mat_reciclavel_brasil.pdf.

Stefaniu, Luciana, and Luciana Di Raimo. 'O espaço urbano, o grafite e a identidade do sujeito catador.' *Revista Rua* 1, no. 22 (June 2016): 18–32.

Walker, Lucy, dir. *Wasteland.* Performed by Vik Muniz; England/Brazil: Midas Film, 2010, film.

Escola de Ativismo, *Journey for Activism and Sustainability*, Manaus (Brazil), 2012

"Demonstrations and direct actions such as marches and street protests, whether spontaneous or planned, are common in the history of activism and are part of the fight for rights in most societies. But isolated actions, however impactful, in most cases do not solve complex problems, nor create the desired change in the medium or long term. **The need to think about the future**, to achieve lasting results and to have a broader scope and political influence than those resulting from one-off actions, **leads activists to enter the field of strategy.**"

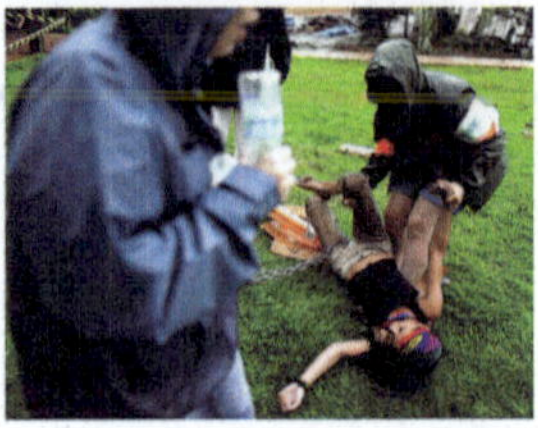

Image credit: Rodrigo Baleia

Escola de Ativismo, *Journey for Activism and Sustainability* 2012

ESCOLA DE ATIVISMO (School of Activism) is a politically independent collective with the mission to strengthen the transformative and creative capacity of activism in Brazil through innovative learning processes looking to deepen democracy, fight injustice and defend human rights and sustainability. On an ongoing basis since 2011, the Escola de Ativismo has partnered with NGOs in Brazil to promote the political sustainability of grassroots organizations, movements and collectives. The collective's principles are: nonviolence; nonpartisanship; financial, political, pedagogical and operational independence from corporations, unions, governments, political parties, banks and churches; practical learning combined with a consistent theoretical base; horizontality; collaboration; equality and equity; freedom; sharing; and transparency.

In 2012, the collective launched its first series of "Journeys for Activism and Sustainability" —multi-day workshops designed to teach strategies for creative activism and advocacy. The third of these courses was held near Manaus, in the state of Amazonas. It brought together activists, community leaders, environmental researchers and journalists to discuss the complex relations between economics, sustainability, and social inequality. Learning modules included theory and practice of nonviolent action; planning and execution of campaigns; activist communications for activism; cyberactivism; street action; legal aspects of activism; information security; artivism; organizing and mobilization.

CHAPTER 8

Sustainable Practices on the US–Mexico Border: inSITE_05, Intervention, and Precarious Communities

Jennie Klein

Gloria Anzaldúa described the U.S./Mexican border as, '*una herida abierta* where the Third World grates against the first and bleeds. And before a scab forms it hemorrhages again, the lifeblood of two worlds merging to form a third country—a border culture.'[1] *La Frontera* is both a place to be avoided at all costs ***and*** a tourist destination, a strangely uninhabited territory of desert, canyons, arroyos, mesas, and scrub, bisected by a fortified yet porous wall that keeps nobody out. When the borderland meets the ocean at San Ysidro/Tijuana, the scrub gives way to ocean grass, beaches, and one of the most populated urban environments in the Americas. The San Diego/Tijuana region is a megacity, and, like most megacities, has incredible disparities between people in terms of access to resources such as housing, drinking water, education, and medical care. Many people are desperate, and many more are exploited.

[1] Gloria Anzaldúa, *Borderlands/La Frontera* (San Francisco: Aunt Lute Books, 1987), 3.

J. Klein (✉)
School of Art + Design, Ohio University, Athens, OH, USA

N. Alvarez et al. (eds.), *Sustainable Tools for Precarious Times*, Contemporary Performance InterActions,
https://doi.org/10.1007/978-3-030-11557-9_8

The border culture is one that has had ongoing issues with conditions that go hand in hand with precarity, including migration, drugs, and human rights violations. Ila Sheren writes, 'this mix of human rights issues, international and cultural conflict, and the very futility of enacting permanent change in such a fluid region has proved irresistible to certain artists.'[2] Artists/activists who live/d on or near the border have tried to ameliorate these conditions, either by making work that calls attention to the plight of the border dwellers or by providing access to social services. In the past 50 years, the San Diego/Tijuana region has seen various activist artist collectives who have been concerned with the plight of the migrants from Mexico. In the seventies, the Chicano Art Movement (which was led in San Diego by Salvador Torres) created Chicano Park under the freeway bridge in protest against the bisecting of Barrio Logan and the lack of a park in the predominantly Mexican American neighborhood.[3] The Border Arts Workshop/Taller de arte fronterizo or BAW/TAF, formed in 1984 in conjunction with the Centro Cultural de la Raza in Balboa Park, whose members included Guillermo Gómez-Peña, David Avalos, Emily Hicks, and Michael Schnorr. BAW/TAF initiated art events, educational projects, and community engagement in order to draw attention to the plight of the border crossers.[4] There were also collaborative public actions organized by

[2] Ila Nicole Sheren, *Portable Borders: Performance Art and Politics on the U.S. Frontera since 1984* (Austin, TX: University of Texas Press), 99–100.

[3] The Chicano Art Movement was formed in opposition to a proposed substation and parking lot for the Highway patrol that was slated for the concrete wasteland under the intersection of Interstate 5 and the Coronado Bridge, an intersection that had been formed only at the expense of Barrio Logan, a predominantly Mexican American neighborhood in San Diego. Enraged that the city had reneged on a promised park, the residents of Barrio Logan—along with radicalized students from San Diego State University—occupied the area for twelve days and began construction on what is presently known as Chicano Park, a grassy area under the pylons that is renowned for its Chicano murals, stylistically reminiscent of the Mexican Muralists with nationalistic subjects that ranged from pre-Columbian symbols to heroes of the Mexican revolution and the Chicano Resistance Movement. Later that same year, the artist group Los Toltecas en Aztlán, led by Salvador Torres, were successful in getting the city of San Diego to grant them a building for a Chicano center in Balboa Park. From 1971 to 1983, an abandoned concrete water tank at the edge of Balboa Park was painted over with murals that echoed the pylon murals at Chicano Park both thematically and stylistically. See Jo-Anne Berelowitz, 'Border Art Since 1965,' in *Postborder City*, ed. Michael Dear and Gustavo Leclerc (New York: Routledge, 2003); Jo-Anne Berelowitz, 'The Spaces of Home in Chicano and Latino Representations of the San Diego–Tijuana borderlands (1968–2002),' *Environment & Planning D: Society & Space* 23, no. 3 (June 2005): 323–350; and on the website http://www.chicanoparksandiego.com/.

[4] BAW/TAF was founded in 1984 by David Avalos, who would later participate in inSITE_97. Avalos brought together a group of artists and scholars to form the BAW/

the artists coalition of Louis Hock, Deborah Small, Elizabeth Sisco, and David Avalos, including *Welcome to America's Finest Tourist Plantation* (1988), a billboard project that called attention to the disparity between undocumented Mexican workers and those coming to see the Superbowl, *N.H.I (No Humans Involved)* (1990), a multimedia event that addressed the plight of 45 murdered women, and *Art Rebate/Arte Reembolso* (1993), a project that involved giving undocumented taxpayers cash that resulted from a grant for the project. For these artists, the border was an actual site, not a metaphor, with specific conditions germane to US/Mexico relations that needed to be addressed. Art and art making was also a local activity—the Chicano artists, BAW/TAF and the artist group with Hock, Sisco, Avalos, and Small were all based at local universities and lived in the area.

This was not the case with the sprawling, site-specific exhibition inSITE_05, which, thanks to the efforts of its curatorial team, redefined the definition of the border as well as what constituted border art. inSITE_05, the fifth incarnation of the exhibition, took place at sites on the San Diego/Tijuana border. The artists who participated in inSITE_05 were not local and thus unfamiliar with the border region. Curators Osvaldo Sánchez, Donna Conwell, Marcela Quiroz, and Tania Ragasol encouraged the participating artists to conceive of public 'interventions' that would insert themselves into the social fabric of the region. A number of projects included in inSITE_05 fell under the label of interventionist or social practice art.[5] The siting of inSITE_05 work on and around the US/Mexico border meant that many of the

TAF. Unlike the earlier Los Toltecas en Aztlán, whose members were local and Mexican American, the membership of BAW/TAF was much more heterogeneous and eclectic, comprised of academics, artists, workers, and dancers that hailed from both sides of the border. Gómez-Peña, along with his then wife Emily Hicks, was a central player in the theorization of the border as a concept and mode of consciousness rather than a literal geographic site. Under the theoretical guidance of Hicks and Gómez-Peña, the BAW/TAF articulated an artistic subjectivity based on the idea of the border subject as a bilingual postmodern trickster who moved between identities, countries, and nationalities. By 1989, the BAW/TAF had achieved international recognition with an invitation to participate in the Venice Biennial. For more information on BAW/TAF, see Berelowitz, 'Border Art Since 1965'; Sheren, *Portable Borders.*

[5] See Nato Thompson and Gregory Sholette, eds. *The Interventionists: Users' Manual for the Creative Disruption of Everyday Life* (North Adams, MA: MASS MoCA Publications and Cambridge, MA: The MIT Press, 2004). Although the MASS MoCA exhibition took place the year prior to inSITE_05 and the catalogue for inSITE_05 was not published until 2006, the curatorial essays, including that by Sánchez, reference relational aesthetics rather than interventionism (although all of the catalogue writers conceptualized the work for inSITE as 'intervening' in public life), social practice, or, in Sholette's terminology, 'dark matter.'

artists, with the encouragement of the curators, were drawn to making work that could address the social fabric of the border.

Under the curatorial guidance of Sánchez and his team, the work produced for inSITE_05 anticipated strategies by which aesthetic interventions could not only say something to the cognoscenti about the politics and publics associated with the border, but possibly help some of the most precarious publics improve their situation. Significantly, the idea that the artwork would be all but unnoticeable was reiterated again and again by the essayists in the catalogue, which was published approximately a year after the event took place.[6] It is important, therefore, to consider what was at stake in these interventions. How did they address and in some cases attempt to improve conditions that would militate against precarity? What kinds of tools did these projects provide that gave agency to those populations that were marginalized in the relatively recent landscape of the postcolonial neoliberal NAFTA economy? This chapter will examine three of the most successful projects: SIMPARCH's *Dirty Water Initiative*, a 'fountain' that recycled dirty water so that it was potable; Mark Bradford's *Maleteros*, a project designed to brand the legitimate and illegitimate porters that carried goods across the border at San Ysidro; and Judy Werthein's *Brinco*, border crossing shoes that were given to workers trying to cross the border, none of which would have been possible without the institutional support of inSITE.

inSITE Background

In order to understand how it was possible that Bradford, Werthein, and SIMPARCH (Matt Lynch and Steven Badgett) were able to conceptualize and realize these projects, it is necessary to give some background on inSITE, how it started, and how it eventually evolved in relationship to its geographical and cultural location. The first iteration took place in the fall of 1992. It was a modest local event based primarily in San Diego; a bid to help stave off the eventual closing of Installation Gallery, which had been founded in 1981. Two members of Installation Gallery's board,

[6] In the opening paragraphs of his catalogue essay, Sánchez stressed that he and the curatorial team decided to eschew the idea of the border region as a 'chic' public platform in favor of subtle interventions and immersions into the flow of public life. Osvaldo Sánchez, 'Fading Tracers,' in *inSITE_05: [Situational] Public*, ed. Osvaldo Sánchez and Donna Conwell (San Diego: Installation Gallery, 2006), 40–41.

Ernest Silva and Mark Quint, organized the exhibition. Participating artists were for the most part local, and the venues were modest with only one venue in Tijuana.

Installation Gallery ultimately lost its lease, but continued as an organization to support the inSITE art event. Two years later, inSITE_94 had expanded to include a number of sites and artists from both sides of the border along with two co-directors—Michael Krichman and Carmen Cuenca. Beginning with inSITE_97, the curatorial team inaugurated the practice of requiring participating artists to spend a significant amount of time in the border region, interacting with local communities, geography, and 'interlocutors'—cultural critics and theorists whose expertise lay in economics, geography, urban development, sociology, and activism. This practice continued for the subsequent manifestations of inSITE in 2000/2001 and 2005. The inSITE_05 curatorial team (Sánchez, Conwell, Quiroz, and Ragasol), along with the interlocutors—Beverly Adams, Ruth Auerback, Joshua Decter, Kellie Jones, and Francesco Pellizzi—asked that the artists respond to two curatorial guidelines: first, that the work should involve co-participation with community members and second, that the work should be of a 'processual' nature. The idea of processual art came from Sánchez, who suggested in his catalogue essay for inSITE_00 that the most relevant aspect of the inSITE projects were 'their capacity to create spaces—not artistic spaces or painstakingly animated public spaces—but spaces that were virtually public domains. They did not seek to build landmarks elevated above the urban fabric, but to catalyze the briefest instants of intense cultural mobility, transforming the established, dominant models of behavior defined by the social group that usually laid claim to that space.'[7] Sánchez was interested in using inSITE as a means of conceptualizing how to create political interventions that could continue after the event for which they were created had ended. For Sánchez, what was crucially important was using everyday experiences as a means of revelation. Writing about Gustavo Artigas's *Rules of the Game* (a contest between soccer and basketball teams from both sides of the border, played simultaneously in the same Tijuana school gymnasium) from inSITE_00, Sánchez suggested that

[7] Osvaldo Sánchez, 'Rito de paso/Rite of Passage,' in *Fugitives sites: inSITE 2000–2001 new contemporary art projects for San Diego–Tijuana*, ed. Osvaldo Sánchez and Cecilia Garza (San Diego: Installation Gallery, 2002), 172.

> The project demonstrated the live self-construction of the public fabric by means of a liberating experience between heterogeneous individuals in unexpected circumstances. For the attending public as well as the co-participants—high school amateur sportsmen—engaging in the performance of the game allowed for a heightened understanding—through a joyful and revealing experience—of the complex conditions of the region.[8]

Sánchez's curatorial strategy thus provided a model by which artists could avoid the pitfalls of 'parachuting' into a site and constructing an art work that used the circumstances of the site as a means of framing the art without interrogating the relationship between the site and the art work. It also provided a model of engaged activism that was relatively quiescent. When drafting the curatorial premise of inSITE_05, Sánchez was at pains to avoid 'the standard participatory procedures and rewards that tend to constitute so-called 'art' or 'public art' today.'[9] inSITE's commitment to 'the public,' according to Sánchez, involved 'convoking spontaneous heterogeneous groups—not institutionalized communities—through a collaborative process that would be specific, focused, and unfold over time.'[10]

The events associated with inSITE_05 actually started in 2003. Beginning in November of that year, Sally Yard, who had previously been on the curatorial team of inSITE_97, organized what would become the *inSITE 05 Conversations*, a series of 16 mini-symposia that included presentations and dialogue that, according to Yard, 'converge in their quest to make sense of the forces that form the places where disparate publics meet.'[11] Many of the conversations circled around what Yard called 'the fraught urban expanse of San Diego-Tijuana.'[12] However, just as many *Conversations* approached the idea of the border from a global perspective, interrogating the economies, cultures, and ideologies that construct artificial borders, particularly those that demarcate the highly technologized and affluent Global North with the resource-rich but underdeveloped Global South. Thus Teddy Cruz, who served as one of the facilitators for the first artist's residency, argued that if one were to trace an imaginary

[8] Sánchez, 'Fading Tracers,' 41.

[9] Ibid.

[10] Ibid.

[11] Sally Yard, 'A Dynamic Equilibrium: In Pursuit of Public Terrain,' in *inSITE_05: A Dynamic Equilibrium: In Pursuit of Public Terrain*, ed. Sally Yard (San Diego: Installation Gallery, 2007), 13.

[12] Ibid.

line around the world, beginning with the border between the US and Mexico, the world would be divided between the parts of the world where advanced technology, financial security, and collective security prevail and the parts of the world with widespread poverty, food insecurity, and politically repressive regimes. Noting that 'this imaginary border' includes some of the most 'contested thresholds,' Cruz suggests that it is along this border that 'the most dramatic socio-economic global dynamics are witnessed as a series of two-way hemispheric crossings.'[13] On the one hand, there are increasing flows of migrants from the poverty stricken countries in search of work that can be found in the stronger economies of the Global North, while on the other hand the centers of manufacture and production have been moved to the Global South, where labor is cheap (the *maquiladoras* in Tijuana, the clothing factories in Pakistan, the call centers in India). The money from the affluent north helps to support the fragile economies of the developing countries whereas the cheap labor in the Global South makes the prolific expansion of global capital possible. What is more, the events of September 11, 2001, had produced a climate in which the fear of terrorism has resulted in borders that are increasingly militarized. Cruz wrote, 'we are witnessing how societies of overproduction and excess are barricading themselves in an unprecedented way against the sectors of scarcity they have produced out of political and economic indifference.'[14]

Countering the effects of the hardening border walls is not easy, but, as Cruz argues, no wall is impermeable. The border wall, however much it is reinforced, will always be transcended by migrating populations and the relentless flow of goods between the two countries it divides. In 2005, the urban borders between the US and Mexico were already heavily reinforced and placed under constant surveillance, forcing many undocumented workers to try to make the dangerous desert crossing with little or no water. In order to counter an already militarized border, Cruz advocated for a practice of encroachment, a sort of 'light, micro-urbanism' that makes use of derelict spaces and brown fields, something that Cruz had done in his collaboration with Casa Familiar, a non-profit, community-based organization located adjacent to the San Diego/Tijuana border in San Ysidro. The collaboration seeks to avoid the homogenizing force of gentrification by creating micro-economic opportunities.[15] These interventions are subtle and

[13] Teddy Cruz, 'Border Postcards: Chronicles from the Edge,' *inSITE_05: A Dynamic Equilibrium*, 69.

[14] Ibid.

[15] Ibid., 72.

inexpensive, often involving the reallocation of cast-off goods into sustainable tools and structures. Cruz's call for performative micro-interventions was echoed by his fellow panelist Shuddhabrata Sengupta, one of the founders of RAQS Media Collective, who pointed out that 'the border is not just a performance that you contemplate. It also demands participation, and our willingness to play a bit part, a walk-on role in the spectacle.'[16]

The *Conversations* set the tone for inSITE_05, expanding upon and echoing Sánchez's curatorial premise. In April 2004, local artists who had been invited to participate in inSITE_05 convened for the first working session. Over the course of three days, the artists engaged in conversations and visited sites on the border in which they had expressed interest. The artists were encouraged to think about how the specific conditions of the site were dictated by the people who used it, and what sort of intervention, if any, would be effective in activating and energizing a new (and micro) public domain. The artists were directed to conceptualize a revitalization of the urban space through minimalist interventions that were performative rather than object-based. Essentially the artists were encouraged to identify communities, ad hoc industries, needs, and spaces around and along the border and encouraged to conceptualize and design clothing and/or tools that could be worn/used.

The synopsis of the residencies included in the inSITE_05 guide made it clear that while the intervention might ostensibly have been conceptualized by the artist who received credit for the piece, most of the interventions were the products of a great deal of collaboration between the curatorial team, the interlocutors—'practitioners from diverse backgrounds who have been invited to participate at a conceptual level in the artists' project development'—and the inSITE staff, who spent hours negotiating permissions for the use of the chosen sites, transporting the artists around, and procuring supplies.[17] Equally important for the success of these interventions were the audiences, or publics, that consumed these interventions. George Yúdice, who participated in the conversations in 2000–2001, argued that this collaboration between the artist and the community has been fetishized at the expense of a broader notion of collaboration, one that also implicates the viewer of the artwork: 'What inSITE calls for, in my view, is to become a user, a collaborator who intervenes in order to have

[16] Shuddhabrata Sengupta, 'Liminal,' in *inSITE_05: Conversations: Compilation: Dialogues 1–2: Liminal Zones, Coursing Flows, Aliens, Denizens, Cosmopolitans*, ed. Sally Yard (San Diego: inSITE_05, 2004), 15.

[17] Osvaldo Sánchez et al., *inSITE_05: Art Practices in the Public Domain San Diego Tijuana* (San Diego: Installation Gallery, 2005), 6.

the labor expended recognized and compensated. Venues like inSITE become important sites for the reformulation of cultural policy in a post-Fordist, globalizing world, not from the vantage point of a government agency, foundation, or university office, but by engaging as an archaeologist-practitioner in the process.'[18]

The 22 artists were asked to become archaeologist-practitioners: people who excavated the historical layers of a space and then performatively demonstrated how to productively reuse or newly use that space, much as Cruz and Casa Familiar had suggested a new use for the brown areas along the border. When conceiving of inSITE_05, Sánchez was aware of the history of artwork made on the border that had not enacted permanent change. Artists associated with inSITE_05 were asked to conceptualize a different kind of engagement with the border and border region, one that was less about big statements and more about DIY design and geographical modifications. These goals were realized in SIMPARCH's *Dirty Water Initiative*, Bradford's *Maleteros*, and Werthein's *Brinco*. In the next section, these projects are covered in more detail.

SIMPARCH: *Dirty Water Initiative*

If there was a project/proyecto that fit perfectly within the parameters of inSITE_05 it was SIMPARCH's *Dirty Water Initiative*, a 'fountain' installed on the pedestrian walkway on the Tijuana side of the San Ysidro/Tijuana border checkpoint.[19] The 'fountain' was comprised of solar stills linked together, contaminated water, containers for purified water, and pipe and fittings. The sun heated the contaminated water in glass covered basins, which caused the water to condense onto the glass while the pollutants stayed at the bottom of the basin. The purified water flowed into a channel where it was collected in the containers designated for the purpose. After inSITE_05 closed in November 2005, the stills were relocated to nearby communities that were without running water, situated, as SIMPARCH put it, 'on the 'technophagic fringe' of development (Fig. 8.1).'[20]

[18] George Yúdice, *The Expediency of Culture: Uses of Culture in the Global Era* (Durham, NC: Duke University Press, 2003), 337. Yúdice's chapter on inSITE, 'Producing the Cultural Economy: The Col*labor*ative Art of inSITE' was excerpted in *inSITE 2000–2001: Fugitive Sites*, 78–84.

[19] Unless otherwise indicated, most of the information in this paragraph is taken from SIMPARCH's web site, http://www.simparch.org.

[20] SIMPARCH, 'Dirty Water Initiative,' http://www.simparch.org/dirty-water-initiative/.

Fig. 8.1 SIMPARCH *Dirty Water Initiative* inSITE_05. 2005. Lynch and Steven Badgett. Stainless steel, glass, silicone, plastic bottles, hardware. Photo from SIMPARCH/Matthew

Dirty Water Initiative worked well in conjunction with inSITE_05 for a number of reasons. First, and most significantly, it called attention to an ongoing problem in the geographical region of Bajalta California: a lack of water, particularly a lack of potable water in a very urban area. Access to water in the *Colonias*, or the squatter neighborhoods constructed with recycled materials that had sprung up or already existed near the *Maquiladoras* to provide housing for the factory workers, was an ongoing problem. As Cruz demonstrated in his contribution to the *Conversations*, there is little to no infrastructure in the *Colonias*, which are constructed from the detritus of San Diego's cast-offs, after which services from the city are requested. At the time Cruz was working with The Manufactured Sites project, which was attempting to facilitate a collaboration between a San Diego NGO and the Municipal Planning Institute in Tijuana in order to channel funding for urban and housing policies. The goal of the

Manufactured Sites project was to create a prefabricated and *maquiladora*-produced aluminum frame that could be used to construct a house. Significantly, the proposed frame included a bracing system that could support a two-week water supply pouch.[21] SIMPARCH's stills could either supplement and recycle the existing water supply, or even replace it depending on the availability of non-potable water. Individually the stills were not very large, making it possible to have many of them in a cramped neighborhood.

Another factor in the success of this project was the nature of SIMPARCH's previous work and their longstanding collaboration, which began in 1996 and has continued at least through 2015, the date of *River Monument (glomus)*, a site-specific, tree-like geodesic sphere covered with driftwood installed along the Ohio River in Louisville, KY. When SIMPARCH was invited to contribute an intervention to inSITE_05, they had a nine-year history of making work from recycled industrial material that was relatively cheap to construct, site specific, and could be read and used as an architectural or a sculptural installation. SIMPARCH had had experience working with Center for Land Use Interpretation (CLUI), for which they made living/working spaces for CLUI's residency site in Utah. They were accustomed to negotiating public space and to working with a team of people to realize their projects. *Dirty Water Initiative* was aesthetically attractive, a long silver industrial construction linked together with curving tubes that ended with the large bottles. Its placement on the pedestrian walkway resembled a public fountain. The high visibility of the piece helped to call attention to the shortage of water in the region, an effect that was enhanced by the Dirty Water Initiative stickers that were handed out: *!TOMA EL AGUA! Hecho in México www.SIMPARCH.org* and *DRINK THE WATER! Made in Mexico www.SIMPARCH.org*. The separate stills provided a micro solution to the problem that could be easily replicated by other families. Indeed, SIMPARCH planned to donate the stills to several families and did so upon the closure of the exhibition.

SIMPARCH completed their first residency in October and November 2003. At that time, they had still not completely solidified their project. By the time of their second residency in October 2004, SIMPARCH had settled on researching water and its purification for human consumption.[22]

[21] Cruz, 'Border Postcards: Chronicles from the Edge,' 87.

[22] The information for this chronology is found in the SIMPARCH chronology that is part of 'Unfolding Process: Summaries of Key Moments during the Projects' Development,' in *inSITE_05: [Situational] Public*, 6.

They visited Ecoparque, where they studied the treatment of wastewater in Tijuana, and Fundación Esperanza México, a non-profit agency dedicated to the development of community projects. Fundación Esperanza México facilitated contact with some of Tijuana's informal communities. For their third residency in April 2005, they stayed in Posada Esperanza so that they could interface with the communities of La Morita and the Ejido Lázaro Cárdenas. A family from each of these communities installed a prototype of the distillery in their homes. In August 2005 Badgett travelled to El Paso, TX and Ciudad Juarez, Chihuahua to visit communities that had implemented solar light water purification plants. By the time that *Dirty Water Initiative* was installed in the San Ysidro Pedestrian corridor, SIMPARCH had literally filtered out all of the bugs (and all other contaminants). Subsequently, SIMPARCH would go on to work with the table distilleries again in 2006, for the installation *Hydromancy*, a series of table stills that descended down a hillside.[23]

Mark Bradford: *Maleteros*

Although Mark Bradford is best known for his large-scale paintings made from house paint and cast-off building material that he salvages from the industrial area in downtown Los Angeles near his studio, like SIMPARCH, he sought to address an under-represented group who worked on the border. Bradford's project, *Maleteros*, was designed to intervene in an informal border economy: that of the porters, or *maleteros*, who operated on both sides of the border carrying goods for people who were crossing from the US to Mexico or vice versa. Bradford worked with three distinct groups of porters who operated at various entry points across the San Ysidro border crossing. He attempted to give the porters an identity, similar to the identity of African American train porters from the first part of the twentieth century. His proposal outlined the three different groups of porters: the official porters who had passed a background check, had a VISA as well as identification, and were authorized to cross the border; the unofficial porters based at the San Ysidro Trolley Platform who were US residents and did not cross into Mexico; and the so-called gypsy porters based at the Tijuana border bridge who worked the bridge only.[24] Whereas

[23] SIMPARCH, 'Hydromancy,' accessed January 21, 2018. http://www.simparch.org/hydromancy/.

[24] Mark Bradford, 'Proposal,' 2004, Box 182, inSITE Archive ca. 1992–2006 MSS 0707.

the official porters had a certain amount of recognition and legal protection, the unofficial and 'gypsy' porters did not. The 'gypsy porters,' in particular, were often the recipients of police harassment and could be fined for loitering. Nevertheless, the porters, many of whom worked day in and day out for about $20 a day, were a tight-knit group.

Bradford proposed to give the unofficial and 'gypsy porters' an identity. Through the supply of customized equipment, the informal branding of key work areas, and the provision of a temporary workspace, Bradford hoped to make visible this informal economy of passage across and around the border, an economy that was based on a knowledge and use of the 'soft city' or the perceptual and physical experience of the urban architecture of the border.[25] Bradford used the oral networks that were already in place between the porters in order to get the word out about this project. He designed easily recognizable and functional carts, found a temporary workspace where the porters could rest, and provided tools and a place to lock everything up so that the carts and tools would not be stolen. The maleteros/porters were given new vests and caps, which made them more recognizable. A two-dimensional map of the paths of the various maleteros groups that reflected Bradford's interest in mapping the informal uses of urban spaces was displayed on the wall of the headquarters. The map, which reflected the trajectories of the maleteros, demonstrated the city of this disenfranchised but economically necessary industry—a series of routes that reflected the passage of goods across the border, a passage that was circumscribed by where and what the maleteros were permitted to do based on their documentation. As Bradford's interlocutor Kellie Jones wrote, 'Bradford's project demonstrated art's ability to reveal and intervene in these realities. It shed light too on the changing nature of notions of site-specificity and public art.'[26]

Bradford's *Maleteros*, as Jones noted, created an opportunity for a group of people who were often at odds as they competed for the same customers to work together to create visibility and thus a political presence for their industry. Unfortunately, the conceptual underpinning of Bradford's project was never completely realized. By drawing attention to the maleteros, Bradford had hoped not only to create an official identity for the unofficial and 'gypsy porters,' but also map an unofficial, psychogeographical trajectory of the three groups of porters across the terrain of

[25] Donna Conwell, 'Maleteros/Mark Bradford,' *inSITE: Art Practices in the Public Domain* (2005), n.p.

[26] Kellie Jones, 'Just Across the Way,' *inSITE_05: [Situational] Public*, 227.

the urban border, revealing 'the underground economy of those who have carved out social spaces at the border in order to ease the cross-border flow of goods and people.'[27] An important component of this mapping was to have been the installation of the project on both sides of the border. In spite of the best efforts of inSITE's curatorial and administrative team, Bradford was unable to obtain permission to install a workstation on the US side of the border, thus undermining the idea of the circular flow of the economy of the maleteros. What remained was an installation only on the Tijuana side. In the end, Bradford found that the longstanding differences between the groups—particularly between the official and unofficial/'gypsy' porters—were difficult to surmount. And while the synopsis in the catalogue suggested that individual porters would attempt to continue the project, 'hoping to secure a degree of solidarity in order to defend their work at the border, underline its importance, and work towards a unified *maleteros* (sic) presence,'[28] it remains unclear whether or not this actually happened. In the end, Bradford did not seem satisfied with the project, which has subsequently been erased from his oeuvre. The catalogue that accompanied his 2010–2012 traveling retrospective *Mark Bradford* makes no mention of his project for inSITE_05.[29]

Judi Werthein: *Brinco*

Judi Werthein created a brand of sneakers called *Brinco* (Jump) that were simultaneously marketed in Blends, a high-end shoe store in downtown San Diego, and given out for free to undocumented migrants who were potentially planning to cross the border illegally. What distinguished Werthein's intervention from that of all the other participating artists including Bradford and SIMPARCH was that the public that she sought to address—the undocumented workers—were exceptionally vulnerable, desperately poor, and often without recourse to food, water, shelter, or any kind of legal protection. Werthein's *Brinco* trainers were designed for border crossing: little boots that included a compass, a flashlight, and a map, printed on the removable insole, that showed the most popular illegal routes between Tijuana and San Diego. An Aztec eagle, the symbol of

[27] Conwell, 'Maleteros/Mark Bradford,' n.p.

[28] Sánchez, et al., 'Mark Bradford/*Maleteros*,' *inSITE_05: [Situational] Public*, 220.

[29] Christopher Bedford, ed., *Mark Bradford* (Columbus, OH: Wexner Center for the Arts and New Haven, CT: Yale University Press, 2010).

Mexico, was embroidered on the heel of the shoe, and an American Eagle on the toe, symbolizing the direction in which the migrant is travelling. Even the name of the shoe, Brinco, suggested its intended use, as Brinco was also a shorthand term for crossing the border.[30]

When Werthein was initially approached by the curatorial staff at inSITE to come up with an idea for an intervention, she wanted to do a project on consciousness. She met with Christof Koch and other scientists from the Salk Institute in San Diego. By December 2004, Werthein was unhappy with how her proposal for a consciousness project was shaping up. She presented the proposal for Brinco instead. Aided by inSITE's curatorial and production teams, Werthein conducted extensive research. She met and conversed with people on both sides of the Tijuana/San Diego border including activists, academics who wrote about migration, undocumented migrants, and even *coyotes*, who help migrants to cross the border for a fee. Werthein met as well with sneaker designers in the US to come up with Brinco.[31] Werthein's initial design was for a shoe that looked a lot like the Adidas Art no. 012548 with the colors olive green, musk green, cocoa brown, and blood red. The tongue was supposed to hold an extra pocket for the map with a compass attached to the laces. A limited run of 750 sneakers in the two most common sizes for men and women were to be manufactured in China by HengJiaLi Shoes Inc. After receiving several prototypes not to her liking, Werthein traveled to China where she was able to meet with the factory designers and convey her vision. As Werthein noted in an interview with María Fernanda Cartagena for *LatinArt.com*, 'they spoke very little English and, what with one translation and another, the message that arrived in the factory in China was like what you'd get over a bad phone line. Finally, I went to China and got a lot of things decided there personally.'[32]

In August 2005 Werthein began distributing the Brinco shoes. Some of the shoes were sold for $215 in Blends. The rest were distributed to undocumented migrants who were either living in shelters in Tijuana or in the ditch along the border fence where migrants waited for *coyotes*. For many of the recipients, the Brinco shoes were the first pair of new shoes

[30] Amy Isackson, 'State-of-the-Art Shoes Aid Migrants: The World Programme, San Diego,' *BBC News*, November 17, 2005. http://news.bbc.co.uk/2/hi/4445342.stm.

[31] Sánchez, et al., 'Unfolding Process: Judi Werthein,' *inSITE_05: [Situational] Public*, 63.

[32] María Fernanda Cartagena, 'Interview with Judi Werthein,' *LatinArt.com*, December 1, 2005.

that they had ever had. Werthein also donated any profits made from the sale of the shoes in Blends to the Casa Migrante and Casa Madre Asunta in Tijuana. In November 2005, the Associated Press and the BBC reported that Werthein was distributing the Brinco trainers to undocumented workers who were attempting to cross the border. The story quickly went viral, and Werthein was inundated with requests for interviews, while the inSITE_05 blog exploded with comments, many of them virulently opposed to Werthein's piece. Ironically, Conwell and Sánchez had anticipated that there might be problems with the intervention even before the shoes were manufactured. In an email correspondence with Werthein, Conwell mentioned that she and Sánchez were concerned that the dedication tag sewn onto the shoe seemed to support illegal immigration and suggested that it simply acknowledge the migrants as an inspiration.[33] Werthein, who was born in Buenos Aires in 1967 and had lived through the Dirty War during which thousands of people had been disappeared due to their political views, was also concerned, and asked that Sánchez and Conwell consult an immigration lawyer prior to launching the project.[34] The tag/sticker included the statement, 'These sneakers were specifically designed for migrants who cross the Mexico–US border, by foot, daily.' And in very small print it stated that 'this art work does not encourage, condone, or support illegal immigration.'[35]

In spite of the effort on the part of Conwell and Sánchez to avoid controversy with *Brinco*, it proved to be one intervention that did not go unnoticed in the cultural fabric in which it operated. Just the opposite: *Brinco* generated more controversy than any of the other interventions for inSITE_05. This was, in part, because the project attempted to ameliorate the conditions of a group of people whose lives were so precarious that they were often targets of criminals and law enforcement. With no safe haven where they could find protection, many would-be immigrant workers slept in a ditch near the wall that was used for the waste runoff of Tijuana. When Werthein had finally obtained her shoes, she went to this site to distribute them. *Brinco* certainly helped a few people whose feet were the right size for the shoes and who were able to wear protective footgear as they made the dangerous trek across the border. However, the amelioration made by Werthein was, as she put it, 'miniscule. A million

[33] Donna Conwell, 'Email to Judi Werthein,' May 31, 2005, Box 201, inSITE Archive.
[34] Judi Werthein, 'Email to Donna Conwell,' June 7, 2005, Box 201, inSITE Archive.
[35] Information about Brinco Shoe, n.d., Box 201, inSITE Archive.

and a half people attempt an illegal crossing each year, and this is totally outside of my control. It's not something I engender or don't engender. It's just something that happens, and that has always happened, and the only thing I do with my intervention is call attention to a critical situation that merits a certain amount of reflection by both sides, and I expose it as a conflict. Then, as an artist, I try to produce an object that reveals everything that goes on in the background.'[36]

Werthein's characterization of *Brinco* recalls what Claire Bishop, drawing upon the work of Jacques Rancière, has termed an aesthetic of antagonism, an aesthetic that favors rupture and ambiguity, allowing the meaning of artistic forms to shift in relationship to the uses of these forms made by society at large.[37] *Brinco* operated in what Bishop termed 'a state of antagonism or negativity.' It provided no simple, ameliorative 1:1 relationship with the art, in this case the shoes, and social improvement. The project didn't better the lot of the public that Werthein addressed as the undocumented migrants still had to cross the border and find work in the US under tremendously hostile conditions. Nor was *Brinco* easily replicated. Unlike the components of SIMPARCH's water distillery, which could be quickly obtained and assembled, the Brinco shoes had to be assembled in China, the cheapest place to fulfill a micro-sized order after Werthein and Conwell had attempted to find a *maquiladora* that could manufacture the shoes with no luck. The shoes were largely a symbolic gesture that pointed to the conflict between the need for cheap labor in the agricultural sector of the US and the neoliberal policies of US Presidents Bill Clinton (1993–2001) and George W. Bush (2001–2009) that promoted free trade while simultaneously closing and militarizing the border between the US and Mexico. *Brinco* also demonstrated how global economic models of circulation and exchange produced huge inequities in the world populations, with Chinese factory workers and undocumented South American immigrants that worked long hours and in some cases risked their lives for substandard wages and art collectors in San Diego who were able to pay $215 for a pair of shoes that cost about $17 to make. It was the perfect project for a well-funded art festival that purported to speak to and about the border, through interventions, dialogues, conversations, and catalogues. The public that Werthein addressed was not only those whose lives

[36] Cartagena, 'Interview with Judi Werthein.'

[37] Claire Bishop, *Artificial Hells: Participatory Art and the Politics of Spectatorship* (London: Verso Books, 2012), Kindle edition.

were precarious, it was also those whose lives were decidedly not. Werthein accomplished this through the agency of inSITE, which provided the platform and financial backing from which she could operate.

Sheren, who has argued that with inSITE the border became both actual site and portable metaphor, has pointed out that the festival, by bringing in big-name artists from outside of the region and facilitating the interventions with interlocutors, academic publications, generous funding, and a helpful curatorial staff, had become the authority on border art. However, as Sheren points out, the phenomenon of inSITE raises several significant questions: 'What is the value (and ultimately, the effect) of widespread public attention on the US–Mexico border? How can art projects generate social change while remaining aesthetically grounded? In the case of inSITE's festivals, what, if any, new knowledge is gained from such focused attention on the physical border?'[38] inSITE was an apparatus, according to Sheren, 'complete with its funding and distribution channels, manufactured art projects and performances ready-made for mass consumption. In the guise of sponsoring art that sought to remake the border region, inSITE turned border art into a brand.'[39] The interventions for inSITE_05, particularly those discussed in this essay, certainly beg these questions. Socially engaged art work does not necessarily fit very well within the context of an art festival or biennial[40] that was originally designed to attract money and art tourists. Mark Bradford, whose strength has always been in his ability to work within the ambiguity generated by the tension between abstract painting and, in some cases, sculpture that actually speaks very specifically to particular instances of social inequity, injustice, racism, and homophobia in contemporary culture, seemingly

[38] Sheren, *Portable Borders*. Kindle Edition.

[39] Ibid.

[40] inSITE is usually considered to be a biennial or triennial—the designation is murky because there were two years between 1992 and 1994, three years between 1994 and 1997, three years again between 1997 and 2001, and then technically three years between 2001 and 2005, since inSITE_05 began in 2004 with panels and residencies. Jens Hoffmann, in *Showtime: The Fifty Most Influential Exhibitions of Contemporary Art* (New York: D.A.P, 2014), placed inSITE in the category of 'Beyond the White Cube,' and not in Biennials. On the other hand, Royce W. Smith, writing for *XTRA*, included inSITE in a discussion of contemporary biennials, although he acknowledged that inSITE was considerably different than a standard biennial. See Smith, 'A Crisis of Supersized Proportions (or Why the Next Great Art Biennial Should Not Be Curated by a Super Platinum Frequent Flyer),' *XTRA* 13, no. 2 (Fall 2010). http://x-traonline.org/article/a-crisis-of-super-sized-proportions-or-why-the-next-great-art-biennial-should-not-be-curated-by-an-uber-platinum-frequent-flyer/.

found himself hamstrung by the idea of eschewing an aesthetic impact, whereas SIMPARCH and Werthein were more successful.

The success of inSITE_05 should not be measured in terms of the success or lack of success of the interventions commissioned and executed for the event. Instead, the interventions in inSITE_05 should be understood in relationship to the sixth iteration of inSITE: inSITE/CasaGallina, sited in Mexico City from 2014 to 2020. In his catalogue essay for inSITE_05, Sánchez referred frequently to relational aesthetics rather than interventions or social practice. Sánchez was primarily interested in using artists, an art platform, and communities in pursuit of socially just projects. With inSITE/CasaGallina, it appears that Sánchez has realized this goal. The premise of inSITE/CasaGallina, situated in the historic district of Mexico City, was 'to inoculate/transgress/crash daily life through interventions and gestures with the potentials to activate flows of group empathy.'[41] This version of inSITE was not conceived within the art festival or biennial model, but rather as a cultural platform from which artistic interventions could unfold over time. A six-year project, inSITE/Casa Galina was to serve as a space of exchange in an unstable community, a social model of operations based on experimental art practices. inSITE/Casa Galina is realizing the goal of serving as a community center for exchange and support. A glance at the website today, a much abridged and less verbose version of previous web sites for inSITE, lists a preserves workshop for restaurant owners, a neighborhood lending service that shares tools and other necessities, and a presentation by Ana María Millán on the collaborative process.[42] What is missing are the gala events, big-name artists, and touristy spectacles that characterized the previous incarnations of inSITE.

For inSITE/CasaGallina and Sánchez, all socially collaborative projects that lead to better forms of social engagement and collaboration are a good thing. It would seem that the best way to create sustainable tools is to follow this most recent model, one operating from an embedded center over a period of time. As an intervention into the urban border fabric, inSITE_05 was only partially successful; its initial role as an art tourist spectacle came into conflict with the stated goals of the curatorial staff. Nevertheless, it suggested a model of art practice that existed outside of the high-end art fairs, biennials, triennials, and festivals. The events at inSITE/CasaGallina points to the desire that underpinned the curatorial

[41] '6th edition of inSITE,' listserv email from e-flux, March 1, 2015.

[42] inSITE/Casa Galina, accessed February 3, 2018. http://inSITE.org.mx/wp/en/.

premise of inSITE_05: namely, to search for sustainable practices and tools that can ameliorate living conditions for those peoples left behind by the global, late capitalist society. It is no accident that inSITE/CasaGallina is based in an actual house and designed to be an 'incubator of cultural production and generator of public domain within the neighborhood.'[43] Nor is it an accident that many of the projects bear a strong similarity to SIMPARCH's *Fountain*, Bradford's *Maleteros*, or Werthein's *Brinco*. inSITE/CasaGallina has a long list of collaborators/invited artists (many who are known for their political work in the Global South) and a much shorter list of supportive institutions and centers that have lent their support to the initiatives begun by inSITE/CasaGallina. Collaborators/artists are invited to experience long residencies at Casa Gallina that allows them to work with the local communities in a sustained fashion—in 2017, for example, the artist Erick Meyenberg collaborated with a Mexico City High School marching band to stage public performances in sites such as Monumento a la Revolución, which commemorates the Mexican Revolution, and Plaza de Tlatelolco, where hundreds of striking students were massacred in 1968. Meyerberg's video *the wheel bears no resemblance to a leg* was based on these performances.[44]

Conclusion

While inSITE/CasaGallina continues as an ongoing project, it has important implications for the intersection of art and sustainable tools and practices. The groundwork for this important project, a project whose audience is not the art world but the public domain/people based in Mexico City, was done before, during, and after inSITE_05 with projects such as the three described above. Significantly, these three projects avoided the pitfalls of the artist/activist parachuting in for a one-off event that leaves little or no impact. By way of comparison, I would like to close with an anecdote about an earlier inSITE, a project designed to address a precarious population, and the difficulty in successfully realizing such a project, even or in spite of an artist's long-term involvement of addressing injustice and racism at the US–Mexico border.

[43] Ibid.

[44] Claire Voon, 'Wielding Instruments Like Weapons, A Marching Band Sweeps Through Mexico City,' *Hyperallergic*, July 27, 2017. https://hyperallergic.com/391598/wielding-instruments-like-weapons-a-marching-band-sweeps-through-mexico-city/.

For inSITE_92, Ulf Rollof and Michael Schnorr collaborated to create an installation at the Playas de Tijuana entitled *Abandonado II*, brick outdoor furniture with built in firepits where people could sit in comfort while waiting on the Tijuana side of the border. Schnorr had cofounded the BAW/TAF with David Avalos, and *Abandonado II* was one of the few installations that year that was designed to address the needs of a vulnerable local population, created for 'abandoned children along the international boundary.'[45] *Abandonado II* was reactivated for inSITE_94, with fires lit in the pits so that the art tourists could sit or even lie down on the warm brick seats and contemplate the beauty of Playas de Tijuana. Good intentions notwithstanding, with no one to ensure that the fires remained lit or to collect and care for the abandoned children, *Abandonado II* was quickly abandoned. In 2001, what remained of *Abandonado II* could be seen by the inSITE_00 art tourists who had alighted from the bus to view Valeska Soares's installation *Picturing Paradise/Visualizando el Paríso*, large reflective metal sheets with excerpts from Italo Calvino's *Invisible Cities* installed onto the border fence between Playas de Tijuana and Border Field State Park.[46] By 2001 *Abandonado II* had been literally and figuratively abandoned. Serving no population and no purpose, unused and unloved, it was reabsorbed into the landscape. Although the art tourists walked right past it, *Abandonado II's* presence and purpose went unremarked and unnoticed, even by the public—inSITE art tourists and guides—who *should* have acknowledged it. The projects/interventions for inSITE_05 were also deliberately unmarked, but, unlike *Abandonado II*, they were not unnoticed. And, significantly, they were used and remarked upon by a very different audience than the traditional art going public. It is thus with inSITE_05, and, subsequently inSITE/CasaGallina, that we might look to a model for activism in the second millennium. It is not a model designed for a Biennial format—inSITE_05 actually took place over two years, and inSITE/CasaGallina is occurring over an even longer period of time. This model is about a long-term and thoughtful engagement with the community. As such, it addresses the title of this essay and this anthology; it is a model of sustainability that can continue long after the art context is no longer relevant.

[45] Ulf Rollof and Michael Schnorr, 'Abandonado II,' *inSITE94 Guide* (San Diego: Installation Gallery, 1994), 158–159.

[46] Accessed February 3, 2018. http://valeskasoares.net/work/untitled-from-picturing-paradise/.

References

'6th edition of inSITE.' 2015. listserv email from *e-flux*, March 1.

'Information about Brinco Shoe.' n.d. Box 201. inSITE Archive.

inSITE/Casa Galina. http://inSITE.org.mx/wp/en/.

Anzaldúa, Gloria. *Borderlands/La Frontera*. San Francisco: Aunt Lute Books, 1987.

Bedford, Christopher, ed. *Mark Bradford*. Columbus, OH: Wexner Center for the Arts and New Haven, CT: Yale University Press, 2010.

Berelowitz, Jo-Anne. 'Border Art Since 1965.' In *Postborder City*, edited by Michael Dear and Gustavo Leclerc, 143–182. New York: Routledge, 2003.

———. 'The Spaces of Home in Chicano and Latino Representations of the San Diego–Tijuana Borderlands (1968–2002).' *Environment & Planning D: Society & Space* 23, no. 3 (June 2005): 323–350.

Bishop, Claire. *Artificial Hells: Participatory Art and the Politics of Spectatorship*. London: Verso Books, 2012.

Bradford, Mark. 'Proposal.' Box 182, inSITE Archive ca. 1992–2006 MSS 0707, 2004.

Cartagena, María Fernanda. 'Interview with Judi Werthein.' *LatinArt.com*, December 1, 2015. http://www.latinart.com/transcript.cfm?id=72.

Conwell, Donna. 'Email to Judi Werthein.' May 31, Box 201. inSITE Archive, 2005.

Cruz, Teddy. 'Border Postcards: Chronicles from the Edge.' In *inSITE_05: A Dynamic Equilibrium: In Pursuit of Public Terrain*, edited by Sally Yard, 68–91. San Diego: Installation Gallery, 2007.

Dear, Michael and Gustavo Leclerc, eds. *Postborder City: Cultural Spaces of Bajalta California*. New York: Routledge, 2003.

Isackson, Amy. 'State-of-the-Art Shoes Aid Migrants: The World Programme, San Diego.' *BBC News*, November 17, 2005. http://news.bbc.co.uk/2/hi/4445342.stm.

Jones, Kellie. 'Just Across the Way.' In *inSITE_05: [Situational] Public*, edited by Osvaldo Sánchez and Donna Conwell, 227. San Diego: Installation Gallery, 2006.

Ollman, Leah. 'Perils of Public Art: Pavilion to be Dismantled.' *Art in America* 86, no. 9 (September 1998): 33–36.

Pedrosa, Adriana, ed. *inSITE_05: Farsites/Sitios distantes*. San Diego: Installation Gallery, 2005.

Sánchez, Osvaldo. 'Rito de paso/Rite of Passage.' In *Fugitives Sites: inSITE 2000–2001 New Contemporary Art Projects for San Diego–Tijuana*, edited by Osvaldo Sánchez and Cecilia Garza, 166–175. San Diego: Installation Gallery, 2002.

———. 'Fading Tracers.' In *inSITE_05: [Situational] Public*, edited by Osvaldo Sánchez and Donna Conwell, 40–49. San Diego: Installation Gallery, 2006.

Sánchez, Osvaldo, et al. *inSITE_05: Art Practices in the Public Domain San Diego Tijuana*. San Diego: Installation Gallery, 2005.

Sánchez, Osvaldo and Donna Conwell, eds. *inSITE_05: [Situational] Public*. San Diego: Installation Gallery, 2006.

Sengupta, Shuddhabrata. 'Liminal.' In *inSITE_05: Conversations: Compilation: Dialogues 1–2: Liminal Zones, Coursing Flows, Aliens, Denizens, Cosmopolitans*, edited by Sally Yard, 13–24. San Diego: inSITE_05, 2004.

Sheren, Ila Nicole. *Portable Borders: Performance Art and Politics on the U.S. Frontera Since 1984*. Austin, TX: University of Austin Press, 2015.

SIMPARCH. 'Dirty Water Initiative.' http://www.simparch.org/dirty-water-initiative/.

Smith, Royce W. 'A Crisis of Supersized Proportions (or Why the Next Great Art Biennial Should Not Be Curated by a Super Platinum Frequent Flyer).' *XTRA* 13, no. 2 (Fall 2010). http://x-traonline.org/article/a-crisis-of-super-sized-proportions-or-why-the-next-great-art-biennial-should-not-be-curated-by-an-uber-platinum-frequent-flyer/.

Reich, Robert. 'Six Reasons Why Trump's Wall is Even Dumber Than Most of Trump's Ideas.' *robertreich.org*, January 13, 2017. http://robertreich.org.

Rollof, Ulf, and Michael Schnorr. 'Abandonado II.' In *inSITE94 Guide*, 158–159. San Diego: Installation Gallery, 1994.

Thompson, Nato, and Gregory Sholette, eds. *The Interventionists: Users' Manual for the Creative Disruption of Everyday Life*. North Adams, MA: MASS MoCA Publications and Cambridge, MA: MIT Press, 2004.

Voon, Claire. 'Wielding Instruments Like Weapons, A Marching Band Sweeps Through Mexico City.' *Hyperallergic*, July 27, 2017. https://hyperallergic.com/391598/wielding-instruments-like-weapons-a-marching-band-sweeps-through-mexico-city/.

Werthein, Judi. 'Email to Donna Conwell.' June 7, Box 201. inSITE Archive, 2005.

Yard, Sally. 'A Dynamic Equilibrium: In Pursuit of Public Terrain.' In *inSITE_05: A Dynamic Equilibrium: In Pursuit of Public Terrain*, edited by Sally Yard, 12–31. San Diego: Installation Gallery, 2007.

Yúdice, George. *The Expediency of Culture: Uses of Culture in the Global Era*. Durham, NC: Duke University Press, 2003.

micha cárdenas, Patrisse Cullors, Chris Head, Edxie Betts
***UNSTOPPABLE*, 2015-2017**

Materials testing by micha cárdenas, photo by Brett Stalbaum 2015

Edxie Betts in Kevlar tube dress designed by micha cárdenas, photo by micha cárdenas 2015

"What would technology for black lives be?"

Bulletproof backpack prototype designed by micha cárdenas, photo by micha cárdenas 2015

micha cárdenas, Patrisse Cullors, Chris Head, Edxie Betts
UNSTOPPABLE, 2015-2017

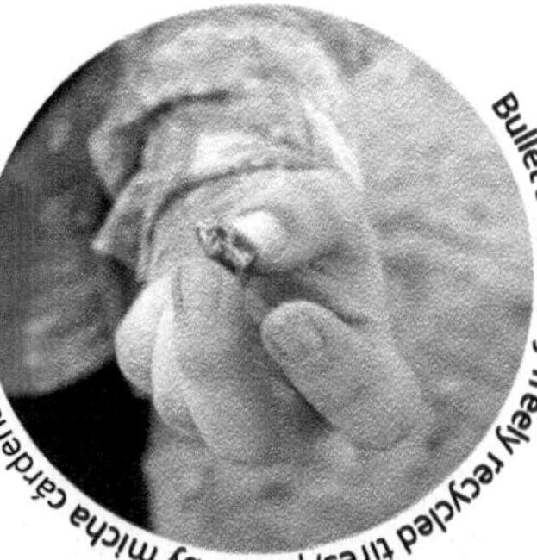
Bullet stopped by freely recycled tires, photo by micha cárdenas 2015

"At the 2015 Allied Media Conference opening ceremony, Patrisse Cullors asked 'what would technology for black lives be,' while wearing a shirt designed by Foremost and Damon Turner with the words ***BULLETPROOF #BlackLivesMatter*** *emblazoned across her chest in gold. Inspired by this idea, micha cárdenas, Patrisse Cullors, Edxie Betts and Chris Head are collaborating to develop* UNSTOPPABLE, *a set of materials and processes for producing DIY bulletproof clothing at low to no cost.* UNSTOPPABLE *is art as intervention.*

"These clothes and prototypes were exhibited at the INCA gallery in Seattle, and used as the basis for a conversation about direct action approaches to ending the murder of black people, in particular black trans women. The project name comes from the words of Sylvia Rivera, a trans Latina leader of the movement for liberation for transgender people: 'A lot of heads were bashed [at Stonewall]. But it didn't hurt their true feelings—they all came back for more and more. Nothing—that's when you could tell that nothing could stop us at that time or any time in the future.'

"While a larger movement to change ideas and laws is of the utmost importance, UNSTOPPABLE *is an intervention now to stop the bullets from killing black people."*

—micha cárdenas

MICHA CÁRDENAS, PhD, is Assistant Professor of Art & Design: Games + Playable Media at the University of California, Santa Cruz. cárdenas is writing a new algorithm for gender, race and technology. She is the author of *Poetic Operations* (in progress), and co-author of *The Transreal: Political Aesthetics of Crossing Realities* (2012) and *Trans Desire / Affective Cyborgs* (2010), both with Atropos Press. **PATRISSE CULLORS** is cofounder of Black Lives Matter and founder of Dignity and Power Now. An artist, organizer, Fulbright scholar and NAACP History Maker, she's received many awards for activism, including the Sydney Peace Prize. Cullors is the author of *When They Call You a Terrorist: A Black Lives Matter Memoir* (2018). **EDXIE BETTS** is a black, filipin@, black footed, trans femme, gender nonconforming, queer anti-authoritarian art healer whose aims are to uplift those on the margins of margins. **CHRIS HEAD** is an artist whose work focuses on the intersection of software design and art practice to produce projects that take a variety of forms including computer visualization, simulation, games, and hardware hacking. Christopher received his MFA at the University of California San Diego.

CHAPTER 9

INTERVIEW
Art as Process in Everyday Life

Wilfredo Prieto and Zaira Zarza

Wilfredo Prieto is a graduate of Havana's Instituto Superior de Arte (ISA). From 1998 to 2002 he was a member of Galería DUPP (Desde Una Pragmática Pedagógica), with whom he was awarded the UNESCO Prize for the Promotion of the Arts. Prieto has exhibited widely on an international level and his work can be found in prestigious collections around the world.

Much has been written about Cuba's world-leading role in sustainable agriculture.[1] The island is a model of organic urban farming and guerrilla

[1] See Fernando Funes, *Sustainable Agriculture and Resistance: Transforming Food Production in Cuba* (Oakland, CA: Food First Books, 2002), http://www.infinitejourney-project.com; María Caridad Cruz and Roberto Sánchez Medina, *Agriculture in the City: A Key to Sustainability in Havana, Cuba* (Kingston, Jamaica: Ian Randle Publishers, 2003); and Pamela Stricker, *Toward a Culture of Nature: Environmental Policy and Sustainable Development in Cuba* (Lanham, MD: Lexington Books, 2007).

Foreword and translation by Zaira Zarza

W. Prieto (✉)
Havana, Cuba

Z. Zarza
University of Montreal, Montreal, Quebec, Canada

N. Alvarez et al. (eds.), *Sustainable Tools for Precarious Times*, Contemporary Performance InterActions,
https://doi.org/10.1007/978-3-030-11557-9_9

gardening initiatives that involve the use of natural fertilizers and peasant labor. Agriculture develops in the country with minimum environmental impact: self-provisioning neighborhoods are sustained by harvests yielded from the so-called *organopónicos*. However, sustainability is not a concept openly discussed in other realms of Cuba's everyday life. Both its geographical and ideological isolation—an island nation and the only socialist country in the West—has also meant that Cuba has been estranged from global conventional markets. Over five decades of US embargo have prevented free trade and caused dependency on the tourism industry as well as limited commerce with countries such as the former USSR and Venezuela. This controlled exchange has resulted in a broad lack of ecological consciousness in Cuba. Procedures such as massive recycling are non-existent because the level of garbage produced is still mainly organic. Cans and plastic are not yet an essential part of day-to-day use within the general population and do not approach the scale of consumption in post-industrial societies. A culture of refurbishment and reuse has imposed what architect and planner Orlando Inclán calls 'an "accidental sustainability" borne of necessity.'[2]

Decades of ideological discourse on Cuba's exceptionalism have also weighed heavily on the political stance of several generations. A single party—the Partido Comunista de Cuba (PCC) or Cuba's Communist Party—leads the country which has had a long-term hostile relationship with its closest, most powerful neighbor: the United States. And yet, unparalleled access to free education, medicine, and culture has made Cuba an example of social development in the Americas. Not unlike ecology, politics, particularly in the aftermath of the Cuban Revolution (1959), has been threaded into Cubans' quotidian practices. This is instanced in the sense of pride around the island nation's highly-educated citizenry, the control on international capitalist intervention, and the way in which people have survived periods of harsh economic crisis using their creativity. Most official media are still state-run, and they exemplify what María Caridad Cumaná has called, 'the burden of revolutionary representation.'[3] That is probably why many socially engaged artists today do not frame their work in activist terms. Political art still tends to be largely associated with strict ideological concerns—in favor of, or in opposition to, the

[2] J. Marshall Brown, 'Accidental Sustainability: An American Planner Wonders Whether Cuba's Culture of Reuse Will Persist,' *Planning* 83, no. 8 (2017): 25.

[3] María Caridad Cumaná González, 'Cuban Film and the Burden of Revolutionary Representation,' in *New World Coming: The Sixties and the Shaping of Global Consciousness*, ed. Karen Dubinsky, et al. (Toronto: Between The Lines, 2009), 153–160.

extremely Leftist government—rather than committed critical interventions attempting to unsettle the status quo. The memory of the Revolution, the histories of massive migration waves—the first one in the early 1960s, the Mariel Boatlift in 1980, and the *balseros* (rafters) crisis in the early 1990s[4]—and the hardships of the Special Period[5] after the fall of the Soviet Bloc are certainly present in the discourse of Cuban contemporary artists. But more often than not these political narratives live symbolically in the intricate nature of their work.[6]

Wilfredo Prieto is one of the few Cuban artists who has managed to combine environmental sustainability with artistic practices that emphasize prolonged community engagement. Born in Zaza del Medio (Sancti Spíritus, Cuba) in 1978, Prieto is a graduate of the Instituto Superior de Arte (ISA, Cuba's University of the Arts) where he participated in the project Galería DUPP (*Desde Una Pragmática Pedagógica*, 1997–2001).

[4] The first significant migration wave in the 1960s comprised a large number of white, upper-class Cubans who fled to the United States expecting a quick fall of the Revolution and a prompt return to the island. Two decades later, from the port of Mariel, a second mass exodus occurred and was composed of a more diverse groups in terms of class and racial identities; many were either members of the working class or released from Cuban jails and mental health facilities. The event deeply impacted Florida's demographics. After the fall of the Berlin wall, the collapse of the Soviet Bloc and its economic support to Cuba, a third and final massive exodus occurred. The *balseros* crisis reached its most dramatic point in 1994, as Cubans despaired facing the conditions of the Special Period.

[5] After the fall of the Berlin Wall in 1989, trade relationships between Cuba and the socialist countries of Eastern Europe collapsed. Over 70 percent of the island's consumed products were imported from those nations. This was the beginning of a post-Cold War era of dramatic scarcity and social crisis characterized by an 'economy of survival' and by the intensification of the US blockade which led to many social transformations distanced from the utopian conception that the Revolution envisioned for the Cuban society. This crisis was baptized—note the euphemism—as the *Período Especial en Tiempo de Paz* (Special Period in Time of Peace). From that moment on, tourism became one of the country's main sources of income.

[6] It is important to consider the political censorship that many artists and writers faced in Cuba during the first decades of the revolutionary process. Its aftermath has certainly affected younger generations as well. The conflicts of the Cold War made Cuba a defensive state where ideological controversy was punished and political paranoia became frequent. Pronounced by Fidel Castro in June 1961, the discourse *Palabras a los Intelectuales* stated that 'dentro de la Revolución, todo; contra la Revolución, nada' ('Inside the Revolution, everything; outside the Revolution, nothing'). That argument defined the cultural policy of the nation and impacted the arts in three ways: (1) it drove artists to the diaspora; (2) it marginalized a few trenchant artists who decided to stay in Cuba; and (3) it turned forms of very explicit political art into conceptual criticism to be read between the lines. Wilfredo Prieto's work belongs to this third group.

DUPP was an alternative educational project under the guidance of renowned artist René Francisco Rodríguez that included several generations of ISA students. Prieto was part of the first cohort of graduates encouraged to leave the classroom and enter the streets, engaging in community-based artistic research. This approach inspired students to venture outside the gallery and question traditional institutions as the locus for the exhibition of artworks.

Traversing the categories of 'superminimalist,'[7] 'conceptual,'[8] and 'experimental,'[9] Prieto's unconventional art is a 'direct gesture'[10] pinned between sharp irony and simplicity. And yet, despite these wide-ranging categories, his practice is deeply invested in the context in which the work develops. Throughout his career, Prieto has addressed social, philosophical, and political issues using subtle, sarcastic, and even ludic means. His narratives on food insecurity in the Cuban context are present in pieces such as *Arte Óptico* (*Optic Art*, University of the Arts, Cuba, 1999), *Sin título—Mapa del mundo* (*Untitled, World Map*, Martin van Zomeren Gallery, 2002), and *Pan con Pan* (*Bread with Bread*, Centro de Arte Dos de Mayo, Madrid, 2011). In these works, he has respectively painted on an unripe mango to make it look like it was ready to eat; drawn a map of the globe on a yellow pea—one of Cuba's most consumed products during the financial crisis of the early 1990s; and placed a bread bun inside another one—a reminder of the slim diet he was forced to follow when he moved to Havana for art school. These pieces portray Cuba's everyday economic precarity as a condition of resistance and a source of ever-flowing creativity.

In 2015, Prieto co-organized, with curators Gretel Medina and Direlia Lazo, the exhibition *Mountains with a Broken Edge* in the semi-ruins of a former bicycle factory in Cuba. One of the most visited collective projects of the 12th Havana Biennial, this exhibition gathered twelve artists from over seven countries with a broad variety of projects.[11] In this case, the artist

[7] Michael Slenske, 'Method Making: Wilfredo Prieto Embodies Every Aspect of Kurimanzutto,' June 21, 2016, https://www.wallpaper.com/Art/Cuban-Artist-Wilfredo-Prieto-Takes-Over-Mexico-Citys-Kurimanzutto-Gallery.

[8] Guillaume Désanges, 'Una rosa es una rosa es un camión,' s.l. Mousse Publishing (2012): 220–221.

[9] Dalida López Arbolay, 'Les intuitions illogiques de Wilfredo Prieto,' *Parachute* 125 (2007): 145–149.

[10] Laura Bardier, 'Essays: Wilfredo Prieto and the Work of Art as a Direct Gesture,' *Review: Literature and Arts of the Americas* 44, no. 1 (2011): 143–148.

[11] Gretel Medina and Direlia Lazo, 'Mountains with a Broken Edge: A Dossier,' *Public* 26, no. 52 (December 2015): 125–134.

acted as both a producer and mediator, a cultural agent through which other creative partners were able to connect. This experience inspired one of Prieto's most important projects to date: his collaborative studio in Havana.

Prieto's new studio revitalizes an abandoned government-owned space. Supported by a national law that allows individuals to rent unutilized sites owned by the state to develop cultural events, the artist negotiated with the Ministry of Industry to access the area. The venue, a former shipyard, has been remediated and now invites multidisciplinary artists and their projects. As a result, an insalubrious zone conquered by mosquitos and wild vegetation turned into a beautiful garden that contributes to strengthening the socio-ecological and formally experimental awareness of that community. Located on the ground floor of an apartment building, the studio shares its space with the neighbors living on the bottom floor. That coexistence has impacted both the artists' work and the tenants' everyday lives. Elderly residents practice Tai Chi in the front yard, and neighbors of all ages participate in all events. The presentations are promoted at the university, in cultural institutions, and through text messages across Havana, but the main advertising happens via word of mouth.[12]

At the same time that Prieto founded his studio, he was producing *El viaje infinito* (*The Infinite Journey*, 2013–ongoing). This is perhaps the most relevant piece of land art developed in Cuba since Ana Mendieta's (1948–1985) earth-body work in the 1980s. This site-specific effort will be developed on a currently useless terrain subjugated by harmful and invading plants, and turned into a 2000-meter highway designed in the shape of the infinity symbol. Working with a team of engineers, scientific researchers, and community members, the highway will include a high-level bridge and serve as an agro-ecological project that involves forestry. The road will lead nowhere and anywhere. The utopianism of the proposal could be read as the critique of a long-term political stasis. However, it emerged in a moment of transition for Cuba where the tourism industry had exploded with American visitors, foreign investment, and business revival. The production will be made with ecological cement LC3, a

[12] Oscar-nominated Austrian filmmaker Hubert Sauper organized a public screening of his social justice documentary *We Come as Friends* (2014) with a question-and-answer session at the end. Sauper and his team—who worked for nearly a year on site in Havana filming their new production—continued to visit and use Prieto's space for meetings, and so on. *Ensayos de Duración* (2017) was a series of performance pieces by choreographers/dancers Gabriella Burdsall and William Ruiz Morales, and visual artist Kiko Faxas. The workshop was also the venue of Irving Vera's installation *Giraluna* (2017) during the *Havana Art Weekend* (November 30–December 3). An average of 150 persons have attended each of these events.

much less toxic substance that reduces CO_2 emissions by 20–30 percent in comparison to other concrete.[13] With this piece, Prieto is co-creating an experience in order to instigate conversations that awaken consciousness of decolonial politics around land, agriculture, the environment, and the way these questions shape community rituals and ways of life (Fig. 9.1).

Cuba has been listed among the 25 nations with the least number of vehicles per person in the world.[14] By 2010 there were only 38 vehicles (including 27.5 cars and 2 buses) per 1000 inhabitants on the island, and most of those automobiles circulated in Havana. Due to the price of imported cars, these numbers have not increased dramatically. In a country where the average wage is US$20 a month, the cost of a car can be nearly ten times its original price.[15] In this context, it is reasonable to

Fig. 9.1 Viaje Infinito, oil and acrylic on canvas, 2014. Credit: Jose Perdomo and Wilfredo Prieto

[13] Ángel Freddy Pérez Cabrera, 'Cemento de bajo carbono gana espacio en el mundo,' *Granma*, September 2, 2015, http://www.granma.cu/cuba/2015-09-02/cemento-de-bajo-carbono-gana-espacio-en-el-mundo.

[14] 'Vehículos por mil habitantes,' *Foresight Cuba*, March 8, 2015, 2018, http://foresight-cuba.com/vehiculos-por-mil-habitantes.

[15] 'Cubans Shocked at Prices as Foreign Cars Go on Sale,' *British Broadcasting Corporation*, January 4, 2014, http://www.bbc.com/news/world-latin-america-25595674.

imagine that *El viaje infinito* will likely be used by cyclists and pedestrians rather than by drivers, discouraging car emissions that contribute to air pollution and global warming. Prieto conceived the shape and location as ecologically and socially sustainable gestures in the sense that they criticize the industrial dynamics of urban traffic in capitalist regimes overflowing with private forms of transportation. He returns to his rural birthplace with a tool of collaboration, working to create a physical and symbolic space of relations across different social sectors. Unlike his previous ephemeral pieces, this sculpture implies direct action and strategies for continuous community engagement as it becomes a landmark in the area and attempts to invigorate the local economy and culture of Zaza del Medio. Prieto has financed *El viaje infinito* with the support of the Cuban government and an international grant.

Projects like these have become extremely significant given the current climate in which Cuba finds itself. The years 2016–2017 imposed many challenges for the world in general and Cuba in particular. Donald Trump took power as the 45th President of the United States. Fidel Castro passed away. Hurricanes Irma and María affected the economy of the whole Caribbean region like no other climate event had done in years. The American embassy in Havana drastically reduced its functions due to an alleged—and unlikely—'sonic attack' that, to date, has not been resolved. What seemed like a potential time of prosperity and broad openness, after Barack Obama and Raúl Castro re-established diplomatic relations, became an uncertain path. In this framework, workers within the creative industries—specifically, contemporary visual artists—engaged in initiatives that functioned as alternatives to the cultural programs planned by state institutions. Carlos Garaicoa's project *Artista x Artista* (Artist x Artist) offers art residencies to both foreign and local artists in Havana since 2015. A year later, the private gallery *El Apartamento* (The Apartment) started to run with a group of relevant artists moving between photography, architecture, and design. Wilfredo Prieto is also participating in this emergence. His studio opened in 2017, and it has functioned as a laboratory for creative experimentation and artistic events. This collective space invites artists from different disciplines—installation, performance, filmmaking, dance—to develop their work and present it to the public.

The ever-influential experimental approach to the arts that Prieto learned with Galería DUPP has enabled him to track a creative path that centers on the process as much as—or even more than—the product. The value of Prieto's practice lies in the way he conceives of art making, his level of commitment to, and investment in, the material, and his new role as a facilitator and mentor of younger generations. I understood the ongoing value of his creative performance, especially in the precarious environmental and political climate that I describe above. To delve into Wilfredo's new sustainable projects, I met him in December 2017 in his studio, and in January 2018 at his home in Havana.

Zaira Zarza: As a visual artist you have developed projects in traditional exhibition spaces such as galleries and museums as well as in public and repurposed sites. How do you see the relationship between these two environments? In terms of organization and public reception, what is the difference between working in those distinct environments?

Wilfredo Prieto: I believe that both are necessary experiences. I compare them to the act of eating. Sometimes you sit at the table with all the cutlery, the plates, the glasses. There is a ritual that begins with the starter and ends with the dessert. That causes a specific kind of pleasure. But there is also another pleasure that occurs when eating on the streets, while standing or sitting on the floor, at a park, with the plate in your hand. Food acquires a different flavor. The same happens with exhibitions. There are multiple ways to communicate ideas. It is not the same to display an exhibition in a place understood and agreed upon to 'read' art than to do it in a place where art is not often present. This interaction gives a different plasticity and value to the work with another type of staging or *mise-en-scène*.

Each project has unique indicators. There are works that have a mutual plasticity. They can be inside the white cube and also in spaces of real/daily life. This gives a different symbolic quality to the work, as it is enriched with other nuances, spiced in other ways. On the contrary, there are pieces that are only meant to live in the public space, to interact with the open landscape and the environment. These could not be confined to a white cube because they would lose freedom, spontaneity, content, meaning. Similarly, some artworks cannot leave the white cube because they would vanish. They would lose their essence and significance. I think we have to see each project in their specific terrain. But we must also understand the freedom of the works that have that double capacity. There is no denying either of the two spaces. We should not limit ourselves to those possibilities but enrich our practice with them.

Art can also adapt to specific conditions. In organizational terms, there are pieces that need a whole system of permissions for their execution. There is an absolute dependence on a determined terrain, because there are rules that govern the public sphere. Other public interventions, on the contrary, do not need any permission because they are so subtle that they almost disappear in the terrain. Factors to take into account are also the durability of the piece, the dimensions, and, above all, the relationship with a public of passers-by. Sometimes art is interactive because of its presence or formal structure and sometimes it is not. Ultimately, each work has an autonomy, a personality, a different need.

Zaira Zarza: Although you have been in Cuba for most of your life, you have also had the possibility to live abroad. You have participated in artist residencies and won fellowships in Spain, Mexico, and the United States. How has the experience of living abroad impacted your work?

Wilfredo Prieto: When you face new life experiences this certainly influences the way you make art. In my case, it helped me to recognize my culture. Issues that one can understand as virtues become defects and the other way around. Those contexts put in crisis the knowledge of my own culture. One's aesthetic evaluations and formal assessments also change under the influence of the new surroundings. And this, of course, is reflected in the work. The most important thing is that you learn to discard elements that you thought were previously important. The gain of a comparative perspective is relevant. For me it is key that artists travel and have that experience of exchange. I returned to my place of origin because I had the privilege, but also the cultural anchorage that it allows me. There is a way of life that we never lose and that makes us feel we do not belong as migrants.

Zaira Zarza: I believe education is one of the most sustainable tools a person can claim. We carry forms of knowledge throughout our entire lives and we learn to embrace and repel them, whether indistinct or simultaneously. You had a very peculiar learning experience when you were a student at the University of the Arts. What do you owe to Galería DUPP as an educational project, and to your formative years in Cuba's art education system? What do you think are the main challenges now for younger generations of art students?

Wilfredo Prieto: I owe DUPP everything: the exchange, the coexistence, the understanding of how pure ideas do not really belong to you. I learned from that project that pedagogy and art cannot be detached from the personal. We were fourteen artists working together during four years, respecting each other's individuality but also working tightly as a collective under the premise that life is art and art is life. We grew from the solid ground of an education system that no longer exists.

There is a serious problem with education across the globe. There seems to be a divorce between pedagogic tools and the learning process, mediated by information and communication technologies. The Cuban University of the Arts, for example, is in crisis as we speak. There is a disconnect between older and younger generations, a change of concept for education itself, and a different approach to teaching methods. I think the best educational tools can be found these days not in traditional institutions—schools, universities—but in other spaces that coexist with them. The alternative work of artists today and the spaces of exchange they are facilitating is replacing some of those former learning methodologies and venues. The instruction works more now at the level of art production and exhibition. It has a practicum component where intuition continues to be relevant.

I am a consequence of the cultural, social, and political reality of Cuba. I think education in Cuba was something unique and a rare experience compared to other countries of the world. That makes me think about art in a different way, maybe with a more romantic attitude. It is a reality that can change, of course. But right now many of us almost feel an unconscious need to give back. If someone invites you to her/his house and gives you coffee, then when the person comes to your house, you give them coffee. But if when you visit, they sell you a cup of coffee, you will probably do the same. The relationship changes. And something similar happens in the case of art education. In Cuba one receives a free, long-term education and we logically feel indebted.

Zaira Zarza: After graduating from ISA, you continued to develop your career as a conceptual artist. Today, you still work with unsettling ideas as an individual producer, but now you are interested in generating spaces for more collective practices where collaboration becomes important. Where does this interest come from? What are the functioning principles of your studio/lab and how are you developing relationships with the community?

Wilfredo Prieto: First of all, in terms of the global context, I believe that business-oriented art is an international circumstance nowadays. This is not necessarily an advantage and I think it will eventually change in Cuba too. It is just another part of the contemporary 'trash culture' depending on the power of information and on the institutions of art: markets, galleries, museums. There is a commercial bubble that surrounds art production, and to be instituted in those circuits does not unavoidably mean that artists are creating 'good' art. Secondly, professional development, experience, age, and the different moments of one's life are also an important feature when it comes to creative production. I did not need a studio before. I worked anywhere. Now that I am 40 years old, I need a certain security, or a centered space. I need my house, my plants, my monotony. The same happens with the art practice. At the beginning, my work was more physically aligned with my life, with my daily experiences: on planes, in airports, at friends' houses. I worked anywhere and with any kind of material. That changes with time, with a different type of maturity or need. I do not believe in that dependence though. I do not think there is a precept that states how the artist needs to be attached to a space, to certain materials and financial possibilities to be able to work. Creativity does not need that. In my case it is a need related to a new stage of maturity—or maybe immaturity—because one risks losing the freshness in the work. I think sometimes creativity is more free when it is not dependent on space or funding. The challenge is to continue to work without losing spontaneity even with those advantages. And a space could become dangerous if it turns into a sort of gallery—a boring temple—where one can generate a self-hierarchizing environment. Then the work would become 'lighter' and insipid.

The concept of the studio has also changed. It is no longer the traditional space with the painter, the easel, and the model in a room. Today, we are interacting with art historians, curators, engineers, gardeners, cooks. We should be conscious of that and magnify it in order to understand why and how these interactions are happening. We want to make each element a protagonist, so that they can nurture each other and make us grow as artists, curators, and neighbors. Thus, we can develop as a community. This is more about building an environment than about only producing cold and decontextualized pieces of artwork. The studio then becomes a platform that functions as a museum, as a lab, as a meeting point, as a brainstorming center. It becomes a comfort zone of emotional stability where we can create a dialogue of thought. I think this can create a terrain to refresh cultural activity in Cuba. The idea is for people to meet in Havana. As long as there is a tuning of ideas with the projects that approach us, or that we invite, we will provide a space and equipment for free. We work with a trial and error system that includes imperfect works. We are interested in the workshop dynamic of a collective space. We want an exchange with both experienced and younger artists in order to build spaces of collaboration. Cuba has always inhabited a complex and changing set of contexts. It cannot be alienated from the global 'trash culture.' Therefore, the island is poised to align with an injection of both tangible and mental markets. The mental one suggests an attitude linked to the myth of desire. Artists fall into that trap too. And there is a need to create zones to oxygenate that. I think the studio is trying to bring in that oxygen.

Zaira Zarza: In recent years, there have been many changes in Cuba's creative economies. The possibility to buy and sell property and the proliferation of business licenses issued for modest private enterprises have impacted artistic production. Migratory laws that prevented people from traveling freely outside of the country without the government's permission have also been revised, relaxed, and updated. These transformations have allowed the emergence of new investments in the island, and more mobility to and from Cuba. How would you describe the state of the arts in these times of transition? How do you think the studios of independent artists or galleries are influencing Cuban cultural practices today?

Wilfredo Prieto: I think that there is a current suspension or brake in the world economy, and an immense warring tension after Trump's election. This generates a situation of global tension and Cuba is part of that. I am optimistic though, and I still believe that Cuba is a different society. There are possibilities to go in the right direction without depending on the United States. These are slow changes happening on the island. I see a positive evolution. The best aspect of these transformations is that there is constant dialogue among independent artists and between them and the state-run institutions. Unlike what could happen in other contexts, the relationship between studios in Cuba is much more open and generous to the local culture. This is perhaps due to an initiative of the artists to return a modest contribution to a cultural context that offers so much in the formative period. There is a large diversity, a positive dialogue, and a posture of collaboration and exchange.

Many of us who graduated from that era believe that the best way to return what we have learned is through a commitment to the quality of our labor. That is the challenge and the greatest effort as an artist: to be as demanding as possible with oneself, to work from the purest respect for research and experimentation, and to stay away from making concessions. Beyond direct projects that can socially or pedagogically affect a community, the example you can create with your own work can leave the best legacy for younger generations. That is what I aspire to. I think it is very difficult to achieve it, but it is the most appropriate thing to do, especially considering an international society where what prevails is the garbage of cultural trivialization. The only thing you can do against that is the clean gift of quality by establishing pure aesthetic and conceptual patterns that do not become contaminated with market needs.

Zaira Zarza: Probably your most personal project so far has been *El viaje infinito* (*The Infinite Journey*, 2013–present; expected completion in 2020), which you are currently developing in Zaza del Medio, your home town in central Cuba. This is a major project that includes research in such diverse disciplines as engineering, forestry, topography, sociology, and cultural studies. What is this research project about and how has the local community received your idea?

Wilfredo Prieto: *El viaje infinito* is a highway in the shape of the infinity symbol in the middle of nowhere, in the countryside. But just placing it there was not possible. It became something else because the project generated a social interaction with the peasants, with the neighbors of that place. When you modify their landscape, and their environment, you are also changing people's way of life. That required a social responsibility that I did not normally have in art. In previous projects, I had to be accountable from an aesthetic and contextual point of view, but not directly for people's lifestyles. Through this project, farmers are already changing some ways of doing agriculture. We are all starting to deforest an area where the sculpture will be located. It is a place full of *aroma*, a plague that locals have been fighting for quite a while. A very important exchange is starting to occur: forms of traditional agriculture are guiding contemporary agriculture, and forms of contemporary agriculture are refreshing traditional growing practices. This relation gives a new nuance to life in that space and generates new ways of living together. Neighbors may work and cultivate differently. The environment in this case has really qualified the basic artwork and generated a different coexistence. There will be an external audience that will arrive there to start interacting with that community. Neighbors might move. The work gained a scientific and social relevance that was not in my hands anymore.

The project has been very well received by both residents and the local government because it is about revitalizing a space. It is a very long process with obstacles and critics. We have to work very hard. I have calculated ten years for its completion. The sculpture has the original design of a real highway. It is an official ready-made road with paving and traffic signs. It is interesting for the field of contemporary art as we will create a work in a space that is not designed to exhibit such art. But there is also a scientific interest because we are testing some materials that are being developed in a laboratory with students. We are collaborating with several ministries, and we depend on state budgets, resources, and planning materials. There is a logic of project development that went beyond my control and my knowledge. I did not know this was going to happen. It has transcended my understanding of sculpture and my idea of artistic intervention to become a social project.

Zaira Zarza: As you develop a socially engaged art practice today, how would you respond to the notion of 'sustainable strategies' in your work?

Wilfredo Prieto: I think that not unlike life itself, art today is not sustainable. But artists can certainly generate tools and mechanisms to balance their work and be consequential. I think my most sustainable strategy is a combination of lived experiences, commitment to research, and respect for what I do. Contemporary art is full of fake effects. I believe in the truthfulness of art making. It is also very important that art goes beyond its limits, that it has a life of its own that expands outside its zones of origin. A project has different levels of content, and it becomes complete in its capacity to transgress a local environment, an individual taste or interest. Art has the possibility to generate a butterfly effect. It can conduct a different sensitivity, and create reflections that you never expected in people.

Zaira Zarza: Cuban visual arts critic and curator Gerardo Mosquera has stated about you: 'Although Prieto is an artist of ideas, he is not a critical artist, inasmuch as he doesn't set out to produce political or social commentary. He seeks to unravel a grid of meanings that opens itself to a long-range perspective [...] [T]he way he constructs meaning in his works refers to his country through suggestions that are as indirect as they are potent.[16] [...] Prieto is a critical artist who does not "do" criticism: it emerges from the very context of his work.'[17] Do you consider yourself a political artist?

Wilfredo Prieto: I am part of a political generation. As medieval artists responded to religious art, we now live in a time when we respond to political, economic, and media interests. One reflects—and is a consequence of—one's society. It is logical then that my art has a greater political influence. But I am

[16] Gerardo Mosquera, 'Wilfredo Prieto: The Tension of the Image,' *Art Nexus* 7, no. 69 (2008): 53.

[17] Ibid., 55.

also a romantic, philosophical, and social artist, as well as a media critic. I think there are many manipulated concepts when it comes to political art. To be a political artist does not mean that you have to be exaggeratedly complacent with either side. I call that an *artista turista* (a tourist artist). There are cases in which the artists who pronounce themselves against the government are the ones who are commercially successful. But to be a political artist does not mean to be partial. One can be a political artist that recognizes virtues and defects in a system both at local and global scales.

Zaira Zarza: Do you feel that you have freedom to do the work you want to do in Cuba despite the allegedly crude censorship of the system? Is there anything specific about your work, or your context that incites or prevents your autonomy as an artist?

Wilfredo Prieto: I have to start my answer by saying that Cubans are a very critical and honest public that will give their opinion on art without hesitation. To have a relationship like this is very constructive. In addition, I understand censorship in two ways. One way is related to the artists who provoke censorship to achieve promotion. Unlike what happens in other countries, public figures in Cuba express controversial criteria about the regime and the next day they make the news in media sources around the world. It has been an effective strategy for some Cuban artists in the past. There is a second way that I relate to the lack of metaphoric capacity that some artists have. If you work in an extremely direct way, your art will be so explicit that it will become propaganda. There is a lack of technical capacity of that work when it is not able to filter in and say more complex things. If the work is not rich enough in terms of language and content, then it is censurable. Censorship is sometimes the best measurement for 'bad art.'

More importantly, there is a tendency to talk about political censorship. It has been many years since political censorship changed morphologically. To speak about it today is a bit outdated. Economic censorship is the new face of political censorship. It is much stronger and more overwhelming. Even artists do not have reflective relations with their society and their environment because of the economic censorship that neutralizes them to make complacent art. The whole world is doing 'pretty' art; docile works prostituted to the market and to the power of information. That creates a global neutrality, a symbol of trash culture. That is why I say that in Cuba there is a very important expressive freedom because that economic censorship has not yet arrived. We can still have our feet on the ground and talk about society and philosophical conflicts that are being lost elsewhere. I feel free and I think that, overall, the arts in Latin America are in good health. But when you go to some places in Europe or the United States there is a deficit of art that really engages with society. Censorship has changed its face. Currently, artists are absolutely censored everywhere and do not realize it because the form has changed. It is necessary to look at contemporary forms of economic censorship instead of focusing on previous forms of political censorship. There has not been a time in the world where there was more censorship than today. However, I am optimistic.

References

Bardier, Laura. 'Essays: Wilfredo Prieto and the Work of Art as a Direct Gesture.' *Review: Literature and Arts of the Americas* 44, no. 1 (2011): 143–148.

Brown, J. Marshall. 'Accidental Sustainability: An American Planner Wonders Whether Cuba's Culture of Reuse Will Persist.' *Planning* 83, no. 8 (2017): 22–28.

Castro, Fidel. *Palabras a los intelectuales*. Havana: Ediciones del Consejo Nacional de Cultura, 1961.

Cruz, María Caridad, and Roberto Sánchez Medina. *Agriculture in the City: A Key to Sustainability in Havana, Cuba*. Kingston, Jamaica: Ian Randle Publishers, 2003.

Cumaná González, María Caridad. 'Cuban Film and the Burden of Revolutionary Representation.' In *New World Coming: The Sixties and the Shaping of Global Consciousness*, edited by Karen Dubinsky, et al., 153–160. Toronto: Between The Lines, 2009.

Désanges, Guillaume. 'Una rosa es una rosa es un camión,' 1961. s.l. Mousse Publishing, 2012.

Funes, Fernando. *Sustainable Agriculture and Resistance: Transforming Food Production in Cuba*. Oakland, CA: Food First Books, 2002. http://www.infinitejourneyproject.com.

López Arbolay, Dalida. 'Les intuitions illogiques de Wilfredo Prieto.' *Parachute* 125 (2007): 145–149.

Medina, Gretel, and Direlia Lazo. 'Mountains with a Broken Edge: A Dossier.' *Public* 26, no. 52 (December 2015): 125–134.

Montes de Oca, Dannys, et al., eds. *Havana*. Special Issue, *Public* 26, no. 52 (December 2015).

Mosquera, Gerardo. 'Wilfredo Prieto: The Tension of the Image.' *Art Nexus* 7, no. 69 (2008): 50–55.

Pérez Cabrera, Ángel Freddy. 'Cemento de bajo carbono gana espacio en el mundo.' *Granma*, September 2, 2015. http://www.granma.cu/cuba/2015-09-02/cemento-de-bajo-carbono-gana-espacio-en-el-mundo.

Sánchez, Suset. 'Skirmishes to Manage Reality: Collaborative Strategies in Contemporary Cuban Art.' *Artecontexto* 34–35 (2012): 63–69.
Slenske, Michael. 'Method Making: Wilfredo Prieto Embodies Every Aspect of Kurimanzutto.' *Wallpaper*, June 21, 2016. https://www.wallpaper.com/art/cuban-artist-wilfredo-prieto-takes-over-mexico-citys-kurimanzutto-gallery.
Stricker, Pamela. *Toward a Culture of Nature: Environmental Policy and Sustainable Development in Cuba*. Lanham, MD: Lexington Books, 2007.

Syrus Marcus Ware, *Listen to Black Women*, 2017

Syrus Marcus Ware, *Listen to Black Women*, 2017

"I am an activist. I have rallied, protested, hosted discussions, created art and lectured about the movement for black lives and about the concept of our lives mattering. Because black people deserve to live. Black people deserve to thrive. Black people's lives matter. It matters that there is currently an open season on black bodies, an attempted genocide of our people through state sanctioned white supremacy at the highest levels of decision-making. And yet still, people have a hard time embracing this loving concept, this idea that should be the least radical thing to utter: Black Lives Matter.

Instead we are faced with the demand for explanation, for softening, and for a dilution of our messaging. We are faced with the call for All Lives Matter. All lives. As if Kimberlé Crenshaw hadn't written in 1991 about intersectionality, and about how when we make space safe for those most marginalized it makes it safer for everyone else. And so Black Lives Matter. As if the Combahee River Collective hadn't said in 1973 that making the world a better place for black women necessarily meant making a better place for all others on this planet. And so Black Lives Matter.

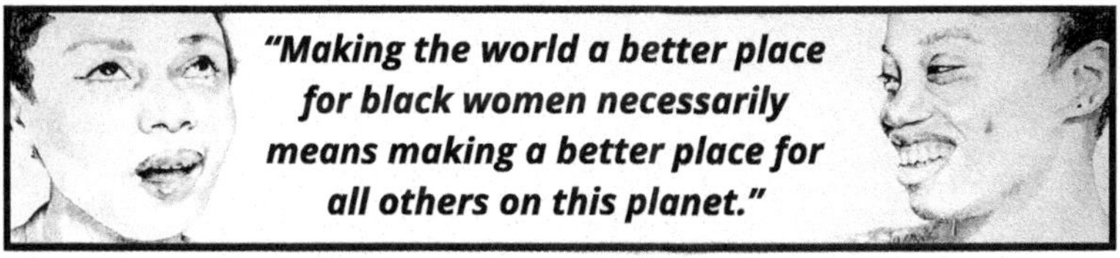

*Instead we are confronted by those who do not know or do not understand these important genealogies of resistance, and we have to justify how much and in what context it matters if we live. But I choose to move, to roll with my people, over to a place where loving and living is central to our organizing, where all black lives matter. How do we get to this place of loving and living? I get to this magical place every single time that I get to connect with my people. We sit outside on apartment stoops and tell stories, we text each other about our days, we laugh until our bellies hurt during our nightly meetings for this rally or that demo, stretching into the night long after we have put the kids to bed, and worked a full day's work. And we eat together. We share this love with each other, and we fall in love with the idea of loving. Because we believe, as Che Guevara told us, "that the true revolutionary is guided by a great feeling of love. It is impossible to think of a genuine revolutionary lacking this quality."**

—excerpt from Syrus Marcus Ware, "Love and Living," Creative Time Summit, Toronto, October 2017

SYRUS MARCUS WARE is a visual artist, activist and curator whose work explores social justice frameworks and black activist culture. A core member of Black Lives Matter-Toronto and a member of Blackness Yes!/Blockorama, he was awarded the Steinert and Ferreiro Award for LGBT community leadership in 2012. Ware's works have been mounted at galleries and festivals across Canada, including *Cripping The Stage* (Toronto, 2016), *Complex Social Change* (Lethbridge, 2015) and *Decolonizing and Decriminalizing Trans Genres* (Winnipeg, 2015). Ware is a PhD candidate in Environmental Studies at York University.

* Ernesto "Che" Guevara, "From Algiers, for *Marcha*: The Cuban Revolution Today" (March 1965)

CHAPTER 10

'CAVCA Buries BIACI': Activating Decolonial Tools in Cartagena de Indias

Martha Herrera-Lasso Gonzalez and Kimberly Skye Richards

This chapter tells the story of the First International Biennial of Contemporary Art Cartagena de Indias (BIACI), held in Cartagena de Indias in the Republic of Colombia from February to April 2014, and the creation of an artist-activist collective forged in response to the lack of support for the region's artists. Keeping with the rampant proliferation of festivals, arts fairs, and biennials as markers of status for cities signaling their readiness to participate in an ever more global (art) system, the BIACI was designed to promote Cartagena as a center for the visual arts at a time when the state was attempting to improve its international image and present a new Colombia—one committed to peace. Although the peace talks would not conclude until November 2016, the agreement between the government of Colombia and the Revolutionary Armed Forces of Colombia-

With appreciation to Muriel Angulo, Alexa Cuesta Flórez, Helena Martin-Franco, Guadalupe González González, Consuelo Salas Leguizamón, and Linda Mae Richards for their encouragement and assistance developing this chapter.

M. Herrera-Lasso Gonzalez • K. S. Richards (✉)
University of California, Berkeley, Berkeley, CA, USA
e-mail: krichar@berkeley.edu

N. Alvarez et al. (eds.), *Sustainable Tools for Precarious Times*, Contemporary Performance InterActions,
https://doi.org/10.1007/978-3-030-11557-9_10

People's Army (FARC-EP) to meet and earnestly discuss bringing an end to 50 years of conflict and violence in Colombia in 2012 was a landmark occasion, especially since efforts to talk to FARC had commenced in 1982. Although the BIACI explicitly shied away from making an overt political statement, or contextualizing itself within Colombia's political situation, it is a clear example of biennials conducting politics by other means, and attempting to provide a 'salve' for extraordinary violence.[1] As such, BIACI prompts an examination of precarity and precariousness within a context of festivalization even as we attend to the complex overtures of grief and anger that correspond with living in precarious times.

The BIACI was produced by the International Biennial of Contemporary Art Foundation of Cartagena de Indias, a nonprofit foundation created and promoted by a group of Colombian entrepreneurs and private entities, and supported by the Ministry of Culture.[2] The biennial brought together 137 artists from 47 countries in a festival and educational program spanning the city. The event was designed to attract the globetrotting art elite, as well as serve as a pedagogical tool about contemporary arts to the people of Colombia, and particularly the youth of Cartagena through school programs, free conferences, art appreciation talks, and workshops. When the BIACI was announced, a group of local artists petitioned the curator for inclusion, suggesting people and places that would add value to the biennial. When they realized local arts and local artists would not be included in BIACI's programming, three Carthagenian artists, Muriel Angulo, Alexa Cuesta Flórez, and Helena Martin-Franco, who

[1] On politics and Biennials, see Caroline Jones, 'Biennial Culture: A Longer History,' in *The Biennial Reader: An Anthology of Large-Scale Perennial Exhibitions of Contemporary Art*, ed. Elena Filipovic, Marieke Van Hal, and Solveig Øvstebø (Bergen: Bergen Kursthall, 2010), 66–86.

[2] The Ministry of Culture primarily provides support for cultural initiatives such as the BIACI Foundation allocating funds through the Programa Nacional de Estímulos as well as granting permission to use spaces under the Ministry's jurisdiction. The Ministry of Culture and its regional entities have no direct involvement in the selection processes or the content of the projects they support. Nevertheless, one of the harshest critiques that CAVCA made was the permissiveness and complicity of cultural authorities in the use of local infrastructure and public funds at the service of the BIACI Foundation's agenda. See 'Manifiesto Emputao!' *CAVCA: Comunidad de Artistas Visuales de Cartagena y Bolívar*, February 7, 2014. http://cavca-cartagena.blogspot.mx/p/manifiesto-emputao.html. For more on the National Incentives Program see 'Programa Nacional de Estímulos,' *MinCultura*. http://www.mincultura.gov.co/planes-y-programas/programas/programa-nacional-estimulos/Paginas/default.aspx.

had previously organized together as Colectivo Feminista in 2010, a feminist artist collective, led the creation of an artistic collective and nonprofit entity, entitled the Community of Visual Artists of Cartagena and Bolívar (CAVCA) so as to represent the interests of a faction of contemporary visual artists from the area. In order to convey CAVCA's grievances, and draw attention to the colonial processes in operation, Angulo, Cuesta Flórez, and Martín-Franco created *Las Meninas Emputás!*, a performance project consisting of disruptive interventions online and in public spaces in Cartagena during the biennial. The group takes its name from Diego Velázquez's famous 1656 portrait of the Spanish infanta Margarita de Austria surrounded by her servants—the *meninas*. In the painting, servants surround the infanta as she entertains the sovereign (King Philip IV of Spain), whose image is reflected in a mirror in the background. Similar to an illustration of the process of creating a royal painting, *Las Meninas* captures the spectacle of artistic production from the vantage point and subject position of the sovereign and calls into question a history of art about kings and queens.

In alluding to this artwork, one with which an international art audience would be familiar, the artists of CAVCA conjure a European model of 'excellence,' and draw attention to the servant's anger at the labor serviced behind the scenes of artistic production. Viewers of Las Meninas Emputás' performance actions are framed as the elite for whom the spectacle is designed to entertain. Las Meninas, in their large, powdered wigs, matte white clown paint, and rouged lips, are '*emputás*'—'very fucking angry' about being infantilized by the sovereigns they serve. By parodying the 'grand masters,' and alluding to the European colonial aesthetic models and values that would later be implemented around the world, Las Meninas Emputás! launch a critique of the colonial machinery at the biennial, one that is especially poignant given that the court of Louis XIV represented an aesthetic aspiration for the rest of Europe at the time when Europe was colonizing the Americas. Moreover, by employing the language of the core/periphery in their protests, the local artists exposed the colonial logic through which the BIACI operated, articulating the nuanced internal politics of Colombia that could easily remain opaque to international eyes (Fig. 10.1).

Inspired by the performance actions of Las Meninas Emputás!, this essay draws attention to the ways in which Colombia's centralized political organization affected the administration and curation of the BIACI, and how Bogotá, Colombia's capital, continues to serve as the semi-periphery in the implementation of international values on the centuries-

Fig. 10.1 *Las Meninas Emputás!* Alexa Cuesta Flórez, Helena Martin-Franco, and Muriel Angulo dramatize the aggrandizement of European art and culture. Credit: Las Meninas Emputás

old colonial stage that is Cartagena de Indias. The concept of core/periphery as understood here aligns with Immanuel Wallerstein's formulation of a world-system as a social system that can be used to explain the dynamics of a capitalist world economy. According to Wallerstein, a world-system operates within an internal logic in which the core produces the ideological principles and structures of the system, the periphery provides the labor force that sustains the core, and the semi-periphery mediates between the two and produces its own core–periphery dynamics in various shifting configurations.[3] Given the political organization of Colombia as a central republic (as opposed to a federal republic), in which

[3] Immanuel Wallerstein, *The Modern World-System: Capitalist Agriculture and the Origins of the European World-Economy in the Sixteenth Century* (New York: Academic Press, 1976), 226.

all nation-wide political and administrative functions are concentrated under a central organ in the capital city, and the power of the oligarchy, Bogotá's role as semi-periphery was essential to incorporating outside values and aesthetics into Cartagena. Although a move toward decentralization of culture has been an important part of Colombia's official cultural policies in the last 20 years,[4] Colombian participation in the BIACI Foundation and curatorial team was primarily made up of Colombians based in Bogotá who were already elite. This read to many artists in Cartagena and in the province of Bolívar as yet another centralist operation acting in the service of a Eurocentric core (mediated by Colombian oligarchies) that could legitimize Colombia as both a peaceful and a modern actor on the global (art) stage, while sustaining the values of the existing world-system.

In order to draw attention to these processes, CAVCA developed a repertoire of strategies to launch their complaints, including art-activist postering, digital vandalism, the parodying of 'great art' through performance, and the staging of mock funerals. By comparing the strategies the BIACI employed with those generated by CAVCA, this chapter speaks of the sustainability of colonial logic through the arts and the conditions of possibility for its undoing. It begets the question: what does it mean to seek out 'sustainable' practices from subjects living in such precarious situations that they do not have the resources to plan for the long term? Can staging one's own precarious existence produce the tools to sustain its undoing? And how might precariousness be used as a basis for exercises, alliances, and coalitions that seek to overcome precarity?

[4] In order to meet the expectations of the 1991 Constitution (which defines the political system as a 'unitary decentralized republic' and introduce reforms granting certain levels of autonomy to the 32 territorial entities), efforts to decentralize aspects of Colombian administration were set into motion. Amongst them was the creation of the Ministry of Culture (1997) and the National System for Culture. Fundamental to their objectives was the decentralization of cultural administration, and the promotion of civic participation at a local and regional level. To these ends, the Regional Development initiative was launched, which consisted of the creation of cultural public entities in provinces and municipalities, as well as training in arts administration, awards and recognition for local cultural initiatives, and in 2010, the creation of the Strategy for Regional Promoters. The Ministry of Culture acknowledges some of the shortcomings and limitations of these initiatives in *Sistema Nacional de Cultura: Estado, Retos y Perspectivas* (Bogotá: Ministerio de Cultura, 2013). http://www.mincultura.gov.co/areas/fomento-regional/Documents/sistema_nal_cultura_FINAL_baja.pdf.

BIACI's Frame; Cartagena's Stage

Before moving into an analysis of the art-activist strategies deployed by Las Meninas Emputás!, it is necessary to provide some context to the BIACI to understand their anger. It is not coincidental that a biennial was staged in Cartagena in 2014 given the extraordinary event of the 2012–2016 peace talks between the Colombian government and the FARC-EP, which aimed to bring an end to the armed political conflict and guerilla warfare in Colombia. The origin of the conflict goes back to 1920s agrarian disputes in which peasants fought over ownership of coffee lands. Since independence, the Colombian government has been commanded by oligarchs (such as coffee growers) with little interest in economic or social reform, or institutional development to protect peasants and workers. The absence of labor laws and the distribution of land perpetuated a colonial system that left much of the country in dire poverty. In the 1960s, left-wing guerrilla insurgencies gained considerable public support as they advocated for the redistribution of land and greater equality. Eventually, FARC became involved with the drug cartels, resorted to bombings and kidnappings to gain territory and finances, and lost much of its popular support, but it had a considerable militant presence that the federal army could not defeat. In 2002 the country elected President Álvaro Uribe Vélez after he promised to defeat the guerillas and bring an end to the terrorist activities and drug trafficking. He allied with the United States military to improve army training and intelligence and successfully weakened the guerrilla's power. But the geography of Colombia combined with the diffuse structure of guerilla warfare meant that the war could not end militaristically. The peace process commenced in September 2012 in Havana, Cuba, at which the Colombian state, represented by former defense minister Juan Manuel Santos, and FARC announced consensus on a plan toward peace and reconciliation, and the government began a process of reparation for victims of conflict.

The postcolonial history of Colombia is extraordinarily violent—so much so in fact, that historians and cultural critics often describe conflict as that which defines Colombia as a nation.[5] Both the guerrilla and paramilitary

[5] For example, Andrea Fanta Castro, Alejandro Herrero-Olaizola, and Chloe Rutter-Jensen write that conflict 'continues to permeate [Colombia's] political discourse and cultural production (almost) to the point of no return.' Andrea Fanta Castro, Alejandro Herrero-Olaizola, and Chloe Rutter-Jensen, 'Introduction: Territories of Conflict through Colombian Cultural Studies,' in *Territories of Conflict: Traversing Colombia through Cultural*

groups were accused of engaging in drug trafficking and terrorism, and all parties (including the state) have been criticized for numerous human rights violations. According to a study by Colombia's National Centre for Historical Memory, 220,000 people died in the conflict between 1958 and 2013, most of them civilians, and more than five million civilians were forced from their homes between 1985 and 2012, generating the world's second largest population of internally displaced persons.[6] Staging high-profile cultural events alongside transitional justice endeavors is a common strategy for states to frame and narrate a shift from an authoritarian regime to democratic social forms in the aftermath of mass violations of human rights.[7] Such a process often deploys performative celebrations to herald its enactment. The BIACI at once functioned within this model and against it, for it generated an image of Colombia as a safe space all the while avoiding any explicit political commentary. The biennial was not given an overarching theme, but was curated with the idea that the 'powerful presence of the past' in the streets of Cartagena would serve as a remarkable backdrop. The colonial history of Cartagena presented an intriguing context for international guests that also worked to overpower more recent, sometimes state-sanctioned forms of violence.

The staging of the event in Cartagena de Indias, Colombia's signature tourist destination and cosmopolitan center, was specific to the re-imagining of Colombia as 'post-conflictual.' Cartagena has always been a colonial 'destination city': an essential link in the route of the West Indies; a haven for the treasures and riches of the Spanish crown; a port for trade between Spain and its overseas empire; a site of the Caribbean slave trade and the Spanish Inquisition; and, more recently, an urban core transformed by industrialization and immigration. Cartagena is robust with museums, churches, public monuments, statues, plazas, colonial architecture, a bilingual hotel infrastructure, and a frivolous tourist economy of

Studies, ed. Andrea Fanta Castro, Alejandro Herrero-Olaizola, and Chloe Rutter-Jensen (New York: University of Rochester Press, 2017), 1.

[6] 'Estadísticas del conflicto armado en Colombia,' *Centro Nacional de Memoria Histórica*. http://www.centrodememoriahistorica.gov.co/micrositios/informeGeneral/estadisticas.html.

[7] For example, the Havana Biennial (1984) was born in the utopian context of the Cuban Revolution, and was part of Cuba's strategy for crafting a positive image of itself and fighting the isolation imposed by the United States. As well, the Johannesburg Biennial, which began in 1995 after years of isolation and cultural boycotts, attempted to formulate an international platform at a time when the nation was grappling with the legacy of apartheid.

partying and vacations that only seems to contribute to the enormous social problems, poverty, and resentment around it.[8] The BIACI thrust Cartagena into the 'global biennial phenomenon,' the trend of cities staging large-scale international exhibitions curated by guest (foreign) curators in order to signify participation in a global community by contributing to the display and consumption of international contemporary art, all the while promoting their city's image to boost their profile abroad and encourage tourism.[9]

Although biennials share nationalist and developmental agendas, their politics of internationalism and cosmopolitanism is linked to (neo-)colonial and neoliberal agendas. These points are made clear in the history of Cartagena presented in the biennial catalog, which omits any indication of political violence or of local artistic production. Although Cartagena was relatively protected from the violence taking place across the country because of its location on the coast, the BIACI catalogue narrative services a political agenda that dissipates the violence of Colombia's past, and substantiates George Yudicé's claim that nearly any invocation of culture today is expedient in relation to economic or political purposes or goals.[10] While it would have been an error for BIACI's organizers to fall into the trap of reinvesting in Colombia's violent history as its predominant marker of cultural distinction, the failure to generate spaces for the people of Colombia to speak to the conditions of their life was remiss.

[8] For centuries, Cartagena was a focal point of confrontation between the principal European powers vying for control of the 'New World.' Defensive fortifications were built by the Spanish in 1586 and extended until the eighteenth century, leaving it as an eminent and extensive example of military architecture of the sixteenth, seventeenth, and eighteenth centuries recognized by UNESCO as having outstanding universal value. Today, Cartagena has a population of nearly 850,000, and exists as two cities: one inside the colonial Spanish wall that caters to tourists, and one outside, where most Colombian people live. As a World Heritage site, it already receives an influx of international funds through tourism and real estate speculation, which have caused processes of gentrification in which the people and the culture of the city are being devalued. The period between 1950 and 2000 has been described as the 'second golden age of Cartagena' due to the development of the petrochemical sector and port service expansion projects. As well, the second half of the twentieth century brought a new appreciation for the arts with the reopening of The Institute of Music and Fine Arts in 1958, and the creation of several galleries, museums, and festivals, and made Cartagena the ideal host for cultural events and tourism.

[9] See Jones, 'Biennial Culture,' 69, on the contemporary art biennial's links to nineteenth-century expositions, tourism, and spectacular urbanism.

[10] George Yudicé, *The Expediency of Culture: Uses of Culture in the Global Era* (Durham, NC: Duke University Press, 2003).

BIACI's organizers were not sensitive to the deep forms of systematic violence and precarity as a result of Colombia's centralized economic, political, and cultural power that has otherwise caused anger and grievances.

Thus, while a human rights emergency frames this case study, the precarious subjects under discussion are not performing in response to the human rights violations, though they are making visible the continuation of key political conditions that enabled such violence to occur in the first place. Argentinian philosopher Enrique Dussel describes the Latin American semi-periphery as 'the educated neocolonial elites, loyal to the empires in turn, who distanced themselves from their own "people", and used them as hostages to their political dependency.'[11] The oligarchic nature of Colombian society is revealed by the persistence of deep economic and social inequalities. According to World Bank estimates, despite some advances in the fight against poverty, by 2015 Colombia was the eleventh most unequal country in the world.[12] The power of Colombian elites is mainly rooted in the second highest unequal distribution of land in Latin America given that 1.15% of Colombia's population owns 52% of the country's land.[13] Politicians are linked by family ties and clientelistic mechanisms, and economic elites have been able to block redistributive public policies and social reforms. The 'crisis' that the local artists of Cartagena face is not directly the result of Colombia's history of violence, but the cultural eugenics of cultural management: the exclusion and continual invisibilizing of regional artists (specifically from the Caribbean region of Colombia) in the programming of cultural events with this degree of international visibility, and that power's ignorance of the local context of art beyond small-scale public initiatives to promote regional art and participation. It is about a deeply ingrained colonial logic that has

[11] Our translation. Dussel understands neocolonialism as the ways in which the role once played by Spain or Portugal in these Latin American countries is substituted by a self-imposed dependency on other European or North American countries. These elites adapt to an empire 'in turn,' reproducing the colonial logic that governed their relationship to Spain or Portugal in their relationship to other actors. Enrique Dussel, *Filosofía de la cultura y la liberación* (Ciudad de México: UACM, 2006), 30.

[12] World Bank, 'World Development Indicators.' https://data.worldbank.org/indicators/SI.POVERTY.GINI.

[13] *Informe Nacional de Desarrollo Humano 2011. Colombia Rural: Razones para la esperanza. Resumen Ejecutivo* (Bogotá: PNUD, 2011), 50. http://www.co.undp.org/content/colombia/es/home/library/human_development/informe-nacional-de-desarrollo-humano-2011.html.

normalized these forms of precarity for artists situated in the periphery, and that has been adapted into the cultural institutions of Colombia. And it is about cultural policies designed to service Colombia's oligarchy.

The art-activist actions of CAVCA draw attention to a precarious condition unlike those typically described in the Global North and Anglophone discourse. The point is not the transformation of labor practices in advanced capitalist systems under the impact of globalization and information technologies, or public funding cuts to the arts and social welfare institutions. Precarity in this context designates 'that politically induced condition in which certain populations suffer from failing social and economic networks of support more than others, and become differentially exposed to injury, violence, and death.'[14] For the artists under discussion, their precariousness is defined in relation to the colonial machine of the art system and the absence of funding and opportunity for local artists to perform on the global stage, and make a sustainable life.[15] The presence of the BIACI showed that the arts can attract significant investments to the region, yet this doorway to exchange and investment is heavily policed by centralist oligarchies and the colonial logics they service.

In the face of this precariousness, artists of Cartagena formalized and created a united front. Las Meninas Emputás! came out of a series of conversations (mostly online) in which Martin-Franco, Angulo, and Cuesta Flórez combined their individual art practices with video and sound, collage, and public space with their primary resources: their bodies and their voices.[16] Martin-Franco, Cuesta Flórez, and Angulo produced a series of

[14] Judith Butler, *Notes Towards a Performative Theory of Assembly* (Cambridge, MA: Harvard University Press, 2015), 34.

[15] Following Yates McKee, we use the term 'art system' as a way to 'displace the deeply engrained figure of the "art world".' Where 'art world' connotes a 'unitary, self-enclosed cultural universe of like-minded cogniscenti making, viewing, judging, and sometimes buying and selling works of art,' the phrase 'art system' refers to the core elements of that system that remain within 'the relatively comfortable *habitus* of "art" as a professional field.' Yates McKee, *Strike Art: Contemporary Art and the Post-Occupy Condition* (London: Verso, 2016), 12.

[16] It is interesting to note the distinct geographic locations of the artists - Cuesta Flórez based in Cartagena is closest to the site and her livelihood is most directly connected to her reputation there; Angulo, based in Bogotá, moves between the centralized dynamics of Bogotá and its dependent province of Bolívar. Martín-Franco, based in Montreal since 1999, extends the reach of this alliance into the Northern Hemisphere and provides a comparative perspective to how notions of precarity are lived differently, and how activists' practices travel and unfold in diverse sites. In our conversation, Martin-Franco commented that she has

loud and visible on- and offline performances that accompanied the biennial, which have been re-engaged to protest institutionalized art practices in the years since. They variously act as individuals, as Las Meninas Emputás!, and as the public face of CAVCA—an ambiguity that allows them to protect each other and the artist community of Cartagena. Las Meninas Emputás have found that although many local and regional artists privately support CAVCA, they have few public allies, since openly supporting CAVCA risks their reputations and exposes them to further vulnerability. 'Tenemos muchos respeto, pero poco aliados públicos. Estamos solas [We have a lot of respect, but few public allies. We're on our own].'[17] As Martin-Franco expressed in our interview, they face a long and difficult struggle, trying to build trust against all odds since people do not want to lose the few exhibition spaces they have.

Moreover, the BIACI employed over 350 Cartagenians as floor managers, aides, technicians, and production assistants during the biennial. Many of the artists who belonged to CAVCA made up this number (since they had both the knowledge of local context and the specialized labor, they were perfect candidates for these jobs), and given the precarious economic conditions under which many of them live, work was not an easy thing to turn down. This aspect of the event structure is not only linked to apparatuses of knowledge production, but is indicative of the placement of the Cartagenian artists within the world picture that determines their value as merely service workers in the context of the international art system. The employment of local artists as exhibit guides or specialized labor in the execution of artworks by invited artists resonates with Wallerstein's description of the interdependency between the core and the periphery, in which the periphery provides the labor force that sustains the core.

For Martin-Franco, Cuesta Flórez, and Angulo, these performances are *un*sustainable: they are risky to maintain (and indeed, their individual professional trajectories and reputations have suffered as a direct result of their

never done this type of protest work in Montreal since she has been unable to find other artists to take these risks with her. She says that many people would support her if she were to do it herself, but they are not willing to protest alongside her, and she insists protest is collective work. Although there is frustration in Montreal on many fronts, she attributes this unwillingness to engage to fear: as there is more support, there is more to lose. Helena Martin-Franco, Skype interview, January 9, 2018. Quotations by the artists in Spanish are included in both languages. We find it important to retain the original language the artists work and live in, offering translation only as a resource to readers who otherwise would not have access.

[17] Ibid.

protests on- and offline); yet, they are simultaneously the only means by which they feel their situation as Cartagenian artists might become less precarious. They illustrate Judith Butler's acute observation that 'acting in the name of that support, without that support, is the paradox of plural performative action under conditions of precarity.'[18] Precariousness is the result of our interdependence—that life and work are dependent upon one another, and the fact that our livelihood is dependent on anonymous others and on infrastructure—be that the environment, social relations, or networks of support and sustenance. Recognizing this interdependency and the inequities of our dependence on particular others often leads to fear and the suspension of dissent, further perpetuating cycles of violence and the continuation of power as is. It is a more subtle, less spectacular, institutionalized set of colonial practices that constitutes these artists' precariousness than the large part of the Colombian population who lives in fear of assassinations, disappearances, extrajudicial executions, or massacres, especially under the siege of the guerillas. Yet while the precariousness under discussion refers specifically to a group of artists, their situation points to the possibility of generating new, alternative narratives about the conditions of precarity on international stages by allowing art to operate as 'a restorative agent of life and of the social fabric.'[19]

The performance interventions by Las Meninas Emputás disrupted the BIACI and the image of Cartagena it attempted to cultivate, and propelled the precariousness of artistic production in Cartagena into light. The biennial was never staged again, despite initial plans for a second event in 2016. While it would be a leap to claim that CAVCA's performance actions engendered the 'death' of the BIACI, the performance intervention, 'CAVCA buries BIACI' in the public space of Cartagena did produce actions beyond the event horizon of the biennial. CAVCA continues to be a formalized society of artists and the interlocutor of the artist community before various cultural entities, public and private administrators, political and social institutions at local, regional, national, and international levels. The collective works to 'dignify and highlight the work of the artist of this region in today's society,' and protest the usurption of the name 'Cartagena de Indias,' and allocation of public resources (infrastructure, buildings, and money) for private events. Beyond the localized injustices CAVCA protests, the artist-activist strategies deployed in 'CAVCA buries BIACI' help us to better understand the power of performing one's vulnerability as an embodied strategy of resistance.

[18] Butler, *Notes*, 65.
[19] 'Manifiesto Emputao!'.

CAVCA Buries BIACI

When the BIACI commenced on February 7, 2014, CAVCA launched their *Manifesto Emputao!* (online and on the streets), whereby they publicly rejected the exclusionary tactics employed by the BIACI. Las Meninas Emputás staged readings of the Manifesto Emputao on the interactive installation 'Say it Loud' located in Plaza del Polo. Designed by Satch Hoyt to investigate freedom of expression, the installation was composed of a metallic ladder surrounded by a mountain of books covering civil and human rights, the African diaspora, and cultural and social issues in Colombia. At the top of the ladder, a microphone rested on the book *Seize the Time* by Bobby Seale, a member of the Black Panther Party, and James Brown's classic 'Say it Loud! I'm Black and I'm Proud!' served as a soundscape. Visitors ascending the ladder were able to declare what they pleased. Las Meninas Emputás usurped Hoyt's installation to manifest their rejection to the exclusionary practices of the BIACI, which they detail under eight headings: (1) Invisibility and Exclusion; (2) Critical Discourse vs. The Art Market; (3) Centralism; (4) Disdain for Local Context; (5) Usurpation; (6) Improvisation; (7) Abuse of Power; (8) Paternalism.[20] The language of the manifesto speaks of 'una visión centro-periferia [a center-periphery vision]' by which the BIACI was conceived, operating through 'procesos curatoriales centralistas y colonizadores [centralist and colonizing curatorial practices].' It ends with a rejection of the BIACI 'por ser un evento privatizado, elitista, mediático e invasor [as a privatized, elitist, mediatized and invasive event]' and demands an explanation by Cartagena authorities 'por la permisividad y complicidad [for their permissiveness and complicity]' with the biennial organizers. This manifesto does not manifest the new; it does not announce, it denounces old hegemonic practices, thus exposing the logic that has fashioned the terrain in order to make room for cultural forms that have continued to exist in a place of exteriority.[21] By reading the manifesto on Hoyt's platform, Las Meninas Emputás leveraged a space sanctioned by the biennial

[20] Ibid.

[21] In his decolonial theory of transmodernity, Enrique Dussel takes Emmanuel Levinas's notion of exteriority to situate the Other historically and politically, and uses it to refer to the totality of alterity, considering 'lo declarado por la Modernidad como la *Exterioridad desechada, no valorizada*, lo "inútil" de las culturas [that which Modernity has declared as *discarded, non-valuable exteriority*, what is "useless" of Other cultures].' Enrique Dussel, *Filosofías del Sur* (Ciudad de México: Ediciones Akal, 2015), 29.

for their own art-activism. Yet, they did not merely assimilate the domain of speakability within the biennial, they broke open the authority of its regime.

This feat might be considered an example of 'the art of complaining,' a strategy associated with the Guerilla Girls, a group of female artists who have, since 1985, used humor and statistics in performance actions, posters, and billboards to draw attention to sexism, racism, and corruption in the art system, and call for a history of art that reflects a diversity of experience rather than preserving the history of white men, and their wealth and power. Communicating a complaint, or vocalizing a dissatisfaction or injustice, requires identifying a target audience, and articulating a small aspect of that critique in a creative way in a manner that will catch their attention and change their mind. The Guerrilla Girls found that dressing in gorilla costumes concealed their identities, played with the notion of them being guerillas (as in freedom fighters), as well as comically represented the dehumanization of women's bodies in art and as muses, objects rather than agents of history. Las Meninas' colonial costumes similarly create a comic politics of subversion that desecrate that which has been deemed 'great art.'

Amongst CAVCA's objections, Las Meninas Emputás spoke of the *Colombia Hoy* (Colombia Today) initiative, describing it as an improvisational tactic through which local content was excluded from the biennial. *Colombia Hoy* consisted of a two-month open call for Colombian artists, and it presented the only opportunity for Colombian and Cartagenian artists who had not been invited directly by the BIACI to display their work in the biennial—though in a separate exhibit. Of the initiative, Bonilla commented,

> We felt it was important that the Colombian artists be placed in a context where the national movements in art could be evaluated and seen together. Many of our visitors of the biennial may have never been to Colombia before and we wanted to ensure that they came away with a greater understanding of the current trends in Colombian art, as well as the ways that Colombian artists are responding to broader international movements. The point is not to set them aside but rather to make sure Colombian artists are given adequate space and really a larger presence in the biennial.[22]

[22] Ashton Cooper, 'Exploring the Presence of the Past at Colombia's First Biennial,' *Blouin Art Info*, February 7, 2014. http://www.blouinartinfo.com/news/story/1006822/exploring-the-presence-of-the-past-at-colombias-first.

These statements verify that Bonilla was aware of the importance of incorporating a narrative of Colombian art into the biennial, and producing a larger space for Colombian artists. CAVCA's main criticism of this initiative was that the BIACI failed to put out a public and timely call, with at least a year of administration, circulation, participation, and evaluation by the artists and academics of Cartagena. Without denying merit or relevance to the artists exhibited, the design of the open call, and the fact that only nine artists were selected (out of nearly four hundred applications), shows that those artists that the *Colombia Hoy* exhibit claimed to represent had in fact very little or no agency on how 'current trends in Colombian art' were curated.

Another reason that Las Meninas Emputás' parody of canonical European art was so befitting was because of the education initiatives implemented by the BIACI. In an interview, Sichel commented that she hoped that the BIACI would serve as a catalyst for generating greater interest in art in the region: 'I hope this biennial, in a couple of years, will have taught people to see what contemporary art is.'[23] Such sentiments align with BIACI's claim that there is no presence of contemporary art in Cartagena, and that the festival would endow the Colombian population with an education on contemporary art. As part of BIACI's educational initiative, 2500 schoolchildren in Cartagena and 380 students from 12 universities in Colombia attended the event; 75 students from fine arts institutions, such as the University of Cartagena, the Fine Arts University of Medellín, and the University of the Atlantic, did internships with the BIACI Foundation, and more than 100 young people from Cartagena acted as gallery guides. Organizers boasted about introducing international art to local children—'many of [whom] have never seen any international work of art up close'—and offered 12 'art appreciation' workshops directed to children in impoverished areas of Cartagena.[24] The exposure of youth to international art appealed to schools as a mechanism of introducing students to different cultures and contemporary art, and yet this intercultural dialogue was essentially a monologue.

This goal of education is explicitly colonial, and it speaks directly of several points outlined in the manifesto, including a disdain for local culture and a paternalistic approach. Enrique Dussel makes a distinction

[23] Ashton Cooper, 'Notes from Colombia: Why the World Needs Another Biennial,' *Blouin Art Info*, April 4, 2014. http://www.blouinartinfo.com/news/story/1022190/notes-from-colombia-why-the-world-needs-another-biennial.

[24] Ibid.

between three forms of revolution/liberation: the patriotic revolution that refers to national liberation, the social revolution that works toward the liberation of the oppressed classes, and the cultural revolution that takes place on the terrains of pedagogy, youth, and culture.[25] The efforts exerted by the BIACI around educating Cartagena youth to consume art according to the Eurocentric values prove the importance of a revolution that exposes these strategies in an attempt to reclaim local values in the eyes of international visitors and, more importantly, in the eyes of its own youth. Dussel asks, 'How can one deny the disdain of what one is, if not by initiating the path towards discovering one's own value? Postcolonial cultures must indeed decolonize, and in order to do so, they must value themselves.'[26] The possibility of sustaining CAVCA's decolonial project depends on the possibility of reclaiming these pedagogical and cultural spaces as their own, and exposing the ways in which colonial logics are reproduced.

In addition to the public stagings of the manifesto, Las Meninas Emputás organized a series of burial performances around Cartagena designed to enact the mourning of the death of local art and the burial of the BIACI. They postered over BIACI promotions with images that read 'Aquí yace el arte local. Cartagena, Febrero 7–Abril 7 de 2014. Descansa en la "Paz" de la BIACI-RNC [Here lays local art. Cartagena, February 7th–April 7th 2014. Rest in the "Peace" of the BIACI-RNC].' Dressed in their colonial garb, they walked the city, mourning, crying, putting up posters, laying flowers made out of these posters under BIACI signs and at BIACI venues as they recited their prayer in a tone of lamentation:

> ¡Exponme! ¡internacionalízame! ¡asimílame! Espíritu de la BIACI ¡hibrídame! ¡tolérame! ¡escúchame! ¡conóceme! ¡descúbreme! Espíritu de la BIACI ¡infantilízame! ¡globalízame! ¡blanquéame! Espíritu de la BIACI, descanse en paz, Amen [Exhibit me! Internationalize me! Assimilate me! Spirit of the BIACI, hybridize me! Tolerate me! Listen to me! Know me! Discover me! Spirit of the BIACI, infantilize me! Globalize me! Whiten me! Spirit of the BIACI, rest in peace, Amen].[27]

[25] Dussel, 31.

[26] Our translation, Dussel, 50.

[27] Helena Martin-Franco, 'CAVCA Entierra la BIACI,' *YouTube video*, April 10, 2014. https://www.youtube.com/watch?list=PL6XhSMVHlyW_zOWj9R1ZUJMxdHannr1O5&v=E2XvvIUv66M.

The artist's comic portrayal of Las Meninas proved to be an effective albeit risky tactic of taking to the street and speaking truth to power. On one occasion, Angulo and Cuesta Flórez were harassed by the police who claimed their posters visually polluted public space. These same images proclaiming the death of local art were included as online comments in all posts on the BIACI Facebook page with such fervor and consistency that CAVCA and Las Meninas Emputás were collectively and individually blocked from the BIACI account, all the while generating traffic and discussion on their own Facebook page and blogs.[28] Although these actions share similarities with the work of internet trolls, who use the space of 'comments' to make mischief, the content and purpose of these actions go beyond a desire to provoke, humiliate, or abuse for their own enjoyment, and are not masked in anonymity or protected by the distance of the web. The term 'digital vandalism,' then, indicates a stylized direct action on social media, one that accompanies and magnifies a series of in-person activist actions. Moreover, the term 'vandalism' evokes a sense of the proprietary relations that relate to conflicts over space and the legal sense of precarious as describing 'the situation wherein your tenancy on your land is in someone else's hands.'[29]

When making demands did not work, Martin-Franco, Angulo, and Cuesta Flórez developed art of complaint that sought to correct the inadequacies of the present through parodic performance and demystification. For Las Meninas Emputás, and many of the CAVCA artists who performed these burials alongside them, the precarity of their circumstances as local artists in Cartagena denies them even the right to mourn:

> Es hora de hacer balances. No tenemos tiempo para hacer duelos porque se nos han negado todos los espacios. El duelo se hace cuando se ama y se respeta una pérdida. No es el caso con la primera Bienal de Cartagena ni con respecto al Salón Inter, que todavía no está muerto, pero que es nuestro deber ayudar a morir. [It's time to put things into balance. We don't have time to mourn because we have been denied all spaces. You mourn when you love and when you respect a loss. This is not the case with the first Cartagena Biennial nor with the Salón Inter, which are not yet dead, and which it is our duty to help die.][30]

[28] In places like Cartagena, where there is limited access to technology, and many do not have artist webpages, Facebook is an essential tool in the dissemination of artwork.

[29] Lauren Berlant, *Cruel Optimism* (Durham, NC: Duke University Press, 2011), 192.

[30] Jorge Peñuela, 'Elogio de las Emputadas Cartageneras,' *Liberatorio.org*, April 11, 2014. http://liberatorio.org/?p=1638.

Their strategy was to stage the death of a more valuable life (BIACI's) in order to draw attention to their own exclusion, their own death. In this way, CAVCA artists exposed the hierarchies of value that prize certain lives over others, exposing 'the differential distribution of precariousness.'[31] Martin-Franco poignantly remarks, 'Recently I was reading a very interesting text by Judith Butler where she says that these people who [...] have a status of precarity—don't even have the status of human. And if on top of that we are invisibilized, imagine where we are left [...]. I think that's what I'm most fucking angry about.'[32] In order to begin to think of sustainability, both in their lives and of their tactics, these subjects find they must first address and situate their conditions of precarity in relation to the colonial machinery that has normalized this distribution of precariousness. The decolonial move here insists on the need to expose a colonial logic in order to undo it, and thus realign social, economic, and political conditions from the perspective of the periphery, from a place of exteriority: 'That denied "exteriority," the living and latent alterity that indicates the existence of an unsuspected cultural richness that is slowly being reborn like fire from the embers.'[33]

The curatorial policies of the BIACI not only deemed what art is valuable and what is not, but who is valuable and who is not. Curation prescribes the limits of the sayable—of what can be said and shown and sanctioned within the public sphere. Judith Butler clearly articulates, 'the public sphere is constituted in part by what can appear, and the regulation of the sphere of appearance is one way to establish what will count as reality, and what will not.'[34] At this pivotal moment in Colombia, the stakes of representation to the international community were especially high for those in power. Yet, the BIACI created the optimal conditions for CAVCA to reveal the reality of their vulnerability to the political situation. Through

[31] Butler, *Notes*, 34.

[32] 'En estos días me estaba leyendo un texto muy interesante de Judith Butler en donde decía que estas personas que están invizibilizadas por la sociedad, que tienen ese estatus de precariedad, no tienen ni siquiera el estatus de persona. Y si nos invizibilizan más aún, pues imagínate cómo quedamos. Yo creo que es una cosa supremamente—una falta de ética total. Y yo creo que eso es lo que más emputá me tiene.' 'Emputaó testimony by Muriel Angulo,' ed. Helena Martin-Franco, February 26, 2014. https://www.youtube.com/watch?v=sThaywRenLI.

[33] Our translation. Dussel, 47.

[34] Judith Butler, *Precarious Lives: The Powers of Mourning and Violence* (London: Verso, 2003), xx.

the formation of CAVCA, Carthaginian artists insisted on their continuing and collective 'thereness,' organizing themselves without hierarchy, and exemplifying the principles of equal treatment that they are demanding.[35]

The story of CAVCA also reminds those of us spectating the BIACI from outside that precariousness is not a recent phenomenon bound predominantly to neoliberal expansion in a post-Fordist age, but is also, in many places in the Americas, the continuation of colonial practices in new formations of civic and national engineering, and that an explicitly decolonial resistance to unsupportive institutions and cultural industries must be the basis for alliance, coalition building, and resistance. As Paula Moya writes, 'the problem is that transnational flows of goods and resources affect the process of knowledge production just as they affect the production of any other commodity. Since its entrance into the emerging capitalist world-system some 500 years ago, Latin America is not and never has been situated as a *producer of knowledge*.'[36] CAVCA's interventions during the biennial reminded both the international art community and their own community that Cartagenians are, indeed, producers of knowledge, and that in order to move beyond their conditions of precarity, it was essential to resist being once again situated within the geopolitics of knowledge as nothing more than labor or producers of raw materials. As Angulo writes on the CAVCA webpage, 'A esos que con su paternalismo tratan de exotizarnos, queremos exigirles mayor rigor en sus investigaciones, y recordarles que en Caribe, también se hace Academia [To those whom with their paternalism try to exotify us, we demand more rigor from your research, and remind you that the Caribbean also produces Academia].'[37]

The story of the BIACI and CAVCA reveals the profound interdependence of the core–periphery dynamics and the privatized and elitist interests that are constitutive of the biennial model, and of the global art system more generally. The decolonial call of these artist-activists is less about attempting to dissolve this interdependence than it is about exposing the

[35] Judith Butler and Athena Athansiou, *Dispossession: The Performative in the Political* (London: Polity, 2013), 197.

[36] Paula Moya, 'Who We Are and From Where We Speak,' *Transmodernity* (Fall 2011): 82–83.

[37] Muriel Angulo, '¿El nuevo traje del emperador?' *CAVCA: Comunidad de Artistas Visuales de Cartagena y Bolívar*, September 4, 2014. http://cavca-cartagena.blogspot.mx/p/la-meninas-emputas.html.

colonial logics that govern it. They attempt to shift the dynamics through which these sectors interact, thereby reaffirming Butler's poignant observation that 'the opposite of precarity is not security, but, rather, the struggle for an egalitarian social and political order in which a livable interdependency is possible.'[38] The tools put forward by CAVCA artists provide useful possibilities not only for those living in precarious situations, but for those situated at the core, inviting them to see more clearly their role within this (neo-)colonial machinery, and conscientiously adjust the terms of our interdependence.

References

Angulo, Muriel. '¿El nuevo traje del emperador.' *CAVCA: Comunidad de Artistas Visuales de Cartagena y Bolívar*, September 4, 2014. http://cavca-cartagena.blogspot.mx/p/la-meninas-emputas.html.

Berlant, Lauren. *Cruel Optimism*. Durham, NC: Duke University Press, 2011.

Butler, Judith. *Precarious Lives: The Powers of Mourning and Violence*. London: Verso, 2003.

———. *Notes Toward a Performative Theory of Assembly*. Cambridge, MA: Harvard University Press, 2015.

Butler, Judith, and Athena Athansiou. *Dispossession: The Performative in the Political*. London: Polity, 2013.

Castro, Andrea Fanta, Alejandro Herrero-Olaizola, and Chloe Rutter-Jensen. 'Introduction: Territories of Conflict through Colombian Cultural Studies.' In *Territories of Conflict: Traversing Colombia through Cultural Studies*, edited by Andrea Fanta Castro, Alejandro Herrero-Olaizola, and Chloe Rutter-Jensen, 1–22. New York: University of Rochester Press, 2017.

CAVCA: Comunidad de Artistas Visuales de Cartagena y Bolívar. 'Manifiesto Emputao!' February 7, 2014. http://cavca-cartagena.blogspot.mx/p/manifiesto-emputao.html.

Centro Nacional de Memoria Histórica. 'Estadísticas del conflicto armado en Colombia.' http://www.centrodememoriahistorica.gov.co/micrositios/informeGeneral/estadisticas.html.

Cooper, Ashton. 'Notes from Colombia: Why the World Needs Another Biennial.' *Blouin Art Info*, April 4, 2014. http://www.blouinartinfo.com/news/story/1022190/notes-from-colombia-why-the-world-needs-another-biennial.

———. 'Exploring the Presence of the Past at Colombia's First Biennial.' *Blouin Art Info*, February 7, 2014. http://www.blouinartinfo.com/news/story/1006822/exploring-the-presence-of-the-past-at-colombias-first.

[38] Butler, *Notes*, 69.

Dussel, Enrique. *Filosofía de la cultura y la liberación*. Ciudad de México: UACM, 2006.

Informe Nacional de Desarrollo Humano 2011. Colombia Rural: Razones para la esperanza. Resumen Ejecutivo. Bogotá: PNUD, 2011. http://www.co.undp.org/content/colombia/es/home/library/human_development/informe-nacional-de-desarrollo-humano-2011.html.

Jones, Caroline. 'Biennial Culture: A Longer History.' In *The Biennial Reader: An Anthology of Large-Scale Perennial Exhibitions of Contemporary Art*, edited by Elena Filipovic, Marieke Van Hal, and Solveig Øvstebø, 66–86. Bergen: Bergen Kursthall, 2010.

Martin-Franco, Helena. 'CAVCA Entierra la BIACI.' *YouTube video*, April 10, 2014. https://www.youtube.com/watch?list=PL6XhSMVHlyW_zOWj9R1ZUJMxdHannr1O5&v=E2XvvIUv66M.

———, ed. 'Emputaó testimony by Muriel Angulo.' February 26, 2014. https://www.youtube.com/watch?v=sThaywRenLI.

———. Interviewed by Kimberly Richards and Martha Herrara-Lasso. January 9, 2018.

McKee, Yates. *Strike Art: Contemporary Art and the Post-Occupy Condition*. London: Verso, 2016.

Ministerio de Cultura. 'Programa Nacional de Estímulos.' *MinCultura*. http://www.mincultura.gov.co/planes-y-programas/programas/programa-nacional-estimulos/Paginas/default.aspx.

———. *Sistema Nacional de Cultura: Estado, Retos y Perspectivas*. Bogotá: Ministerio de Cultura, 2013. http://www.mincultura.gov.co/areas/fomento-regional/Documents/sistema_nal_cultura_FINAL_baja.pdf.

Moya, Paul. 'Who We Are and From Where We Speak.' *Transmodernity* (Fall 2011): 82–83.

Peñuela, Jorge. 'Elogio de las Emputadas Cartageneras.' *Liberatorio.org*, April 11, 2014. http://liberatorio.org/?p=1638.

Wallerstein, Immanuel. *The Modern World-System: Capitalist Agriculture and the Origins of the European World-Economy in the Sixteenth Century*. New York: Academic Press, 1976.

World Bank. 'World Development Indicators.' https://data.worldbank.org/indicators/SI.POVERTY.GINI.

Yudicé, George. *The Expediency of Culture: Uses of Culture in the Global Era*. Durham, NC: Duke University Press, 2003.

Fred Moten and Stefano Harney
Notes on Sustainable Tools

Suné Woods, *Falling to get here*, 2017, TRT 9 minutes 39 seconds, single channel video

Michel Foucault presents his 'tips' on non-fascist living in anticipation of a cultivation of the self he may well have seen as a counter-strategy to the production of the individual. But he sends his self-help text into a world of interpersonal relations, one he also documents in his account of the intimate rise of neo-liberalism. Another way to say this is that he sends his text into the mouth of democratic despotism. Neo-liberalism was nothing other than the completion of the Southern strategy, as Nixon and his aides refined it. The Southern strategy was of course never simply about the Southern United States. It was about the global hegemony of the planters. A global plantocracy made possible by democratic despotism. In this regard, Nixon's U.S. political strategy is an extension of the Dulles brothers' foreign policy, which was, in turn a transnational echo of the repression of "black reconstruction in America."

Neo-liberalism sealed the global deal on democratic despotism. As DuBois explains, democratic despotism was an innovative form of the global color line. Workers would be designated as white and offered deputy positions in the rule of each country, in exchange for aligning with the ruling classes against people of color inside and outside the borders of that nation. But reading DuBois carefully we see a second dimension to this deputization, securing the deal through a promised, though always thwarted individuation for these workers. Or today, for these home-owners. That is, democratic despotism was also about a certain democratization of despotism. We have referred to this democratization as policy. But such a hacked word should not hide the brutality of the agreement. Each of these persons was offered the opportunity to individuate through despotic violence against blackness (best understood, here, as the refusal of refused access to the unity of whiteness and personhood). Indeed, this despotic violence was the core manufacturing process of the thwarted individual. The production of white people on an industrial scale required this democratization of despotism. Of course, signing up to a world of despotism, proving one's 'self' through ongoing predatory violence against those who claim the differences they enact, required accepting the democratization of despotism as a general principle, and that meant accepting it in the military, in the state, and especially at work, or in other words, Fordism, and later, logistical capitalism, which each, in their own way, necessitate and manufacture a brutal little dictator in every workplace. And once despotism is accepted by white people, in and as every little ritual of their own self-acceptance, all of which amount to an endless lag, an eternal deferral, the interpersonal becomes the only way to mollify it. If interpersonal relations form the reservoir of whiteness into which the people tap for dead energy and unsustainable sustenance, then the intersectional becomes the only way for the ones who wait on waiting, whose doubly interminable wait takes the form of critique, to mollify the constantly redoubled despotism they face. Either way, every body waits in vain.

But the interpersonal is not only not up to the task of mollification, it actually reproduces and refines thwarted individuation and democratic despotism. These are the conditions under which the Southern strategy flourished; this is the spread soil of the plantocracy. And now the pulling down of the Confederate statue proves the strategy has triumphed. The global plantocracy reigns. But how could we call Foxconn or Goldmans Sachs planters? Because they work to fulfill the condition of any and all plantocracies. Planters try to control and concentrate all the land, all the water, all the air, all the food, animals, and plants. Pushing people into factories was just a temporary tactic in this control and concentration, not the endgame. Marxism misunderstood this. The endgame is that no one can survive outside their rule, everyone and everything must walk into the jaws of the planter, or in other words that the earth itself is what they aim to consume. Finance is completely explicit about using its menacing means to do this. So is logistics. They are sciences of the planter. But understanding this regime as a plantocracy thriving in the individuating violence of democratic despotism does not lead to the thought that there is no outside to the world.

It leads to getting some land. Because in the face of this despotism we need somewhere to really care, which is the collective destruction of the interpersonal, and with and through it the delusion of the individual, in open practices of welcome and visitation. That cannot be done in conflict with the plantocracy, where the interpersonal, or freedom, or non-fascist living, becomes our faulty weapon. It is a battle that can only be won in militant, self-defensive, self-annihilative retreat. And given the nature of the rule under plantocracy, retreat means finding land that is fugitive from the rule over land, water, air, etc. And then setting that land up anautonomously enough to start the treatment. That land may be a squatted garage in the city or an abandoned mill in the countryside. That treatment may entail forming a band, hosting a barbeque, a dance and a drink. It may be a farm and a daycare, an experimental writing collective, or a mechanics shop. Any form of detoxification from the interpersonal.

If we do go back to battle democratic despotism it will not be through the interpersonal. There will be no white people, no people of colour, no allies, no microaggression. And when we win blackness will rain in sun showers while the time disappears.

Illustration: Mick Agustin

FRED MOTEN and **STEFANO HARNEY** are co-authors of *The Undercommons: fugitive planning and black study* (2013) and the forthcoming *All Incomplete*, both published by Automedia/Minor Compositions. Fred's *Black and Blur* (2017) is the first in a trilogy of books published by Duke University Press. Stefano was Artistic Co-Director, with the *freethought* collective, of the 2016 Bergen Assembly in Norway. Fred teaches at New York University and Stefano teaches at Singapore Management University.

SUNÉ WOODS is an artist whose practice examines absences and vulnerabilities within cultural and social histories. She has participated in residencies at Headlands Center of the Arts, Vermont Studio Center, The Center for Photography at Woodstock, and Light Work. Woods is a recipient of the *Visions from the New California* initiative, *The John Gutmann Fellowship Award, and The Baum Award for an Emerging American Photographer.* She lives in Los Angeles.

CHAPTER 11

INTERVIEW
Performance in the Peace Process: Creating Cultural Brigades

Patricia Ariza and Beatriz Pizano

Patricia Ariza is a renowned producer and artist who has worked on the front lines for justice and social change in Colombia for over 50 years. For the past 26 years, she has produced vast works and massive performances that bring together professional artists and victims—particularly women—of Columbia's armed conflicts.

Beatriz Pizano is artistic director of Toronto's Aluna Theatre known for creating award-winning intercultural, interdisciplinary, and intermedial performance. Founded in 2001, Aluna is recognized for its unique approach to creation and its daring political work.

Translated by Bruce Gibbons Fell

P. Ariza (✉)
Corporación Colombiana de Teatro and Teatro la Candelaria,
Bogotá, DC, Colombia

B. Pizano
Aluna Theatre, Toronto, ON, Canada

N. Alvarez et al. (eds.), *Sustainable Tools for Precarious Times*,
Contemporary Performance InterActions,
https://doi.org/10.1007/978-3-030-11557-9_11

Beatriz Pizano: How would you describe the current state of 'art-activism' in Colombia today?

Patricia Ariza: There are a lot of people making art and a lot of people doing activism. There are a few of us who do both. Doing activism, without having art lose its specificity, is not an easy thing to do. That's the most important challenge: to put art and creativity at the service of peace during this crucial moment in Colombia's history.

So, I see it as a bit difficult because all the years at war have produced a kind of mutation in Colombia's collective imagination. People are afraid. There's a lot of depoliticizing. Neoliberalism has influenced people in a pragmatic way. It doesn't make it easy for the artistic community. We live in a very big and dispersed country, but people are doing great things all over. That is what we are trying to do now. We are going to have an art and culture summit for reconciliation, so as to gather all these experiences and see how we can present them to the country and the world.

Beatriz Pizano: Over the course of your career, you've directed mass actions in public spaces as well as performances in theatre spaces proper. How do you see the relationship between these two sites? Why have you often turned to performance actions in public spaces throughout your career?

Patricia Ariza: I am part of an emblematic company that develops plays over long periods of time. It's a company that is dedicated to doing a research process for every play. It takes us a great amount of time to create a play, but plays usually take a long time in Colombian theatre. So, this is the great school that allows me to go out to the streets. On the streets, we do other kinds of things.

I am also a political activist. I work with many victims, specifically with victims, and we've done massive pieces. And it's become almost like a habit. Many organizations ask me to do things for demonstrations, celebrations, or commemorations. For example, I work with Corporación Reiniciar[1] and we create a large performance every year paying homage to the victims of the Unión Patriótica.[2] I work with other organizations as well, and sometimes I work alone. There are things I come up with and we do them on a smaller scale, but we're always creating performances. I also work with the women's movement often.

[1] Corporación Reiniciar: a Colombian corporation for the defense and promotion of human rights.

[2] Unión Patriótica (Patriotic Union): leftist Colombian political party, founded in the 1980s by the FARC and the Colombian Communist Party.

La Candelaria also does performance pieces, but in theatre spaces. The most interesting thing that's happened is that these two things have begun to connect. Sometimes, for example, what we do in the performances we do outside influences what we do in the theatre. We steal images from the performances for theatre, and the other way around too. The theatre has allowed what we do on the streets to have a possibility of presence and aesthetic elaboration that is interesting for people to watch and participate in.

Beatriz Pizano: You've done performances in the streets with an impressive amount of people. What are the challenges you have as a director when it comes to presenting these performances in the streets? What is needed of you that is not needed in a theatre space?

Patricia Ariza: It's a very interesting thing because it's like interrupting day-to-day life. When people go to the theatre, they go prepared: they know they are going to see a play, they know what play they are going to see, and they pay for it. Not in the streets, where people are living their everyday lives, their routine, and suddenly this interrupts their life. It's very risky and it's very interesting. I'd say it's simply something else. It also creates a very interesting connection to politics, which doesn't mean it doesn't happen in theatre, but with theatre there is usually a longer process.

Theatre is also political. We can see everything from a political perspective, but let's say, in a play, one by La Candelaria or other groups I work with, the playwriting process takes a long time. In contrast, the performances we work on are always about issues that are immediate, about things that are happening in the pain of the people, in the hearts of the people. So, we prepare them very quickly. Some have taken four months to prepare, others a month, and some in a week [...]

Beatriz Pizano: In three hours! I've seen pieces you've done. There's one you uploaded to YouTube, where you immediately jumped into it [...]

Patricia Ariza: If there's an urgent matter, of course. A year and a half ago we occupied a church close to here, because social leaders were being murdered. So, we occupied a church and that's where we began to come up with things to do. That's a way of making people stop and watch and ask themselves what is going on. Not only what is happening here, but also what is happening now, and the reason why these women have come out to do this.

Beatriz Pizano: Pieces such as *Vivir sin Miedo*, a performance that decries rampant femicide, bring the power of a mass public action to the stage with its ensemble of 50 women. What is your method of working with such a large ensemble? How critical is the large ensemble to your work's overall aims?

Patricia Ariza: I come from the school of collective creation, of a company, of a group, and because of it I am always surrounded by people. So, when something very big comes up I always ask for help: from dancers, singers, and other people that come and help me. For example, when we did the performance at the Hemispheric Institute's Encuentro in 2009, we worked with 350 women and had a team of 20 people. Each of the team members would take care of a group. For example, there was a model to create the dance pieces from, as well as other spontaneous things.

Some things were relatively planned, but order is what allows spontaneity. Spontaneity alone, I don't think it works. So, we would put these two things together: planning and people's spontaneity. For example, there was a moment where the women came out and screamed all over the plaza, and there was another moment where they all gathered in a prayer or a demand of sorts, which became something very intimate and something very public.

Beatriz Pizano: What inspires you as an artist? Your images are impressive, whether they come from your plays in the theatre or the performances you are part of. You get all these great ideas. A couple of festivals ago, there were all these Manuelas[3] in the park. It was stunning. Where do these images come from?

Patricia Ariza: I think my training ground has mostly been Teatro La Candelaria. Not just Teatro La Candelaria though, but also the theatrical movement, as well as the demonstrations in the streets. I'm an activist. The performances are done by the people: workers, laborers doing performances every time they go out to the streets. In fact, they make their costumes and different things to create a satire or a critique. There are many alliances with artists to do this so that it can have an impact. So, that's where I began.

Beatriz Pizano: What new possibilities for politics do you feel the ensemble work models?

Patricia Ariza: Every possibility in the world. Because when one works in alliance with other artists or other people—sometimes they are not artists but people who give ideas, who are there, helping—it becomes

[3] *Cien Manuelas en el parque por la paz en Colombia*, paying homage to Manuela Sáenz (1797–1856), who was part of the Independence process in Colombia, Ecuador, and Peru.

a sort of collective passion, like collective creation, and that is inspiring for all of us. I direct and coordinate, but I'm not the only one. Many others are helping us all the time.

Beatriz Pizano: This book is interested in how art-activism engages in sustainable strategies—strategies that are designed to *exceed* the moment of protest to encourage a sustained and ongoing press of political action. You've been using performance as a form of political intervention for over 50 years. How do you understand the idea of 'sustainable activism'?

Patricia Ariza: It's difficult to sustain in a country like Colombia, because people have to make many commitments to survive. It's quite hard to sustain a large group. But I have been able to because, for example, the Mothers of Soacha[4] are always willing to create. Some groups of victims are always there. They even come to me and say: 'We haven't created a performance in some time, let's do another one.'

There are also artists that are always with us, like dancers and actresses. There's a team, and it's like a motor. But there's also a situation out there that makes us step out of our comfort zone. Theatre is somewhat of a comfort zone. We're present, we have a theatre, that theatre has chairs, an audience, and all these other things. So, going out to the streets has been challenging, very challenging. For us it was very difficult at the beginning too, but now it's something that we need very much.

Groups like the Mothers of Soacha keep coming back, and not only them. FESTA[5] offers them a lot, and we have instances where these women keep uniting. And there's the possibility of continuing to work with them.

Beatriz Pizano: These groups work over a long period of time. What's the secret? How do these relationships keep going?

Patricia Ariza: We've been working with the Mothers of Soacha for ten years now. Carlos[6] also worked with them on his last play, *Antígonas Tribunal de Mujeres*. We don't only call them so they can come and act, or for them to do a performance. We are also with them, helping them in their lawsuit, among other things. We're the ones who proposed Luz Marina[7] as a candidate for the Senate. We made the posters for her.

[4] The Mothers of Soacha come from the Bogotá suburb of Soacha, where the Colombian Army abducted and murdered a group of young men in 2008, falsely presenting them as members of a guerrilla who died in combat.

[5] FESTA: Festival de Teatro Alternativo; Patricia Ariza is festival director.

[6] Carlos Satizábal, a Colombian playwright and director, is also a creative partner and colleague of Patricia Ariza.

[7] Luz Marina Bernal is a Mother of Soacha, artist, activist, and Nobel Peace Prize nominee, and is one of the creators of *Antígonas Tribunal de Mujeres*.

We don't invite them to do things that are born out of our ideas: we are in the struggle with them. The same thing happens with Unión Patriótica, with Jahel Quiroga[8] from Corporación Reiniciar. I'm also working with her on other things, supporting her. It's a two-way process: 'Don't come and work for me. Let's work together on pieces that speak about what happens with you and with theatre and art.' They are also speaking like actresses now, they're incredible.

Beatriz Pizano: Yes, they're fantastic. That piece was very beautiful. I think it had a huge impact in Toronto. When they presented, Colombia had recently voted against the agreement to end the Colombian conflict.[9] The performance was something different that night. I wondered: 'Why is the surtitle operator not following the piece?' But it was because the women jumped straight into it and got off script. It was fascinating.

Patricia Ariza: Imagine the tragedy we felt. We did a great amount of performances for the SÍ.[10] So many of them.

Beatriz Pizano: And performances in the streets.

Patricia Ariza: Yes. Many. Big ones, small ones, medium-sized ones. We did many videos, like 40 of them.

Beatriz Pizano: The book's interests in sustainable strategies stem, in part, from that post-protest malaise of 'Now what?' that so often follows mass public actions: the moment of protest happens, people disperse, and questions linger about the overall impact and efficacy of the action. How do you sustain the energy and investment of the mass action? Are there strategies you employ that work in durational ways to sustain the press of resistance beyond the moment of action?

Patricia Ariza: I think that maintaining a relationship with people is very helpful. Not having a performance ending and then saying goodbye, thank you so much for your work. We continue having a relationship, not as permanent as we'd like, because it's a lot of people. But we maintain our relationship with them to the best of our abilities, and that creates enthusiasm for the possibility of another performance.

We are also part of different causes. The ones who are more willing to participate are the women. That's a very important thing. We also work with men, but it's not as easy to sustain permanent relationships with them. With women, it is easier.

[8] Jahel Quiroga is an activist who works with the Unión Patriótica.
[9] This result followed a referendum on October 2, 2016.
[10] The referendum option that voted for peace in Colombia.

Beatriz Pizano: Why do you think it's different?

Patricia Ariza: I don't know, I have no way of explaining it. But there are some that are always present, though not as directly: taking photos or helping with technical things. But it's the women who have always been at the heart of these performances.

Beatriz Pizano: How do you maintain the impact of these performative actions?

Patricia Ariza: By continuing a relationship with their causes, because many of them have a cause to fight for. Besides, there have been many exciting things. Some of them have called me on two occasions to support performances they are devising. It was very moving for me because that's what it's about. This is not private property: the idea is to create a movement. And there are a lot of people creating performance work, but some performances—which I don't criticize—are very hermetic. It's hard for one to communicate with them, though they may have interesting aesthetic imagery. But I can't manage to unravel their meaning. The social serviceability of performance is very important to me: to make it something useful for the people, for those who are part of it and those who see it, or participate, because some are participatory. That, for me, is fundamental.

Beatriz Pizano: Since 1994, the Festival Alternativo has been a vital meeting place for artists and activists. Beyond its reputation for curating works that are at the frontier of aesthetic developments in Colombia, in what respects has FESTA become a hub for artists committed to socially engaged art?

Patricia Ariza: FESTA is an alternative theatre festival that happens at the same time as another gigantic festival, the Iberoamericano,[11] which nowadays is going through many economic problems and problems of all kinds. There's a movement of artists that signed a letter saying that they would not participate in the Iberoamericano. We obviously didn't sign the letter because we decided to go our own way many years ago. Our festival is a tribute to Colombian theatre, because Colombian theatre is constantly being denied. We don't have a chauvinistic view. We admire, need, and learn a lot from what comes from other countries. But we can also sometimes have a very colonized mentality, denying what is made here, all the time, rejecting it systematically, and when there are political reasons to deny it, well, they deny it twice, right? So, it's something very hard.

[11] Festival Iberoamericano de Teatro (FITB).

FESTA is a festival of resistance, even though we have a great track record. For example, the state's budget allocation for us is minimal, less than minimal. It makes it very difficult for FESTA to become the encounter that we would like it to be, because we want people to stay for the whole festival, for people to have in-depth discussions of what is happening in the world, what is happening in the theatre, and what happens inside of us as well.

It's hard, but we've made considerable progress. Everybody wants to come to FESTA, and the most interesting thing about FESTA is the audience, because it's an astonishing thing, especially since the ticket prices are extremely low. A lot of people come to Colombia exclusively to see theatre, and they can see what is happening at the Iberoamericano in the streets, which is free of charge, and what is happening at FESTA in the streets and in theatres, because it's very cheap.

We want this festival to be an encounter festival, not a showcase festival. Just like the Festival de Mujeres en Escena por la Paz.[12] Every morning we are having meetings with companies, having discussions, learning, listening. We sometimes do performance pieces that we all come up with. Well, that's what we can do and it's what we do. I believe it's leaving a mark.

Beatriz Pizano: It's beautiful. I remember two years ago at ten in the morning when the box office opened. I saw that almost every single performance was sold out. I would see a lot of people there and think: 'These people are not from the theatre community.' It was a very diverse audience, and once they heard there were barely any tickets left, they'd reply: 'Well, what's available for today?' They weren't there for a specific artist or company.

Patricia Ariza: They just wanted to know where they could get in.

Beatriz Pizano: They wanted to see everything. It made a huge impression on me. It's beautiful. One can see those who are part of the theatre community and who are not, and it makes up a very diverse audience.

Patricia Ariza: It's been an impressive audience, hungry for theatre.

Beatriz Pizano: The companies have been impressive too, because it's very intense work. They have very few hours to set up. And then they finish a show and another one begins immediately. That doesn't happen in Canada. There's something very exciting happening. Plays are being performed because people want to see the different groups' artistic proposals.

[12] Festival de Mujeres en Escena por la Paz focuses on women in art and politics.

Patricia Ariza: We want to make theatre a popular passion, and it does happen during those days. It's phenomenal.

Beatriz Pizano: And so many students come, young people, during Easter, which is a pretty busy time.

Patricia Ariza: They're on holiday and they travel by land. They often ask us for discounts. Some people come walking from their neighborhoods and ask for a discount that can even get to 2000 Colombian pesos.[13] It's amazing. This audience makes it all worthwhile.

Beatriz Pizano: FESTA cannot disappear.

Patricia Ariza: No. I was so sad when I found out about the funding, we got this year, but well [...]

Beatriz Pizano: What a struggle, right? It's never over.

Patricia Ariza: La Candelaria is an emblem in Colombian theatre history. First, because it's an ensemble with its own venue, its own methodology, and because it has a project, a utopia. It makes it a benchmark for us, a benchmark for the audience. A benchmark that is sometimes denied: sometimes we are hit very hard, but La Candelaria always creates a sense of confusion for the audience. People expect to see a theatre company that repeats itself, and La Candelaria never repeats itself because we are always doing new pieces. We're constantly challenging ourselves, trying to create something we may not easily understand. We don't do what we already know, rather what we are investigating. I think our legacy is that insatiable pursuit: making theatre because one has a lump in one's throat. Not because making theatre is cool, or to get prestige or money, which is legitimate too, but it's not our reason to do it. We spend all the time in our lives creating.

Beatriz Pizano: Colombia is at a critical political moment. With the signing of the revised peace agreement with FARC in December 2017 and the end of 53 years of armed struggle, civilians and former rebels are now tasked with the project of sustaining peace. What role do you see your work taking at this juncture? Has this political shift changed your methods or ways of working?

Patricia Ariza: Yes, of course. In the encounters we've had with artists, we've stated that the conflict has been not only an armed, social, and political conflict, but also a cultural one. There's a cultural mutation happening in Colombia, which makes it necessary to convince the state, convince society, convince the artists, and convince ourselves that cultural

[13] Equivalent to approximately one Canadian dollar (March 18, 2018).

work is essential. We need to change people's worldview. It cannot be done only through traditional pedagogy or through politics, because we need to work on it from an emotional point of view as well.

The warmongering media has managed to take peace out of people's hearts. It's terrible and very sad, because we say that a peace that is not sung, that is not told, that is not represented or painted in the streets is a peace that can even die. Because if things are not emotional—we artists know that—they're simply not there. Logic alone is not enough. That's our main effort, to work from the sphere of cultural debate.

And it's not easy. Because every project focuses on pedagogy or politics, which is legitimate and necessary, but not many of the projects focus on culture, and less on art and creativity. We're working on it on a practical level. Some of us have visited rural areas to work with people there, and even work with women from the insurgency. We've been asking them, and the country, to make peace for 30 years. And when they decide to make peace, it's not accepted, it's not welcomed. They do not have space.

The problem is that there's a lack of implementation of agreements, which is very dangerous because it creates a sense of hopelessness in people. Right now, we're in a very difficult situation. There's a genocide happening against social leaders, and many are dead. Many insurgents have laid down their arms and are now being killed.

So, what happens to those who remain? What can we ask of them? What can society ask of people who are not complying? We believe that cultural and artistic work is not the only way, but it's fundamental. This is the moment we are in, and it's forced us to work differently, to go out to those areas. We have some beautiful videos of what we've done. For example, for the Festival de Mujeres en Escena, we brought a group of thirty young women from the insurgency that came to announce the end of the war to civil society. It was very moving because they delivered a military announcement in the context of an act of war. They came to say: 'We are announcing to civil society that the war is over.' It was very exciting. We decided to do it through performance. They transform themselves, put on white dresses, and express themselves through the language of art. Some of them have even enrolled in theatre school.

We're working on this, but what is ideal is to have a collaboration with actresses and women from the rural areas. That's the big challenge I always wish to undertake. We worked with victims but also with actresses. In *Antígonas Tribunal de Mujeres*, they did it too. The challenge now is this: how do we all unite to stop the killing? How can we find a way for agreements to be respected? Now, even though this is an enormous tragedy, peace is moving forward. I mean we can't have a negative, pessimistic point of view, though there are reasons to have one. No. Peace is progressing. Many creative projects are created in many places. But it's not enough. It's progressing slowly, very slowly. There is something that currently is not advancing peace: the upcoming elections. It's created an atmosphere where hate and exclusions have been rejuvenated in a terrible way.

Beatriz Pizano: Does Patricia Ariza have hope regarding peace in Colombia?

Patricia Ariza: Yes. All the hope in the world. I'm sure that the war does not have a reason to exist anymore. There was a moment where it could have had one. There have been armed movements in all Latin America. In Colombia, it has lasted too long. Too long. Many of us don't know a day of peace since we can remember. So, this moment is an extraordinary moment, a wonderful one, but not all the country is part of it.

What happens is that war is a massive business, which brings a lot of resistance to peace. That's the fight we are in: how do we put peace back in people's hearts? International cooperation can help with that. Friendly countries are working on this alongside many countries. It's not easy. Now, even though social, productive projects are necessary, cultural work is not considered to be very effective.

Beatriz Pizano: How do you think the international community can participate in this process?

Patricia Ariza: Germany is working on the creation of an Institute for Peace, and they are going to create a University for Peace. Many countries are giving out scholarships. For example, Cuba has given out thousands of scholarships so the people from the insurgency can study medicine. But they complain, saying they don't only want to study medicine. Some want to study art, for example. A lot of people want to study art.

Beatriz Pizano: How does one learn to live in peace?

Patricia Ariza: That is something very hard, even for those of us who have fought for peace. It's hard because it's not only a matter of disarming bodies. It's a spiritual matter too.

Beatriz Pizano: Is there anything else you would like to mention?

Patricia Ariza: We need to do co-productions. We can't do it all by ourselves. We need teamwork. We need to have a lot of people coming over. I believe that at this moment we need a lot of people to come over, to help, creating cultural brigades. I say cultural brigades, but we need every kind of brigade. People could come and do temporary work, for a month, and create a performance piece. I think that would be fundamental for Colombia right now.

Let's see what government is elected, which one comes next, because we have hope that the new government—whichever one is elected—will ensure the implementation of the agreements. If this doesn't happen, we don't know where this sense of despair will take us. In Colombia, war has been wild. It's happened everywhere and very easily. It's impressive. The war still goes on, and we need to end it. The Havana Agreements are the doorway to end the war completely.

Our effort now is for the ELN[14] to also be part of the peace process. It doesn't only depend on them. It depends on the government too. But they have a fundamental role. I believe that the FARC[15] have the advantage of a unity of command and they now have a clear purpose, though this is costing them their lives.

Beatriz Pizano: How about the paramilitary? How can that be disbanded?

Patricia Ariza: That's the heart of the matter. It's not only about not complying with the agreements: it's the paramilitary. It's a problem of political will. The state could put an end to the paramilitary if it wanted to. But the state is not strong enough to do so, because there has been an alliance with them all these years, during Uribe's government. So, to dissolve that alliance is a very complicated thing to do.

In our parliament, the obstacles for peace are enormous, because there are senators and members of parliament that have ties with the war. That's the tragedy: that these alliances exist in our politics. It's not as if the paramilitary operates like a loose cannon. No. These relationships are very strong and have existed in our politics for a very long time. And there's a lot of money involved. Hence, this is the country of threats.

Every electoral campaign is happening with threats. There's also something new that's happening with Gustavo Petro.[16] He's like a phenomenon. I believe this is a product of the peace process. People can live without machinery, without corruption, without all of it. But who knows if he will be elected or not. That's what we fear, that violent spirit that still brutally survives.

Beatriz Pizano: Thank you, Patricia.

Patricia Ariza: Thank you.

[14] ELN: National Liberation Army.

[15] FARC: Revolutionary Armed Forces of Colombia.

[16] Presidential candidate, founder, and leader of the center-left Movimiento Progresistas.

Cannupa Hanska Luger, *The Mirror Shield Project*, 2016

Mirror Shield Project at Oceti Sakowin Camp, 2016. Image credit: Rory Wakemup

"As artists, we live on the periphery. But we are the mirrors. We are the reflective points that break through a barrier."

Standing Rock on Thanksgiving Day 2016, police in reflection. Image Credit: Rob Wilson Photography

Cannupa Hanska Luger, *The Mirror Shield Project*, 2016

"This project represents how just one person can acquire one sheet of plywood and cut it into six shields; those shields stand on the frontline protecting hundreds behind them in prayer for the water, and right behind that line stands a camp where there are thousands of people standing for the water protection for the eight million people down river, who all use the Missouri River as their water source. And so the *Mirror Shield Project* demonstrates how one person can help protect eight million."
—Cannupa Hanska Luger

Bertolt Brecht famously declared that "Art is not a mirror held up to society but a hammer with which to shape it." In Cannupa Hanska Luger's *Mirror Shield Project*, Brecht's maxim is reconfigured and given new life on the frontlines of Standing Rock, as the mirror *becomes* the hammer to shape a new reality of Indigenous rights in the Americas. In April 2016, members of the Standing Rock Sioux Indian Reservation in North Dakota launched a massive collective action against the approved construction of the Dakota Access Pipeline under the Missouri River, which they believed would threaten the region's water supply. By winter of that year, thousands of water protectors had converged on the protest camps, including Luger, who was born and raised in Standing Rock. Inspired by women in the Ukraine who, that same year, confronted riot police with mirrors to remind them of their shared humanity, Luger invited supporters to make and send mirror shields—constructed using reflective Mylar on masonite for safety and durability—to the camps. These were deployed as a kind of "poetic armor," to use Luger's description: protecting the protectors from the rubber bullets of DAPL security guards while forcing these same guards to reflect on their actions. The Mirror Shield project has since been adapted for use in various resistance movements across the U.S.

Born in North Dakoka on the Standing Rock Reservation, multi-disciplinary artist **CANNUPA HANSKA LUGER** comes from Mandan, Hidatsa, Arikara, Lakota, Austrian, and Norwegian descent. His work communicates stories of complex Indigenous identities coming up against 21st century challenges, including human alienation from and destruction of the land. He provokes diverse publics to engage with Indigenous peoples and values beyond the lens of colonial social structuring. Luger's practice combines critical cultural analysis with dedication and respect for the diverse materials, environments, and communities he engages. He is known for his ceramic innovations, and he also tells stories using fiber, steel, cut-paper, video, sound, performance, monumental sculpture, land art installation, and social collaboration.

Cannupa Hanska Luger would like to thank Jack Becker from Forecast Public Art for helping bring *Mirror Shields* to Standing Rock, ND, along with Rory Wakemup at All My Relations Arts in Minneapolis, Minnesota, who facilitated a workshop, hosting Luger as guest artist for the *Mirror Shield Project*.

CHAPTER 12

Pimicikimak Sovereignty: Cree Sustainability and Hydroelectric Inundation in Northern Manitoba

Jessica Jacobson-Konefall

In August 2017, I travelled by vehicle and motorboat with seven academics and activists on a one-week tour of hydro-affected Cree communities in the north of the province of Manitoba, Canada. The Cree, also known as Ininew or Ininewak, are an Algonkian-speaking Indigenous people who occupy the subarctic and northern plains regions of Canada. Cree fishermen, activists, and elders, associated with a research consortium called the Wa Ni Ska Tan Alliance of Hydro-Affected Communities, led our group in visiting and learning about sites impacted by hydroelectric development on the Saskatchewan, Churchill, and Nelson River systems in Manitoba. Contrary to popular beliefs about this form of energy, hydroelectricity exported from Northern Manitoba is not a sustainable energy source. In fact, hydroelectric development has been devastating for Cree peoples and lands inundated by flooding since the 1970s. While remediation of Cree lands remains a possibility and is a matter of political will, the Cree have long fought for just relations with the public utility Manitoba Hydro, the

J. Jacobson-Konefall (✉)
University of Winnipeg, Winnipeg, MB, Canada

N. Alvarez et al. (eds.), *Sustainable Tools for Precarious Times*, Contemporary Performance InterActions,
https://doi.org/10.1007/978-3-030-11557-9_12

province of Manitoba, and Canada's federal government. In this context, the Cree self-government at Pimicikimak, a community we visited on the trip, performs sovereignty in ways that resist the exploitative relationships imposed by the state, the province, and public hydro utility. The Cree have performed—undertaken, constituted, transmitted—their intergenerational practice of sovereignty from time immemorial on their lands.

In my view, Pimicikimak's sovereignty aligns with definitions of performativity focused on embodiment, practice, and social reproduction, or what Dene scholar Glen Coulthard calls grounded normativity: 'the modalities of Indigenous land-connected practices and longstanding experiential knowledge that inform and structure our ethical engagements with the world and our relationships with human and nonhuman others over time.'[1] Coulthard's notion of grounded normativity invites a particular understanding of performativity that centralizes Indigenous land-based practices, in ways that performance, broadly conceived, risks obscuring. Cherokee scholar Lara Evans notes that practices of distinct Indigenous nations are unlikely to be captured by a broad theory of performance,[2] and Stó:lō academic Dylan Robinson similarly questions the concept of performance as a first principle in discussion of Indigenous practices as they are grounded in specific Indigenous ontologies.[3] Coulthard's grounded normativity—a concept preferred by Cree scholar Ramona Neckoway[4]—conveys the integrated and holistic sense in which I invoke the performative in this essay. In the context of embodied praxis and resistance to the colonial impacts of hydroelectric inundation, Pimicikimak's self-governance engages the imposed structures and discursive forms of Canadian law, that is, treaty and Aboriginal rights, as well as those of human rights in ways that are broadly performative, innovative, and self-determined.

The terms 'sustainability' and 'human rights' have complex purchase for Pimicikimak and other hydro-affected Cree communities, who respond to imposed colonial discourses by selectively reframing them as activist

[1] Glen Coulthard, *Red Skin White Masks: Rejecting the Colonial Politics of Recognition* (Minneapolis: University of Minnesota Press, 2015), 27.

[2] Lara Evans, 'What to Do When Theory Does Not Work For You: Native Performance Art and Performance Theory Revised,' *Not Artomatic* (blog), accessed July 7, 2018, https://notartomatic.wordpress.com.

[3] Dylan Robinson, 'Enchantment's Irreconcilable Connection: Listening to Anger, Being Idle No More,' in *Performance Studies in Canada*, ed. Laura Levin and Marlis Schweitzer (Montreal: McGill-Queens University Press, 2017), 211.

[4] Ramona Neckoway, in discussion with author, August 2017.

tools. In Canadian public discourse, environmental sustainability has, for decades, functioned as an alibi for exploitative hydroelectric development. At the same time, human rights discourses often figure as an imaginative framework for an abstract vision of 'equality' that fits easily within the Canadian state's aims to assimilate Indigenous peoples. Pimicikimak sovereignty, as embodied practice, provides a distinct engagement with human rights discourse. Namely, it openly questions the efficacy of that discourse in the context of Indigenous rights struggles, which Peter Kulchyski highlights in his work *Aboriginal Rights are Not Human Rights*. First, Pimicikimak are committed to their lands through ancient, sustainable, and ongoing cultural practices and attachments. Second, Pimicikimak ground their use of human and Indigenous rights discourse in historically specific struggle, based on their own commitment as Cree people to sustainable relationships at multiple scales. The related question of 'whose sustainability' is relevant: Cree gathering and hunting cultures in Northern Manitoba, ongoing for tens of thousands of years, are reflective of one of the most sustainable forms of social organization humans ever developed; but since the 1970s, this practice has been radically disrupted by hydroelectric inundation.

Following the flooding of hundreds of acres of their land without meaningful consent or warning, five communities negotiated a treaty with the province, federal government, and the utility in 1977 called the Northern Flood Agreement (NFA). The NFA resulted from the advocacy and demands of five communities for compensation of the hydro development's impacts: Pimicikimak, Nisichawayasihk, Norway House, Tataskweyak, and York Factory. In signing a modern treaty, the Cree exercised their sovereignty. The provincial government and its public utility, while having signed the NFA, have defied their commitments by interpreting the treaty in the narrowest possible terms and attempting to extinguish it at every opportunity. This relationship between communities and the utility highlight how the form and content of rights emergencies caused by hydroelectric development in Northern Manitoba are 'hand in glove' with Canada's colonial governance writ large. While the state, province, and public utility occupy, bureaucratically dominate, and work to disaggregate the Cree as peoples on their lands, the Cree perform continued sovereignty and resistance through activism.

Pimicikimak's performance of self-governance addresses the rights emergencies that hydro development, and the related abrogation of treaty relationship, precipitated. The material context of self-governance encloses and reformulates the intensely colonial tool of written law within the nation's own performance of sovereignty. By adopting the language of Aboriginal, human, and treaty rights, Pimicikimak affirms, as any sovereign nation today must, the complex relationships with other peoples in which it is embedded. As Pimicikimak incorporates human, Aboriginal, and treaty rights language into its accounts of Cree self-government and relationships with other governments, it articulates these relationships in ways that directly oppose colonial processes.

The struggles that hydro-affected communities face contradict Canada's global reputation as a human rights leader, and I describe my experience of travelling with and learning from Cree advocates on the Wa Ni Ska Tan hydro tour to provide experiential context for my reading of Pimicikimak's use of rights language. I read Pimicikimak's 1998 discussion paper, 'A New Relationship,'[5] alongside a narrative legal analysis of their governance produced by settler lawyer Collin Gillespie in collaboration with Pimicikimak. The advocacy of Cree activists, elders, and fishermen on the Wa Ni Ska Tan Hydro Alliance tour resonates with Pimicikimak's approaches, together conveying Cree understandings of sustainability and rights.

Community members from Pimicikimak and other hydro-affected communities, with numerous activists and cultural workers, created the Wa Ni Ska Tan Alliance of Hydro-Affected Communities in 2014 with scholars from Southern Canada and the United States, with whom our group traveled in 2017. Wa Ni Ska Tan Hydro Alliance (WHA, or Hydro Alliance) takes its name '*Wa Ni Ska Tan*' from the Cree word for "Wake Up" or "Rise up"' and it 'emerged out of the priorities and voices of impacted Indigenous communities.' The group 'consists of representatives from 24 Cree (Ininew/Inniniwak), Anishinaabe, and Métis nations; 22 researchers; 14 social justice and environmental NGOs; 9 universities from Canada and the US; and multiple levels of government.'[6]

[5] I am citing this discussion paper because it resonates with the perspectives shared with us on the tour and because it is in the public domain. Many communities have had to sign indemnity agreements in order to access any compensation from Manitoba Hydro. Cree scholar Ramona Neckoway (Nisichawayasihk) advises that it can be valuable to cite the public record where possible.

[6] 'Who We Are,' *Wa Ni Ska Tan*, 2015, http://hydroimpacted.ca/.

Wa Ni Ska Tan scholars, Peter Kulchyski, settler scholar (University of Manitoba), and Cree scholar Ramona Neckoway (University College of the North) facilitated our group from Southern Manitoba to visit and learn from Cree communities affected by Manitoba Hydro's development on their land. For me, this process entailed learning about the treaties that I am beholden to in Manitoba from Cree perspectives, and pursuing with others, including activists from the Manitoba Energy Justice Coalition, how to act in ways that honor sovereignty, longstanding agreements, and material relationships.

Ours was the fourth iteration of the tour to date. Initiated in 2014, and run annually, the hydro tour is funded by a Social Sciences and Humanities Research Council of Canada (SSHRC) Partnership grant, headed by University of Manitoba geographer Stéphane McLachlan. An internal University of Manitoba grant to Peter Kulchyski funded the tour originally. For Kulchyski, the goal of the tour has been to take people with a wide range of social skills and possible or actual influence and expose them to the impacts of hydroelectric development. Most of the participants on the tour in each of its iterations were aware in advance of the fact that hydroelectric development has negatively impacted Northern Cree communities, and wanted to meet with affected communities to learn more and make connections, get a better sense of the environmental impacts firsthand, and offer to contribute to the aims of communities wherever possible. Kulchyski has taken artists, writers, academics, intellectuals, and activists on the tour. Many forms of resistance have been enhanced or initiated through Wa Ni Ska Tan, including art projects, journalistic productions, academic works, publicity/education endeavors, and Cree-led community collaborations. The work of the Alliance has concretely contributed to hearings with the National Energy Board of Canada, and ongoing legal challenges to Manitoba Hydro. Proposals for artistic, intellectual, educational, and activist projects are submitted to the SSHRC Partnership grant committee biannually. In 2017, the tour continued and we went to six communities in the following order: Misipawistik (Grand Rapids), Norway House, Pimicikimak (Cross Lake), Gillam (home of Fox Lake Cree Nation), Tataskweyak (Split Lake), O-Pipon-Na-Piwin (South Indian Lake), and Nisichawayasihk (Nelson House), spending roughly a day in each community.

Local organizations endorse the hydro tour at times, while development impacts and compensation agreements under imposed colonial governance systems create significant challenges for people seeking to improve their circumstances. This year, Norway House First Nation, Tataskweyak (for the first time), and Pimicikimak officially supported the tour. At South Indian Lake, Wa Ni Ska Tan works with the Community Association of South Indian Lake (CASIL) but not closely with the band councils. While Fox Lake Cree Nation is agnostic toward the group, their senior elder Noah Massan works with the Alliance. Massan, as the senior elder in the community, is highly respected and the First Nation frequently relies on his knowledge in negotiations with Manitoba Hydro. Nisichawayasihk is not supportive of Wa Ni Ska Tan, but this year we visited local activists with Ramona Neckoway, herself from Nisichawayasihk. Pimicikimak, who, of these communities, has retained a unique degree of legal autonomy from Manitoba Hydro, has supported Wa Ni Ska Tan from its inception.

Pimicikimak's sovereign governance system performs in striking and effective ways when it comes to fighting for ethical relationships to lands and peoples—relationships that those taking the hydro tour and Wa Ni Ska Tan's numerous related activist and political projects seek to create and affirm. Pimicikimak's self-governance functions to sustain distinctively accountable relationships within their community, thus positioning Pimicikimak to engage relationships outside their community on the same bases. The hydro tour itself attempts to respond to their call for accountability. In undertaking the tour, participants bear witness to the negative impacts of hydroelectric inundation. Further, face-to-face conversations with Cree people at Pimicikimak and other communities, facilitated by the tour, build ongoing relationships that frame southern academic, artistic, and activist work. This ongoing conversation combats the marginalization of Cree voices in both public discourse and colonial policy broadly.

On the tour, we were asked to bear witness and 'take on' or commit to the advancement of the communities' goals. For example, Dr. Melanie O'Gorman, who was on the 2017 tour, works as an economist with communities negotiating settlements with Manitoba Hydro. Laura Tyler, activist with the Manitoba Energy Justice Coalition (MEJC), responded by working to reframe the MEJC's mandate to attend to the impacts of hydroelectric development rather than only those of oil and gas development. As a writer and researcher, I aim to amplify the voices and perspectives of community members with whom we shared boat trips, meals, car rides, meetings, and from whom we were privileged to hear many stories. As the impacts of hydroelectric development on Cree communities have been largely erased from southern Canadian consciousness, due to 'green washing' by Manitoba Hydro, as well as the marginalization of Northern Cree communities, the hydro tour galvanizes tour participants by occasioning our listening to Cree activists, elders, and fishermen, whose expert knowledge framed all that we saw. Indigenous and non-Indigenous scholars leading the tour, through research and lived experience, also shared expert knowledge that deepened our understandings. Further, while a panel in the south or readings might also contribute to grasping aspects of the situation at a distance, the emotional impact of direct testimony and witnessing inspires a heightened degree of commitment to the issue. Flooding has inundated and eroded hundreds of acres of land, destroyed fisheries and trap lines, profoundly reduced employment opportunities, cultural practices, and knowledge, and forced relocations, disaggregating communities and causing social issues to accrue. These profound losses were crystallized (again and again) through personal stories that I had the privilege of hearing as a guest on Indigenous territories during the Wa Ni Ska Tan hydro tour.

In centering Cree perspectives on their sovereignty in the context of hydroelectric development and its impacts, and amplifying Pimicikimak's use of rights discourses, I perform accountability and witnessing. This is my small step toward embodying the rearticulation of sustainability and rights discourses within my province, as well as the material foundations of my own life, into alignment with Cree sovereignty. I am a non-Indigenous beneficiary: a white woman raising her young family in Winnipeg, teaching settler and Indigenous university students, and residing on Treaty 1 territory (having grown up in Thompson, Manitoba in Treaty 5). I am a Manitoban bound by three treaties including the Northern Flood Agreement and I hope that this writing contributes to my provincial and national communities honoring our agreements.[7] When we visited them

[7] Living in Winnipeg, I am a Treaty 1 person within the Métis homeland. I am aware that Canada and the non-Indigenous community in Treaty 1 territory do not honor Treaty 1 terms articulated by the Anishinaabe to any meaningful extent. I continue to learn about these relationships as a community participant in Indigenous-led social movements, and by studying, for example, Aimee Craft's book *Breathing Life into the Stone Fort Treaty: Anishinaabe Perspectives on Treaty One.* Having lived in Thompson, Manitoba, close to many hydro-affected Cree communities and where, as in Winnipeg, Manitoba, Hydro supplied

in August 2017, Cree community members explained to us their experiences and struggles due to inundation, and their continued thriving as Cree peoples. By listening to their accounts with others, discussing community needs and collaboration opportunities, I have been able to join in ongoing and forthcoming activist projects. While the tour is a singular event or experience for visitors, it occasions relationships based in the embodied knowledge of Cree community members and tour visitors who, in relating to one another, are committed to creating an ethical and honorable historical present.

Misipawistik (Grand Rapids)

In Grand Rapids, we visit Cree/Métis fisherman Gerald McKay on August 5, 2017. In his kitchen, he fried pickerel for us, recounting his firsthand experience of the Grand Rapids dam construction from 1960 to 1968. McKay recalls that when thousands of workers descended upon the small fishing community, Grand Rapids became unsafe for children even within residents' homes, and interpersonal racism became a profound force in the lives of the community. The community was traumatized by the dam's development and McKay, in a personal revelation, said it permanently altered the rest of his mother's life. He describes the impacts of the dam further, recalling water swallowing islands and animals swimming in circles until they drowned. His grandmother worried it was a biblical flood, praying for seven hours a day at the local church. This story resonates with a memory McKay conveys to me while we stand at the dam; he tells me he recently saw an island floating by in the reservoir, with a living deer standing on it. We see the silenced rapids of 'the town that lost its name' (there is no longer a rapids at Grand Rapids) and discuss the mental health impacts for his parents' generation of rapids replaced by ubiquitous electrical humming. We visit graveyards that were destroyed and replaced; a site we attended is called 'apartment graveyards,' because the area all

heat and electricity, I also recognize Treaty 5 as foundational terms for my existence. The Cree negotiated two treaties, Treaty 5 in 1875, and the Northern Flood Agreement with the Crown: Canada, Manitoba, and Manitoba Hydro, in 1977. In addition, the Northern Flood Agreement, signed in 1977, a treaty that focused on hydro-electrical development, has enabled my access to heat and electricity—requirements of life—on an ongoing everyday basis.

around the sacred site was razed for gravel and dam building. After having lunch, looking at the dam, the dried-up rapids, and apartment graveyards, our group continues by car to spend the night in Norway House. In the morning, Cree fisherman Langford Saunders shows us erosion on the northernmost tip of Lake Winnipeg.

Playgreen Lake, Boat Trip from Norway House

On August 6, 2017, we visit the Playgreen Lake by boat, connected by both a diversion outlet and a natural waterway to the northernmost tip of Lake Winnipeg. We see astonishing erosion at the mouth of the outlet, which our guide compares to virtually no erosion on the natural waterway. Saunders is very familiar with northern Lake Winnipeg; his family has lived seasonally in fishing lodges here all his life, as have countless generations before. He points out that Manitoba Hydro claims the erosion near the diversion outlet is 'naturally caused by the wind.' Saunders and Neckoway structure this experience to fill in for us in no uncertain terms the fact of erosion and the way it impacts Cree fisherman throughout the system. Generational family campsites have disappeared or are unsafe due to deadheads in the water. Saunders' narrative of his community's resilience and grief gives personal context for island after island, shoreline after shoreline, beach after beach having disappeared (Fig. 12.1).

Tataskweyak (Split Lake)

In Tataskweyak, on Kitchee Sipi (Nelson River), we meet with Chief Doreen Spence, and two fishermen from the fishermen's association take us on motorboats to see destroyed cabins on the islands in the lake, erosion and 'apple core' islands, so-called because they erode under the surface of the water before sinking into the lake (like so many before), and unending devastation to shorelines. Our guides explain the local histories and current realities for fishing practice and familial and communal relationships. Amid testimony of lost land, lost access to sites, mercury in fish, sediment in water, we witness how multifaceted the impacts of hydro development are and have been: the daily, moment to moment, cumulative impact over years, the emotional labor of coping, the decades of legal battling, constant self-advocacy and citizenship practice against a colonial onslaught: the vast

Fig. 12.1 Flooded and eroding shorelines at South Indian Lake, Wa Ni Ska Tan boat tour, August 11, 2017. Photo by Whitney Light

magnitude of what has happened. This process benefits hydro users like me with very low energy rates within Winnipeg homes, producing my home through multifaceted Indigenous dispossession. In witnessing and listening on the Wa Ni Ska Tan tour, I am hailed as a settler scholar and citizen, as someone responsible to these relationships, as a beneficiary of the power thus produced, as a beneficiary of the colonial processes of dispossession of which this development is a piece. During our next visit to Pimicikimak, elder Rita Monias ties these themes together (Fig. 12.2).

Pimicikimak | Cross Lake Reserve

At Pimicikimak Okimowin, we visit the new governance center. In this space, we meet Rita Monias, member of the women's council of Pimicikimak's four councils of government. She tells us of her occupation of Manitoba Hydro's Jenpeg dam in 2014. For Monias, it is hydro that is occupying Pimicikimak land, and not the other way around. Monias points out that she occupied the dam's spillway—or made tea on her land, rather—in 2014 because she 'was lonely' for the elders in her community,

Fig. 12.2 Flooded cabin on Split Lake, Wa Ni Ska Tan boat tour, August 9, 2017. Photo by Whitney Light

and for what they saw unfolding in their community. Monias' activism performs her belonging on the land; her belonging thwarts Canadian ideas of land, nature, and identity that falsely view the Manitoban North as by-and-large empty, and freely available for resource exploitation by southerners. This land, as Monias and other Cree activists emphasize, is intergenerationally inhabited and used by the Cree (Fig. 12.3).

Monias further described the significant loss of economic and cultural opportunity for her community. She says, 'Our people need to work, especially children. For future generations, jobs, homes. This is cultural genocide. These agreements collect dust, centuries of dust, burying us alive.' What struck me in what she said is in part that practical experiences of home and belonging for non-Indigenous peoples in the southern parts of Manitoba rely on these processes, the significance of which is disavowed: the fragmentation and alienation of Indigenous relational worlds that Monias describes. Kulchyski calls this the 'racial reconfiguration and redistribution of wealth,' wherein capitalist development destroys Cree forms of wealth—time, land, culture, and relationships—converting these into

Fig. 12.3 Jenpeg dam, August 9, 2017. Photo by Whitney Light

abstract capital for southerners.[8] Monias' references to dust offer a harrowing metaphor for the multifaceted weight of the inundation's impacts: suffocating deadly dust piling up due to neglect and inattention. Sociologist Caroline Desbiens writes of settlers in Quebec that their relationship to hydroelectric power produces their subjectivity: 'national and provincial subjects are produced in the relationship between Northern and Southern [Manitoba], whose desires, aspirations, interests, and beliefs are generated through their interaction with water,' whether this interaction be self-aware or, as Monias describes, deadly in its inattentiveness.[9] In occupying the Jenpeg dam/making tea on her land, Monias identifies and interrupts, with her body, the colonial dynamics that rest upon what Mark Rifkin calls 'settler common sense.' Rifkin writes:

[8] Peter Kulchyski, 'A Step Back: The Nisichawayasihk Cree Nation and the Wuskwatim Project,' in *Power Struggles*, ed. Thibault Martin and Steven M. Hoffman (Winnipeg: University of Manitoba Press, 2008), 132.

[9] Caroline Desbiens, *Power from the North: Territory, Identity, and the Culture of Hydroelectricity in Quebec* (Vancouver: UBC Press, 2013), 14.

> [T]he workings of settler colonialism [mean] an entrenched inattention to the ways non-Native conceptions and articulations of personhood, place, property, and political belonging coalesce around and through the dispossession of Native peoples and normalization of (the) settler (-state's) presence on Native lands.[10]

Monias supports southern social movement building and consciousness raising, such as that of the MEJC, which builds awareness of the impacts of hydroelectric development on northern communities, and interrupts the naturalization of colonial 'personhood, place, property and political belonging' in response to and in alignment with Pimicikimak's efforts. After meeting with Rita and spending the night at a hotel in Thompson, Manitoba, we move forward to Gillam and Fox Lake, a town split in two sections: Fox Lake reserve, where Cree people live, and Gillam, a town for mostly non-native hydro workers. The striking contrast of poverty and affluence, street-to-street and side-by-side, speaks exactly to the assumptions that Rifkin and Desbiens describe, and that Monias and Pimicikimak confront with their performance of sovereignty.

Gillam and Fox Lake

In Gillam and Fox Lake, on August 9, 2017, we drive along the trapline of Cree trapper Noah Massan, who tells us many stories while we see the present state of the Keeyask dam's construction, and the clear-cut forests and disturbed trap lines, in particular Massan's own. The clear-cut forest is an apocalyptic scene. The view back in town is not much better: in addition to the glaring imposed poverty on the First Nation, we witness two meter boxes on each of the homes for hydro employees in Gillam, who receive subsidized hydropower. The people on the First Nation do not; they only have one meter, and have had to pay astronomically high rates ($800 a month at times). Manitoba Hydro cut off their heat in the wintertime for being in arrears, until it was legally obligated to cease such an inhumane practice. The spatial arrangement of Gillam/Fox Lake renders in stark relief the oppression of 'settler common sense' as the utility, the province, and the state embody it, and as their structures make manifest in on-the-ground relationships: annihilated ecosystems, hierarchical built environments, openly racist infrastructures.

[10] Mark Rifkin, 'Settler Common Sense,' *Settler Colonial Studies* 3 (2013): 324.

After witnessing impacts and listening to stories, we spend the night in Thompson before coming to O-Pipon-Na-Piwin for our next-to-last community visit. Like Massan, the Dysarts, a fishing family, frame my experience of witnessing in terms of the complex details of community relationships with hydro: most significantly, the impacts on lands and waters and the energy/labor of the people we meet in confronting and negotiating the onslaught. The sustainability of the work of this trip relies in part on the actions of tour participants: will we amplify voices, engage in social movement, teach in our communities, lobby government, and lend our skills to the effort? My role as a participant focuses on acknowledging responsibility to what I have been given: all of the people I have met have shared their time, knowledge, personal experience; accountability means in part amplifying their voices in the domains within our reach.

O-Pipon-Na-Piwin (South Indian Lake)

Les Dysart, fisherman at O-Pipon-Na-Piwin, recounts the history of their commercial fishery, fifth largest in the world during the mid-twentieth century. Their transnational trade with Chicago and New York fish markets meant that Rabbis from New York City regularly came up to bless the boats for gefilte fish. Hydro destroyed the fishery in the 1970s. Fishing and hunting, including guided hunting at a community-owned hunting lodge, do continue: we visit a bush camp. Our hosts and some visitors, including filmmaker Kevin Lee Burton (Swampy Cree), from God's Lake Narrows 800 miles north of Winnipeg, together collect Labrador tea.

These acts of relationship with the land speak to longstanding connections. Intimate relationships between land and people are apparent here and in other moments, such as when Noah Massan receives tobacco from a Cree hydro worker, asking if Massan can collect Labrador for him, as we move through a checkpoint on the way to see a dam site. These dynamics are alive and resonant across communities including Nisichawayasihk, the last community we visit.

Nisichawayasihk (Nelson House)

While I grew up in northern Manitoba, on the Wa Ni Ska Tan tour I saw for the first time how environmental menace and outright destruction coalesce with colonial policy to profoundly stress Cree relationships. In Nelson House, we visit a bush camp, and share fish and moose with

Ramona Neckoway's mother and aunties and uncles. Neckoway's uncle Moses describes to me how he lost his brother, due to deadheads floating in the water that caused a boating accident. He rhetorically asks me, with some anger: 'how can they compensate for life?' When we visit, the family is setting up an annual youth camp for the following week. After having lunch in the camp, we visit two sacred sites, the Footprints, and the Circle, the former a place of mourning adjacent to a cemetery. According to Peter Kulchyski, the Footprints site

> was flooded [in the 1970s] as part of a hydroelectric grand project called the Churchill River Diversion and Lake Winnipeg Regulation. Two of the Footprints were removed and set in a concrete slab, which sat at a variety of destinations until it was returned to rest on the bank of the river near its original site. Although there is evidence of traditional activity at the site, at least some local elders believe these are not the real Footprints but a copy, attesting in my view to the fact that they feel the site has lost its power.[11]

Stranded boats and beaver dams, due to sudden falling water levels, are the last disquieting environmental vision with which our guides leave us.

The labor of our guides in each site reflects commitments made by members of their community in the 1970s, when all five of these communities formed the Northern Flood Committee (NFC) and negotiated a treaty. Still, shoreline erosion and deadheads, destroyed camps, fisheries, habitats, and sacred sites surround us on our travels. There is mercury in the fish and methane in the air, released by stirred water. The strategies of the NFC, the Cree community members we meet on the tour, and Pimicikimak's self-governance refuse to accept the assumption that they as a people do not exist or matter, that their lands are 'empty,' and their sovereignty voided. The people who led us on the tour showed through their narratives and actions the commitment they have to relationships with and on the land: to themselves and each other and the land. The Northern Flood Committee set a legacy of advocacy in motion, grounded in pre-existing sovereignty. The latter is the basis for the ongoing relationships that we on the tour witnessed and entered into as guests and treaty beneficiaries in the present.

[11] Peter Kulchyski, 'Bush Sites/Bush Stories: Politics of Place and Memory in Indigenous Northern Manitoba,' *MLA Commons*, July 13, 2016, https://profession.mla.hcommons.org/2016/07/13/bush-sites-bush-stories-politics-of-place-and-memory-in-indigenous-northern-canada/.

Northern Flood Committee

The NFC negotiated the Northern Flood Agreement (NFA) in part by arguing flooding and land appropriation violated Treaty 5,[12] and while the NFA promised meaningful compensation, the province and Manitoba Hydro did not honor their agreement. Instead, they eventually offered a number of 'Implementation Agreements' or one-time cash buyouts, as the utility claimed that the NFA, which committed to 'the eradication of mass poverty and mass unemployment' for impacted communities, was too onerous. While the federal government supported the NFC in asserting their treaty rights to negotiate with the province and Manitoba Hydro,[13] the five communities represented by the NFC were in a precarious position when they agreed to sign the already-completed hydroelectric development. Most communities, all but Pimicikimak, enduring poverty directly caused by the impacts of flooding accepted badly needed monies when the subsequent implementation agreements were offered. In Manitoba Hydro's commissioned book, *A History of Electrical Power in Manitoba*, they detail how the NFA addressed 'mitigation works, compensation, training, employment and [...] community planning'; however, they claim that 'by the mid-1980s, it was apparent the arbitration process set out in the NFA was an inefficient mechanism to resolve outstanding issues.'[14] Inefficiency is an interesting word here, since the Implementation Agreement sums up that the compensation offered was exceedingly modest when compared to the compensation of the Cree in northern Quebec for Hydro Quebec's development, for instance, or to what the NFA has promised.

The spirit and intent of the treaties from many Cree perspectives, of mutual benefit and sharing the land, have yet to be treated with seriousness by Crown parties in Manitoba or federally. Traditional economies continue to be impacted, despite enormous profits accruing for the

[12] Namely, the NFC argued for the section of the treaty that states: 'the aforesaid reserves of land, or any interest therein, may be sold or otherwise disposed of by her Majesty's Government for the use and benefit of the said Indians entitled thereto, with their consent first had and obtained.'

[13] Ramona Neckoway, 'Amiskuk Boo-koo Ta Ki Oosey-ta-chik Ki-piikuna: "Only Beavers Should Build Dams",' Master's Thesis, University of Manitoba, 2007, 36.

[14] Manitoba Hydro, *A History of Electrical Power in Manitoba* (Winnipeg: Manitoba Hydro, 2005), 65.

corporation every year from the sale of power to the United States. In addition, impacted communities have had to sign 'indemnity clauses' in order to access desperately needed (and insufficient) compensation monies, and thus cannot legally speak of any ongoing negative impacts on their communities. Pimicikimak performing their Cree sovereignty enhances intergenerational hope within their community as well as personal, communal, and national identity. At the same time, their performative strategies of framing their relationships—both within and without their community—increase the power of their sovereignty and related conceptual framings in the intersocietal context of relationships between Canadians, Manitobans, and the Cree in northern Manitoba.

Framing 'A New Relationship': Pimicikimak Discussion Paper and Self-Governance

Pimicikimak, refusing an Implementation Agreement in favor of the NFA, affirms the modern treaty as a document of Pimicikimak's sovereignty. While national sovereignty, according to British legal traditions inherited by Canada, means that the nation is a body politic deriving its authority from 'no temporal source other than itself,'[15] Pimicikimak draws upon transnational and intersocietal rights language in articulating its sovereignty: treaty, human, and aboriginal rights. Pimicikimak Cree Nation's (PCN) 1998 discussion paper 'A New Relationship' asserts their treaty, Aboriginal, and human rights, insisting that Crown treaty signatories honor their agreements on the basis of alliance and good faith.[16] Gillespie points out that the international human right 'to exist as a people' in this context becomes a decolonial tool, as it recognizes Pimicikimak's existing sovereignty. Aboriginal rights, enshrined in the Canadian constitution, are a form of law distinct from either Pimicikimak laws or Canadian laws—yet Pimicikimak draws upon them: Gillespie notes the deep dissonance and tension in Aboriginal rights discourse between individual rights (on which Canadian law is based) and relationships and responsibilities (Cree law).[17] Pimicikimak draws upon Aboriginal rights language, which originates from colonial contact, as a way to describe—in a cross-cultural context—their sovereign responsibilities within both their nation and intersocietal relationships.

[15] Colin Gillespie, *Portrait of a People: A Study in Survival* (Winnipeg: Big Fizz, 2017), 26.
[16] Pimicikimak Cree Nation, 'A New Relationship,' *Pimicikimak Cree Nation* (1998), 24.
[17] Gillespie, *Portrait of a People*, 9.

The language of rights and their violations affords Pimicikimak one of many means to articulate the impacts of colonial impositions in language shared with other nations, rendering legible how inundation has infringed on Pimicikimak's right to exist as a people. In this way, it lends weight to their arguments that the National Flood Agreement must be honored. The 'implementation agreement' proposed by Manitoba Hydro, ceasing treaty relationships, opposes their approach, defining Pimicikimak's relationship with the state in terms of the Indian Act and the Band Council system of governance (as opposed to self-governance and sovereignty). Further, through the Implementation Agreement approach, colonial disruptions of Pimicikimak's relationships to their land will be inadequately remediated. In response, 'Pimicikimak has adopted a strategy of visibility [...] to focus public attention on the NFA *performance* of Crown parties and officials' (my emphasis). In Pimicikimak's view, this attention should lead to sustained changes by those who commit to the repair of Cree 'society and economy,' with a focus on the spirit and intent of the treaty relationship from Cree perspectives.[18]

Understanding the NFA relationship as performance grounds it in experience, relational visibility, embodiment, and materiality, rather than in the bureaucratic abstractions that form the basis of colonial governance. Colonial governance provides a scalable capitalist framework for abstract (liberal) individuals—the very logic enshrined in many iterations of human rights discourse. The Cree, exercising their sovereignty in making treaty, continue their embodied and material relationships from time immemorial as present and continuous: not abstract but performative, 'from the ground up.' 'A New Relationship' underscores that the NFA is a treaty relationship that requires ongoing good faith and engages rights discourse to emphasize it.

While Canadian law designates the terms 'modern treaty' and 'land claim' as interchangeable, Pimicikimak argues that the term 'claim' is reductive. Their use of human rights language underscores this fact by affirming their existence 'as a people.' Pimicikimak argues that 'the treaty relationship provides a basis for reconciling the constitution of the Nation and the Constitution of Canada—and indeed may be the only viable basis for reconciling them.' This vision sees the NFA treaty as a sacred promise, in view of the Crown's honor and Cree governance approaches, that ensures 'substantive fair and equitable treatment [with]

[18] Pimicikimak Cree Nation, 'A New Relationship,' 8.

effective and meaningful structures [...] in place' to resolve hydroelectric development's 'devastat[ion of] the Nation's spirit, culture and economy and dissipation of its lands.'[19] They write: 'our people suffer under permanent and inflicted conditions of dispossession, mass poverty, unemployment and despair, in breach of our fundamental human rights,'[20] including the right to exist as a people. Detailing the UN articles in which their human rights are enshrined, including Articles 1.1 and 1.3 of the International Convention on Civil and Political Rights, as well as Articles 1.1 and 1.3 of the International Convention on Social, Economic and Cultural Rights, Pimicikimak invites 'ongoing human-rights scrutiny' on the basis of these conventions. Such scrutiny invites other nations to intervene in 'ensuing our human rights are respected.'[21] Here, human rights are a tool within the purview of already-existing Cree existence and governance.[22]

Not all thinkers see value in the language of human rights for Indigenous communities. Kulchyski, for example, argues that social justice activists need to understand the difference between Aboriginal and human rights if they want to be of use in contributing to Indigenous struggles, and he decries the totalization implied and enacted in many uses of human rights discourse.[23] Further, Cherokee scholar Jeff Corntassel argues that, in settler–colonial contexts, rights discourses are commensurate with those of reconciliation and resource extraction, or what he calls the 'politics of distraction.' Against these, he advocates autonomous Indigenous approaches centered on responsibilities, resurgence, and relationships. Corntassel argues for autonomy from the colonial state and its language, and a rejection of 'the performativity of rights discourse geared toward state affirmation and recognition [...] embracing instead a daily existence conditioned by place-based cultural practices.'[24] In line with

[19] Ibid., 17.

[20] Ibid., 9.

[21] Ibid., 23.

[22] PCN practices Aboriginal rights in its self-government methodologies, which include four councils of government, and differ from the Cross Lake First Nation, which it regards as an arm of Indian and Northern Affairs, created through the Indian Act to abrogate self-governance. It aims for Cross Lake to increasingly serve as an arm of PCN as autonomous self-governance accrues greater strength in the rebuilding of national practices and Cree-determined identity.

[23] Peter Kulchyski, *Aboriginal Rights are not Human Rights* (Winnipeg: Arbeiter Ring, 2013), 8.

[24] Jeff Corntassel, 'Re-envisioning Resurgence: Indigenous Pathways to Decolonization and Sustainable Self-Determination,' *Decolonization: Indigeneity, Education & Society* 1, no. 1 (2012): 88.

Corntassel's insights, Pimicikimak distinguishes itself from the band name that was instituted by Indian and Northern Affairs: Cross Lake First Nation, under the authority of the settler state and governed through Canada's Indian Act. To date, the federal government of Canada requires on-reserve Indigenous peoples to have band councils in order to receive federal funding. Pimicikimak, through their resurgence of Cree law, deliberately diminishes the power of Cross Lake First Nation, by increasingly turning its function toward the collective will expressed through Pimicikimak's sovereignty and four-council Cree government structure. For Pimicikimak, rights discourses and band councils are not used here to gain state affirmation, but to ground the language and infrastructure of the state in the form and content of Cree self-governance.

When we were on the hydro tour, Monias explained that the nation's First Written Law, written in English text and legal dictum, and displayed and encased in glass in the Governance Building's foyer, provides a contemporary ground for Pimicikimak's nationhood. Cree oral tradition is the basis of the law. Like Corntassel, Pimicikimak emphasizes community resurgence, against 'fram[ing] community relationships in state-centric terms.'[25] They frame relationships with the state, including state discourses of rights, in community-centric terms. Human rights as delineated by Pimicikimak are not the 'distraction' of their community from better, more resurgent priorities. Rather, they are provided for the understanding of all peoples, performing visibility and legibility from within Pimicikimak's relational framework.

Conclusions on Home and Manitoba Hydro

While the settler state and global capitalism have aimed to erase Cree existence, including through the application of rights language, Cree people have resisted by bringing rights into the purview of dynamic, land-based, and relational responsibilities. This is a sustainable strategy, drawing upon pre-existing sovereignty and using language developed by others for self-determined Cree use in the context of intersocietal relations. In the wake of the Wa Ni Ska Tan tour, I continue to build relationships of Cree-led collaboration, educate myself on intersocietal and treaty relationships, and align myself with the ongoing performance of sovereignty by

[25] Taiaiake Alfred and Jeff Corntassel, 'Being Indigenous: Resurgences against Contemporary Colonialism,' *Government & Opposition* 40 (2005): 600.

Pimicikimak and other Cree communities. Scrutinizing the Crown parties' NFA performance can potentially contribute to repairing treaty relationships, by uniting settler-Canadians' vision of ourselves and Manitoba territory to that of Pimicikimak's sovereignty, exercised rather than extinguished in signing treaties.[26] Pimicikimak embodies and performs sovereignty and self-government as sustainable methods in the face of colonial onslaught, using the language of rights while subsuming them into Cree self-determination.

References

Corntassel, Jeff. 'Re-envisioning Resurgence: Indigenous Pathways to Decolonization and Sustainable Self-Determination.' *Decolonization: Indigeneity, Education & Society* 1, no. 1 (2012): 86–101.

Coulthard, Glen. *Red Skin White Masks: Rejecting the Colonial Politics of Recognition*. Minneapolis: University of Minnesota Press, 2015.

Desbiens, Caroline. *Power from the North: Territory, Identity, and the Culture of Hydroelectricity in Quebec*. Vancouver: UBC Press, 2013.

Evans, Lara. 'What to Do When Theory Does Not Work for You: Native Performance Art and Performance Theory Revised.' Not Artomatic, March 4, 2010. https://notartomatic.wordpress.com/2010/03/04/what-to-do-when-theory-does-not-work-for-you-native-performance-art-and-performance-theory-revised/.

Gillespie, Colin. *Portrait of a People: A Study in Survival*. Winnipeg: Big Fizz, 2017.

Kulchyski, Peter. *Aboriginal Rights are Not Human Rights*. Winnipeg: Arbeiter Ring Press, 2013.

———. 'Bush Sites/Bush Stories: Politics of Place and Memory in Indigenous Northern Manitoba.' *MLA Commons*, July 13, 2016. https://profession.mla.hcommons.org/2016/07/13/bush-sites-bush-stories-politics-of-place-and-memory-in-indigenous-northern-canada/.

———. 'A Step Back: The Nisichawayasihk Cree Nation and the Wuskwatim Project.' In *Power Struggles*, edited by Thibault Martin and Steven M. Hoffman, 129–144. Winnipeg: University of Manitoba Press, 2008.

Neckoway, Ramona. 'Amiskuk Boo-koo Ta Ki Oosey-ta-chik Ki-piikuna: "Only Beavers Should Build Dams".' Master's Thesis, University of Manitoba, 2007.

———. Conversation with the Author, August 2017.

Pimicikimak Cree Nation. 'A New Relationship.' Discussion Paper. 1998.

Rifkin, Mark. 'Settler Common Sense.' *Settler Colonial Studies* 3 (2013): 322–34.

[26] I am currently working on an art project to this effect.

Robinson, Dylan. 'Enchantment's Irreconcilable Connection: Listening to Anger, Being Idle No More.' In *Performance Studies in Canada*, edited by Laura Levin and Marlis Schweitzer, 211–235. Montreal: McGill-Queen's University Press, 2017.

'Who We Are.' *Wa Ni Ska Tan*, 2015. http://hydroimpacted.ca/.

Leah Decter with Stop Violence Against Aboriginal Women Action Group, *The Human Billboard Project*, 2010

"Ending violence against Aboriginal women and girls lies with both men and women, with both Aboriginal and non-Aboriginal communities. It ends with recognition, responsibility and cooperation."
—Native Women's Association of Canada (NWAC), April 2010

Image credit: SVAAWAG

Leah Decter with Stop Violence Against Aboriginal Women Action Group, *The Human Billboard Project*, 2010

In 1971, a young Cree student named Helen Betty Osborne was kidnapped, sexually assaulted and brutally murdered by four white men in the town of The Pas, Manitoba. It wasn't until 1987 that one of the men was charged and convicted. In the intervening years, hundreds—perhaps thousands—of Indigenous women and girls would be murdered or go missing across Canada, and activists and advocates would begin to identify an epidemic of racism, sexism, indifference and impunity that continues to put lives in danger. **NO MORE STOLEN SISTERS**, they demanded.

In 2010, the Winnipeg-based collective Stop Violence Against Aboriginal Women Action Group collaborated with artist Leah Decter on a series of performances designed to call public attention to the issue. After meeting with affected women and families, the team called on community members to occupy several public spaces in the city—a shopping mall, a big box store parking lot, a sports stadium—wearing t-shirts with messages of mourning, resilience, and solidarity. **NO MORE STOLEN SISTERS**, read the human billboard.

In 2016, a National Inquiry into Missing and Murdered Indigenous Women and Girls was launched with a mandate to "examine the systemic causes of all forms of violence against Indigenous women, girls and members of the LGBTQ2S community in Canada." While the ongoing Inquiry has been mired in confusion and controversy, activists and advocates continue to mobilize around a simple but powerful message:

NO MORE STOLEN SISTERS.

"They came together across race, class, gender and experience, and they used their bodies to bring palpable presence to urgent words and thoughts. In this way, the project insisted the issue into public space at a time when it was decidedly underrepresented. It was made visible on site in real time and subsequently in mainstream media, social media, and in continuing public actions —extending the scope of the project both further into the community and into concrete actions that can be taken by individuals." **—Leah Decter**

Formed in 2009, **STOP VIOLENCE AGAINST ABORIGINAL WOMEN ACTION GROUP** is a grassroots collective of Indigenous and non-Indigenous women working to address violence against Aboriginal women and girls. Members come to the collective through a commitment to action, and with experience in community, program and economic development, research, social practice and inter-media art practices, front line and antiracism work, counselling, activism, and lobbying. **LEAH DECTER** is an intermedia artist and scholar based in Winnipeg, Treaty 1 territory. Her work has been exhibited and screened internationally at venues including the Winnipeg Art Gallery, Trinity Square Video, the Dunlop Art Gallery, Film Festival Rotterdam, Malta Contemporary Art and the Images Festival in Toronto. Her practice focuses on contested spaces and decolonial interventions through a critical white settler lens. Decter holds a PhD in Cultural Studies from Queen's University.

CHAPTER 13

INTERVIEW
Already-And: The Art of Indigenous Survivance

Cheryl L'Hirondelle, Natalie Alvarez, and Keren Zaiontz

Cheryl L'Hirondelle is an Indigenous (non-status treaty Indian and a mixed-blood: Cree/Métis; German/Polish) award-winning interdisciplinary artist, singer/songwriter, and new media curator originally from the land now known as Canada. Her creative practice is an investigation of the intersection of a Cree worldview (*nêhiyawin*) and contemporary time-place.

C. L'Hirondelle (✉)
University College Dublin, Dublin, Ireland

N. Alvarez
Ryerson University, Toronto, ON, Canada
e-mail: natalie.alvarez@ryerson.ca

K. Zaiontz
Queen's University, Kingston, ON, Canada
e-mail: keren.zaiontz@queensu.ca

N. Alvarez et al. (eds.), *Sustainable Tools for Precarious Times*,
Contemporary Performance InterActions,
https://doi.org/10.1007/978-3-030-11557-9_13

Keren Zaiontz: Cheryl, in a 2012 conversation entitled 'Songlines, Stories and Community Engagement,'[1] you reflect on your five-year residency in northwest Saskatchewan for the Meadow Lake Tribal Council. As a community-engaged artist, you came to recognize that '*nêhiyawin* (a Cree worldview) is my tool for survival.' Can you tell us about the centrality of *nêhiyawin* to your artistic practice? What does that mean to you, and how does it function as a tool?

Cheryl L'Hirondelle: Cree worldview is a way to experience and be in the world. To help unpack: *nêhiyawin*—Cree worldview—Cree people, or *nêhiyawak*, are called 'four-directions' people[2] because it is thought that the first syllable '*nê*' refers to *nêwo* or the number 'four.' We're also known as being precise speakers. Etymologically, the first syllable is thought to also reference '*nahi*,' meaning 'accurate' or sometimes people will say, 'correct speaking.' The language itself is *nêhiyawewin* and the diphthong '*wew*' in the middle connotes 'to sound'—hence, the language is 'the sounding of the worldview.' Conceptually, if I'm sounding out into four directions and in doing so experiencing the relationship of language and land, then I'm very grounded. Like a table with four legs, it's a stable base or framework. It is this incredible grounding with which I make work, and how I proceed in the world. Like a portal, it became the most accurate and authentic way to be in the world, and from this vantage point, I also started to know who I am. And as it explained me, this process empowered and grounded me and I became more connected with the world. 'Survivance,' as Gerald Vizenor writes extensively about,[3] is a concept of what I'd translate as: 'already-and.' In Cree one would say: *âsay mîna*. You could translate it into English roughly as, 'again' but it's not a repeat or a reoccurrence—as if anything stopped and needed to be started. It really translates to: 'already-(continuing)-and.'

Keren Zaiontz: This language of continuance takes our thinking about sustainability into philosophical territory and yet, is still very much tied to the survival of body and soul. I'm wondering, could you talk

[1] See Cheryl L'Hirondelle, Elwood Jimmy, and Chris Bose, 'Songlines, Stories and Community Engagement,' *West Coast Line* 74 46, no. 2 (2012): 94–107.

[2] Mary Lee, 'Cree (*Nehiyawak*) Teaching,' *FourDirectionsTeaching.com*. Aboriginal Online Teachings and Resource Centre, 4D Interactive Inc., 2006. http://www.fourdirectionsteachings.com/transcripts/cree.html.

[3] As Gerald Robert Vizenor writes, 'Survivance is an active sense of presence, the continuance of native stories, not a mere reaction, or a survivable name. Native survivance stories are renunciations of dominance, tragedy and victimry.' See *Manifest Manners: Narratives on Postindian Survivance* (University of Nebraska Press, 1999), vii.

about your relationship to the Cree language, how you came to learn it, and its tie to your artistic practice?

Cheryl L'Hirondelle: My mother used to speak some Cree words to us when we were kids—mostly utilitarian or scolding phrases [*laughs*]. It wasn't until my early 20s that the language started showing up in my mouth. I remember waking up one morning, and as I was brushing my teeth, all of a sudden I started uttering sounds. I went to visit my mom later that day and she said, 'Oh, I think you're trying to say ________. ' It was like my body already knew the language; sounds I would have heard as a really young child. In the summer of 1995, I had the opportunity to go to northern Saskatchewan on the Beaver River—at Beauval and La Plonge First Nation. My mom had lived along the Beaver River, but down river in Alberta where she grew up, and I knew the Cree language would be similar, so a perfect place to learn.

Victor Masayesva [Jr.] asserts that Indigenous aesthetics begins with the sacred.[4] There are many beyond rational realities encoded within the worldview I experienced those next few years living amongst elders, knowledge keepers, and ceremonialists. It was during this time that I recognized deep in my subconscious and dreams someone was always there shining a light and hinting at concepts, though I wasn't quite sure who or what they were at first. I looked back at earlier performance work that I had made and could finally begin to understand what they were about. So *nêhiyawêwin was* useful and became a vital part of a new way of conceptualizing work, though it was not based on, 'when am I going to have my solo show?' and all the calculating that goes along with a contemporary urban practice.

Natalie Alvarez: What precipitated the move into *songs because of the land*? I wonder if you can tell us a little bit of the backstory of how you arrived at that project.

Cheryl L'Hirondelle: Not long after I moved to Saskatchewan, I was writing songs and performing in a musical duo called Nikamok[5] and then in 1996 I began working for the Meadow Lake Tribal Council (MLTC) as

[4] Steven Leuthold, *Indigenous Aesthetics: Native Art, Media, and Identity* (University of Texas Press, 1998).

[5] In 1995, L'Hirondelle had been awarded a Toronto Arts Council Composer Award, and used the funds towards her first year in Saskatchewan. It serendipitously dovetailed with her then newly formed musical duo, Nikamok (with Joseph Naytowhow).

a co-storyteller.[6] The work required constant traveling to visit elders from all of the nine MLTC First Nations. Nikamok, was regularly touring and performing at other First Nations, music festivals, and events all around Saskatchewan—and beyond. Around that time, I think I started to become cognizant that while we were driving and witnessing these beautiful vistas, with every turn in the road, there was another spontaneous song to sing.

I moved to Vancouver, and in 2005 when I had a roommate, we would go for walks around the Kitsilano—or *Khatsahlano*—area. I would be humming little song shards, and when we would turn to go down another street, I would sing something slightly different. One day she pointed out to me: 'You've got songs for all these streets.' It was unconscious, but I think the practice was well rooted/routed. Glenn Alteen [program director] from grunt gallery commissioned me to make a performance art piece, but I was already moving toward a more integrated interdisciplinary approach in my work. I was already making [online] database driven net. art projects by then, and I also had an ongoing practice as a musician—and I didn't want to have a siloed practice. So, I suggested that I would create something like a website that cataloged these singings, but that I would also include performative elements—that I would sing to individual people living on the streets.

Glenn, in his curatorial essay for *nikamon ohci askiy (songs because of the land)*, states that I based the project on the practice of Aboriginal Australian. It was actually my production team, who were helping me develop the web interface who begged me not to use a Cree title as the domain. Their rationale was that because no one would know how to consistently spell (let alone pronounce it), that visits to the site would be affected, hence the domain name: vancouversonglines.ca.[7]

Natalie Alvarez: How might *songs because of the land* link back to this idea of 'sounding,' because it seems that was the original place from which it emerged. In a 2010 talk you gave in Winnipeg, you discuss how this work has served as a way of mapping the land for Indigenous peoples since time immemorial. But I wanted to ask what makes this practice of sounding newly urgent for you in this particular historical moment, in

[6] From 1996 to 2000, she was a co-storyteller in residence (also with Joseph Naytowhow) for Meadow Lake Tribal Council in northwest Saskatchewan. He had been hired in 1995, but after one year she had proven to be a good collaborator and resource to help expand the outreach and impact of their work.

[7] The web project was later given an honorable mention in their net.art category at the prestigious Webby Awards (2009).

what is now called Canada. You touched originally on how it's important for your artistic practice but is there something that it's doing for you now, in this particular moment?

Cheryl L'Hirondelle: I think I may have stated that because in 2008, as I was in development of *nikamon ohci askiy*, I met and performed with a couple Sami joikers at a colloquium[8] and they shared their practice of how joiking related to their landbase, and the next year, I heard the Indigenous music group Digging Roots talk about a similar process they were engaged in.[9]

As a visual artist, I lack the dexterity or knowledge of a material practice and therefore can't render. One material I *do* have knowledge of, and considerable ability with, is sound and, specifically, my voice. So, I decided to make a sonic drawing, a sonic map of the places I walked. I was singing out into all directions, echolocating and substantiating myself in the process. What makes it urgent now? In the last ten years, there has been a shift toward decolonial work—insurgence, resurgence—and indigenizing place. During a *Doing Sovereignties* gathering at Western Front,[10] I was invited to take some people around Vancouver on sound walks to listen and shed some insight on my process. Two participants were from the West Coast. When I asked them what they heard, they commented on mechanized sounds from buses or vehicles. As they intoned these sounds, one said: 'Oh, there used to be bears here, this is the sound that a bear would make.' The other said of their observance: 'This is actually a sound from my language, even though it's the bus hydraulics.' I thought that was interesting, that those sounds are still in the land. We can still hear them, we can still listen for them. As much as we may think of sounding as something that you utter, there's actually a more resonant relationship to the deep listening involved.

Natalie Alvarez: Where did the maps live? Were they bodily or did you actually put them to paper? Were they mapped with imagery, or was it completely improvisational and site-responsive, moment-to-moment?

Cheryl L'Hirondelle: The website housed audio files of the various song shards of my journeys around Vancouver. It was intuitive and not a visual rendering, because I was drawing with my voice—in the air, so to speak. I

[8] Niila Stålka Per, Ulla Pirttijärvi, and Frode Fjellheim, 'Indigenous Music and Dance as Cultural Property,' May 2–4, 2008, and 'Global Spirit: An Indigenous Showcase,' May 4, 2008, Toronto, ON.

[9] See Digging Roots explaining their latest album concept: https://www.youtube.com/watch?v=4jE8P3NJNK4&t=36s.

[10] 'Doing Sovereignties' gathering, coordinated by Dylan Robinson and Candice Hopkins, Western Front Gallery, Vancouver, BC, May 2016.

was very conscious about not wanting to make the piece traceable. As we know, a lot of these technologies we use in our creative practices are still military technologies: Global Positioning Systems (GPS) and Geographic Information System Mapping Technology (GIS) have not been decommissioned by the army or by defense. Because of this, I didn't want to make people vulnerable, for you to find out where people are, or pinpoint them on a map and I wanted to *sing* this place. The community-engaged part of the project was interactions with people on the streets [homeless and precariously housed people], so the lyrics were almost all in English. I didn't want to make anybody vulnerable. I didn't want to have a Google map or a Twitter feed locate me nor have an art audience show up. The performance aspect of the project was situated around a community-engagement fund. I subverted it somewhat and instead paid homeless guys to listen to me sing my song shards. It was winter, so it was really lovely to know that they could get into a shelter or buy a meal that day. It was also important for me to subvert the practice of people paying to hear the musician, and reverse the transaction so that the singer was in service to the community.

Keren Zaiontz: Is that something that you often do, subvert traditional artist-spectator categories, or redirect your art capital in ways that might benefit different communities or create new interlocutors?

Cheryl L'Hirondelle: Yes, I've been doing it in many projects and in various ways. I think it is important to share the focus, since I'm not the only bird singing, you know? One project I did for several years that hasn't been discussed much was one I called *The NDN Storytelling Bus Tour* for a couple years (2011–2014) in Regina as part of Sâkêwêwak Artist Centre's annual Storytellers Festival. For this project, the festival provided me a city transit bus equipped with a small battery powered amplifier and a handheld microphone with a 25-foot cable. Because I'd previously been a storyteller-in-residence people assumed that I would be telling the stories. It was the coldest time of the year with temperatures dipping to −30° Celsius during the day, but the sun was shining, so a free ride on a warm bus must have sounded fun. I was the MC, singing intermittently and the only rule I had, once we were all aboard, was that the bus driver could be instructed to go anywhere in the city, but once there, the passenger/participant who selected the location needed to tell a story of that place. The ride lasted two hours and in subsequent years, participants started adding extra stipulations: that the bus driver would pick up people at bus stops and drive them right to where they wanted to go, provided they either told a story or sang a song. In the end, it was a feel good afternoon where people stayed warm together sharing their stories, speaking up, and daring to be heard—and I was *performing* a useful role for community.

So yeah, I definitely think subversion has been a big part of my work and I think it's connected to a lateral, inventive way of doing things. It is me authentically being me and still being free (Fig. 13.1).

Natalie Alvarez: I know it's been a number of years, but on the website for the project you describe the performative act of *songs because of the land* as 'transitory wanderings' and 'temporary autonomous zones.' Yet, it's conceived as an ongoing action that moves through different cities with a continued life online that extends the work to new users who are invited to remix sonic clips. How has the work's online life been conceived as a way of turning your transitory movements into sustained actions, so that users, in effect, participate in the work of mapping Indigenous space?

Cheryl L'Hirondelle: The website had a couple areas where people were asked to participate, to upload sounds that they didn't hear reflected. That was a complete failure, it never had any uptake.

Natalie Alvarez: Why?

Cheryl L'Hirondelle: I think what actually happened was that instead of users uploading audio from around the greater Vancouver area, the website was perhaps a remix engine. I preferred this over having a load of subscribers to maintain and entertain. There are all kinds of interesting

Fig. 13.1 NDN Storytelling Bus Tour, by Cheryl L'Hirondelle—Sâkêwêwak Storytellers Festival, Regina SK (2011). Credit: Carey Shaw

sounds on the site: you can hear street sounds, you can hear animals, you can hear birds, you can hear a lot of small snippets of conversations from many of the people I visited. They are represented as embers that are released if the user puts a log on the fire. There are the little song shards—a phrase or two of a lyrical melody resulting from my walks—represented by notches in the tipi poles.

In terms of the reference I made to 'temporary autonomous zones' that emerged from Hakim Bey's book by the same title—TAZ.[11] It's the notion that I'm *not* putting up a flag here or claiming this place. I'm just here doing what I need to do right now. In Vancouver, I was thinking about how homeless people are always in a sort of temporary autonomous zone. There were these moments where I was singing and we were visiting—with me gifting them. And with regard to 'transitory wanderings,' people always reference [Guy] Debord and the Situationists, the fláneur versus *dérive*, and my response to that imposition of the western explorer (disguised here in anti-capitalist dress) will continue to be—no, it's more like our trickster who goes wandering out of curiosity and to visit relatives, and that's actually how the world was created. I was also thinking about the 'sneak up,' *nâciyôscikewin*—this notion of stealthily moving through time/space in an unauthorized manner. Now, as a side note, if I was to go back to Vancouver and do that project again—or anywhere really—I've shifted my position, and would definitely go and talk to the people whose place it is, and make a different kind of relationship.

Natalie Alvarez: Even though it wasn't a success in terms of users participating in this work of mapping, was that originally part of your hope for the online life of the project?

Cheryl L'Hirondelle: I wanted to create a database that people could play around with and in that way witness my activities. I think that aspect was successful, since a lot of visitors have done that with the site. We built the site in Flash, which was a mistake, because shortly after the piece was created and mobile technology spiked, Adobe did not extend Flash into a mobile environment. The work has been in several exhibitions, so it has netted out with a fair amount of participation or play. But net.art has had its day. There's a Black Elk teaching that has been of consequence to me. It says: '[…] a man who has a vision is not able to use the power of it until

[11] See Hakim Bey, *TAZ: The Temporary Autonomous Zone, Ontological Anarchy, Poetic Terrorism* (New York: Autonomedia, 1985).

after he has performed the vision on earth for the people to see.'[12] So really, I manifested it. It wasn't just this idea that I had in my head. So, there it is, the beta version.

Keren Zaiontz: Can you talk about the *Why the Caged Bird Sings* project with Indigenous women, men, and youth in prisons and detention facilities across Canada? In the same 2012 interview, you talk about how this project extends the tradition of insisting on bodily and psychic survival—or maybe more precisely, survivance—through voice. You say: 'There have always been work songs that help sustain people through really trying times.' How did you adapt the idea of the 'work song,' most commonly recognized as chain gang music from the southern US, to your collaborations with inmates and correctional staff in Canada's prisons?

Cheryl L'Hirondelle: When we're talking about the notion of *songlines*, there's a difference between singing ***about*** land and singing land. *Why the Caged Bird Sings* was not about composing songs ***about*** people in prison. Instead, we wrote some songs ***together***. Songs about life, without diminishing anyone's life experiences, but also not specifically focusing on the trouble, the hard times. Again, my approach was to ask this question: can we write some lyrics about what we want that might make life better? As an icebreaker, one of the very first things—after I introduced myself—I'd tell that joke: 'What do you get when you play a country song backwards?'

Keren Zaiontz: What do you get?

Cheryl L'Hirondelle: You get back your house, your dog, and your car [...] [*laughs*] So one of the things I would then relate to start the process of collaboration was that the 'M.O.' of ***nêhiyawin*** is ***miyo pimâtisiwin*** and it means 'good life.' So, these songs—creating them, singing them—are life affirming. Cree language is based on metaphor and metonymy, so how could we then use those life experiences as a metaphor in the same way Cree language operates?

Also, I was triggered, and outraged—and still am—to think about archivists such as Alan Lomax Jr. When people think about 'work songs,' they generally don't think about the people who composed whose songs. They are considered Lomax's songs, and I think that authorial claim is very problematic. So, I wanted to make it my personal mission that these songs belong to the real composers. All of the participants creating the song, writing the

[12] Black Elk, *Black Elk Speaks: Being the Life Story of a Holy Man of the Oglala Sioux* (Lincoln: University of Nebraska Press, 1932).

song, singing the song, performing the song, recording the song, have their names attached as their song. When I worked in the detention center, all the guys got aliases because they were under-age, but thanks to social media, I stay in touch with a fair amount of the past co-writers.

My work in prisons was also my Master's project in Inclusive Design at OCAD University (2013–2015), which I entitled, 'Why the Caged Bird Sings: radical inclusivity, sonic survivance and the collective ownership of freedom songs.' 'Radical Inclusivity' was including the correctional staff as well as the inmates, because if you think of many of the facilities, some of the staff *are* actually the lifers—they spend their whole life 'inside.' I work specifically with program staff, but there would be guards around, and their two cents worth was always considered. 'Sonic survivance' is about the continuance of the voices of my co-writers—all remarkable human beings. Over time, they got targeted as the sector of society that no one wants to hear. 'Collective Ownership' was the fact that everybody who contributed to the song, owns the song in equal shares. I've co-written with over 80 collaborators!

Natalie Alvarez: Can you speak to the connection you make between the 'freedom song,' and the word 'freedom' in Cree, which signifies self-determination? Is there a way in which this project extends the methodology of sounding as a tool that inmates use to remap the very terms of their own incarceration? I think you hinted at this in your last response, but if you could elaborate [...]

Cheryl L'Hirondelle: As you alluded to in your question, *tipêy-imisowin* means 'freedom or independence,' but in Cree, it doesn't denote wild abandon. It is more about a sense of self-control or self-determination. I did create a framework but the participants liked the idea that there was a bit of structure that supported a life-affirming worldview, where they wrote from. We did talk, I think early on, about how it could be a positive mantra of what you wanted to manifest in your life, worth singing over and over again. Once they got the hang of what was going on, it was really interesting to see the equity happening in the room where a self-determining kind of process was self-initiated by my co-writers. There might be points where I needed to rein it back to do pronoun shifts or think about rhythm, but the fact they took ownership and a lead was really really inspiring.

Natalie Alvarez: I'm just wondering if there's a through line, because at the beginning of our conversation you talked about how sounding the Cree worldview has been so foundational to opening up your practice.

Does it also undergird, *Why the Caged Bird Sings*? Were you hoping to share the tools of sounding with inmates, share the kind of agency it gave you, and the ways in which it grounded you?

Cheryl L'Hirondelle: I'm glad you ask that. One of the reasons I stopped making performance art pieces was because I had this new tool—songwriting and all it afforded me in expressing myself. Though I had begun songwriting many years previous, it wasn't until I released *Giveaway*, my first solo EP in 2008, that I had a better command of the craft of songwriting, working in the recording studio and with *Why the Caged Bird Sings*, in co-producing. And my knowledge, practice, and use of Cree meant I didn't need to flail my body about anymore—acting out what I was so earnestly trying to articulate from deep inside myself. I thought songwriting was something that I could share with the amazing people who I collaborated and co-wrote with 'inside.' They could have their own soundtrack to their life, something that they had created, and they are really good songs too. Only one song to date (*Live the Life that was Meant for Me*, 2016) has a bit of Cree and Dene in the lyrics. The reason there isn't more is because many of the inmates don't speak 'their language.' Several had been adopted and grew up in non-native families and there was always an agreement that as many of their families, friends, and communities as possible should be able to sing their song.

I wrote about the initial realization for the project in my master's thesis.[13] It is a known fact that recidivism drops dramatically when there are special programs, or *any* programs. What happens inside the correctional system in this land we know as Canada is that once someone is sentenced, they are assessed by the program section of the facility. The facility looks at: literacy, skills, cognition, and addictions in their assessment. My project was part of the literacy and cultural programming (as in the case of the one detention center I was at). On some level I think I was invited 'inside' because initially I'd proved a song could be written and recorded in five days and because I didn't want to 'babysit' nor was I expecting the facility to pay me an artist fee—I raised my own money or had partnering organizations pay for expenses and fee. A lot of musicians and poets might go into facilities, and all they're going to do is give a concert. I wanted the end result to be tangible and not about someone else's credence and 'stardom.' And maybe, instead, a manifestation in one's hand, in one's

[13] Cheryl L'Hirondelle, 'Why the Caged Bird Sings: Radical Inclusivity, Sonic Survivance and the Collective Ownership of Freedom Songs,' Master of Design thesis, OCAD University, 2015, 7–9, http://openresearch.ocadu.ca/287/.

head, or on one's tongue—something my co-writers could also prove they created in five days. And something so beautiful and good! Without sounding overly sentimental, I think we all need to have that kind of opportunity, and definitely for everyone who is or has been incarcerated.

Keren Zaiontz: It doesn't seem at all sentimental to me, especially when you consider the ways in which the biopolitics of incarceration strips inmates of agency over their bodies. The prospect of regaining property over yourself through the authorship of a song—a song that is yours, that you can sing under your breath, in your head, by tapping it out—strikes me as incredibly powerful.

Cheryl L'Hirondelle: I agree, and that is what music always did for me. Growing up, whenever I was in a tricky or dangerous situation, choosing music always saved my ass. [*laughs*]

Keren Zaiontz: In 2005 and 2006, you receive the imagiNATIVE New Media Award for your net.art projects, *treatycard*, *17:TELL*, and *wêpinâsowina*. Can you talk about the ways in which projects such as *treatycard* take up strategies of cyberactivism to advance the struggle for Indigenous sovereignty?

Cheryl L'Hirondelle: When I created *treatycard v1* in 2003, there weren't many Indigenous websites. It was also just before social media became so pervasive (*Myspace* started in 2004 and *Bebo*—where many native people were initially inhabiting—started in 2005). I had been going to Bristol, UK, a couple times a year to learn on a collegial and informal basis, from Heath Bunting[14] about DIY, redundant technology, Linux, the 'command line,' and coding such as PERL. I made a few earlier sites in basic HTML and with some a PERL CGI script that Heath had written: Slangclaims, All My Relations, and World Indigenous Register (2002).[15] What I was trying to accomplish with *treatycard* was both a database (because is it generative and can grow with user interaction) and a website in which you could alter the page and thus exercise a bit of self-representation; plus I was making a statement about colonial government sanctioned identity politics. Up until that point, most websites were 'point and click' only, and for Native people it meant that we could go to a site and read about what someone else (usually non-Indigenous) was publishing about us. It was also extremely rare for people to have their own websites and personal pages back

[14] Heath Bunting is accredited as one of the first creators of net.art. http://irational.org/cgi-bin/cv2/temp.pl.

[15] Only the index pages of these sites are currently operational though provide a bit more information: https://sparror.cubecinema.com/ndnnrkey/.

then—and *treatycard* was the site I was proposing where you would add your name, image, and where you were from. Also, you could change your name from your colonized name to what might have been your ancestral name, or maybe an alias you prefer to be called by, or maybe your 'NDN' name. It was a way to situate yourself and say: 'This is my land base, this is where I am *from*.' The term 'treaty card' is a misnomer for the status Indian card, used mostly on the prairies. Because of that—if you think of what a treaty is, it's an agreement between two parties—so I also invited non-Indigenous people to participate. It was my way of letting non-native people know they have a role and a responsibility too. And the list generated operates also as a virtual 'band roll' but by adding yourself you're learning you're part of the treaties. The piece went through a bit of versioning and was in several exhibitions.[16] Throughout the years there have been several—mostly middle-aged—Native men who made cards. I can only imagine that they had typed, 'treaty card' into a search engine and somehow happened upon my site instead of a governmental page. And they signed up and a few guys made several entries using different photos and aliases. It was touching and I was grateful I could make something that allowed someone who had been previously excluded from having an Indigenous identity could now be included.

17:TELL (2004) was a commission from the Banff New Media Institute (BNMI) that was part of the online magazine, *Horizon Zero*. They commissioned me to be the guest creative editor of an issue called 'TELL' about Indigenous digital storytelling (or 'Aboriginal,' which was the term at the time). The edition was a collection of projects and essays that showed how Indigenous people were already using technology as this 'already-and,' this continuance, this survivance—proving technology was a tool that serves a good purpose. As a bit of background to contextualize why I had been

[16] *treatycard* was featured in the following exhibitions: 2003 'Wild Fire on the Plains' curated by Morgan Wood—Mendel Art Gallery; 2004–2006 'Database Imaginary' curated by Steve Dietz, Sarah Cooke, Anthony Kiendl—Walter Phillips Gallery, Dunlop Art Gallery, Blackwood Gallery, Saidy Bronfman Centre; 2005 'Subverting Virtual Territories' curated by Elwood Jimmy—Godfrey Dean Gallery; 2005 '5th annual imagineNATIVE Film + Media Arts Festival'; 2006 'Grrls, Chicks, Sisters & Squaws: Le citoyennes du Cyberspace' curated by Skawennati, MAWA; 2007 '21' curated by Elwood Jimmy, Dunlop Art Gallery, Paved Media Arts, A Space Gallery; 2011–2015 'Decolonise Me' curated by Heather Igloliorte, Ottawa Art Gallery, Robert McLaughlin Art Gallery, Oshawa Art Gallery, Foreman Art Gallery, Art Gallery of Windsor, Thunder Bay Art Gallery, Vernon Art Gallery, Reach Gallery Museum, Tom Thomson Art Gallery; 2012 'Re-Story' curated by Charo Neville, Kamloops Art Gallery; 2012 'Night Kitchen' curated by Lisa Myers, Scotia Bank Nuit Blanche/OCAD University; 2016 'Canadian Belonging(s) 'curated by Ellyn Walker, Art Gallery of Mississauga.

invited to guest edit the issue: in 1994, I had been part of a think tank at the Banff Centre, called *Drum Beats to Drum Bytes.* At that think tank Osage sociologist George Baldwin was there and was discussing why we shouldn't become road kill on the information superhighway (a phrase he and colleague Randy Ross had coined). TELL was a ten-years-later survey of some of my favorite projects, developments, and critical thinking. And simply put, *wêpinasowina* (2006) was my prayer offering. The project was to remind people that the spirit world existed, even in cyberspace.

In an essay for the volume *Coded Territories*,[17] I offer a provocation: that internet technology started as small packets of information sent on telephone lines as a US Defense project, though the physical roots and routes of those telephone lines have deep Indigenous ties. We've always been on the move, initiating movement, '[…] toward a specific goal, cause or objective.'[18] I would surmise we even are at the core of cyberactivism—our survivance is proof.

References

Bey, Hakim. *TAZ: The Temporary Autonomous Zone, Ontological Anarchy, Poetic Terrorism*. New York: Autonomedia, 1985.

Elk, Black. *Black Elk Speaks: Being the Life Story of a Holy Man of the Oglala Sioux.* Lincoln: University of Nebraska Press, 1932.

Lee, Mary. 'Cree (Nehiyawak) Teaching.' Accessed April 16, 2018. http://www.fourdirectionsteachings.com.

Leuthold, Steven. *Indigenous Aesthetics: Native Art, Media, and Identity.* Austin: University of Texas Press, 1998.

L'Hirondelle, Cheryl. 'Codetalkers Recounting Signals of Survival.' In *Coded Territories: Tracing Indigenous Pathways in New Media Art*, edited by Steven Loft and Kerry Swanson, 152–153. Calgary: University of Calgary Press, 2014.

———. 'Why the Caged Bird Sings: Radical Inclusivity, Sonic Survivance and the Collective Ownership of Freedom Songs.' Master of Design thesis, OCAD University, 2015.

L'Hirondelle, Cheryl, Elwood Jimmy, and Chris Bose. 'Songlines, Stories and Community Engagement.' *West Coast Line* 74.46, no. 2 (2012): 94–107.

Vizenor, Gerald Robert. *Manifest Manners: Narratives on Postindian Survivance.* Lincoln: University of Nebraska Press, 1999.

[17] Cheryl L'Hirondelle, 'Codetalkers Recounting Signals of Survival,' in *Coded Territories: Tracing Indigenous Pathways in New Media Art*, ed. Steven Loft and Kerry Swanson (Calgary: University of Calgary Press, 2014), 152–153.

[18] https://www.techopedia.com/definition/27973/cyberactivism.

About the Editors

Natalie Alvarez is Professor of Theatre and Performance Studies at Ryerson University's School of Performance in Toronto, Canada. She is the author of *Immersions in Cultural Difference: Tourism, War, Performance* (2018) and the editor of two books on Latina/o Canadian theatre and performance (2013). She is working on *Theatre & War* for Palgrave Macmillan's Theatre & series.

Claudette Lauzon is Assistant Professor of Contemporary Art History and Theory in the School for the Contemporary Arts at Simon Fraser University in Vancouver, Canada. She is the author of *The Unmaking of Home in Contemporary Art* (2017) and co-editor, with John O'Brian, of the forthcoming edited collection, *Through Post-Atomic Eyes.*

Keren Zaiontz is Assistant Professor and Queen's National Scholar in the Department of Film and Media at Queen's University in Kingston, Canada. Her co-edited work on the cultural politics of contemporary art and performance includes special issues in *Contemporary Theatre Review*, *PUBLIC*, and *Canadian Theatre Review*. She is the author of *Theatre & Festivals* (2018) for Palgrave Macmillan's Theatre & series.

N. Alvarez et al. (eds.), *Sustainable Tools for Precarious Times*,
Contemporary Performance InterActions,
https://doi.org/10.1007/978-3-030-11557-9

Notes on Contributors

Patricia Ariza is a renowned producer and artist who has worked on the front lines for justice and social change in Colombia for over 50 years. For the past 26 years, she has produced vast works and massive performances that bring together professional artists and victims—particularly women—of Columbia's armed conflicts. Her not-for-profit organization, Corporación Colombiana de Teatro creates performances and events with widows and children from the most violent regions of the country. The company also organizes the Festival Alternativo de Teatro and the internationally acclaimed Festival de Mujeres en Escena. In 1966, Ariza co-founded Colombia's first alternative theatre, Teatro La Candelaria. In 2007, she was awarded a Culture and Conflict Prince Claus Award from the Netherlands and, in 2014, the National Award for Human Rights in Colombia and the LPTW Gilder/Coigney International Theatre Award for her endeavors toward peace and greater awareness of women's issues during armed conflicts.

Daniella Wittern Bush is a writer, translator, editor, yoga teacher, and once upon a time professor, who has temporarily broken up with academia to focus on being a mother. She holds a PhD in Hispanic Studies from Brown University, where she wrote a dissertation on the political performances latent in contemporary Chilean author Diamela Eltit's work. On the scholarly front, her articles on Eltit's performances of trauma, memory, and urban space, as well as on the work of Fernando Vallejo, Carlos

N. Alvarez et al. (eds.), *Sustainable Tools for Precarious Times*, Contemporary Performance InterActions,
https://doi.org/10.1007/978-3-030-11557-9

Fuentes, and Luis Buñuel, have been published. Her most recent work probes the intersections of performance, community, and politics in the Chilean student movement. Daniella's current writing, however, is mostly creative, either exploring the performances of everyday life and the tangled webs of relationships created by language, memory, and trauma, or pondering ways to make the practice of yoga—both on the mat and beyond it—kind and sustainable for all bodies. You can find her musings at yogawithdani.com.

Martha Herrera-Lasso is a PhD candidate in Performance Studies at UC Berkeley. She holds an MA in Theatre from the University of British Columbia and a BA in Playwriting from the National University in Mexico City (UNAM). She has worked as a playwright, a translator, and a dramaturge across North America and, as an artist and a scholar, she is interested in reimagining the region. Her current research is concerned with the practical and theoretical implications of international theatre collaborations between Mexico and Quebec, read through the politics of linguistic, cultural, and aesthetic translation.

Jessica Jacobson-Konefall is a Social Sciences and Humanities Research Council (SSHRC) postdoctoral research fellow at the University of Toronto in the Department of Art History (2017–2019). Her work explores Indigenous/settler relationships and environmental aesthetics and artworks. Current projects include a chapter in the anthology *Wordless: The Performance Work of Rebecca Belmore* (ed. Florence Belmore, Vancouver: Grunt Gallery), an essay on the challenges of art historical approaches to an Ininew sacred site, Wesakejack's Footprints, in Northern Manitoba, Canada (with Peter Kulchyski), and her forthcoming book, focused on her own work as an archivist within two archives of Indigenous contemporary art (in progress; McGill-Queen's UP). Since 2014, she has worked as assistant and archivist to artists Rebecca Belmore and Osvaldo Yero.

Jennie Klein is Professor of Contemporary Art History at the School of Art + Design, Ohio University. She has written on second wave feminist art, performance art, and the relationship between art institutions and contemporary art. Klein is presently working on a book, co-edited by Natalie Loveless, on the work of Marilyn Arsem, which is under contract with Intellect Press.

Cheryl L'Hirondelle is an Indigenous (non-status treaty Indian and a mixed-blood: Cree/Métis; German/Polish) award-winning interdisciplinary artist, singer/songwriter, and new media curator originally from the land now known as Canada. Her creative practice is an investigation of the intersection of a Cree worldview (nêhiyawin) and contemporary time-place. Since the early eighties, she has created, performed, and presented work in a variety of artistic disciplines including music, performance art, theatre, performance poetry, storytelling, installation, and new media. She was the first Indigenous artist from Canada to be invited to present her new media work at DAK'ART Lab (2004), as part of the sixth edition of *the Dakar Biennale for Contemporary African Art*, Dakar, Senegal, and is proud to have contributed backing vocals to Buffy Sainte Marie's award winning album *Power in the Blood* (2015). Most recently, she was nominated for the 2018–2019 Keith Haring Art and Activism Fellowship at Bard College. L'Hirondelle is an original member of OCAD University's Indigenous Education Advisory, and is a PhD candidate with SMARTlab at UCD in Dublin, Ireland.

Carla Melo is a theatre/performance artist, educator, and scholar whose creative and academic research lives at the intersections of performance and activism in the Americas, focusing on the ways in which theatricality and/or the body in public space foreground, trouble, and contest marginalized histories and collective memory. Her work has appeared in the *Canadian Theatre Review*, *TDR: The Drama Review*, *Theatre Journal*, *E-misférica*, *Latin American Theater Review*, and *Latin American Cultural Studies*, among others. Melo is working on a monograph titled *Rite(s) to Remember: Performance and Collective Memory in Contemporary Brazil*. She is graduate faculty at Arizona State University, College of Liberal Arts and Sciences and has also taught at UCLA, York, McMaster, and Brock universities. Melo is also artistic director of Toronto-based CorpOLuz Theatre and co-founder of the former Corpus Delicti Performance Lab.

Jimena Ortuzar holds a Postdoctoral Fellowship, funded by the Social Sciences and Humanities Research Council of Canada, at Ryerson University's School of Performance. She completed her PhD at the University of Toronto's Centre for Drama, Theatre and Performance studies with a collaborative program at the Centre for Diaspora and Transnational Studies. Her research explores how labor associated with the reproductive sphere is visibilized and politicized through aesthetic and everyday practice. She has contributed essays to *TDR*, *Canadian Theatre Review*, *alt.theatre*, and *Journal of Curatorial Studies*, and co-edited a *CTR* journal issue on performance and human rights in the Americas. Her writing has also appeared in *Latina/o Canadian Theatre and Performance* and *Fronteras Vivientes: Eight Latina/o Canadian Plays* (Playwrights Canada Press).

Beatriz Pizano is artistic director of Toronto's Aluna Theatre known for creating award-winning intercultural, interdisciplinary, and intermedial performance. Founded in 2001, Aluna is recognized for its unique approach to creation and its daring political work. Pizano is an accomplished director, playwright, and actor. She has received a number of prestigious awards including the John Hirsch Prize and the Chalmers Fellowship. In 2014, she received the K.M. Hunter award and this year she was recognized by President J.M. Santos as one of the *100Colombians* who have made significant contributions to their communities outside Colombia. In 2012, she co-founded the biennial festival on contemporary performance and human rights, RUTAS panamericanas, followed by its alternating biennial CAMINOS in 2014, both of which showcase work from across the Americas.

Wilfredo Prieto studied at the Escuela Profesional de Artes Plásticas (Trinidad, Cuba) between 1992 and 1996. He graduated from Havana's Instituto Superior de Arte (ISA) in 2002. From 1998 to 2002 he was a member of Galería DUPP (Desde Una Pragmática Pedagógica) with whom he was awarded the UNESCO Prize for the Promotion of the Arts. Prieto has held residencies at Headlands, San Francisco (2015), Gasworks, London (2008), Le Grand Café, St. Nazaire (2007), the Guggenheim Foundation, New York (2006), and the Kadist Art Foundation in Paris (2005). His exhibitions include *System error*, Museo de Arte Contemporáneo del Zulia, Venezuela; *Ping-pong grid*, Museo Nacional de Bellas Artes, Cuba (2015); *Speaking badly about stones*, S.M.A.K, Belgium (2014); *Leaving something to chance*, Sala de Arte Público Siqueiros, Mexico; and *Balancing the curve*, Hangar Bicocca, Italy (2012). He has been invited to showcase his works in the Istanbul Biennial (2011), the Biennale di Venezia (2011 and 2007), the Lyon Biennial (2011), the São Paulo Biennale (2010), and several other Havana Biennials.

Kimberly Skye Richards is a PhD candidate in Performance Studies at UC-Berkeley. Her dissertation examines a range of performance practices on oil frontiers in which petro-politics are negotiated, extractive ideologies are staged, and theatrical tactics are deployed to impede the expansion of petro-imperialism. She has contributed to *Theatre Journal*, *TDR: The Drama Review*, and *Room One Thousand*.

Jennifer Beth Spiegel holds a PhD in Cultural Studies from Goldsmiths College, the University of London and is a research fellow at Simon Fraser University. Spiegel has previously taught courses in performance history and critical theory at McGill and Concordia University. Grounded in deep involvement with social movement collectives, her work explores the intersection of creativity, social movements, and policy. Spiegel's contributions include video and performance research pieces, several book chapters, as well as multiple articles published in diverse journals including *Theatre Topics*, *TDR*, *Social Movement Studies*, *Critical Inquiry*, and *Antipode Journal of Radical Geography*, amongst others. She is co-leading a collective project on *The Art of Collectivity: Social Circus and the Cultural Politics of a Post-Neoliberal Vision* to be published in English with a version adapted for a Spanish language readership. Her single authored book *Creative Protest* is also slated for completion in 2019.

Micah White, PhD, is a lifelong activist who co-created Occupy Wall Street, a global social movement that spread to 82 countries, while an editor of *Adbusters* magazine. White has a 20-year record of innovative activism, including conceiving the debt-activism tactic used by the Rolling Jubilee, popularizing the critique of clicktivism, and identifying the emerging trend of 'social movement warfare.' He is the author of *The End of Protest* which has been translated into German and Greek. His essays have been published in the *Washington Post*, the *New York Times*, and the *Guardian* among others. He has been profiled by the *New Yorker*, *Esquire*, and more. He is the co-founder of Activist Graduate School, an online school taught by, and for, experienced activists.

Zaira Zarza is Assistant Professor in the Department of Art History and Film Studies at the University of Montreal. She was an Izaak W. Killam Memorial Postdoctoral Fellow in the Department of Modern Languages and Cultural Studies at the University of Alberta between 2016 and 2018. She holds a PhD in Cultural Studies from Queen's University and holds both bachelor's and master's degrees in Art History from the University of Havana. She worked for several years in the Department of Social Research of the Cuban Film Institute. Her book *Caminos del cine brasileño contemporáneo* was published by Ediciones ICAIC in 2010 and she co-edited the special issue 'Havana' for the Canadian journal *PUBLIC* in the winter of 2016. She is the founder and coordinator of *Roots and Routes: Cuban Cinemas of the Diaspora in the 21st Century*, a platform for the promotion and study of film and media works by young Cuban artists who live off the island. Her most recent project focuses on creative industries and new economies of film production in transitional Cuba. Since 2017, Zarza has been the Toronto International Film Festival's Programming Associate for Latin America, the Caribbean, Spain, and Portugal.

Index[1]

[1] Note: Page numbers followed by 'n' refer to notes.

N. Alvarez et al. (eds.), *Sustainable Tools for Precarious Times*, Contemporary Performance InterActions,
https://doi.org/10.1007/978-3-030-11557-9

J

Z

Printed by Printforce, the Netherlands

Contemporary Performance InterActions

Theatre's performative InterActions with the politics of sex, race and class, with questions of social and political justice, form the focus of the Contemporary Performance InterActions series. Performative InterActions are those that aspire to affect, contest or transform. International in scope, CPI publishes monographs and edited collections dedicated to the InterActions of contemporary practitioners, performances and theatres located in any world context.

More information about this series at
http://www.palgrave.com/gp/series/14918